Essentials of Employm

EIGHTH EDITION

David Lewis
and
Malcolm Sargeant

:S CENTRE

Chartered Institute of Personnel and Development

The Chartered Institute of Personnel and Development is the leading publisher of books and reports for personnel and training professionals, students, and all those concerned with the effective management and development of people at work. For details of all our titles, please contact the publishing department:
Tel: 020–8263 3387
Fax: 020–8263 3850
E-mail: publish@cipd.co.uk
The catalogue of all CIPD titles can be viewed on the CIPD website:
www.cipd.co.uk/bookstore

Essentials of Employment Law

EIGHTH EDITION

David Lewis
and
Malcolm Sargeant

David Lewis is Professor of Employment Law at Middlesex University and Programme Leader for the LLM in Employment Law. Apart from teaching on a range of degree courses and being a regular contributor to specialist commercial seminars, he has considerable experience as a consultant. He is a member of the editorial committee of the *Industrial Law Journal* and was appointed an ACAS arbitrator in 1999.

Malcolm Sargeant is a Reader in Employment Law at Middlesex University. He has written widely on employment law subjects, especially on issues related to transfers of undertakings, discrimination in employment and parental rights. Prior to becoming an academic he was personnel manager of a large financial services company and director of a recruitment and management consultancy. He teaches a range of employment law topics on the LLM in Employment Law at Middlesex University.

© David Lewis and Malcolm Sargeant 2004

This edition first published in 2004

© David Lewis and Malcolm Sargeant 2002

© David Lewis 1983, 1986, 1990, 1994, 1997, 2000

First published 1983
Second edition 1986
Third edition 1990
Fourth edition 1994
Fifth edition 1997
Sixth edition 2000
Seventh edition 2002

The right of (the authors) to be identified as the authors of this work has been asserted by them in accordance with the Copyright, Designs and Patents Act 1988.

Design by Pumpkin House

Typeset by Fakenham Photosetting Ltd, Fakenham, Norfolk

Printed in Great Britain by
the Cromwell Press, Trowbridge, Wiltshire

British Library Cataloguing in Publication Data
A catalogue record of this book is available from
the British Library

ISBN 1 84398 000 2

The views expressed in this book are the authors' own and
may not necessarily reflect those of the CIPD.

Chartered Institute of Personnel and Development, CIPD House,
Camp Road, London, SW19 4UX
Tel: 020 8971 9000   Fax: 020 8263 3333
E-mail: cipd@cipd.co.uk   Website: www.cipd.co.uk
Incorporated by Royal Charter.   Registered Charity No. 1079797

Contents

Abbreviations

AC	Appeal Cases
ACAS	Advisory, Arbitration and Conciliation Service
ACOP	Approved Code of Practice
All ER	All England Law Reports
AMRA	Access to Medical Reports Act 1988
CA	Court of Appeal
CAC	Central Arbitration Committee
Ch	Chancery Division
CMLR	Common Market Law Reports
CO	Certification Officer
CRE	Commission for Racial Equality
CRTUPEA Regulations	Collective Redundancies and Transfers of Undertakings (Protection of Employment) (Amendment) Regulations 1999
DDA	Disability Discrimination Act 1995
DDAA	Disability Discrimination Act 1995 (Amendment) Regulations 2003
DPA	Data Protection Act 1998
EA	Employment Act 2002
EAT	Employment Appeal Tribunal
EC	European Community
ECA	European Communities Act 1972
ECHR	European Court of Human Rights
ECJ	European Court of Justice
ECR	European Court Reports
EESO Regs	Employment Equality (Sexual Orientation) Regulations 2003
EOC	Equal Opportunities Commission
EPA	Equal Pay Act 1970
ERA	Employment Rights Act 1996
ERel Act	Employment Relations Act 1999
ETA	Employment Tribunals Act 1996
EU	European Union
EWC	Expected Week of Confinement
EWC Directive	European Works Council Directive 1997
GOQ	Genuine Occupational Qualification
HASAWA	Health and Safety at Work Act 1974
HRA	Human Rights Act 1998
HSC	Health and Safety Commission
HSCE	Health and Safety (Consultation with Employees) Regulations 1996
HSE	Health and Safety Executive
ICR	Industrial Cases Reports
IRLB	Industrial Relations Law Bulletin
IRLR	Industrial Relations Law Reports
LBPIC Regulations	Telecommunications (Lawful Business Practice) (Interception of Communications) Regulations 2000
LWTL	Lawtel
MHSW Regulations	Management of Health and Safety at Work Regulations 1999
MLP	Maternity Leave Period

MPL	Maternity and Parental Leave, etc Regulations 1999
MPP	Maternity Pay Period
NMW	National Minimum Wage
NMWA	National Minimum Wage Act 1998
PTW Regulations	Part-time Workers (Prevention of Less Favourable Treatment) Regulations 2000
QB	Queen's Bench
RB Regulations	Employment Equality (Religion or Belief) Regulations 2003
RIDDOR	Reporting of Injuries, Diseases and Dangerous Occurrences Regulations 1995
RIP	Regulation of Investigatory Powers Act 2000
RRA	Race Relations Act 1976
RTOST Regulations	Right to Time off for Study or Training Regulations 2001
SDA	Sex Discrimination Act 1975
SI	Statutory Instrument
SMP	Statutory Maternity Pay
SNB	Special Negotiating Body
SRSC Regulations	Safety Representatives and Safety Committees Regulations 1977
SSCBA	Social Security and Benefits Act 1992
SSP	Statutory Sick Pay
TICE Regulations	Transnational Information and Consultation of Employees Regulations 1999
Transfer Regulations	Transfer of Undertakings (Protection of Employment) Regulations 1981
TUC	Trades Union Congress
TULRCA	Trade Union and Labour Relations (Consolidation) Act 1992
TURERA	Trade Union Reform and Employment Rights Act 1993
WLR	Weekly Law Reports
WT	Working Time
WT Regulations	Working Time Regulations 1998

List of Cases Cited

PREFACE

It is only two years since the previous edition of this text, and the pace of change in employment law has not slackened. Several important legislative provisions have come into force, including the Employment Act 2002, the Flexible Working Regulations 2002, the Equal Pay Act 1970 (Amendment) Regulations 2003, the Sex Discrimination Act 1975 (Amendment) Regulations 2003, the Race Relations Act 1976 (Amendment) Regulations 2003, the Employment Equality (Religion or Belief) Regulations 2003 and the Employment Equality (Sexual Orientation) Regulations 2003.

In this edition we are including a new chapter on Information and Consultation as well as updating the material in the light of statutory changes and court decisions. An Employment Relations Bill was published in December 2003 and we have indicated the areas upon which the new statute is likely to impact. We shall provide detailed consideration of this measure in the next edition.

David Lewis
Malcolm Sargeant

January 2004

The Sources and Institutions of Employment Law

CHAPTER 1

OVERVIEW

This chapter will introduce you to both the way in which employment law is made and the institutions that develop, supervise and enforce it. We start with the distinction between civil and criminal law and a basic introduction to the legal system in this country. Employment law is created by primary and secondary legislation which is then interpreted by the courts, especially by employment tribunals and the Employment Appeal Tribunal. They are influenced by Codes of Practice and, importantly, by EU law and the decisions of the European Court of Justice. Finally we look at those organisations set up by Parliament to regulate industrial relations and dispute resolution.

CIVIL AND CRIMINAL LAW

Criminal law is concerned with offences against the state and, apart from private prosecutions, it is the state which enforces this branch of the law. The sanctions typically imposed on convicted persons are fines and/or imprisonment. Civil law deals with the situations where a private person who has suffered harm brings an action against (ie sues) the person who committed the wrongful act which caused the harm. Normally the purpose of suing is to recover damages or compensation. Criminal and civil matters are normally dealt with in separate courts which have their own distinct procedures.

In this book we shall be concentrating largely on civil law but we shall be describing the criminal law in so far as it imposes duties in relation to health and safety and restricts the activities of pickets. In employment law the two most important civil actions are those based on the law of contract and the law of tort. The essential feature of a contract is a binding agreement in which an offer by one person (for example, an employer) is accepted by someone else (for example, a person seeking work). This involves an exchange of promises. Thus, in a contract of employment there is a promise to pay wages in exchange for a promise to be available for work. As we shall see later, the parties to a contract are not entirely free to negotiate their own terms because Parliament imposes certain restrictions and minimum requirements. The law of tort places a duty on everyone not to behave in a way that is likely to cause harm to others, and in the employment field the tort of negligence has been applied so as to impose a duty on employers to take reasonable care of their employees during the course of their employment. Various torts have also been created by the judiciary in order to impose legal liability for industrial action – for example, the tort of interfering with trade or business – but Parliament has intervened to provide immunities in certain circumstances (see Chapter 21).

LEGISLATION AND CODES OF PRACTICE

In this country the most important source of law governing industrial relations is legislation enacted by Parliament. Often the government will precede legislation by issuing Green Papers or White Papers. Traditionally the Green Paper is a consultative document and the White Paper is a statement of the government's policy and intentions, although this distinction does not always seem to be adhered to. The government will announce its legislative programme for the forthcoming session in the Queen's Speech. A Bill is then introduced into the House of Commons (sometimes this process can begin in the House of Lords) and is examined at a number of sessions (readings) in both the House of Commons and the House of Lords. The agreed Bill becomes an Act (or statute) when it receives the Royal Assent. It is then referred to (cited) by its name and year, which constitutes its 'short title' (eg Employment Rights Act 1996).

The provisions of an Act may not be brought into operation immediately, for the government may wish to implement it in stages. Nevertheless, once the procedure is completed, the legislation is valid. The main provisions of a statute are to be found in its numbered sections, whereas administrative details, repeals and amendments of previous legislation tend to be contained in the schedules at the back. Statutes sometimes give the relevant Secretary of State the power to make rules (regulations) to supplement those laid down in the Act itself. These regulations, which are normally subject to parliamentary approval, are referred to as statutory instruments (SI) and this process of making law is known as delegated or subordinate legislation. Statutory instruments are cited by their name, year and number (eg the Equal Pay Act 1970 (Amendment) Regulations 2003 S.I. No 1656).

Codes of Practice

Legislation sometimes allows for an appropriate Minister or a statutory body to issue Codes of Practice. The primary function of these codes is to educate managers and workers by publicising the practices and procedures which the government believes are conducive to, say, good industrial relations. Under section 199 of the Trade Union and Labour Relations (Consolidation) Act 1992 (TULRCA 1992) the Advisory, Conciliation and Arbitration Service (ACAS) has a general power to issue codes 'containing such practical guidance as [ACAS] thinks fit for the purpose of promoting the improvement of industrial relations'. Following representations by interested parties ACAS submits a draft code to the Secretary of State for approval before it is laid before Parliament. At the time of writing, ACAS Codes of Practice exist on the following topics: *Disciplinary and Grievance Procedures*; *Disclosure of Information to Trade Unions for Collective Bargaining Purposes*; and *Time Off for Trade Union Duties and Activities*. The Equal Opportunities Commission (EOC), Disability Rights Commission (DRC) and the Commission for Racial Equality (CRE) have also issued codes of the same standing as those of ACAS and, by virtue of section 16 of the Health and Safety at Work Act 1974 (HASAWA 1974), the Health and Safety Commission (HSC) has the power to approve Codes of Practice provided it obtains the consent of the Secretary of State on each occasion. The Information Commissioner also has powers to produce Codes of Practice for data controllers (see Chapter 18). Finally, sections 203–6 TULRCA 1992 entitle the Secretary of State to issue codes, but before publishing a draft he or she is obliged to consult ACAS. However, no such duty exists if a code is merely being revised to bring it into conformity with subsequent statutory provisions.[1] Although emerging by different means, all these codes have the same legal standing – ie nobody can be sued or prosecuted for breaching a code – but in any proceedings before a tribunal, court (if the code was issued under TULRCA 1992 or HASAWA 1974) or the Central Arbitration Committee (CAC) a failure to adhere to a recommendation 'shall be taken into account'.

COMMON LAW AND THE COURT HIERARCHY

The feature which distinguishes the English legal system from non-common-law systems is that in this country judicial decisions have been built up to form a series of binding precedents. This is known as the case-law approach. In practice this means that tribunals and judges are bound by the decisions of judges in higher courts. Thus employment tribunals, which are at the bottom of the English court hierarchy, are required to follow the decisions of the Employment Appeal Tribunal (EAT or Appeal Tribunal), the Court of Appeal and the Appeal Committee of the House of Lords, although they are not bound by other employment tribunal decisions. The Employment Appeal Tribunal is bound by the decisions of the Court of Appeal and the House of Lords and normally follows its own previous decisions. The Court of Appeal has a civil and criminal division and, while both are bound by the House of Lords' decisions, only the civil division is constrained by its own previous decisions. The House of Lords has stated that it will regard its own earlier decisions as binding unless in the circumstances of a particular case it is thought just to depart from them.

In addition all English and Scottish courts must follow the guidance given by the European Court of Justice (ECJ). Much of this guidance comes as a result of national courts' referring matters to the ECJ by a procedure under Article 234 of the EC Treaty (previously Article 177 EC). Thus when a court or tribunal decides that clarification of European Union law is required in order for it to make a decision, it will refer the matter to the ECJ for guidance.

What constitutes the binding element of a judicial decision is for a judge or tribunal in a subsequent case to determine. Theoretically what has to be followed is the legal principle or principles which are relied on in reaching the decision in the earlier case. In practice judges and tribunals have a certain amount of discretion, for they can take a broad or narrow view of the principles which are binding upon them. If they do not like the principles that have emerged, they can refuse to apply them so long as they are prepared to conclude that the facts of the case before them are sufficiently different from the facts in the previous decision. Not surprisingly, this technique is known as 'distinguishing'. Thus, while it is correct to argue that the doctrine of precedent imports an element of certainty, it is wrong to assume that there is no scope for innovation in the lower courts. In addition to interpreting the law, the judiciary can and does make law.

The court hierarchy

The court structure in England and Wales, is shown in diagrammatic form in Figure 1 (below). Most proceedings involving individual employment rights are commenced at employment tribunals and appeals

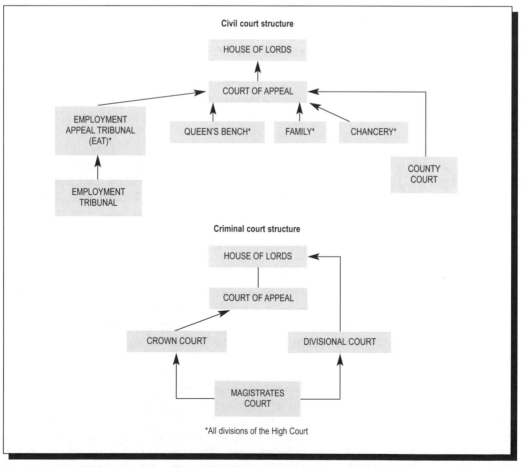

Figure 1 *Court structure in England and Wales*

against an employment tribunal decision can normally be heard by the EAT only if there has been an error of law. An error of law occurs when a tribunal has misdirected itself as to the applicable law, when there is no evidence to support a particular finding of fact, or when the tribunal has reached a perverse conclusion, ie one which cannot be justified on the evidence presented.[2] Further appeals can be made on a point of law to the Court of Appeal and the House of Lords, but only if permission is granted by either the body which made the decision or the court which would hear the appeal. Other civil actions can be started in the County Court or High Court. Appeals on a point of law against a decision made by either court can be lodged with the Court of Appeal and, if permission is granted, further appeal lies to the House of Lords. There is also a 'leapfrog procedure' which enables an appeal against a decision of the High Court to go directly to the House of Lords so long as all the parties involved give their consent.

Criminal proceedings are normally commenced in magistrates' courts – for example, if pickets are charged with obstructing police officers in the execution of their duty. The defence can launch an appeal on fact which goes to the Crown Court, but it is also possible for either party to appeal on a point of law to the Divisional Court of the Queen's Bench and then on to the House of Lords. Prosecutions for serious offences – for example, under section 33 of HASAWA 1974 – are dealt with in the Crown Court, and appeals on a point of law go to the Court of Appeal and the House of Lords in the usual way.

EUROPEAN UNION LAW

The United Kingdom joined the European Economic Community in 1973. Since then there have been a number of Treaties by which the Member States have agreed to develop the scope of the law of the European Union (EU), the most recent being the Treaty of Amsterdam 1998. Article 249 of the EC Treaty (previously Article 189 EC) allows the EU to introduce different types of legislation, the most important ones being regulations and directives. Regulations tend to be of a broad nature and are directly applicable in all Member States. Most EU legislation that affects employment law is introduced, however, in the form of directives. Directives are legislative instruments that require a Member State to translate (transpose) the contents of the directive into national law. Member States are usually given a period of two to three years to carry this out.

If a Member State fails to do this, a citizen may, in certain circumstances, rely on the EU law rather than on existing national laws. The directive is then said to have direct effect. This can be the result of the Member State's either failing to transpose the directive or inadequately transposing it. Direct effect is, however, usually only vertically effective, ie it can only be relied upon against the state or 'emanations' of the state.[3] This concept of direct effect has proved an important tool in the enforcement of Community law, especially with respect to Article 141 EC (previously Article 119 EC) on equal pay.

Early cases in the European Court of Justice established the supremacy of Community law over national law.[4] National courts also have an obligation to interpret national law so that it gives effect to EU law.[5] This means that national legislation should be interpreted in a way that is consistent with the objects of the Treaty, the provisions of any relevant directives and the rulings of the European Court of Justice.[6] In relation to the interpretation of directives, this principle applies whether the national legislation came after or preceded the particular directive.[7]

It is the European Communities Act 1972 (ECA 1972) which gives effect to the UK's membership of the EU. First, section 2(1) enables directly effective EU obligations to be enforced as free-standing rights. Thus in *McCarthys Ltd* v *Smith*[8] Article 141 EC on equal pay was applied following a reference to the European Court of Justice. Second, section 2(2) facilitates the introduction of subordinate legislation to achieve compliance with EU obligations, eg the fixed-term Employees (Prevention of Less Favourable Treatment) Regulations 2002.[9] Articles 226 EC and 228 EC (previously 169 and 171 EC) enable the European

Commission to take steps to ensure that the UK complies with its obligations to give effect to directives.[10] In addition, an individual may be able to obtain damages as a result of a Member State's failure to carry out its obligations under European Union law.[11]

THE KEY INSTITUTIONS

Employment tribunals

Industrial tribunals were first established under the Industrial Training Act 1964 but their jurisdiction has been greatly extended. Their name was changed to 'employment tribunals' by section 1 of the Employment Rights (Dispute Resolution) Act 1998. In this book they will always be referred to by this new name, even though many of the cases cited will refer to them as industrial tribunals.

The Employment Tribunal Service was established in 1997 to provide administrative and organisational support for employment tribunals and the Employment Appeal Tribunal. There are 33 local tribunal offices in England and Scotland. The President of these tribunals is a barrister or solicitor of seven years' standing who is appointed by the Lord Chancellor for a five-year term. Normally tribunal cases are heard by legally qualified chairpersons and two other people who are known as lay members.[12] Tribunal appointments are for five years initially, and whereas the chairpersons are appointed by the Lord Chancellor and are subject to the same qualification requirements as the President, the lay members are appointed by the Secretary of State. They are drawn from two panels; one is formed as a result of nominations made by employer organisations, and the other consists of nominees from organisations of workers. Since 1999 the government has also advertised in the press so that individuals may nominate themselves for one of the panels. However, while lay members are expected to have an understanding of workplace practices and how people work together, they are not supposed to act as representatives of their nominating organisations.

Representation at hearings

Hearings at employment tribunals are relatively informal.[13] The parties, known as applicants and respondents, may represent themselves or be represented by a legal practitioner, a trade union official, a representative from an employers' association or any other person. In practice, employers tend to be legally represented more often than employees, one reason being the unavailability of legal aid at present. (Applicants may be able to obtain advice and assistance in preparing their case under the legal aid scheme.) Human resource managers should give very serious thought to the question of representation, because the manager who understands how the shop floor operates and is familiar with the types of argument that may be raised during the disciplinary process may prove more effective than a lawyer from outside.

Apart from appeals against improvement or prohibition notices issued under HASAWA 1974, costs are not normally awarded unless either party (or their representative) is deemed to have acted vexatiously, abusively, disruptively, or otherwise unreasonably, or the bringing or conducting of the proceedings was misconceived.[14]

Challenging tribunal decisions

Tribunal decisions can be challenged either by review or by appeal. The power of review, which enables the whole or part of a case to be re-heard and set aside or vary the original decision, may be exercised only on one of the following grounds:

- the decision was wrongly made as a result of error on the part of tribunal staff
- a party did not receive notice of the proceedings
- the decision was made in the absence of a person entitled to be heard

- new evidence has become available since the making of the decision and its existence could not have been reasonably known of or foreseen
- the interests of justice require a review.[15]

Applications for review must be made within 14 days of the tribunal's decision being entered on the register which is kept by the Secretary of the tribunals. The review may be heard by the tribunal responsible for the original decision or by a differently constituted one. An appeal to the Employment Appeal Tribunal can normally be made only on a point of law and must be lodged within 42 days of the decision or order being sent to the appellant.[16]

The Employment Appeal Tribunal (EAT)

The EAT, which was established in 1976, is serviced by Employment Tribunal Service offices in London and Edinburgh. It can sit anywhere in England, Wales or Scotland and consists of High Court judges nominated by the Lord Chancellor (one of whom serves as President) and a panel of lay members who are appointed on the joint recommendation of the Lord Chancellor and the Secretary of State. This panel consists of nominees from employers' and workers' organisations. Appeals are heard by a judge and either two or four lay persons, all of whom have equal voting rights. However, a judge can sit alone where the appeal arises from proceedings before an employment tribunal consisting of the chair alone.

Parties can be represented by whomsoever they please, and costs will be awarded only where the proceedings are deemed to have been unnecessary, improper, or vexatious or where there has been unreasonable conduct in bringing or conducting the proceedings.[17] Apart from appeals on points of law, this body can hear appeals on fact from a decision of the Certification Officer under section 2 TULRCA 1992 (entry on the list of trade unions), and section 6 TULRCA 1992 (certificates of independence)[17A]. The EAT has the same review powers as employment tribunals. Finally, the Appeal Tribunal may adjourn proceedings where there is a reasonable prospect of a conciliated settlement being reached.[18]

The Advisory, Conciliation and Arbitration Service (ACAS)

ACAS has been in existence since 1974. Its work is directed by a council consisting of a chairperson and between nine and fifteen members appointed by the Secretary of State. Three or four members are appointed after consultation with trade unions, the same number following consultation with employers' organisations, and the remainder are independent. The Service is divided into seven regions which perform most of the day-to-day work – for example, handling direct enquiries from the public. Although ACAS is financed by the government, section 247(3) TULRCA 1992 states that it shall not be 'subject to directions of any kind from any Minister of the Crown as to the manner in which it is to exercise its functions'.

ACAS has the general duty of promoting the improvement of industrial relations, in particular by exercising its functions in relation to the settlement of trade disputes.[19] It also has specific functions which merit separate consideration.

Advice

ACAS may, on request or on its own initiative, provide employers, their associations, workers and trade unions with advice on any matter concerned with or affecting industrial relations.[20] In practice the forms of advice range from telephone inquiries to in-depth projects, diagnostic surveys and training exercises. In 2002/3, 1828 advisory meetings were held and 458 advisory projects were completed.

Conciliation

Where a trade dispute exists or is likely to arise, ACAS may, on request or of its own volition, offer assistance to the parties with a view to bringing about a settlement. This may be achieved by conciliation or other means – for example, the appointment of an independent person to render assistance. Before attempting to conciliate in collective trade disputes, ACAS is required to 'have regard to the desirability of encouraging the parties to a dispute to use any appropriate agreed procedures'.[21] According to its Annual Report for 2002/3. in 94 per cent of the 1325 cases completed collective conciliation was successful. Pay and other terms and conditions of employment were the most frequent issues in the disputes conciliated (48 per cent) and 49 per cent of requests for assistance came from both parties jointly.

In addition to collective matters, ACAS has the task of conciliating in employment tribunal cases. When a complaint is presented to an employment tribunal, a copy of it will be sent to a conciliation officer who has the duty to promote a settlement without the matter having to go to a hearing. Conciliation officers can intervene if requested to do so by the parties or where they believe they could act with a reasonable prospect of success. At the instigation of either party the officer may act before a complaint has been presented in respect of a matter which could be the subject of tribunal proceedings (for the conciliation officer's particular duty in unfair dismissal cases, see Chapter 16). So as not to undermine the conciliation process it is stipulated that anything communicated to an officer in connection with the performance of his or her functions shall not be admissible in evidence in any proceedings before an employment tribunal without the consent of the person who communicated it.

The Employment Tribunal Service Annual Report for 2002/3 reveals that 24% of tribunal applications reached a hearing, although the rate of settlement, withdrawal and abandonment varied according to the particular jurisdiction. 46% of the 39,882 unfair dismissal cases and 45% of the 2481 disability discrimination cases were settled. However, only 27% of the 7912 sex discrimination cases and 15% of the 1158 equal pay claims were settled.

Arbitration

At the request of one party but with the consent of all the parties to a collective dispute (or potential dispute), ACAS may appoint an arbitrator or arbitration panel from outside the Service or refer the matter to be heard by the Central Arbitration Committee (CAC). In performing this function ACAS is obliged to consider whether the dispute could be resolved by conciliation, and arbitration is not to be offered unless agreed procedures for the negotiation and settlement of disputes have been exhausted (save where there is a special reason which justifies arbitration as an alternative to those procedures).[22] CAC awards can be published only with the consent of all parties involved. According to the ACAS report for 2002/3, 66 per cent of the 80 cases referred to arbitration and dispute mediation involved disputes over pay and terms and conditions of employment, and 19 per cent were concerned with discipline and dismissal; 70 cases went to a single arbitrator, one to a board of arbitration and eight to a single mediator.

In addition, since May 2001 ACAS has operated a voluntary arbitration scheme which provides an alternative to employment tribunals for the resolution of disputes over unfair dismissal. Where the parties agree to use the scheme, they must waive the rights they would otherwise have in relation to an unfair dismissal claim. Arbitrators are appointed from the ACAS Arbitration Panel, and hearings, which are held in private, are intended to be relatively speedy, cost-efficient and non-legalistic. The parties can reach an agreement settling their dispute at any stage. However, where an arbitrator makes an award the parties cannot appeal on a point of law except where the Human Rights Act 1998 or EC law is relevant.[23] According to the ACAS Report for 2002/3, there were only 23 applications under this scheme.

Inquiry

ACAS may inquire into any question relating to industrial relations generally, in a particular industry or in a particular undertaking. Any advice or findings which emerge may be published so long as the views of all concerned parties have been taken into account.[24]

Other duties

Apart from the general power to issue codes of practice, ACAS has an important conciliation role to play in statutory recognition claims and in those situations where a recognised union has lodged a complaint that an employer has failed to disclose information which it requires for collective bargaining purposes (see Chapter 19).

The Central Arbitration Committee (CAC)

The CAC consists of a chairperson, deputy chairpersons and other members, all of whom are appointed by the Secretary of State after consultation with ACAS. The members must have experience as employer or worker representatives, while the deputy chairpersons tend to be lawyers or academic experts in industrial relations. Like ACAS, the CAC is not subject to directions from a Minister. Apart from receiving requests to arbitrate directly from parties to a dispute, the CAC receives arbitration requests from ACAS (see above). Additionally, the CAC is required to make determinations under sections 183–5 TULRCA 1992 (dealing with complaints arising from a failure to disclose information). CAC awards are published and take effect as part of the contracts of employees covered by the award. Unless it can be shown that the CAC exceeded its jurisdiction,[25] breached the rules of natural justice or committed an error of law,[26] no court can overturn its decisions.

The CAC is also required to resolve disputes under the Transnational Information and Consultation of Employees Regulations 1999[27], and the Employment Relations Act 1999 (ERel Act) added an important new role in relation to the recognition and de-recognition of trade unions. The CAC receives the application for recognition and supervises the process, including the holding of a ballot amongst the affected employees, leading to a decision on whether recognition or de-recognition should be granted (see Chapter 19). It is required to establish a panel consisting of an independent chair and an experienced representative of employers and an experienced representative of workers to fulfil these functions. In dealing with these cases the Act requires the CAC to have regard to the object of encouraging and promoting fair and efficient practices in the workplace (so far as is consistent with its other obligations under the Act). According to the CAC Annual Report for 2002/3, trade unions submitted 80 applications for statutory recognition, and seven complaints about disclosure of information were received.

The Certification Officer

The Certification Officer is also appointed by the Secretary of State after consultation with ACAS and is required to produce an annual report for them. He or she is responsible for maintaining a list of trade unions and employers' associations and if an application is submitted has to determine whether or not a listed union qualifies for a certificate of independence. If the application is rejected, the union can appeal to the EAT on a point of law or fact[27A]. The Certification Officer also handles:

- disputes which arise from trade union amalgamations and mergers and the administration of political funds
- complaints that the provisions of Chapter IV TULRCA 1992, concerning trade union elections, have been infringed (see Chapter 20), and can determine the procedure to be followed on any application or complaint received[28]
- complaints by a member of breach of a trade union's own rules relating to a union office, disciplinary proceedings, ballots (on any issue other than industrial action) and the constitution and proceedings of the executive committee or of any decision-making meeting.[29]

In relation to these jurisdictions an appeal can only be lodged if a point of law is involved.

Under the Trade Union and Labour Relations (Consolidation) Act 1992, the Certification Officer can direct a trade union to produce documents relating to its financial affairs. Where there appears to have been impropriety, the Certification Officer can appoint inspectors to investigate (see Chapter 19).[30]

The Information Commissioner

This officer replaced the Data Protection Commissioner. The Information Commissioner has a number of general duties, including the preparation and dissemination of codes of practice for guidance (see Chapter 7).[31]

KEY POINTS

- The most important source of law governing industrial relations is legislation enacted by Parliament.
- Legislation sometimes allows for a Minister or a statutory body to issue Codes of Practice.
- The most relevant Codes of Practice for employment law are issued by ACAS, the EOC, CRE, DRC, Information Commissioner and the Secretary of State.
- The case-law approach of the courts means that they are bound by the decisions of judges in higher courts.
- National courts must follow the decisions and guidance given by the European Court of Justice.
- European laws take precedence and are directly effective against the state or emanations of the state, if not transposed correctly.
- Employment Tribunals are specialist bodies, whose decisions can be appealed against, on points of law, to the Employment Appeal Tribunal.
- ACAS has the general duty of improving industrial relations and provides advice, individual and collective conciliation and arbitration services.
- The Central Arbitration Committee deals with complaints about failure to disclose information for the purposes of collective bargaining.
- The Central Arbitration Committee also has an important role to play in the procedure for the statutory recognition of trade unions.
- The Certification Officer maintains lists of employers' associations and trade unions and issues certificates of independence.

NOTES

1 See section 205 TULRCA 1992
2 *British Telecom* v *Sheridan* (1990) IRLR 27
3 See *Marshall* v *Southampton and South West Hampshire Area Health Authority* Case 152/85 (1986) IRLR 140
4 See *Amministrazione delle Finanze* v *Simmenthal* Case 106/77 (1978) ECR 629
5 See *Litster* v *Forth Dry Dock Engineering Co Ltd* (1989) IRLR 161
6 *Pickstone* v *Freemans plc* (1988) IRLR 357
7 See *Marleasing SA* v *Comercial Internacional de Alimentacion SA* Case 106/89 (1990) ECR 4135
8 (1980) IRLR 208
9 SI 2002/2034
10 See *Commission* v *UK* (1994) IRLR 292
11 See Cases 46/93 and 48/93 *Brasserie du Pêcheur SA* v *Federal Republic of Germany* and *R* v *Secretary of State for Transport ex parte Factortame* (1996) ECR 1029
12 Certain claims can be heard by a chair sitting alone. See Employment Tribunals Act 1996 and the Employment Rights (Dispute Resolution) Act 1998
13 On tribunal practice and procedures see specialist texts
14 Rule 14 Schedule 1 Employment Tribunal (Constitution and Rules of Procedure) Regulations 2001 SI No.1171
15 Rule 13 (see note 14)
16 Rule 3 Employment Appeal Tribunal Rules 1993 SI No.2854
17 Section 34 Employment Tribunals Act 1996

17A The Employment Relations Bill 2003 proposes to restrict appeals to questions of law only
18   Rule 36 (see note 14)
19   Section 209 TULRCA 1992
20   Section 213 TULRCA 1992
21   Section 210(3) TULRCA 1992
22   See section 212(3) TULRCA 1992
23   See ACAS Arbitration Scheme (England and Wales) Order 2001 SI No.1185 and *The ACAS arbitration scheme for the resolution of unfair dismissal disputes: a guide to the scheme*, May 2001
24   See section 214 TULRCA 1992
25   See *R* v *CAC ex parte Hy-Mac Ltd* (1979) IRLR 461
26   See *R* v *CAC ex parte BTP Tioxide* (1982) IRLR 61
27   SI No.3323
27A See 17A above.
28   See section 256 TULRCA 1992
29   Section 108 TULRCA 1992
30   See sections 37A–E TULRCA 1992
31   See section 51 DPA 1998

Formation of the Contract of Employment (1): The Sources of Contractual Terms

CHAPTER 2

OVERVIEW

This chapter and the next one are concerned with the contract of employment and how it comes into existence. We consider the influences that contribute to establishing the contents of the contract. Express terms agreed between the employer and the employee, or the employee's representatives, normally take precedence over all other terms. There is a statutory requirement for the employer to issue written particulars of employment to new employees within two months of their start date. These particulars are considered in detail here, as is the influence of collective agreements, workforce agreements, works rules, and custom and practice.

CONTRACTS OF EMPLOYMENT

Apart from those of apprentices and merchant seamen, who can only be employed under written deeds and articles respectively, contracts of employment may be oral or in writing.[1] A contract of employment is like any other contract in the sense that it is subject to the general principles of law. In theory this means that the parties are free to negotiate the terms and conditions that suit them so long as they remain within the constraints imposed by statute and the common law.[2] In practice a significant proportion of the workforce do not negotiate on an individual basis. An important proportion are engaged on such terms and conditions as are laid down in currently operative collective agreements, although these agreements are, in practice, confined to the minority of employers because almost two thirds of workplaces in the UK do not have any employees covered by collective agreements.

Illegal contracts

One aspect of the common law which has been relied on, particularly in unfair dismissal cases, is the principle that courts will not enforce an illegal contract.[3] Thus, if employees receive additional payments which are not taxed, they may be debarred from exercising statutory rights on the ground that they were not employed under valid contracts of employment. However, an occasional payment by an employer to an employee without deduction of tax does not render the contract of employment unenforceable.[4]

Whether the employee is affected by the illegal performance of the contract by the employer depends on whether the employee was a party to or knew of the employer's illegality.[5] In *Coral Leisure Ltd* v *Barnet*[6] the EAT ruled that a distinction had to be drawn between cases in which there was a contractual obligation to perform an unlawful act, and cases where contractual obligations were capable of being performed lawfully and were initially intended to be so performed, but which had, in fact, been performed by unlawful means. The doing of an unlawful act by a party does not, of itself, preclude the further enforcement of that contract. Thus in *Hewcastle Catering* v *Ahmed*[7] the employee's involvement in a VAT fraud devised by the employer, and from which only the employer benefited, did not preclude a claim of unfair dismissal. According to the Court of Appeal, the general principle that a contract is unenforceable on grounds of illegality applies if in all the circumstances the court would appear to encourage illegal conduct. However, the defence of illegality will not succeed where the employer's conduct in participating in the illegal contract is so reprehensible in comparison with that of the employee that it would be wrong to allow the employer to rely on its being unenforceable.

Although a contract of employment can be entered into quite informally, because of the consequences of having an employee on the books (see Chapter 4) a considerable degree of formality is desirable. Indeed, if practical as well as legal difficulties are to be avoided, great care should be taken to ensure that all the relevant terms and conditions are understood at the time employment commences.

EXPRESS TERMS AND STATUTORY STATEMENTS

Express terms are those which are expressly stated to form part of the contract and they are binding irrespective of whether they differ from those contained in a job advertisement.[8] Apart from statutorily implied terms, which cannot be undermined, express terms normally take precedence over all other sources, ie common law implied terms and custom and practice. Not later than two months after the start of employment of a person whose employment continues for a month or more, the employer must supply written particulars of key terms of employment.[9] Indeed, in *Lange* v *Schünemann GmbH*[10] the European Court of Justice indicated that Article 2(1) of Directive 91/53 (on proof of the employment relationship) obliged an employer to notify an employee of any term which must be considered as an essential element of the contract. The reasoning behind this is clear: if employees receive written statements of the main terms of employment, disputes over the nature and scope of their contracts will be minimised.

Statement of particulars

The following information must be given to employees individually, although in relation to the matters mentioned in 6, 7, 9 and 15 below it is sufficient to make the information reasonably accessible to them by means of a document to which they are referred.[11]

1   *The identity of the parties*
    Sometimes the identity of the employer can be in dispute, eg where people are 'hired out' to other organisations[12] or where the employer consists of a management committee running a charity.[13]

2   *The date on which the employee's period of continuous employment began* (taking into account any employment with a previous employer which counts towards that period)
    Section 211 ERA 1996 defines the meaning of 'continuous employment' (see Chapter 16). It begins with the day that a person starts work for an organisation, except that any period worked before the age of 18 years does not count towards the length of service needed to qualify for a redundancy payment. Also not counted in the length of service are periods spent taking part in a strike (sections 215 and 216 ERA 1996). The period of continuous employment is important because certain statutory rights are associated with length of service, eg the right not to be unfairly dismissed and the right to redundancy payments (see Chapter 15). Section 218 ERA 1996 acts to preserve continuity of employment in certain circumstances, as do the Transfer of Undertakings (Protection of Employment) Regulations 1981[14] (Transfer Regulations). If continuity is not preserved, for whatever reason, qualified employees are entitled to redundancy payments from their previous employer. According to Regulation 5(1) of the Transfer Regulations, where there is a transfer of an undertaking (or part of an undertaking), employees who are transferred are to be treated as if they had originally made contracts with the transferee employer. This provision excludes even a consensual variation in the terms of the contract of employment if the transfer is the reason for the variation.[15] It should also be noted that Regulation 5(1) is not limited to those obligations that arise out of the particular contract in existence at the date of the transfer. It also applies to anything done before the transfer in respect of 'a person employed in that undertaking or part'.[16] (On the scope of the Transfer Regulations see Chapter 16.)

3 *The scale or rate of remuneration, or the method of calculating remuneration, and the intervals at which remuneration is paid*
The word 'remuneration' is not defined in the statute and ought to be regarded as including all financial benefits (see Chapter 5 on the National Minimum Wage Act 1998).

4 *Any terms and conditions relating to hours of work and normal working hours*
The concept of normal working hours is crucial (see Chapter 16), so in order to avoid confusion, employers should specify whether or not overtime is mandatory, ie forms part of the normal working hours. Care is especially needed when considering annualised hours contracts, where it may still be advisable to define the working week for the purpose of calculating holiday entitlement and any overtime payments due to people who leave during the working year. The courts or tribunals will not necessarily be prepared to fill gaps left by agreements that are not comprehensive. In *Ali* v *Christian Salvesen*[17] the Court of Appeal concluded that the parties to a collective agreement, which was expressly incorporated into a contract of employment, might deliberately have omitted provisions dealing with termination of employment during the calculation period on the grounds that it was too complicated or too controversial to include. Working hours are usually a matter for the parties to determine, but see Chapter 10 on the impact of the Working Time Regulations.[18]

5 *Any terms and conditions relating to holidays and holiday pay*
Employees are entitled to be paid if holidays are taken in accordance with the terms of their employment during their period of notice.[19] According to the EAT, the daily rate of pay for the purposes of accrued holiday entitlement should be calculated by dividing the annual salary by the number of working days.[20] Those employees protected by the Working Time Regulations are entitled to four weeks' paid holiday per leave year (Regulation 13). The leave year can be the subject of agreement or, if there is no such agreement, it will commence on the day employment began and each subsequent anniversary thereafter (see Chapter 10).

6 *Any terms and conditions relating to incapacity for work due to sickness or injury*
This includes any provision for sick pay (see Chapter 5).

7 *Any terms and conditions relating to pensions and pension schemes* (on stakeholder pensions, see page 51).

8 *A note stating whether a contracting-out certificate is in force*
This book does not generally address the complex issues of pension entitlement. However, it should be noted that where it is a contractual term that employees are entitled to benefits under a pension scheme, employers must discharge their functions under such a scheme in good faith and, so far as it is within their power, procure the benefits to which the employees are entitled.[21]

9 *The length of notice which the employee is entitled to receive and is obliged to give*
See Chapter 11.

10 *The title of the job or a brief description of the employee's work*
If, in the interests of flexibility, a job description is widely drawn, it should be pointed out to employees that the ambit of their contractual obligations may be wider than the particular duties upon which they are normally engaged.[22]

11 *Where the employment is temporary, the period for which it is expected to continue or, if it is for a fixed term, the date when it is to end*
On fixed-term contracts see Chapter 4.

12 *The place of work or, if the employee is required or permitted to work at various places, an indication of the employer's address*
If an employee works in a number of different countries, the place of work has been defined by the European Court of Justice as the place where the employee habitually carries out his or her work.[23]

13 *Any collective agreements which directly affect the terms and conditions of employment, including, where the employer is not a party, the person by whom they were made*

Such agreements can be incorporated into a contract of employment (see below) and may even be transferred to a new employer by the Transfer Regulations.[24]

14 *Where the employee is required to work outside the UK for more than a month*
The period of work outside the UK, the currency in which payment will be made, any additional pay and benefits to be provided by reason of the work being outside the UK, any terms and conditions relating to the employee's return to the UK.

The Posted Workers Directive[25] provides added protection for people working in a Member State other than that in which they normally work. Any rules in force, concerning terms and conditions of employment, as a result of law, regulation, administrative provision or by collective agreements in the State to which the employee is posted are to be guaranteed. These rules can include maximum work periods; rest periods; paid holidays; minimum rates of pay (although not supplementary occupational pensions); conditions for hiring out temporary workers; health and safety; protective measures for pregnant women and those that have recently given birth; and equal treatment between men and women.

15 *Any disciplinary rules applicable to the employee and any procedure applicable to the taking of disciplinary decisions (including dismissal) relating to the employee*[26]

16 *The name or description of the person to whom employees can apply if they are dissatisfied with any disciplinary decision or seek to redress a grievance*
The statement must indicate the manner in which any such application should be made. Section 29 and Schedule 2 EA 2002 introduce statutory dispute resolution procedures and, when section 30 EA 2002 comes into force, every contract of employment will be deemed to oblige the employer and the employee to comply with their requirements

17 *Any further steps consequent upon an application expressing dissatisfaction over a disciplinary decision (including dismissal) or grievance*
Three points should be noted here. Until section 36 EA 2002 comes into force, if the employer has fewer than 20 employees on the date the employment commences, the statement need not refer to disciplinary rules or procedures.[27] Secondly, although ERA 1996 does not state that employers must have disciplinary rules, the *Code of Practice on Disciplinary and Grievance Procedures* emphasises their desirability (see Chapter 13). Finally, rules, disciplinary decisions (including dismissals), grievances and procedures relating to health and safety at work are exempted because separate rules and procedures are thought to be appropriate in this area and should be referred to in the information provided by employers under section 2 HASAWA 1974 (see Chapter 9).

If there are no particulars to be entered under any of the above headings, that fact must be mentioned in the written statement. It should also be noted that information relating to items 8, 11, 13, 14 and 16 may be given in instalments within the two-month period. The other items must be dealt with in a single document called a 'principal statement'. When section 37 EA 2002 comes into force, the information required can be supplied in the form of a written statement, a contract of employment or a letter or engagement.[28]

Changes cannot be made to a contract of employment without the consent of the employee but, where there is a change in any of the details required by section 1, written notification must be given to the employee within one month.[29] The nature of the changes must be set out in full, although the employer may refer to other documents for the same matters and in the same manner as for the original provision of particulars. There is no provision for the changes to be notified in instalments.

The status of the statement of particulars

It is important to understand that the statement issued does not constitute a contract or even conclusive evidence of its terms, but is merely the employer's version of what has been agreed.[30] Indeed, in *Robertson* v *British Gas*[31] the Court of Appeal decided that a statutory statement could not even be used as an aid to the interpretation of the contract. If agreement has not been reached in a key area, management may choose to include in that statement what it considers to be reasonable arrangements. Technically the statement will be inaccurate (because the terms were on offer rather than agreed at the time they were issued) but if the employee accepts the arrangements or acquiesces in them, ie by not challenging them, the employer's proposals may be deemed to have contractual effect. However, the EAT has suggested that a distinction might be drawn between a matter which has immediate practical application and one which does not. In *Jones* v *Associated Tunnelling Co.*[32] it was thought that it would be asking too much of ordinary employees to require them to object to erroneous statements of terms which had no immediate practical impact on them. The law does not oblige employees to sign the written particulars or even acknowledge their receipt, but if they confirm that what has been issued is an accurate summary of the main employment terms, the particulars may be treated by the courts as having contractual status.[33]

'Mandatory' and 'non-mandatory' terms

Where an employee is given a complete but incorrect statement, ie some of the particulars are wrong in that they do not reproduce what was agreed between the parties, the employee can complain to an employment tribunal, which has the power to confirm, amend or replace the particulars. If there is no written statement or an incomplete one is issued, the tribunal must determine what the missing particulars are.[34] According to the Court of Appeal,[35] the particulars required under 1, 2, 3, 9 and 10 above are 'mandatory' terms in that actual particulars must be given under those headings. On the other hand, the particulars required under 4–7 were viewed as 'non-mandatory' in the sense that no particulars need to be inserted if none has been agreed. As regards 'non-mandatory' terms, the Court of Appeal held that an employment tribunal could not invent a term if nothing had been agreed by the parties. However, where a 'mandatory' term was omitted from a statement a tribunal would probably have to infer one. When the tribunal has decided what particulars should have been included, the employer is deemed to have provided the employee with a statement containing those particulars.[36] Currently, there is no financial sanction on an employer who fails to supply a written statement of initial employment particulars or of particulars of change. However, when section 38 EA 2002 comes into force, in any of the proceedings listed in Schedule 5 EA 2002 a tribunal will be obliged to make or increase an award by a minimum of two weeks' pay (or a maximum of four weeks' pay if that is considered just and equitable.)[37]

COLLECTIVE AGREEMENTS

Terms may be derived from collective agreements as well as being individually negotiated. Such agreements tend to be classed as being of either a procedural or a substantive nature. A procedural agreement aims to govern the relationship between the signatories (employers and trade unions) by establishing methods of handling disputes, whereas a substantive agreement is intended to regulate the terms and conditions of employment of those who are covered by it. Like any other agreement, collective agreements will be construed by giving meaning to the words used in the factual context known to the parties at the time.[38] It is possible to conclude a collective agreement which is legally enforceable (see Chapter 19), although this is not normally the wish of either party. By what mechanism then do individual employees derive the legal right to claim the terms and conditions which have been negotiated on their behalf? The answer lies in the process of incorporation, for by this device collectively agreed terms become legally binding as part of the individual contract of employment.[39] The simplest way of ensuring that substantive terms are incorporated into an employee's contract is by an express provision to this effect. Thus, workers may be employed on the basis of 'terms and conditions of employment which are covered by existing collective agreements negotiated and agreed with specific trade unions or unions recognised ... for collective bargaining purposes'.[40] Commonly, collective agreements will be expressly incorporated because they are referred to in a section 1 ERA 1996 statement of particulars.

In relation to the matters specified above, section 2 ERA 1996 permits employers to refer to 'some other document which is reasonably accessible', and this document may be a copy of the currently operative collective agreement. Equally, it is possible for terms to be incorporated from a collective agreement by implication or custom and practice, although this is less desirable because of the uncertainties involved.[41] Implied incorporation occurs when employees have specific knowledge of the collective agreement and there is conduct which demonstrates that they accept the agreement and are willing to work under it. While this might be relatively straightforward in the case of union members, difficulties can arise in establishing the legal position of non-members. If such employees have habitually accepted and abided by the terms negotiated by the union, an implication arises that they will be bound by future agreements. However, if at any stage non-members declare that they are no longer willing to be bound by such agreements, that implication is no longer valid.[42]

No-strike clauses and collective agreements

It is normally quite easy to decide which terms of a collective agreement are appropriate for incorporation into an individual contract of employment: it is the substantive terms (eg on wages, hours, etc) rather than the procedural ones.[43] However, difficulties have been experienced in relation to no-strike clauses. An undertaking by the union not to call a strike before relevant procedures have been exhausted imposes an obligation on the union alone, but the following clause is clearly capable of being incorporated into individual contracts of employment: 'Employees will not engage in a strike or other industrial action until the grievance procedure has been exhausted.' The situation has been clarified by section 180 TULRCA 1992 which provides that no-strike clauses are binding only if the collective agreement:

- is in writing and contains a provision stating that the clause may be incorporated into a contract of employment
- is reasonably accessible to the employees concerned
- is concluded by an independent trade union and the individual contract of employment expressly or impliedly incorporates the no-strike clause.

Such clauses can be useful in drawing an employee's attention to the illegality of industrial action, but strictly speaking they are unnecessary because most forms of industrial action are likely to breach an obligation imposed on all employees by the common law, ie the duty not to impede the employer's business (see Chapter 21).

WORKFORCE AGREEMENTS

The Working Time Regulations 1998 and the Maternity and Parental Leave Regulations 1999 are examples of where it is possible for 'relevant' agreements to be reached which enable employers to agree variations to the Regulations directly with their employees or with their representatives. These 'relevant' agreements can be reached via a process of bargaining. Where there are no collective agreements, employers can reach workforce agreements with their employees or their representatives. Regulation 23 of the Working Time Regulations allows a workforce agreement to modify or exclude Regulation 4(3) concerning the reference period for calculating the 48-hour average, Regulations 6(1) to (3) and (7) concerning night work, Regulation 10(1) concerning the entitlement to an 11-hour break in each 24 hours, Regulations 11(1) and (2) concerning a weekly or fortnightly break, Regulation 12(1) concerning rest breaks, provided certain conditions are met. These conditions are contained in Schedule 1. An agreement is a workforce agreement where:

- it is in writing
- it has effect for a specified period not exceeding five years
- it applies to all the relevant members of a workforce or all the relevant members who belong to a particular group

- it is signed by the representatives of the group[44]
- copies of the agreement are readily available for reading prior to the signing.

WORKS RULES AND POLICY GUIDANCE

The essential difference between collective agreements and works rules lies not so much in their subject matter but in the fact that the contents of the latter are unilaterally determined by the employer. While both can be expressly or impliedly incorporated into individual contracts of employment (using the mechanisms described above), works rules offer one great advantage to the employer: whereas a collective agreement can be altered only with the consent of the parties to it, management can lawfully change the content of works rules at any time. A refusal to adhere to the revised rules would amount to a breach of contract (ie a failure to obey lawful and reasonable orders) even if there had been no advance warning or consultation with the employees affected. Thus a contractual term to the effect that employees must abide by 'the currently operative works rules' affords management the maximum degree of flexibility.[45]

There may be rules that constitute employer guidance or policy and are therefore not appropriate as contractual terms. Such a situation might arise when the employer is setting out practice and procedures rather than conferring rights on individuals. This occurred in *Wandsworth London Borough Council v D'Silva*[46] where changes to a code of practice on staff sickness were made by the employer without consultation with employees or their representatives. The EAT held that these changes amounted to alterations to a code of good practice, rather than an attempt to unilaterally alter the contract of employment. However, the dismissal of an employee for failing to comply with revised works rules or policy guidance will not necessarily be fair because it will depend on what an employment tribunal regards as being 'reasonable in all the circumstances' (see Chapter 13).

CUSTOM AND PRACTICE

In the days when written contracts of employment were less common and written statements of particulars were not required by statute, custom and practice played an important part in helping to identify the contractual terms. Today custom and practice is not such an important source of law, although it may still be invoked occasionally to fill gaps in the employment relationship. To do so, a custom or practice must be definite, reasonable and generally applied in the area or trade in question. If these criteria are met, the fact that the particular employee against whom the custom is applied is ignorant of its existence appears to be of no consequence.[47] In determining whether a policy drawn up unilaterally by management has become a term of the employee's contract on the grounds that it is an established custom and practice, all the circumstances have to be taken into account. Among the most important circumstances are whether the policy has been drawn to the attention of employees by management or has been followed without exception for a substantial period.[48]

The major drawback of custom and practice is its uncertain legal effect and therefore its unreliability. After what period of time can it be said that a non-union member who has always worked in accordance with current collective agreements is bound to accept future agreements? If a custom and practice is useful to management, it is logical that efforts should be made to convert it into an express term of the contract. This may not always be possible, either because of the imprecise nature of the custom or because unions might oppose such a move as being contrary to the interests of their members. It almost goes without saying that a union will be in a better position to modify a custom or practice if it has not become embodied in a contract of employment. Finally, it should be noted that there may still be a place for custom and practice as an aid to interpreting a contractual term that is truly ambiguous.[49]

TERMS IMPLIED BY STATUTE AND REGULATIONS

There are a number of examples of statues and regulations implying terms into contracts of employment:

1 *Terms and conditions awarded by the CAC*
   Under section 185 TULRCA 1992 (on disclosure of information) these terms operate as part of the contract of employment of each worker affected. However, the terms and conditions imposed may be superseded or varied by a collective agreement between the employer and the union 'for the time being representing the employee' or an express or implied agreement between the employer and the employee so far as that agreement effects an improvement in the terms and conditions awarded by the CAC.

2 *The equality clause*
   This is inserted by virtue of section 1 of the Equal Pay Act 1970 (EPA 1970), as amended (see Chapter 6).

3 *The National Minimum Wage Act 1998*
   This allows the Secretary of State to make provision for determining the hourly rate to be paid. Section 2(3) allows provision to be made with respect to when a person is to be treated as working and when he or she is not.

4 *The Working Time Regulations*
   These provide for maximum hours to be worked in various situations and occupations (see Chapter 10).

5 *Statutory dispute resolution procedures*
   Notwithstanding any agreement to the contrary, section 30 EA 2002 deems every contract of employment to oblige both the employer and employee to comply with the requirements of statutory dispute resolution in procedures.

TERMS IMPLIED BY THE COMMON LAW

There are two distinct types of common-law implied terms. First, where there is a gap in the contract of employment it is possible to imply a term if a court can be persuaded that it is necessary to do so in the circumstances of the particular case (implied terms of fact). Second, there are terms which are regarded by the courts as being inherent in all contracts of employment (implied terms of law). The next chapter will examine the major obligations which are automatically imposed on the parties to a contract of employment.

It is a basic principle that a contractual term can be implied only if it is consistent with the express terms of the contract. However, despite the increased use of written contracts and statements, it is not unusual for the parties to discover that they have failed to provide for a particular contingency. If there is a dispute over something which is not expressly dealt with in the contract of employment, a court or tribunal may be asked to insert a term to cover the point at issue. The party wishing to rely on an implied term must satisfy a court either that such a term was so obvious that the parties did not think it necessary to state it expressly (the 'officious bystander' test) or that such a term was necessary to give 'business efficacy' to the relationship.[50]

KEY POINTS

- Express terms normally take precedence over all other terms apart from those implied by statute.
- Not later than two months after the start of employment the employer must supply written particulars of employment, as provided in sections 1–3 ERA 1996.
- The statement does not constitute a contract of employment. It is merely the employer's version of what has been agreed.
- Terms of a contract may be derived from collective agreements as well as being individually negotiated.
- Substantive terms from a collective agreement may be incorporated into an employee's contract of employment expressly or impliedly or as a result of custom and practice.
- Workforce agreements can provide for a variation in the Working Time Regulations and other specified rights where there is no collective agreement.
- Works rules are normally determined by the employer and can be expressly or impliedly incorporated into a contract of employment.
- Custom and practice, if it is definite, reasonable and generally applied, can be used to fill gaps in the employment relationship.
- Terms, such as the equality clause in section 1 EPA 1970, can be implied in the contract of employment by statute.
- Terms can also be implied by the common law if they are consistent with the express terms.

NOTES

1. On the distinction between a contract of apprenticeship and a contract of employment or training contract see *Wallace* v *C.A. Roofing Ltd* (1996) IRLR 435 and *Edmunds* v *Lawson* (2000) IRLR 391
2. On the application of the Unfair Contract Terms Act 1977 see *Brigden* v *American Express* (2000) IRLR 94
3. Although tribunal jurisdiction in anti-discrimination cases may not depend on the existence of an enforceable contract of employment; see *Governors of Stanhope School* v *Vakante* (2003) ICR 290
4. See *Annandale Engineering* v *Samson* (1994) IRLR 59
5. See *Salvesson* v *Simons* (1994) IRLR 52
6. (1981) IRLR 204
7. (1991) IRLR 473
8. See *Deeley* v *British Rail Engineering Ltd* (1980) IRLR 147
9. Sections 1–2 ERA 1996
10. (2001) IRLR 244
11. See sections 2(2) and (3) ERA 1996
12. For a discussion of this see *Secretary of State* v *Bearman* (1998) IRLR 431
13. See *Affleck* v *Newcastle Mind* (1999) IRLR 405
14. SI 1981/1794
15. See *& anor Martin* v *Southbank University* (2004) IRLR 74 and *Wilson* v *St Helens Borough Council* (1998) IRLR 706
16. See Regulation 5(2)(b) Transfer Regulations and *DJM International Ltd* v *Nicholas* (1996) IRLR 76
17. (1997) IRLR 17
18. SI 1998/1833
19. See section 88(1)(d) ERA 1996
20. See *Leisure Leagues Ltd* v *Maconnachie* (2002) IRLR 600
21. See *Mihlenstedt* v *Barclays Bank* (1989) IRLR 522
22. See *Glitz* v *Watford Electrical* (1978) IRLR 89

23 See *Rutten* v *Cross Medical Ltd* (1997) IRLR 249

24 See *Whent* v *T. Cartledge* (1997) IRLR 153

25 Directive 96/71

26 Section 3(1) ERA 1996

27 See section 3(3) ERA 1996

28 Section 7A ERA 1996

29 See section 4 ERA 1996

30 See *Systems Floors (UK) Ltd* v *Daniel* (1981) IRLR 475

31 (1983) IRLR 302

32 (1981) IRLR 477; see also *Aparau* v *Iceland Frozen Foods* (1996) IRLR 119

33 See *Gascol Conversions* v *Mercer* (1974) IRLR 155

34 Section 11 ERA 1996

35 *Eagland* v *British Telecom plc* (1992) IRLR 323

36 Section 12(2) ERA 1996

37 Section 38(5) EA 2002 deals with exceptional circumstances

38 See *Adams* v *British Airways* (1996) IRLR 574

39 See *Gibbons* v *Associated British Ports* (1985) IRLR 376

40 See *Airlie* v *City of Edinburgh District Council* (1996) IRLR 516

41 See *Hamilton* v *Futura Floors* (1990) IRLR 478 and *Henry* v *LGTS Ltd* (2002) IRLR 472

42 See *Singh* v *British Steel* (1974) IRLR 478

43 On the enforceability of redeployment and redundancy agreements see *Marley* v *Forward Trust Ltd* (1996) IRLR 369; on the enforceability of a recognition agreement see *NCB* v *NUM* (1986) IRLR 439

44 There are provisions which allow employers with fewer than 20 employees to have the majority of those employees sign in order for a workforce agreement to come into being

45 See *Cadoux* v *Central Regional Council* (1986) IRLR 131

46 (1998) IRLR 193

47 See *Sagar* v *Ridehalgh* (1931) Ch 310

48 See *Quinn* v *Calder* (1996) IRLR 126

49 See *Dunlop Tyres Ltd* v *Blows* (2001) IRLR 629 on the interpretation of an ambiguous collective agreement

50 See *United Bank* v *Akhtar* (1989) IRLR 507

Formation of the Contract of Employment (2): Implied Terms of Law

CHAPTER 3

OVERVIEW

In the previous chapter we looked at the different ways in which contractual terms may come into existence and observed that certain terms could be implied into all contracts of employment. We must now examine the major obligations imposed on both employers and employees by law. Some of these are based on long-established common-law principles, while others (such as those to do with unfair dismissal) are of relatively recent origin, having emerged as a result of legislative intervention.

DUTIES OF THE EMPLOYER

To pay wages

This is the most basic obligation of employers and is normally dealt with by an express term. In certain circumstances, however, the law does not leave the parties entirely free to determine the amount of remuneration payable, eg in the application of the national minimum wage or if an equality clause operates. Pay issues are considered in Chapter 5.

To provide work

Employers are generally not obliged to provide work and most employees who receive their full contractual remuneration cannot complain if they are left idle. Nevertheless, in certain circumstances the failure to provide work may amount to a breach of contract.

If a person's earnings depend upon work being provided

Employees who are paid by results or commission or who receive shift premiums must be given the opportunity to work because the payment of basic wages alone would deprive them of a substantial part of what they had bargained for – the opportunity to earn more.

Where the lack of work could lead to a loss of publicity or affect the reputation of an employee

Indeed, in one tribunal case it was held that the higher a person is in the management structure, the more important it is for work to be given when it is available.[1]

Where an employee needs to practise in order to preserve his or her skills

The Court of Appeal has suggested that such employees should be given the opportunity of performing work when it is available.[2] This is linked to the issue of 'garden leave' (see below), which is the practice of continuing to pay an employee for a period, but not allowing him or her to work during that time. It has sometimes been used to prevent a valuable employee from leaving and immediately taking up employment with a competitor. A problem arises when such a period without work can have a detrimental affect on an employee's skills. In *William Hill Organisation Ltd* v *Tucker*[3] the Court of Appeal held that the employer had an obligation to provide work when the work was available. This was partly because of the need to practise and partly because there was a contractual obligation on the employee to 'work those hours necessary to carry out his duties in a full and professional manner'.

To co-operate with the employee

Originally this duty amounted to little more than an obligation not to impede the employees in the performance of their contracts. However, one of the effects of the unfair dismissal provisions has been that the
courts have displayed a greater willingness to accept that employers have a positive duty to ensure that
the purposes of the contract are achieved. Thus it has frequently been stated that employers must not
destroy the mutual trust and confidence upon which co-operation is built without reasonable and proper
cause.[4] However, the House of Lords has ruled that such a term is concerned with preserving the continuing employment relationship and does not apply to the way that the relationship is terminated.[5] There are
also limits as to how positive this obligation should be. In *University of Nottingham* v *Eyett*,[6] for example, a
failure by an employer to warn an employee, who was proposing to exercise important rights in connection
with pension benefits, that the way the employee was proposing to exercise those rights was not the most
financially advantageous was not seen as breaching a duty of mutual trust and confidence. Each case
depends on its particular set of facts, but some examples of situations in which employers have been held
to be in breach of this implied term are:

- the changing of the terms of a transferred employee's bridging loan to his or her detriment[7]
- the operation by an employer of a business in a dishonest and corrupt manner which damaged
  an innocent employee's reputation,[8] although the employee may only be able to claim
  damages if he or she can show that the damage to their reputation has actually caused financial
  loss[9]
- an employer's discretion under a mobility clause being exercised in a way that made it impossible
  for the employee to comply with a contractual obligation to move[10]
- a failure to investigate a genuine safety grievance[11]
- employees not being afforded a reasonable opportunity to obtain redress of a grievance[12]
- a false accusation of theft on the basis of flimsy evidence[13]
- reprimanding an employee in public[14]
- the persistent attempt by an employer to vary an employee's conditions of service[15]
- without reasonable cause, denying the employee the opportunity given to everyone else of signing
  a revised contract with enhanced redundancy payments.[16]

This duty should also inhibit employers from issuing unjustified warnings which are designed not to improve
performance but to dishearten employees and drive them out.[17]

The House of Lords has also accepted that in certain circumstances it will be necessary to imply an obligation on the employer to take reasonable steps to bring a contractual term to the employee's attention.
Such a duty will arise when:

- the contractual terms have not been negotiated with individuals but result from collective bargaining or are otherwise incorporated by reference
- a particular term makes available to employees a valuable right contingent upon action being taken
  by them to avail themselves of its benefit
- employees cannot in all the circumstances reasonably be expected to be aware of the term unless
  it is drawn to their attention.[18]

Although employers should provide sufficient information to enable employees to understand the choices
available to them, the Court of Appeal has ruled that they do not have to ensure that the information was

actually communicated. All the employer has to do is to take reasonable steps to inform the employees about their rights.[19]

To take reasonable care of the employee

In addition to this duty implied by law, there are a number of key statutes in the area of health and safety. We shall be looking at the legislation in Chapter 9, although it is important to note at this stage that a person who is injured in the course of employment in a factory may be able to bring an action for damages based either on the common-law duty or breach of statute or other regulations. 'In the course of employment' means the claimant was doing something that he or she was employed to do, or something reasonably incidental to those things. In *Chief Adjudication Officer* v *Rhodes*,[20] an employee of the Benefits Agency was assaulted at her home, when off sick from work, by a neighbour whom she had reported for suspected fraud. The Court of Appeal decided that although the incident arose out of her employment it did not take place in the course of that employment.

Recognising that employers cannot guarantee that no employees will be injured at work, the standard of care which the law demands is that which 'an ordinary prudent employer would take in all the circumstances'.[21] Generally speaking, if a job has risks to health and safety which are not common knowledge but about which an employer knows or ought to know, and against which she or he cannot guard by taking precautions, then the employer should tell anyone to whom employment is offered what those risks are if, on the information then available, knowledge of those risks would be likely to affect the decision of a sensible prospective employee about accepting the offer.[22] Thus the common law accepts that employers should be held liable only if they fail to safeguard against something which was reasonably foreseeable.[23] In *Pickford* v *ICI*[24] it was held that it was not reasonably foreseeable that a secretary spending 50 per cent of her time in typing would suffer, as a result, from repetitive strain injury. Indeed, it was assumed that a person of intelligence and experience would be able to intersperse the typing with other activities without being told to do so.

It should also be observed that the general duty of care does not extend to taking all reasonable steps to protect the economic welfare of employees, whether by insuring them against special risks known to the employer or by advising them of those risks so that they can obtain appropriate cover.

Employers' single personal duty of care to each employee

Employers are entitled to follow recognised practices in their industry, unless the practices are obviously unsafe, but must make arrangements to ensure that they keep abreast of current developments, eg by joining an employers' association. Once an employer knows of a source of danger, or could have been expected to know of it, it is necessary to take all reasonable steps to protect employees from risks which have hitherto been unforeseeable.[25] The duty is to assess the likelihood of injury and to weigh the risk against the cost and inconvenience of taking effective precautions to eliminate it. Employers owe a single personal duty of care to each of their employees, having proper regard to the employee's skill and experience, etc. Thus even if the employer delegates this duty to another person who is reasonably believed to be competent to perform it, the employer will remain personally liable for injuries to an employee caused by that other person's negligence.[26] Similarly, where an employee's labour is subcontracted, the employer's duty of care is still owed.[27]

Having considered some general issues, it may be useful to subdivide this duty into the following headings:

Safe premises

The case of *Latimer* v *AEC Ltd*[28] provides a suitable illustration of what is required of employers in this connection. Owing to exceptionally heavy rainfall, a factory was flooded. A layer of oil and grease was left on the floor which the employers attempted to cover with sawdust. However, this was not spread across all of the factory floor and an employee slipped in an area which was uncovered. It was held by the House of Lords that the employers had taken reasonable precautions and they could not be expected to close down their factory in order to avoid what was a fairly small risk of injury.[29] More recently it has been acknowledged that in certain circumstances UK-based employers may have to satisfy themselves as to the safety of overseas sites. According to the Court of Appeal, the employer's duty to take all reasonable steps to ensure the safety of employees applies whether the premises where the employee is required to work are occupied by the employer or by a third party.[30]

Safe plant, equipment and tools

If employers know that a tool or a piece of machinery could be a source of danger, it is incumbent upon them to take reasonable precautions to safeguard employees. Where tools or equipment are purchased from a reputable supplier and employers have no reason to suspect that they are defective, they cannot be held liable at common law. If in these circumstances an employee were to sustain an injury as a result of a defect, he or she would be obliged to sue the person responsible, such as the supplier or manufacturer, under the general law of negligence, in order to recover damages.

Safe system of work

Under this heading are included all the matters which relate to the manner in which the work is performed: job design, working methods, the provision of protective clothing, training and supervision. Indeed, it is now accepted that employers have a duty not to cause their employees psychological damage by the volume or character of the work that they are required to perform.[31] However, the Court of Appeal has ruled that, unless an employer knows of some particular problem or vulnerability it is usually entitled to assume that the employee can withstand normal pressures of the job. According to the court, there are no occupations which should be regarded as intrinsically dangerous to mental health.[32] Equally contentious is the view that if the only reasonable way of safeguarding the employee would be to demote or dismiss, an employer will not be in breach of the duty of care in allowing a willing employee to continue in the job. Thus in *Coxall* v *Goodyear Ltd*[33] it was held that the employer was under a duty either to take the claimant off the job or, as a matter of last resort, to dismiss. If safety rules and procedures exist, employees must be informed of their content, and if safety clothing or equipment is required, it must be readily available.[34] Clearly the more dangerous the task or workplace situation, the greater is the need for precautions to be taken – but how far must an employer go to ensure that safety devices are properly used?

In *Crouch* v *British Rail Engineering*[35] the Court of Appeal decided that where an employee is regularly performing tasks which involve a reasonably foreseeable risk to the eyes, the employer has the duty actually to put goggles into the employee's hands. Similarly, employees who are likely to do a great deal of typing should be told that they must take breaks and rest pauses.[36] In *Pape* v *Cumbria County Council*[37] the High Court ruled that an employer has a duty to warn cleaners of the dangers of handling chemical cleaning materials with unprotected hands and to instruct them on the need to wear gloves at all times. It would seem that the circumstances that have to be considered in ascertaining the extent of the duty of care include: the risk of injury; the gravity of any injury which might result; the difficulty of providing protective equipment or clothing; the availability of that equipment or clothing and the distance the worker might have to go to fetch it; the frequency of occasions on which the employee is likely to need the protective equipment or clothing; and the experience and degree of skill to be expected of the employee. Bearing in mind both this common-law duty and the obligations imposed by legislation (see Chapter 9), managers would be advised to ensure that an unreasonable refusal to follow safety rules or procedures is classed as a breach of discipline which could ultimately lead to dismissal for misconduct.

Competent and safe colleagues

Employers are required to take reasonable steps to ensure that employees do not behave in such a fashion that they are a source of danger to others. This means that employers must engage competent staff, or train recruits to a safe-worker level, must instruct their employees in safe working methods, and must then provide adequate supervision to check that these methods are being adhered to. Practical jokers cannot be tolerated, and if they do not respond to warnings their employment should be terminated in accordance with disciplinary procedures. Such people are a threat to everyone and are unlikely to attract the sympathy of their workmates.

This duty extends to a working environment in which an employee's colleagues smoke. In *Walton & Morse* v *Dorrington*[38] a secretary worked in the same office as a number of others, some of whom smoked. This was not a problem to her when working in a well-ventilated room. When they were moved to an office where this was not the case, the smoke became a source of irritation and discomfort. Eventually she left when her employers would not make any changes. The EAT held that her employers were in breach of an implied term to provide their employees with, so far as was reasonably practicable, 'a working environment which is reasonably suitable for the performance by them of their contractual duties'.

To provide references

In *Spring* v *Guardian Assurance plc*[39] the complainant argued that a reference provided by a former employer was a malicious falsehood and/or a negligent misstatement and/or a breach of an implied term in the contract of employment that any reference would be compiled with all reasonable care. The House of Lords concluded that an employer has a duty to take reasonable care in compiling a reference by ensuring the accuracy of the information upon which it was based. The duty is to provide a reference which is in substance true, accurate and fair, and this will usually involve making a reasonable enquiry into the factual basis of any statements made.[40] The provider of a reference must not give an impression that is unfair or misleading overall, even if the component parts of the reference are accurate.[41] This can clearly mean the inclusion of matters not in the employee's favour as well as those that are.

DUTIES OF THE EMPLOYEE

To co-operate with the employer

We are concerned here with the duty to obey lawful and reasonable orders and the duty not to impede the employer's business. In this context the obligation to carry out lawful orders has two distinct aspects. First, it means that employees are not required to comply with an order if to do so would break the law, for example by producing false accounts. Second, it also means that employees are not obliged to accept orders which fall outside the scope of the contract. This is consistent with the view that (at least in theory) the terms of a contract cannot be varied unilaterally. However, as we shall discover later (Chapter 13), this does not prevent employees from being fairly dismissed for refusing to follow instructions which may be outside their contractual obligations.[42]

As regards the duty not to impede the employer's business, it is clear that going on strike breaches a fundamental term of the contract: the essence of the employment relationship is that the employee is ready and willing to work in exchange for remuneration. However, is there a duty on employees not to engage in industrial action which falls short of a strike? In the leading case of the *Secretary of State* v *ASLEF*,[43] which involved a work to rule on the railways, the Court of Appeal gave different reasons for reaching the conclusion that such a duty exists. Lord Justice Roskill thought that there is an implied term that employees ought not to obey lawful instructions in such a way as to disrupt the employer's business. Lord Justice Buckley extended the notion of fidelity (see below) and proclaimed that 'the employee must serve the employer faithfully with a view to promoting those commercial interests for which he is employed'. Lord Denning chose to focus attention on motive, ie the wilfulness of the disruption caused, and his formulation leads to the conclusion that all forms of industrial action are likely to be unlawful. The High Court has also ruled that it is a professional obligation on teachers to co-operate in running schools and that the failure to cover for absent colleagues amounts to a breach of contract.[44] (On the options open to an employer where an employee only part-performs the contract see Chapter 11.)

Fidelity

Employees must avoid putting themselves in a position whereby their own interests conflict with the duty they owe their employer or an employer to whom they have been seconded.[45] Thus employees must not accept any reward for their work other than from their employer, eg a gift or secret commission. However, there is no implied obligation on employees to disclose their own misconduct and whether there is a duty to report the misconduct of fellow employees depends on the individual contract of employment and the circumstances.[46] There are two particular aspects to this duty which we must now consider: the obligation not to compete with the employer, and the obligation not to disclose confidential information.

The obligation not to compete with the employer

Generally the spare-time activities of employees are no business of the employer, although an injunction may be granted to prevent employees from working for competitors during their spare time if it can be shown that the employer's business would be seriously damaged. However, in *Nova Plastics Ltd* v *Frogatt*[47] the EAT rejected the argument that there is a general implication that any work for a competitor should be regarded as being a breach of trust or a failure to give loyal service. It should be noted that the intention to set up in competition with the employer is not in itself a breach of the implied duty of loyalty, although there is a line over which the employee must not go. The renting and equipping of premises in an employee's spare time, and the arranging of financial backing to set up in competition may be construed as a breach of an implied duty of fidelity.[48] If the employer has reasonable grounds for believing that the employee has committed or is about to commit some wrongful act, dismissal may be justified (see Chapter 13).[49]

Restraint clauses

Normally ex-employees are entitled to make use of the skills and knowledge which they have acquired, and are allowed to compete with a former employer provided they do not rely on confidential information (see below). However, this is not the position if there is an express clause in the contract of employment which restrains competition by employees when they leave.[50] Such restraint clauses (restrictive covenants) will be enforced by the courts only if they provide protection against something more than competition alone, if they are shown to be reasonable in the circumstances, and if they are not contrary to the public interest.[51] A clause stopping an ex-employee ever dealing with any of the plaintiff's customers with whom he or she dealt might be unreasonable, but one restricting contact with customers dealt with during the previous six months might be acceptable.[52] The reasonableness of the restraint is to be assessed as at the date the contract was made.[53] Non-competition clauses in a contract may be reasonable to protect the employer's proprietary interests in the customer connections that have been built up by the departing employees, although non-solicitation clauses should not be too broad. It would be an unreasonable restraint of trade to stop employees or ex-employees soliciting even the most junior of employees.[54]

'Garden leave'

What about the enforcement of 'garden leave' clauses, ie clauses which provide that during the period of notice an employee is not obliged to work but will receive full pay and meanwhile must not work for anyone else? Such clauses will not be enforced if it appears that the business for which the employee wishes to work before the notice expires has nothing to do with the employer's business. On the other hand, where the period during which the employee is not required to work is not excessive and there is a risk of damage to the employer's business, it may be appropriate to restrain the employee from taking other employment during the notice period, either under a specific clause or as a breach of duty of fidelity.[55] However, the wrongful or unfair dismissal of an employee will prevent the employer from relying on a restrictive covenant.[56]

Finally, one effect of Regulation 5 of the Transfer Regulations (see Chapter 17) is that the transferee may benefit from a restrictive covenant in contracts of employment made with the transferor. Thus an employee may be restrained from doing or seeking to do business with anyone who had dealt with the transferor during the period stipulated in the original contract.[57] Even if the employee has entered into an agreement, in return for payment, that he or she will not work for a competitor, the employer may find it difficult to enforce this agreement if it took place by way of a variation of contract resulting from a transfer of the undertaking.[58]

The obligation not to disclose confidential information

The following principles have been enunciated by the Court of Appeal.[59] First, an individual's obligations are to be determined by the contract of employment, and in the absence of any express term the employee's obligations in respect of the use and disclosure of information are the subject of implied terms. Second, while the individual remains in employment the obligations are included in the implied term which imposes a duty of fidelity on the employee. The extent of this duty varies according to the nature of the contract and would be broken if an employee copied a list of the employer's customers for use after the employment ended, or deliberately memorised such a list.[60] Third, the implied term which imposes an obligation on the employee as to his or her conduct after the employment has terminated is more restricted than that imposed by the duty of fidelity. The obligation not to use or disclose information might cover secret processes of manufacture or designs, or any other information of a sufficiently high degree of confidentiality as to amount to a trade secret.[61] However, this obligation does not extend to information which is only 'confidential' in the sense that any unauthorised disclosure to a third party while the employment subsisted would be a breach of the duty of fidelity. Fourth, in order to determine whether any particular item of information falls within the implied term thus preventing its use or disclosure after the employment has ceased, it is necessary to consider all the circumstances of the case. Among the matters to which attention must be paid are:

- *the nature of the employment* – a high obligation of confidentiality might be imposed if the employment was such that confidential material was habitually handled

- *the nature of the information* – in deciding whether there is a legitimate trade secret to be protected, a distinction needs to be made between information which can be legitimately regarded as the property of the employer and the skill, know-how and general knowledge which can be regarded as the property of the employee. According to the courts, 'objective knowledge' is the employer's property and 'subjective knowledge' belongs to the employee[62]

- *whether the employer impressed on the employee the confidentiality of the information* – however, an employer cannot prevent the use or disclosure of information merely by telling the employee that it is confidential.

In practice it can be very difficult to differentiate between use and abuse of the knowledge which an ex-employee possesses, for example of the former employer's customers. Thus employers should be advised to draft express restraint clauses which set precise limits on the future employment of key workers. Such clauses must be carefully worded, for it is a court's duty to give effect to covenants as they are expressed rather than to correct errors or remedy omissions.[63] Because breaches are relatively easy to identify, enforcing such clauses should be a fairly simple process. Indeed, the mere presence of a restraint clause can be valuable as a reminder to the employee that disclosure of confidential information will not be condoned. The employer who relies solely on the implied term is at a serious disadvantage, because an employee can be stopped from disclosing confidential information only when the employer has proved that such information has already been divulged. Only then will an aggrieved employer have a remedy against a third party to whom the employee has passed trade secrets or confidential information.[64]

Two further points need to be considered. First, in an appropriate case a court has power to grant injunctions against ex-employees to restrain them from fulfilling contracts already concluded with third parties.[65]

Second, although the Data Protection Act 1998 now imposes additional constraints on an employee's ability to disclose information (see Chapter 18), the Public Interest Disclosure Act 1998 protects workers who make certain disclosures in the public interest (see below).

To take reasonable care

Employees must exercise reasonable skill and care in the performance of their contracts.[66] If they do not do so, apart from any disciplinary action that may be taken against them, there is an implied duty to indemnify the employer in respect of the consequences of their negligence.[67] In theory, therefore, if by virtue of the doctrine of vicarious liability (see Chapter 4) an employer is required to pay damages to an injured third party, the amount paid out could be recovered by suing the negligent employee. In practice, such embarrassing litigation is avoided because it is the employer's insurance company that actually pays the damages.

PUBLIC INTEREST DISCLOSURES

The purpose of the Public Interest Disclosure Act 1998, which primarily amended the ERA 1996, is to protect individuals who make certain disclosures of information in the public interest. Section 43A ERA 1996 defines a 'protected disclosure' as a qualifying disclosure which is made to the persons mentioned in Sections 43C–43H ERA 1996 (below). Section 43B(1) defines a 'qualifying disclosure' as one which a worker *reasonably believes*[68] tends to show one or more of the following: (a) a criminal offence; (b) a failure to comply with any legal obligation;[69] (c) a miscarriage of justice; (d) danger to the health and safety of any individual (ie not necessarily a worker); (e) damage to the environment; or (f) the deliberate concealment of information tending to expose any of the matters listed above. Three general points about these categories should be noted. Firstly, they are not restricted to confidential information. Secondly, there is no requirement for any link between the matter disclosed and the worker's employment. Thirdly, the matter disclosed may have occurred in the past, be currently occurring, or be likely to occur.

Section 43C(1) ERA 1996 protects workers who make qualifying disclosures *in good faith* to their employer or to another person who is responsible for the matter disclosed. According to Section 43C(2) ERA 1996, workers are to be treated as having made disclosures to their employer if they follow a procedure which the employer has authorised, even if the disclosure has been made to someone else such as an independent person or organisation. Thus there is a danger that workers may lose protection if they refuse to follow a procedure which they believe to be defective, for example, because of a lack of confidentiality. Section 43D ERA 1996 enables workers to seek legal advice about their concerns and to reveal to their adviser the issues about which a disclosure may be made. Under these circumstances, Section 43B(4) ERA 1996 provides that the legal adviser is bound by professional privilege and cannot make a protected disclosure.

Section 43E ERA 1996 protects workers in government-appointed organisations if they make a disclosure in good faith to a Minister of the Crown rather than to their legal employer. Section 43F(1) ERA 1996 protects workers who make disclosures in good faith to a person prescribed for the purpose by the Secretary of State.[70] However, the worker must reasonably believe that (a) the matter falls within the remit of the prescribed person, and (b) that the information and any allegation contained in it are substantially true.

Section 43G ERA 1996 enables workers to make a protected disclosure in other limited circumstances. In order to be protected, workers must:

- act in good faith
- reasonably believe that the information and any allegation contained in it are substantially true
- not act for personal gain (according to Section 43L(2) ERA 1996, in determining whether a person has acted for personal gain, a reward payable under any enactment will be disregarded)

- have already disclosed substantially the same information to the employer or to a person pre-scribed under Section 43F ERA 1996, unless they reasonably believe that they would be subject to a detriment for doing so, or that the employer would conceal or destroy the evidence if alerted
- act reasonably. For these purposes regard shall be had, in particular, to:
  - the identity of the person to whom the disclosure is made (for example, disclosure to an MP may be reasonable whereas disclosure to the media may not be)
  - the seriousness of the matter
  - whether there is a continuing failure or one likely to recur
  - whether the disclosure is made in breach of a duty of confidentiality owed by the employer to another person
  - any action the employer (or prescribed person) has taken or might have been expected to take in relation to a previous disclosure
  - whether the worker has complied with any procedure authorised by the employer for making a disclosure.

Section 43H ERA 1996 deals with disclosures about exceptionally serious wrongdoing. Again, in order to be protected:

- workers must act in good faith
- they must reasonably believe that the information and any allegation contained in it are substan-tially true
- they must not act for personal gain
- the relevant failure must be of an exceptionally serious nature
- in all the circumstances it must be reasonable to make the disclosure. In this respect particular regard will be had to the identity of the person to whom the disclosure is made.

Section 43J ERA 1996 prevents employers from generally contracting out of the provisions in Part IVA. In particular, it deals with 'gagging clauses' by invalidating a worker's agreement (whether contained in a con-tract or settlement of legal proceedings) not to make a protected disclosure.

Section 43K(1) ERA 1996 is designed to enable everyone who works to benefit from Part IVA, irrespective of whether they fall within the Section 230 ERA 1996 definition of 'employee' or 'worker'. Thus for these purposes the definition of 'worker' is extended to include certain agency workers; certain workers who would not otherwise be covered because they are not obliged to carry out all of their duties personally; NHS practitioners such as GPs, certain dentists, pharmacists and opticians; and certain trainees. Section 43K(2) ERA 1996 extends the definition of 'employer' accordingly.

Section 47B(1) ERA 1996 gives workers the right not to be subjected to any detriment for making a pro-tected disclosure.[71] For these purposes, the extended meaning of 'worker' in Section 43K applies and it is made clear that 'detriment' covers both actions and a deliberate failure to act. Thus the following would be covered: discipline or dismissal, or being denied a pay rise or facilities that would otherwise be provided.

In addition, workers who have been dismissed for making a protected disclosure and are not qualified to claim unfair dismissal under Part X of the ERA 1996 (the general unfair dismissal provisions) can bring a claim under new Section 47B ERA 1996. The obvious example here is a worker who does not have a con-tract of employment. Section 48(1A) ERA 1996 enables a worker to complain to an employment tribunal that Section 47B has been infringed.

Disclosure and dismissal

Section 103A ERA 1996 makes it automatically unfair to dismiss employees on the grounds that they have (at any time)[72] made a protected disclosure. No qualifying period of service is required and no age restriction operates in these circumstances. Similarly, Section 105(6A) ERA 1996 makes it unfair to select employees for redundancy if the reason for doing so is that they have made a protected disclosure. Finally, it should be noted that there is no limit on the compensation that can be awarded by an employment tribunal if Section 103A ERA 1996 applies.

THE LAW GOVERNING INVENTIONS AND COPYRIGHT

Since section 39(1) of the Patents Act 1977 came into force, an invention belongs to an employer if:

- it was made in the course of the employee's normal duties or those specifically assigned to him or her, and the circumstances in either case were such that an invention might reasonably be expected to result from the carrying out of those duties, or
- it was made in the course of the employee's duties and at the time of making the invention, because of the nature of the duties and the particular responsibilities arising from them, there was a special obligation to further the interests of the employer's undertaking.

In all other circumstances the invention belongs to the employee notwithstanding any contractual term to the contrary. This section was considered in *Reiss Engineering* v *Harris*[73] where the Patents Court held that for these purposes employees' 'normal duties' are those which they are actually employed to do. Section 39(1)(a) was interpreted as referring to an invention which achieves or contributes to achieving whatever was the aim or object to which the employee's efforts in carrying out his or her duties were directed, ie an invention similar to that made but not necessarily the precise invention as that actually made. The extent and nature of the 'special obligation' in section 39(1)(b) will depend on the status of the employee and the attendant responsibilities and duties of that status.

Even if the invention belongs to the employer, an employee can apply to the Patents Court or Controller of Patents for an award of compensation. This may be granted if the patent is of outstanding benefit (in money or money's worth) to the employer and it is just to make an award. The burden of proof lies on the employee to show that the employer has derived benefit from the patented invention. Where inventions belong to employees and their interests have been assigned to the employer, they are still entitled to seek compensation if they can show that the financial benefit they have derived is inadequate in relation to the benefit derived by the employer from the patent and it is just that additional compensation should be paid. However, no compensation can be paid if, at the time the invention is made, there is in force a 'relevant collective agreement' (an agreement between a trade union to which the employee belongs and the employer or an association to which the employer belongs) which provides for the payment of compensation for inventions made by the employee. It is expected that collective agreements will improve upon the statutory rights, yet there appears to be nothing to prevent employers and unions from negotiating less favourable compensation schemes.

According to section 11 of the Copyright, Designs and Patents Act 1988, where a literary, dramatic, musical or artistic work is made by an employee in the course of employment, the employer is the first owner of any copyright, subject to any agreement to the contrary.

KEY POINTS

The law regards employers and employees as having certain obligations to each other. These obligations arise out of long-established common-law principles and more recent statutory intervention in the employment relationship.

The duties of the employer include
- paying wages if an employee is available for work, and not making unlawful deductions
- providing work in circumstances where a lack of work will affect an employee's earnings, reputation or skills
- co-operating with the employee and preserving the mutual trust and confidence upon which this co-operation depends
- taking reasonable care of the employee by providing a safe working environment and safe working practices
- taking reasonable care with regard to references.

The duties of the employee include
- co-operating with the employer and obeying lawful and reasonable instructions
- not damaging the employer's business by competing with the employer in breach of a duty of fidelity
- not disclosing certain confidential information to competitors
- taking reasonable care and exercising reasonable skills in the performance of his or her contract.

NOTES

1 *Bosworth v A Jowett* (1977) IRLR 341
2 *Langston v AUEW* (1974) ICR 180
3 (1998) IRLR 313
4 See *Hilton v Shiner Ltd* (2001) IRLR 727
5 See *Johnson v Unisys Ltd* (2002) IRLR 271
6 (1999) IRLR 87
7 *French v Barclays Bank* (1998) IRLR 647
8 *Malik v Bank of Credit and Commerce* (1997) IRLR 462
9 See *Bank of Credit and Commerce International SA v Ali (No.3)* (1999) IRLR 508
10 *United Bank v Akhtar* (1989) IRLR 507
11 *BAC v Austin* (1978) IRLR 332
12 *Goold Ltd v McConnell* (1995) IRLR 516
13 *Robinson v Crompton Parkinson* (1978) IRLR 61
14 *Morrow v Safeway Stores* (2002) IRLR 9
15 *Woods v WM Car Services* (1982) IRLR 413
16 See *Transco plc v O'Brien* (2002) IRLR 444
17 *Walker v J Wedgewood Ltd* (1978) IRLR 105
18 See *Scally v Southern Health Board* (1991) IRLR 522
19 See *Ibekwe v LGTS Ltd* (2003) IRLR 697
20 (1999) IRLR 103
21 *Paris v Stepney Borough Council* (1951) AC 376
22 See *White v Holbrook Ltd* (1985) IRLR 215
23 See *Hewett v Brown Ltd* (1992) ICR 530 on the duty owed to the employee's family
24 (1998) IRLR 436
25 See *Baxter v Harland & Wolff* (1990) IRLR 516

26 See *McDermid* v *Nash Dredging* (1987) IRLR 334

27 See *Morris* v *Breaveglen Ltd* (1993) IRLR 350

28 (1953) AC 643

29 See also *Smith* v *Scot Bowyers Ltd* (1986) IRLR 315

30 See *Cook* v *Square D Ltd* (1992) IRLR 34

31 See *Walker* v *Northumberland County Council* (1995) IRLR 35 and *Cross* v *Highlands and Islands Enterprise* (2001) IRLR 336

32 *Sutherland* v *Hatton* (2002) IRLR 263. See also *Young* v *Post Office* (2002) IRLR 660

33 *Coxall* v *Goodyear Ltd* (2002) IRLR 742

34 See *Pentney* v *Anglian Water Authority* (1983) ICR 463

35 (1988) IRLR 404

36 See *Pickford* v *Imperial Chemical Industries* (1996) IRLR 622

37 (1991) IRLR 404

38 (1997) IRLR 488

39 (1994) IRLR 460

40 See *Cox* v *Sun Alliance Ltd* (2001) IRLR 448

41 See *Kidd* v *AXA Equity* (2000) IRLR 301

42 See *Farrant* v *The Woodroffe School* (1998) IRLR 176

43 (1972) QB 443

44 See *Sim* v *Rotherham MBC* (1986) IRLR 391

45 *MacMillan Inc* v *Bishopsgate Investment* (1993) IRLR 393

46 See *Sybron Corporation* v *Rochem Ltd (1983) IRLR 253*

47 (1982) IRLR 146

48 See *Lancashire Fires Ltd* v *SA Lyons & Co Ltd* (1997) IRLR 253

49 See *Laughton* v *Bapp Industrial Ltd* (1986) IRLR 245 and *Adamson* v *B & L Cleaning Ltd* (1995) IRLR 193

50 On non-solicitation and non-poaching covenants see *Alliance Paper* v *Prestwich* (1996) IRLR 25

51 See *Office Angels Ltd* v *Rainer-Thomas* (1991) IRLR 214 and *Hanover Insurance Brokers Ltd* v *Schapiro* (1994) IRLR 82

52 See *Dentmaster (UK) Ltd* v *Kent* (1997) IRLR 636

53 See *D* v *M* (1996) IRLR 192

54 See *Dawnay, Day & Co* v *de Bracconier d'Alphen* (1997) IRLR 285

55 See *Eurobrokers Ltd* v *Rabey* (1995) IRLR 206 and *Credit Suisse Ltd* v *Armstrong* (1996) IRLR 450

56 See *Cantor Fitzgerald International* v *Callaghan* (1999) IRLR 234 and *Rock Refrigeration Ltd* v *Jones* (1996) IRLR 675

57 See *Morris Angel* v *Hollande* (1993) IRLR 169

58 See *Credit Suisse First Boston Europe* v *Padiachy* (1998) IRLR 504

59 See *Faccenda Chicken Ltd* v *Fowler* (1986) IRLR 69

60 See *Bullivant Ltd* v *Ellis* (1987) IRLR 491

61 See *Lancashire Fires Ltd* v *SA Lyons & Co Ltd* (note 43)

62 See *SBJ Stephenson Ltd* v *Mandy* (2000) IRLR 233

63 See *WAC Ltd* v *Whillock* (1990) IRLR 23; on the possibility of severing unlawful clauses and enforcing the remainder see *Marshall* v *NM Financial Management* (1996) IRLR 20

64 See *Sun Printers Ltd* v *Westminster Press Ltd* (1982) IRLR 92

65 See *PSM International* v *McKechnie* (1992) IRLR 279

66 See also section 7 HASAWA 1974 (Chapter 10)

67 See *Janata Bank* v *Ahmed* (1981) IRLR 457

68 See *Darnton* v *University of Surrey* (2003) IRLR 133

69 See *Parkins* v *Sodescho Ltd* (2002) IRLR 109

70 See The Public Interest Disclosure (Prescribed Persons) Order 1999 SI 1549

71   See *London Borough of Harrow* v *Knight* (2003) IRLR 140
72   See *Miklaszewicz* v *Stolt Offshore Ltd* (2002) IRLR 344
73   (1985) IRLR 232

Recruitment and Selection

OVERVIEW

In this chapter we raise some of the issues that will have to be considered by the human resources department. Firstly, is it preferable to hire employed or self-employed persons? Secondly, what are the possible implications in outsourcing the work to be done? Thirdly, if employees are engaged, should they have indefinite, fixed-term, part-time or some other form of contract of employment? Fourthly, what are the issues concerned with employing workers on a temporary basis? Lastly, is it necessary to impose a probationary period on new recruits? The latter part of the chapter deals with some of the regulatory constraints which impinge upon the process of recruitment and selection. Rules concerning rehabilitated offenders and rules contained in the Asylum and Immigration Act 1996 are outlined here. The law relating to the employment of disabled persons, and to sex and race discrimination are dealt with in Chapters 6 and 7.

EMPLOYMENT STATUS

Before recruiting or selecting an individual one of the first important decisions to be reached is what sort of contract he or she is to be hired under:

- is it to be a contract of service (i.e. an employee) or a contract for services (i.e. an independent contractor)?
- is it to be a fixed-term or an open ended contract?
- is it to be a full-time or a part-time contract?
- would it be better to utilise the services of an employment agency and take on a temporary agency worker?

Although some statutes apply to all of these categories of workers, such as the Sex Discrimination Act 1975, some do not and some categories of workers are provided with special protection.

Examples include:

- employees gain the benefit of a number of statutory employment rights, such as protection with regard to unfair dismissal, the right to maternity leave and the right to parental leave;
- employees are subject to the unwritten general obligations implied into all contracts of employment (see Chapter 3);
- when employees, rather than self-employed persons, are engaged, employers are required by statute to deduct tax under Schedule E as well as social security contributions. In addition employers are obliged to pay employers' National Insurance contributions and to insure against personal injury claims brought by employees.

Perhaps the most significant difference at common law is that the doctrine of vicarious liability applies to employees but not to the self-employed, although in exceptional circumstances employers will be liable for the tortious acts of their independent contractors, eg if they authorise the commission of the wrongful act or have a responsibility which cannot, by law, be delegated to someone else.

The essence of the doctrine of vicarious liability is that employers are held liable to third parties for the civil wrongs committed by employees in the course of their employment. Determining what is 'in the course of employment' has caused immense difficulties over the years but the position today appears to be as follows. Clearly employees act 'in the course of employment' where they carry out acts which are authorised by the employer. Similarly, where their actions are so closely connected with the employment as to be incidental to it, although prohibited and unauthorised by the employer, employees act 'in the course of employment'. However, if an employee's action is so outside the scope of employment as to be not something the employee was employed to do, then the employer is not liable.[1] In *Lister* v *Hedley Hall Ltd*[2] the employers were held vicariously liable for a warden who sexually abused the claimants whilst they were in his care. According to the House of Lords, the correct approach is to ask whether the employee's wrongdoing was so closely connected with his or her employment that it would be fair and just to hold the employer liable.

Before an employer can be held vicariously liable, some nexus has to be established between the employee's wrongful act and the circumstances of employment. Thus a contractor engaged to clean offices (including telephones) was not vicariously liable when one of the contractor's employees dishonestly used the phones for his own purposes.[3] Employees remain personally liable for their own acts and theoretically may be required to reimburse the employer for any damages paid out as a result of their failure to take care (see Chapter 3). It should also be noted that in some cases the criminal law regards an employee's act as being that of the employer, in which case the latter will be responsible for the wrongs committed by the former.

Additionally, a company might be liable as a substitute employer for the negligence of employees not directly employed by them if it can be shown that the substitute employer had sufficient power of control and supervision properly to be regarded as the effective employer at the critical time.[4]

Distinguishing employees from other types of worker

Given all the consequences of having an employee on the books, is it always possible to discern whether a contract is a contract of service or a contract for services? Unfortunately, the answer must be in the negative, for the courts have ruled that the intention of the parties cannot be the sole determinant of contractual status; otherwise it would be too easy to contract out of employment protection legislation. It is the operation of the contract in practice that is crucial rather than its appearance. According to the Court of Appeal[5] tribunals have to consider 'all aspects of the relationship, no single feature being in itself decisive and each of which may vary in weight and direction, and having given such balance to the factors as seems appropriate to determine whether the person was carrying on business on his own account'. Thus in *Hall* v *Lorimer*[6] the Court of Appeal considered the position of a person who gave up their employment to pursue the same occupation on a freelance basis. The person concerned carried out all their tasks at employers' premises using equipment provided by the employers. The Court held that there was no single path to deciding whether the contracts under which a person worked were contracts of service or contracts for services. One had to stand back from the detail and take an informed and considered view of the whole picture. In this case the crucial factor was that the employee worked for a number of different companies.

Although the element of control is important, it may not be decisive in the case of skilled workers who decide for themselves how their work should be done. In such cases the question is broadened to 'Whose business is it?'[7] The fact that workers pay their own tax and National Insurance cannot be conclusive in determining employment status,[8] and the cases show that people who perform work at home may be classed as employees so long as there is an element of continuing mutual contractual obligation.[9] In

Carmichael,[10] the House of Lords held that the applicant's case 'founders on the rock of the absence of mutuality'. The case concerned the question as to whether two tour guides were employees under contracts of employment and therefore entitled to a written statement of particulars of the terms of their employment (see Chapter 2). An important issue was that there was no requirement for the employer to provide work and for the individual to carry out that work. The Court heard that there were a number of occasions when the applicants had declined offers of work and ruled that there was an 'irreducible minimum of mutual obligation' that was necessary to create a contract of service. There needed to be an obligation to provide work and an obligation to perform that work in return for a wage or some form of remuneration.

Of crucial importance is whether one person working for another is required to perform his or her service in person or not. In *Express and Echo Publications* v *Tanton*[11] a contract allowed a worker to provide a substitute if he was not available. This prevented the worker from being defined as an employee because the obligation to do the work in person was, according to the Court of Appeal, an 'irreducible minimum'. This approach, however, was held not to apply to gymnasts working for a local authority who were able to provide substitutes for any shift that they were unable to work.[12] The difference in approach resulted from the fact that the local authority paid the substitutes directly and that the gymnasts were only able to be replaced by other gymnasts on the Council's approved list.

Unless the relationship is dependent solely upon the true construction of a written contract, whether a person is engaged under a contract of employment is a question of fact for a court or tribunal to determine.[13]

OUTSOURCING

Increasingly employers are choosing to outsource parts of their non-core activities. Outsourcing can mean an arrangement whereby a contractor supplies staff who will be under the supervision of the hirer, or it can mean the outsourcing of the complete activity, so that the hirer is concerned only with the outcomes rather than with the means of achieving them. Activities that are commonly outsourced include in-house catering and the cleaning of premises.

When an organisation decides on outsourcing an activity it must also decide what is to happen to its current employees who work in the part to be contracted out. It also has an obligation to inform and consult those employees at the earliest opportunity. There may not be the need for redundancies because the employees currently working in the part to be transferred may be protected by the Transfer of Undertakings (Protection of Employment) Regulations 1981[14] as amended (these Regulations will be further considered in Chapter 16). Their contracts of employment and their employment relationship are likely to transfer with the outsourcing contract. The contractor will become their employer and be liable for all and any debts arising out of the employment relationship. It will be as if they signed their original contract of employment with the new contractor. Any outstanding claims from employees, whether they concern contractual or other obligations, will transfer. In a case, for example, where two employees had an outstanding claim for sex discrimination at the time of the transfer, the claim was transferred to the contractor who was faced with the need to settle a dispute in which it had not taken part.[15]

Examples of outsourcing situations where the Transfer Regulations have been held to apply include the contracting out of a local authority refuse collection and cleansing work,[16] a contract to deliver Audi and Volkswagen cars around the country,[17] and the transfer of a security guarding contract.[18] It has not always been clear when the Transfer Regulations apply (see Chapter 16) and there has been much litigation on the meaning of a transfer of an undertaking or business.

FIXED-TERM OR INDEFINITE CONTRACT?

Assuming that a decision has been taken that the organisation will engage employees itself, another matter for consideration is whether to hire for a fixed term or for an indefinite period. Concern that employers might abuse the use of fixed-term contracts was the motivation behind the EU Directive on Fixed-Term Work.[19] The aims of the Directive were twofold. Firstly, it aimed to improve the quality of fixed-term work by ensuring the application of the principle on non-discrimination. Secondly, it aimed to establish a framework to prevent abuse arising from the use of successive fixed-term contracts. The Directive was implemented in the United Kingdom by the Fixed-term Employees (Prevention of Less Favourable Treatment) Regulations 2002.[20]

The main features of the Regulations are

- fixed-term employees should not be treated less favourably than comparable permanent employees with respect to their terms and conditions of employment, unless there is an objective reason to justify the treatment[21]
- fixed-term employees should be able to compare their terms and conditions with permanent employees who do the same or similar work for the same employer if they think that they are being treated less favourably[22]
- the use of successive fixed-term contracts should be limited; this can be effected by setting a maximum period of 4 years for such successive contracts (although any period before July 10 2002 does not count) unless there are objectively justifiable reasons for the renewal of such contracts. This four year period depends upon continuity being maintained.

If an employee considers that he or she has been treated less favourably than a comparable permanent employee, then he or she may request in writing a written statement from the employer giving the reasons for the treatment. The employee is entitled to the statement within 21 days of the request and the statement is admissible as evidence in any subsequent Tribunal proceedings.

An employee may present a complaint to an employment tribunal that he or she has received less favourable treatment. It will be for the employer to identify the reason for the less favourable treatment. If the employment tribunal finds that such treatment has taken place, then it may make a recommendation for action by the employer and award compensation to the employee.[23] Employers will, therefore, need to be aware of these legal requirements when deciding whether to employ individuals on a permanent or a fixed-term contract. However, the expiry of a fixed-term contract without its renewal on the same terms amounts to a dismissal in law (see Chapter 12).

PART-TIME OR FULL-TIME?

In deciding whether to employ a full-time or part-time individual, account will need to be taken of the Regulations. The Part-time Workers (Prevention of Less Favourable Treatment) Regulations[24] (PTW Regulations) give effect to the European Council Directive on part-time work.[25] The purpose of the Regulations is to give part-time workers the right not to be treated less favourably than an employer treats comparable full-time workers, as regards the terms of the contract, or be subjected to some detriment by any act or failure to act.[26] This right applies only if the treatment is on the grounds that a worker is a part-timer and that the treatment cannot be justified on objective grounds.

Part-time workers and comparable full-time workers

The principle of non-discrimination applies to 'workers'. This has a wider meaning than 'employees', and the definition given in the PTW Regulations[27] is identical to that in section 230(3) ERA 1996.

Regulation 2 PTW Regulations has a similar definition of both full-time and part-time workers. They are individuals who are paid wholly or in part by reference to the amount of time worked and who are, in relation to other workers employed under the same type of contract, defined as full-time or part-time.

Comparable full-timers, in relation to part-timers, are individuals who are:

- employed by the same employer under the same sort of contract[28]
- engaged in the same or broadly similar work, having regard, where relevant, to whether they have similar levels of qualifications, skills and experience[29]
- based at the same establishment or, if there is no full-time comparator at the same establishment, then at a different one.[30]

The time, according to Regulation 2(4) PTW Regulations, for deciding whether an individual is a full-time comparator is the time when the alleged less favourable treatment takes place. This is a very demanding test for establishing whether an individual's job can be used as a comparator on which to base a claim of discrimination. If there is not a full-timer who meets the criteria, it will not be possible to make a claim for discrimination based upon the PTW Regulations. In a business where all the management staff were full-time and all the operatives were low-paid part-timers, for example, it is unlikely that the PTW Regulations would be of any help to the part-time workers.

There are a limited number of exceptions to these strict rules on comparators. These are:

- workers who become part-time. If a full-time worker varies or terminates his or her contract in order to work fewer hours each week and thus become a part-timer, it is permissible to assume that there is a full-time comparator employed upon the same terms as applied before the variation or termination.[31]
- full-time workers who return to work for the same employer after an absence of less than 12 months, but are now required to work fewer hours per week. This is conditional upon the returning individual working in the same job, or at the same level as that in which he or she worked before the break. In such a situation it is possible to assume that there is a full-time comparator employed on the same terms and conditions as applied to the individual before the break in employment.[32]

Less favourable treatment

In determining whether a part-timer has been discriminated against, the pro rata principle applies, unless it is inappropriate.[33] This means that a part-time worker is entitled to receive pay or any other benefit in proportion to the number of weekly hours that he or she works in comparison with a comparable full-time worker.[34] The one exception to this concerns overtime. Not paying overtime rates to a part-time worker until he or she has worked hours at least comparable to the basic working hours of the comparable full-time worker may not be regarded as less favourable treatment.

In the government's guidance accompanying the PTW Regulations the following are examples given as arising from the application of the principle of non-discrimination:

- previous or current part-time status should not of itself constitute a barrier to promotion
- part-time workers should receive the same hourly rate as full-time workers
- part-time workers should receive the same hourly rate of overtime pay as full-time workers, once they have worked more than normal full-time hours

- part-time workers should be able to participate in profit sharing or share option schemes available to full-time workers
- employers should not discriminate between part-time workers and full-time workers over access to pension schemes
- employers should not exclude part-timers from training simply because they work part-time
- in selection for redundancy part-time workers must not be treated less favourably than full-time workers.

Detriment and dismissal

There is a distinction in the protection offered by the Regulations between employees and workers. Dismissal of employees, for any of the reasons listed below, will be regarded as an unfair dismissal in accordance with Part X of the ERA 1996 (see Chapters 12 and 13).[35] Regulation 6(1) PTW Regulations entitles a worker, who considers that he or she has been treated less favourably, to request in writing a written statement giving particulars of the reasons for the treatment.[36] The worker is entitled to receive this statement within 21 days of the request. The written statement is admissible as evidence in any future proceedings, and a tribunal may draw its own inferences if the statement is not provided or if it is 'evasive or equivocal'.[37]

Workers (which includes employees) have the right not to be subjected to a detriment by any act, or any deliberate failure to act, by the employer on the grounds that the employer believes that the worker has (or intends in due course to have):

- brought proceedings against the employer under the PTW Regulations
- requested from the employer a written statement of reasons under Regulation 6
- given evidence or information in connection with any proceedings brought by any worker
- done anything else under the PTW Regulations in relation to the employer or any other person
- alleged that the employer has infringed the Regulations
- refused, or proposes to refuse, to give up any rights held under the PTW Regulations.

Complaints to employment tribunals

A worker who believes that he or she has suffered less favourable treatment or other detriment in accordance with the Regulations may complain to an employment tribunal.[38] The complaint needs to be made within a period of three months from the date of treatment or detriment, although a longer period will be allowed if the tribunal finds it just and equitable to do so.[39] The options open to the employment tribunal are to:[40]

- make a declaration of the rights of the complainant in respect of the complaint
- order the employer to pay compensation to the complainant. Compensation does not include injury to the complainant's feelings and the complainant has a duty to mitigate his or her losses[41]
- recommend that the employer takes action to obviate or reduce the adverse effect on the complainant of any matter to which the complaint relates. The tribunal may specify a reasonable period during which this action should be taken. If the employer fails to follow the recommendation, without justification, the tribunal may increase the amount of compensation to be paid to the complainant.[42]

SHOULD TEMPORARY EMPLOYEES OR AGENCY STAFF BE HIRED?

In deciding whether to employ on a temporary or 'permanent' basis (see Chapter 11 on notice provisions), it should be noted that temporary staff have exactly the same statutory rights as other employees so long as they possess any necessary qualifying period of service. The only two exceptions to this proposition arise where an individual is employed on a temporary basis as a replacement for a woman on maternity leave or to replace someone absent from work under the statutory provisions relating to medical suspension (see Chapters 9 and 6 respectively).

Occasionally an organisation may ask an agency to provide staff, and if the worker engaged by the client organisation is under a personal obligation to perform the work, a contract of employment may exist. The exact relationship between the client and the individual supplied by the agency is a question of fact for an employment tribunal to decide.

The courts have looked at, firstly, issues relating to the relationship between the individual and the agency and, secondly, issues relating to the relationship, if any, between the individual and the hirer.

The case of *McMeechan* v *Secretary of State for Employment*[43] concerned a temporary worker who completed a series of individual assignments through an employment agency. He was given a job sheet and a standard written statement of terms and conditions for each assignment. The statement specified that he was providing services as a self-employed worker and was not operating under a contract of service, although the agency did deduct tax and National Insurance contributions. When the agency became insolvent, the individual made a claim to the Secretary of State for wages owed. The claim was refused because, it was argued, the individual was not an employee of the insolvent company. The Court of Appeal considered *Wickens* v *Champion Employment*[44] which concerned an attempt to show that all temporary staff of an agency were working under contracts of employment. This failed because the relationship between the agency and the temporaries lacked, according to the Court, the essential elements of continuity and care by the employer that are characteristics of a contract of service.

The question for the Court in *McMeechan's* case was whether the individual assignment could amount to a contract of service or not. The arguments for there being a contract for services were that there was an express statement that the individual was self-employed and that the worker had freedom to work for a particular client on a self-employed basis. On the side of there being a contract of service were the power of the agency to dismiss for misconduct, the power to bring any assignment to an end, the establishment of a grievance procedure and the stipulation of an hourly rate of pay, which in turn was subject to deductions for unsatisfactory timekeeping, work, attitude or misconduct. The Court concluded that, despite the label put on it by the parties, there was a contract of service between the temporary worker and the agency. The courts will, therefore, consider all aspects of the relationship in deciding whether the agency worker has a contract of employment or not.[45]

Mutuality of obligation and control
The second question is whether there can be an employment relationship between the individual, supplied on a temporary basis by an employment agency, and the client employer. In *Montgomery* v *Johnson Underwood Ltd*[46] an individual was placed by an agency with a client company and remained there for two years. Eventually the company asked the agency to terminate the assignment. As a result the individual made a complaint of unfair dismissal (see Chapters 12–13) naming both the client company and the agency as her employer. The Employment Appeal Tribunal found that the agency had exercised little or no 'control, direction or supervision' of the individual during the assignment, and this proved crucial. There had to be the essential elements of mutuality of obligation and control.

The Court of Appeal relied upon *Carmichael*[47] to decide that 'mutuality of obligation' and 'control' are the minimum legal requirements for the existence of a contract of employment. Three conditions have to be fulfilled. These are that:

- the individual agrees, in return for wages or other remuneration, that he or she will provide his or her own work and skill in performance of some duty for the employer (mutuality of obligation)
- he or she agrees, expressly or impliedly, to be subject to the other's control in the performance of the duties (control)
- the other provisions of the contract are consistent with those of a contract of service.

Whether there exists a mutuality of obligation and the necessary level of control is a matter for the employment tribunal to decide. In this case the lack of control by the agency meant that the individual could not be regarded as an employee of that agency. However, an employer–employee relationship was established in *Motorola Ltd* v *Davidson*.[48] This case concerned a long-term agency worker who, eventually, was suspended by the client company after a disciplinary hearing. This led to the client company terminating the individual's assignment. The EAT held that once the individual was at the client's site, he was largely subject to the same control as if he had been an ordinary full-time employee. It was the client who decided 'the thing to be done, the way in which it shall be done, the means to be employed in doing it, the time when and the place where it shall be done'.[49]

The Employment Agencies Act 1973

The Employment Relations Act 1999 amended the Employment Agencies Act 1973 and widened the powers of the Secretary of State to issue regulations concerning the operation of employment agencies and employment businesses.[50] The government's stated objective in producing regulations has been to help promote a flexible labour market, which is underpinned by a set of regulations that ensure fairness and minimum standards in the industry. In seeking the 'proper conduct' of agencies and employment businesses, the government aims to protect the interests of work-seekers and those of hirers. There is an attempt to ensure clarity of agreement between the work-seeker and the employment agency or business. The government's proposals are concerned with the content of the terms to be agreed between the work-seeker and the agency or business. This includes, for example, whether, in the case of an employment business, the work-seeker is to be employed under a contract of service or apprenticeship, or under a contract for services. In either case the terms and conditions of employment are to be included in the agreement between the business and the work-seeker. There is also to be an undertaking that the employment business will pay the work-seeker in respect of work done, whether or not the business is paid by the hirer in respect of that work.

SHOULD A PROBATIONARY PERIOD BE IMPOSED?

We shall see in Chapter 16 that (save in exceptional circumstances) only those who have been continuously employed for one year can claim that they have been unfairly dismissed. In a sense this requirement serves to impose a probationary period but some employers may regard one year as excessive for the purpose of establishing whether a person's appointment should be confirmed. Often a shorter period will be deemed appropriate. Some employers prefer to make an assessment within four weeks in order to avoid having to give statutory notice to terminate the contract (see Chapter 12). The great advantage of operating a probationary period is that new recruits are made aware that they are on trial and must therefore establish their suitability.

REGULATORY CONSTRAINTS

At common law, employers have the right to decide what policies to adopt in relation to recruitment, but this position has now been altered by a series of statutory and non-statutory interventions designed to protect certain categories of job applicant. Such interventions mostly concern provisions designed to prevent discrimination in recruitment and employment on the grounds of gender, race, disability and membership or non-membership of a trade union. These issues will be considered in Chapters 6 and 7.

Rehabilitation of Offenders Act 1974

The law does not require applicants to disclose facts about themselves which could hinder them in getting jobs (unless their silence amounts to fraud). Thus if employers believe that certain information is important, they should seek it specifically before the job is offered.

Section 4 of this Act relieves certain rehabilitated persons from the obligation to disclose 'spent' convictions to a prospective employer and makes it unlawful for an employer to deny employment on the grounds that the applicant had a conviction which was 'spent'. It is the policy of the Act that applicants should not be questioned about spent convictions, although if this situation does arise applicants are entitled to deny that they have ever been convicted. There are a number of exceptions to these rules. Protection under the Act is not given to certain occupations such as doctors, nurses, teachers, social workers and those working with children, including those applying to become registered day-care providers.[51]

Sentences of over two-and-a-half years' imprisonment never become 'spent'; otherwise, convictions become 'spent' after periods which are related to the gravity of the sentence imposed. Thus for a sentence of imprisonment of between six months and two-and-a-half years the rehabilitation period is 10 years. Imprisonment for less than six months requires a seven-year rehabilitation period, and fines or community service orders take five years to become 'spent'. A probation order, conditional discharge or binding over need not be disclosed after a year or until the order expires (whichever is the longer), and absolute discharges can be concealed if six months have elapsed since sentence. Despite the existence of the Act, the courts cannot compel an employer to engage a rehabilitated offender: they can only declare the exclusion of the applicant to be unlawful.

Asylum and Immigration Act 1996

Section 8 of this Act is concerned with restrictions on employment for persons subject to immigration control. Employers commit an offence if they employ a person of 16 years or over if either the employee has not been granted leave to enter or remain in the United Kingdom, or if his or her stay in the United Kingdom is subject to a condition that precludes them from taking up employment.[52] However, if before the employment began the potential employee produced suitable documentation and the employer retained it or kept a photocopy, then this may be a defence. Suitable documentation includes:[53]

- a document issued by a previous employer or a government department, such as the Inland Revenue or the Benefits Agency, which contains the person's National Insurance number
- a passport which gives the person the right of abode or of readmission to the United Kingdom, or which contains a Certificate of Entitlement issued by the government
- a birth certificate issued in the United Kingdom, the Republic of Ireland, the Channel Islands or the Isle of Man
- a passport or identity card issued by a Member State of the European Economic Area.

It is not a defence if the employer knew that the applicant was not entitled to work in the United Kingdom.[54] If this offence is committed by a corporate body, then that body will be liable to a fine, as will those senior individuals in the corporate body who connived in the offence.

The Immigration and Asylum Act 1999 added section 8A to the 1996 Act. This placed an obligation upon the Secretary of State to issue a code of practice to help employers to avoid race discrimination in applying the provisions of the Act to recruitment.[55] The Code of Practice is entitled 'Code of Practice for all employers on the avoidance of race discrimination in recruitment practice while seeking to prevent illegal working'. Failure to observe the Code is not in itself a breach of the law, but such a failure would be admissible as evidence in any proceedings under the Race Relations Act 1976. Paragraph 24 sums up the recommended approach: 'The best way to ensure that you do not discriminate is to treat all applicants in the same way at each stage of the recruitment process.'

KEY POINTS

- Organisations have to decide whether to use employees or independent contractors; there are differences in taxation and employment costs as well as vicarious liability.
- It is not always clear whether a worker is employed under a contract of employment or is working under a contract for services; the intention of the parties is important, but may not be the deciding factor.
- The factors leading to a decision on whether a contract of employment exists or not are likely to include a 'sufficient' level of control by the employer and an 'irreducible minimum' of mutuality of obligation between employer and worker.
- Outsourcing is an option for many employers, but it is important to be aware of the effect of the Transfer of Undertakings (Protection of Employment) Regulations 1981.
- Employers may be faced with decisions regarding whether to employ individuals on part-time, fixed-term or temporary contracts. Care will need to be taken with the regulatory constraints on the way an employer treats such employees/workers.
- New regulations will seek to amend the existing rules on the operation of employment agencies in order, it is said, to give greater clarity to hirers and work seekers'.
- Probationary periods may be useful in deciding whether to confirm an appointment; the law normally places a requirement for one year's continuous employment before there is a right to claim unfair dismissal.
- Rehabilitated offenders have the right, in certain circumstances, not to reveal information about spent convictions.
- There may be a need to obtain documentation to prove that a person has the right to work in the United Kingdom, in order for his or her employer to avoid committing an offence.

NOTES

1 See *Chief Adjudication Officer* v *Rhodes* (1999) IRLR 103
2 (2001) IRLR 472
3 See *Heasmans* v *Clarity Cleaning* (1987) IRLR 286
4 See *Sime* v *Sutcliffe Catering* (1990) IRLR 228
5 *O'Kelly* v *Trust House Forte* (1983) IRLR 286
6 (1994) IRLR 171
7 See *Lane* v *Shire Roofing* (1995) IRLR 493
8 See *Young & Woods* v *West* (1980) IRLR 201
9 See *McCleod* v *Hellyer Bros* (1987) IRLR 232
10 *Carmichael* v *National Power plc* (2000) IRLR 43 HL
11 (1999) IRLR 367
12 *MacFarlane* v *Glasgow City Council* (2001) IRLR 7

13   See *Clark* v *Oxfordshire Health Authority* (1998) IRLR 125

14   SI 1981/1794

15   See *DJM International Ltd* v *Nicholas* (1996) IRLR 76

16   *Wren* v *Eastbourne Borough Council* (1993) IRLR 425

17   *ECM (Vehicle Delivery Services) Ltd* v *Cox* (1999) IRLR 559

18   *Securicor Guarding Ltd* v *Fraser Security Services* (1996) IRLR 552

19   Council Directive 99/70/EC

20   SI 2002/2034

21   Regulations 3 and 4

22   Regulation 2

23   Regulation 7

24   SI 2000/1551; subsequently amended by The Part-time Workers (Prevention of Less Favourable Treatment) Regulations 2001 SI 2001/1107

25   Council Directive 97/81/EC OJ L14/9 20.1.98

26   Regulation 5(1) PTW Regulations

27   Regulation 1(3) PTW Regulations

28   Regulation 2(4)(i) PTW Regulations; amended in 2002 (SI 2002/2035) so that there was no distinction between permanent and fixed-term contracts

29   Regulation 2(4)(ii) PTW Regulations

30   Regulation 2(5) PTW Regulations

31   Regulation 3 PTW Regulations

32   Regulation 4 PTW Regulations

33   Regulation 5(3) PTW Regulations

34   Regulation 2(2) PTW Regulations

35   Regulation 7(1) PTW Regulations

36   If the less favourable treatment is dismissal, the employee would be able to exercise his or her right to request written reasons for the dismissal under section 92 ERA 1996

37   Regulation 6(3) PTW Regulations

38   There are special rules for members of the armed forces; see regulation 13 PTW Regulations

39   Regulation 8(1)–(3) PTW Regulations

40   Regulation 8(7) PTW Regulations

41   Regulation 8(11)–(12) PTW Regulations

42   Regulation 8(14) PTW Regulations

43   (1997) IRLR 353

44   (1984) ICR 365

45   See *O'Kelly* v *Trust House Forte* (1983) IRLR 286 and *Dacas* v *Brook Street Bureau* (2003) IRLR 190

46   (2001) IRLR 269

47   *Carmichael* v *National Power plc* (2000) IRLR 43

48   *Motorola Ltd* v *(1) Davidson and (2) Melville Craig Group Ltd* (2001) IRLR 4. Compare now *Hewlett Packard Ltd* v *O'Murphy* (2002) IRLR 4

49   This was a quotation from MacKenna J in *Ready Mixed Concrete (South East) Ltd* v *Minister of Pensions and National Insurance* (1968) 1 All ER 433

50   Section 31 and schedule 7 ERELA 1999; from April 1 2004 the Regulations governing the industry are the Conduct of Employment Agencies and Employment Businesses Regulations 2003, SI 2003/3319

51   See The Rehabilitation of Offenders Act 1974 (Exceptions) Order 1975 SI 1975/1023 as most recently amended by The Rehabilitation of Offenders Act 1974 (Exceptions) (Amendment) Order 2001 SI 2001/1192

52   Section 8(1) Asylum and Immigration Act 1996

53 See The Immigration (Restrictions on Employment) Order 1996 SI 1996/3225 for a complete list of documentation
54 Sections 8(2) and 8(3) Asylum and Immigration Act 1996
55 See The Immigration (Restrictions on Employment) (Code of Practice) Order 2001, SI 2001/1436

Pay Issues

OVERVIEW

This chapter is concerned with a number of issues related to pay, beginning with the duty to pay wages or salaries. There is then some detailed consideration of the National Minimum Wage Act 1998 and the complexities associated with trying to establish the actual rates paid in a variety of work circumstances. We then consider the employer's duty to provide pay statements and what employee rights are in connection with guaranteed payments when not provided with work. Finally, we examine issues related to pay and sickness, including statutory sick pay and the right of employers to suspend employees on medical grounds.

THE DUTY TO PAY WAGES

This is a basic obligation of employers and is normally dealt with by an express term. There are a number of issues to be considered.

1 *An employer may be required to pay wages even if there is no work for the employee to do*
The general rule is that wages must be paid if an employee is available for work,[1] but everything will depend on whether there is an express or implied term of fact in the contract which deals with the matter. Thus an express term to the effect that 'no payment shall be made during a period of lay-off' will eliminate the possibility of a contractual claim being brought in such a situation.

2 *Deductions from wages or payment by the employee are unlawful unless required or authorised by statute, for example PAYE or social security contributions, or the worker has agreed to it*[2]
Section 27(1) ERA 1996 defines 'wages' as 'any sum payable to the worker in connection with his employment'. This includes holiday pay commission earnings which are payable after an employee has left. Before payment of such 'wages' the employer would be entitled to deduct an amount to repay any advances that had been given to the employee.[3]

The worker must give oral or written consent to the deduction before it is made,[4] and where the agreement constitutes a term of the contract of employment it must be in writing and drawn to the employee's attention (or its effect must have been notified to the worker in writing).[5] To satisfy the requirements of the Act there must be a document which clearly states that a deduction is to be made from the employee's wages and that the employee agrees to it.[6] Even if an employee has entered into a compromise agreement to settle an unfair dismissal dispute over non-payment of wages, he or she may still be able to make a claim for that underpayment.[7] If a tribunal is not persuaded on the evidence that a deduction was authorised by a provision of the employee's contract, the individual is entitled to be paid the money deducted. Thus, in *IPC Ltd* v *Balfour*,[8] the EAT held that a reduction in pay following the unilateral introduction of short-time working amounted to an unauthorized deduction. If, however, the contract of employment allowed the employer to change the hours or shift-patterns of an employee, then the employer would be entitled to adjust the pay levels to reflect those changes.[9]

For these purposes there is no valid distinction between a deduction and a reduction of wages. The issue is whether, for whatever reason, apart from an error of computation, the worker is paid less than the amount of wages properly payable.[10] However, employers who take a conscious decision not to make a payment because they believe that they are contractually entitled to take that course are not making an error of computation.[11] Although section 13(4) refers to an 'error of any description', it does not include an error of law.[12] Where there is a dispute over the justification for a deduction, it is the employment tribunal's task to resolve it.[13] However, tribunals do not have jurisdiction to determine whether a deduction by reason of industrial action was contractually authorised.[14]

Written agreements under which employers pay a proportion of wages to third parties are not affected by this Act, and in retail employment deductions or payments made to an employer in relation to stock or cash shortages are subject to a limit of one-tenth of gross pay, except for the final payment of wages.[15]

3   *Payments in lieu are not wages within the meaning of ERA 1996 if they relate to a period after the termination of employment*
According to the House of Lords, in *Delaney* v *Staples*,[16] the Act requires wages to be construed as payments in respect of the rendering of services during employment. Thus the only payments in lieu covered by the legislation are those in respect of 'garden leave' (see below), since these can be viewed as wages owed under a subsisting contract of employment. In the same case the Court of Appeal accepted that non-payment of wages constitutes a deduction for these purposes, as does the withholding of commission and holiday pay.[17] Indeed, the withholding of commission may amount to an unlawful deduction even where it is discretionary so long as commission was normally expected by the employee.[18]

4   *A complaint that there has been an unauthorised deduction must normally be lodged with an employment tribunal within three months of the deduction being made*[19]
If the complaint is well-founded, the tribunal must make a declaration to that effect and must order the reimbursement of the amount of the deduction or payment to the extent that it exceeded what should lawfully have been deducted or received by the employee. This does not affect the ability of the tribunal to consider references about itemised pay statements as in section 11 ERA 1996. The total awarded, however, must not exceed the total amount of the deductions.[20] The only method of contracting out of the requirements of this Act is if an agreement is reached following action taken by ACAS or there is a valid compromise agreement (see Chapter 15).

5   *Overpayments*
Employers may be entitled to restitution of overpayments made to an employee owing to a mistake of fact but *not* a mistake of law – eg an overpayment that arose as the result of a misunderstanding of the National Minimum Wage Act would be irrecoverable.[21] Indeed, employees may commit theft if they fail to notify the employer of an accidental overpayment.[22] Section 16(1) ERA 1996 makes specific provision for the recovery of overpayments, and tribunals cannot inquire into the lawfulness of a deduction for this purpose.[23]

THE NATIONAL MINIMUM WAGE

The National Minimum Wage Act 1998 (NMWA 1998) provides for a minimum hourly wage for workers. 'Worker' is defined, in Section 54(3), as someone working under a contract of employment or any other contract under which an individual undertakes to do or perform in person any work or service for another. The standard rate was £4.50 per hour in October 2003. There is also a development rate for workers aged 18 years to 21 years inclusive, set at £3.80 per hour in October 2003.[24] Any other allowances paid by the employer to the workers, in relation to their work, cannot be used to offset the fact that an individual's basic hourly rate is less than the NMW. It is possible to reduce those other rates in order to increase the basic rate without contravening the requirements of the NMW Regulations, although doing this might result in the employer being guilty of an unlawful deduction of wages in contravention of section 13(1) ERA 1996.[25] It should be noted, however, that tips can could towards the minimum wage.[26]

Regulation 12 describes those who do not qualify for the national minimum wage at all. These include:

- those under 18 years of age
- a worker under the age of 26 years who is employed under a contract of apprenticeship and is in the first 12 months of that contract, or who has not reached the age of 19 years
- a worker who is participating in a scheme designed to provide him or her with training, work, or temporary work, or which is designed to assist him or her to obtain work[27]
- a worker who is attending higher education up to first degree level or a teacher-training course, and who, before the course ends, is required as part of the course to attend a period of work experience not exceeding one year
- a homeless person who is provided with shelter and other benefits in return for performing work.

When is a worker 'working'?

Workers who work and live in the employer's household and who are treated as members of the family are also excluded.[28] Workers who, by arrangement, sleep on the employer's premises may, however, be entitled to payment for all the hours that are required to be spent at those premises. In *Scottbridge Ltd* v *Wright*[29] a night-watchman was required to be on the premises between 5 pm and 7 am each night. Apart from some minor duties he was mainly required to be present in case of intruders. He was provided with sleeping facilities and allowed to sleep during the course of the night. The Court of Session confirmed the EAT held that he was entitled to be paid at least the national minimum wage rate for the specific hours that he was required to be at work. It was up to the employer to provide him with work, but the fact that he was not required to do any did not nullify his entitlement to be paid. A similar issue was raised in *British Nursing Association* v *Inland Revenue*,[30] where nurses who provided a booking service at night from home were held to be working throughout their shifts, even when watching television while waiting for phone calls. The Court of Appeal endorsed the EAT's view that in deciding when a worker is working for the purposes of the NMW Regulations, an employment tribunal should look at the type of work involved and its different elements to see if it all together could be properly described as work. Aspects to be examined include:

- the nature of the work
- the extent to which the worker's activities are restricted when not performing the particular task
- the mutual obligations of employer and worker, although the way in which remuneration is calculated is not conclusive
- the extent to which the period during which work is being performed is readily ascertainable.

Calculating remuneration

The hourly rate is calculated by adding up the total remuneration, less reductions, and dividing by the total number of hours worked[31] during a pay reference period.[32] Total remuneration[33] in a pay reference period is calculated by adding together:

- all money paid by the employer to the worker during the reference period
- any money paid by the employer to the worker in the following reference period which is in respect of work done in the current reference period
- any money paid by the employer to the worker later than the end of the following pay reference period in respect of work done in the current reference period and for which the worker is under an obligation to complete a record and has not done so
- the cost of accommodation, calculated by an approved formula.[34]

Deductions that can be made from this total remuneration figure are set out in Regulation 31 and include:

- any payments made by the employer to the worker in respect of a previous pay reference period
- in the case of non-salaried work, any money paid to the worker in respect of periods when the worker was absent from work or engaged in taking industrial action
- in the case of time-work, the difference between the lowest rate of pay and any higher rates of pay paid during the reference period
- any amounts paid by the employer to the worker that represent amounts paid by customers in the form of service charge, tips, gratuities or cover charge – that is, not paid through the payroll
- the payment of expenses.

Calculating hours

The calculation of the hours worked can be complex. There are four different types of hours of work. These are:

1 *salaried hours work*[35]
   This is where the worker is paid for a number of ascertainable hours in a year (the basic hours) and where the payment, which normally consists of an annual salary and perhaps an annual bonus, is paid in equal instalments, weekly or monthly.

2 *time-work*[36]
   This is work that is paid for under a worker's contract by reference to the time worked, and is not salaried hours work.

3 *output work*[37]
   This is work that is paid for by reference to the number of pieces made or processed, or by some other measure of output such as the value of sales made or transactions completed. The output hours, in a reference period, will be the total number of hours spent by the worker in doing output work.[38] It is possible, according to regulation 25, for the employer and worker to reach a 'fair estimate' agreement on what number of hours to use.

4 *unmeasured work*[39]
   This is any work that is not salaried hours work, time-work or output work, especially work where there are no specified hours and the worker is required to work when needed or whenever work is available. The unmeasured work hours will be the total hours, in a pay reference period, spent by the worker in carrying out his or her contractual duties.[40] Regulation 28 allows for a 'daily average' agreement to be reached between the employer and the worker.[41]

Underpayment of the NMW

Section 9 of the Act[42] allows the Secretary of State to require employers to keep and preserve records for at least three years. Workers have the right to inspect these records if they believe, on reasonable grounds, that they are being paid at a rate less than the national minimum wage.[43] When inspecting these records a worker may be accompanied by another person of his or her choice.[44] This must be stated in the 'production notice' that the worker gives to the employer requesting the production of the records.[45] The employer must then produce these records within 14 days following receipt of the notice and must make them available at the worker's place of work or some other reasonable place.[46] Failure to produce the records or to allow the workers to exercise their rights can lead to a complaint at an employment tribunal.[47] In these circumstances the tribunal can make an award of up to 80 times the national minimum wage. If a worker has been remunerated, during the reference period, at a rate less than the national minimum wage, then there is a contractual entitlement to be paid the amount underpaid.[48] There is a reversal of the normal burden of proof in that the presumption is that the worker qualifies for the national minimum wage and that he or she is underpaid.[49]

Sections 5–8 of the NMWA 1998 established the Low Pay Commission and gave the Secretary of State discretion to refer matters to it. The Inland Revenue has the task of ensuring that workers are remunerated at a rate that is at least equivalent to the NMW. It has wide powers to inspect records and enforce the Act's requirements.[50] If it is discovered that workers are not being paid the national minimum wage, the Inland Revenue may, according to Section 19, issue enforcement notices requiring payment of the national minimum wage and the payment of arrears.[51] Section 20 allows an enforcement officer to complain, on behalf of a worker, to an employment tribunal if the enforcement order is not complied with. The tribunal may impose a penalty of twice the hourly rate recommended for as long as the lack of compliance takes place.

Workers have a right not to suffer detriment[52] if they assert, in good faith, their right to the national minimum wage or their right to inspect records or their right to recover underpayment.

PAY STATEMENTS

Under section 8 ERA 1996 employers must give their employees an itemised pay statement. The statement must contain the following particulars:

- the gross amount of wages or salary
- the amount of any variable or fixed deductions and the purposes for which they are made (on the legality of such deductions, see below)
- the net wages or salary payable and, where the net amount is paid in different ways, the amount and method of payment of each part payment.

Such a statement need not contain separate particulars of a fixed deduction, eg of union dues, if it specifies the total amount of fixed deductions and each year the employer provides a standing statement of fixed deductions which describes the amount of each deduction, its purpose and the intervals at which it is made. If no pay statement is issued, an employee may refer the matter to an employment tribunal to determine what particulars ought to have been included. Where a tribunal finds that an employer failed to provide such a statement or the statement does not contain the required particulars, the tribunal must make a declaration to that effect. Additionally, where it finds that any unnotified deductions have been made during the 13 weeks preceding the application, it may order the employer to pay compensation to the employee. This refund cannot exceed the total amount of unnotified deductions.[53] Thus, unlike the provisions relating to the enforcement of section 1 ERA 1996 statements, there is here a penal aspect to the discretion that tribunals have to exercise.

GUARANTEE PAYMENTS

Employees with one month's continuous service qualify for a guarantee payment if they are not provided with work throughout a day in which they would normally be required to work in accordance with their contract of employment because of:

- a diminution in the requirements of the employer's business for work of the kind which the employee is employed to do, or
- any other occurrence that affects the normal working of the employer's business in relation to work of that kind.[54]

However, if a contract of employment is not expected to last more than three months, there is no right to a guarantee payment unless the person is in fact employed for more than three months.[55] The words 'normally required to work' are significant for two reasons. First, an employee who is not obliged to work when requested may be regarded as not being subject to a contract of employment.[56] Second, if contracts of employment are varied to provide for a reduced number of working days – for example, four instead of five – employees will be unable to claim a payment for the fifth day because they are no longer 'required to work' on that day. 'Any other occurrence . . .' would seem to comprehend something like a power failure or natural disaster rather than works holidays.

No guarantee payment is available if the workless day is a consequence of a strike, lock-out or other industrial action involving any employee of the employer or any associated employer.[57] The entitlement to a guarantee payment may be lost in two other circumstances:

- where the employer has offered to provide alternative work which is suitable in the circumstances (irrespective of whether it falls inside or outside the scope of the employee's contract) but this has been unreasonably refused;[58] and

- where the employee does not comply with reasonable requirements imposed by the employer with a view to ensuring that his or her services are available.[59] This is to enable the employer to keep the workforce together, perhaps in the hope that the supplies which have been lacking will be delivered.

Calculating guarantee payments

A guarantee payment is calculated by multiplying the number of normal working hours on the day of lay-off by the guaranteed hourly rate. Accordingly, where there are no normal working hours on the day in question, no guarantee payment can be claimed.[60] The guaranteed hourly rate is one week's pay divided by the number of normal hours in a week, and where the number of normal hours varies, the average number of such hours over a 12-week period will be used.[61] Payment cannot be claimed for more than five days in any period of three months.[62] There was a maximum daily sum payable of £17.30 in 2003. This sum increases or decreases each year in line with the retail price index.[63] It should be noted that contractual payments in respect of workless days not only discharge an employer's liability to make guarantee payments for those days[64] but are also to be taken into account when calculating the maximum number of days for which employees are entitled to statutory payments.[65] Where guaranteed weekly remuneration has been agreed, this sum is to be 'apportioned rateably between the workless days'.[66] If an employer fails to pay the whole or part of a guarantee payment, an employee can complain to an employment tribunal within three months of the last workless day. Where a tribunal finds a complaint to be well-founded, it must order the employer to pay the amount which it finds owing to the employee.[67]

If guaranteed remuneration is the subject of a collective agreement currently in force, all the parties may choose to apply for an exemption order. So long as the Secretary of State is satisfied that the statutory provisions should not apply, the relevant employees will be excluded from the operation of section 28 ERA 1996. However, the Secretary of State cannot make an order unless a collective agreement permits employees to take a dispute about guaranteed remuneration to arbitration, an independent adjudicating body or an employment tribunal.[68]

STAKEHOLDER PENSIONS[69]

In 1998 the government published a Green Paper entitled *A New Contract for Welfare*. It suggested that, even though pensioners' income had increased by some 60 per cent in the previous 20 years, many still retired into poverty. The government proposed that those who were capable of doing so should be encouraged to save for their own pension, with government help for those on low incomes. The private sector was to be encouraged to provide a low-cost and flexible scheme to enable this to happen.

The result was the Welfare Reform and Pensions Act 1999, which introduced the concept of stakeholder pensions. From October 2001, employers were required to provide access to a stakeholder pension scheme to relevant employees. The provisions apply to employers who employ five or more employees. Relevant employees are those with three months' service who are not eligible to join an employer's occupational pension scheme.

Once the employer has arranged a stakeholder pension scheme, through a third-party provider, an employee may request that the employer deducts contributions from the employee's pay to invest in the scheme.[70] This must be done 'as soon as possible', but no later than the end of the following pay period. The same rule applies if the employee wishes to vary the contribution. Other obligations of the employer include maintaining a record of payments and ensuring that employees receive a statement at the 'year end'.

PAY AND SICKNESS
The right to sick pay at common law

In the absence of an express term in the contract of employment, the correct approach to finding out if there is an obligation upon the employer to pay wages to an employee absent through sickness is to look at all the facts and circumstances to see whether such a term is implied. Such a term may be implied from the custom or practice in the industry or from the knowledge of the parties at the time the contract was made. The nature of the contract will have to be taken into account and, on occasions, it will be permissible to look at what the parties did during the period of the contract. Only if all the factors and circumstances do not indicate what the contractual term is will it be assumed that wages should be paid during sickness. If such a term is implied, it is likely to provide for the deduction of sums received under social security legislation.[71] In *Howman & Sons v Blyth*[72] it was held that the reasonable term to be implied in respect of duration in an industry where the normal practice is to give sick pay for a limited period only is the term normally applicable in the industry. The EAT did not accept that where there is an obligation to make payments during sickness, in the absence of an express term to the contrary, sick pay is owed so long as the employment continues.

Entitlement to benefits and the individual's contract of employment

The courts have intervened to ensure that employees' entitlements to disability benefits under health insurance schemes have not been frustrated by a strict interpretation of the contract of employment. In *Adin v Sedco Forex International*[73] an employee's contract of employment included provisions for short-term and long-term disability benefits. It also contained a clause which allowed the employer, at their sole discretion, to terminate the contract for any reason whatsoever. The Court of Session concluded that because the right to these benefits was established in the contract of employment, the employer could not take them away by dismissing the employee. The courts are also willing to infer terms in contracts which will give effect to agreed health insurance schemes. In *Aspden v Webbs Poultry Group*[74] a management employee had a contract of employment which did not mention the generous health insurance scheme which, the High Court held, had been mutually agreed by the employers and the senior management staff. The employee was dismissed while on sick leave as a result of angina. It was claimed that there was an implied term that the employee would not be dismissed while incapacitated because this would frustrate the permanent health insurance scheme. The court accepted this argument, even though there was an express term in the contract that allowed the employer to dismiss employees for reasons of prolonged incapacity.

An employee can rely on contractual terms to pay long-term benefits, even if the employer has stopped paying the premiums on his or her health insurance policy.[75] In *Hill v General Accident*[76] an employee was dismissed for reasons of redundancy while in receipt of sick pay. The employee was only four months short of qualifying for an ill-health retirement pension. The contract of employment contained an express provision for the retention of sick employees for a period of two years' absence before they were able to qualify for the ill-health retirement scheme. It was held that this express provision did not exclude the possibility of the employee's being dismissed through redundancy, despite the unfortunate consequence. To allow this exclusion would put sick employees at an advantage as compared to those who were well and at work when it came to selecting those who would be dismissed.

STATUTORY SICK PAY

The Social Security Contributions and Benefits Act 1992 (SSCBA 1992) and the Statutory Sick Pay Act 1994 make employers responsible for paying statutory sick pay (SSP) to such of their employees as work within the EU. SSP will be paid for up to 28 weeks of absence due to sickness or injury in any single 'period of entitlement' (see below).[77] As well as those who pay full Class 1 National Insurance contributions, married women and widows paying reduced contributions are eligible for SSP. Part-timers who earn more than the current earnings limit (£77 per week) are to be treated in the same way as full-time employees, and there is no minimum service qualification. Indeed, an employee may be entitled to SSP under more than one contract or with more than one employer if the relevant conditions are satisfied.

The current rate of SSP is £64.35 per week, and the daily rate will be the appropriate weekly rate divided by the number of 'qualifying days' in the week (starting with Sunday).[78] Employers must pay the stipulated amount of SSP for each day that an employee is eligible, but any other sums paid in respect of the same day can count towards the SSP entitlement, eg normal wages.[79] Any agreement which purports to exclude, limit or modify an employee's right to SSP or which requires an employee to contribute (directly or indirectly) towards any cost incurred by the employer will be void.[80] For many employees SSP will be worth less than state sickness benefit because the former is subject to tax and National Insurance contributions and will be paid at a flat rate without additions for dependants. It is therefore hardly surprising that trade unions endeavour to negotiate sick pay schemes which ensure that their members do not suffer any detriment as a result of this legislation.

Normally employers cannot recover the sums they pay out by way of SSP. However, if in any tax month the amount of SSP exceeds 13 per cent of National Insurance contributions' liability for that month, the employer can recoup the excess from the contributions due.[81]

Section 14(3) of the Social Security Administration Act 1992 gives employees the right to ask their employer for a written statement, in relation to a period before the request is made, of one or more of the following matters:

- the days for which the employer regards himself or herself as liable to pay SSP
- the reasons the employer considers himself or herself not liable to pay for other days
- the amount of SSP to which the employer believes the employee to be entitled

and, to the extent to which the request is reasonable, the employer must comply with it within a reasonable time.

The duty to keep records

Employers are obliged to keep records showing:

- the amount of SSP paid to each employee on each pay day
- the amount of SSP paid to each employee during each tax year
- the total amount of SSP paid to all employees during the tax year.

Additionally, Regulation 13 of the SSP Regulations 1982 (as amended) stipulates that for three years after the end of each tax year employers must in relation to each employee keep a record of the following matters:

a) any day in that tax year which was one of four or more consecutive days of incapacity for work, whether or not the employee would normally have been expected to work on that day

b) any day recorded under (a) for which the employer paid SSP.

Penalties

An employer who knowingly produces false information in order to recover a sum allegedly paid out as SSP commits an offence.

SUSPENSION ON MEDICAL GROUNDS

Employees with at least one month's continuous service who are suspended from work in consequence of a requirement imposed by specified health and safety provisions or a recommendation contained in a code of practice issued or approved under section 16 HASAWA 1974 are entitled to a week's pay (see Chapter 9) for each week of suspension up to a maximum of 26 weeks.[82] The relevant health and safety provisions are listed in section 64(3) ERA 1996 and cover hazardous substances and processes, eg lead and ionizing radiation. It should be observed that this statutory right can be invoked only where the specified safety legislation has affected the employer's undertaking and not the employee's health. Employees are therefore not entitled to remuneration under this provision for any period during which they are incapable of work by reason of illness or injury. Additionally, if employees unreasonably refuse to perform suitable alternative work (whether or not it is within the scope of their contract), or they do not comply with reasonable requirements imposed by their employer with a view to ensuring that their services are available, no payment is owed.[83]

It is important to note that these sections do not grant employers the right to suspend: they merely give rights to employees who are lawfully suspended. If there is no contractual right to suspend, employees will be entitled to sue for their full wages anyway, although any amounts already paid in respect of this period can be set off against these wages.[84] Where the employer fails to pay remuneration which is owed to the employee by virtue of the statute, the employee can apply to an employment tribunal normally within three months. Section 70(3) ERA 1996 provides that if the tribunal finds a complaint to be well-founded, the employer must be ordered to pay the amount due to the employee. As long as any replacement for a suspended employee is informed in writing by the employer that the employment will be terminated at the end of the suspension, dismissal of the replacement in order to allow the original employee to resume work will be deemed to have been for a 'substantial reason of a kind such as to justify the dismissal of an employee holding the position which that employee held'.[85] However, an employment tribunal must still be satisfied that it was reasonable in all the circumstances to dismiss (see Chapter 13).

KEY POINTS

- Subject to express or implied contractual terms, an employer is normally obliged to pay wages if there is no work.
- Deductions from wages are unlawful unless approved by statute or by agreement with the employee.
- The standard rate for the national minimum wage is set at £4.50 per hour from October 2003.
- The types of hours worked, for the purposes of the NMWA 1998, are salaried hours work, time-work, output work and unmeasured work.
- Employers are obliged to give their employees itemised pay statements.
- Statutory sick pay is payable for up to 28 weeks of absence due to sickness or injury in any single period of entitlement.
- Employees suspended from work as a result of a requirement imposed by any provisions or code of practice under the HASAWA 1974 are entitled to a week's pay for each week of suspension up to a maximum of 26 weeks.

NOTES

1   See *R* v *Liverpool City Corporation* (1985) IRLR 501
2   See sections 13(1) and 15(1) ERA 1996; wages are defined in section 27 and a worker is defined in section 230(3) ERA 1996
3   See *Robertson* v *Blackstone Franks Investment Management Ltd* (1998) IRLR 376
4   See *Discount Tobacco* v *Williams* (1993) IRLR 327
5   Section 13(2) ERA 1996; see *Kerr* v *The Sweater Shop* (1996) IRLR 424
6   See *Peninsular Ltd* v *Sweeney* (2004) IRLR 49
7   See *Dattani* v *Trio Supermarkets Ltd* (1998) IRLR 240
8   (2003) IRLR 11
9   *Hussman Manufacturing Ltd* v *Weir* (1998) IRLR 288
10 See sections 13(3) ERA 1996 and *New Century Cleaning* v *Church* (2000) IRLR 27. On the distinction between a deduction in respect of wages and a deduction in respect of expenses see *London Borough of Southwark* v *O'Brien* (1996) IRLR 240
11 See *Yemm* v *British Steel* (1994) IRLR 117
12 See *Morgan* v *West Glamorgan County Council* (1995) IRLR 68
13 See *Fairfield Ltd* v *Skinner* (1993) IRLR 3
14 See section 14(5) ERA 1996 and *Sunderland Polytechnic* v *Evans* (1993) ICR 196
15 See section 13 ERA 1996
16 (1992) IRLR 191
17 *Delaney* v *Staples t/a De Montfort Recruitment* (1991) IRLR 112
18 See *Kent Management Services* v *Butterfield* (1992) IRLR 394
19 'Or, within such further period as the tribunal considers reasonable in a case where it is satisfied that it was not reasonably practicable for the complainant to be presented within three months': sections 23(2)–(4) ERA 1996. This 'escape clause' applies to other statutory provisions and throughout the rest of the book will be referred to as the 'time-limit escape clause'; see *List Design Ltd* v *Douglas & Catley* (2003) IRLR 14
20 See section 26 ERA 1996
21 See *Avon County Council* v *Howlett* (1993) 1 All ER 1073
22 See *Attorney General's reference (No 1 of 1983)* 1 All ER 369
23 See *SIP Ltd* v *Swinn* (1994) IRLR 323
24 The development rate can also apply to workers aged 22 years and above during their first six months of employment in a new job with a new employer and who are receiving accredited training
25 This was the case in *Laird* v *AK Stoddart Ltd* (2001) IRLR 591
26 See *Nerva* v *UK* (2002) IRLR 815
27 See National Minimum Wage Regulations 1999 (Amendment) Regulations 2001 SI 2001/1108, which ensure that all trainees on government training schemes are excluded from entitlement to the NMW during the first 12 months of their engagement or if they are under 19 years of age
28 Regulation 2 NMW Regulations 1999
29 (2003) IRLR 21
30 (2002) IRLR 480
31 Regulation 14 NMW Regulations 1999
32 Regulation 10 NMW Regulations 1999; a pay reference period is one month or a shorter period if a worker is usually paid at more frequent intervals
33 Regulation 30 NMW Regulations 1999
34 Regulation 36 NMW Regulations 1999
35 Regulation 16 NMW Regulations 1999
36 Regulation 15 NMW Regulations 1999
37 Regulation 17 NMW Regulations 1999
38 Regulation 24 NMW Regulations 1999

39 Regulation 18 NMW Regulations 1999
40 Regulation 27 NMW Regulations 1999
41 See *Walton* v *Independent Living Organisation* (2003) IRLR 469
42 See also regulation 38 NMW Regulations 1999
43 Sections 10(1) and 10(2) NMWA 1998
44 Section 10(4)(b) NMWA 1998
45 Sections 10(5) and 10(6) NMWA 1998
46 Sections 10(8) and 10(9) NMWA 1998
47 Section 11 NMWA 1998; section 11(3) requires that the complaint should normally be made within three months of the end of the 14-day notice period
48 Section 17 NMWA 1999
49 Section 28 NMWA 1998
50 Sections 13–17 NMWA 1998
51 See The National Minimum Wage (Enforcement Notices) Act 2003
52 Section 23 NMWA 1998
53 Section 12(4) ERA 1996
54 Section 28(1) ERA 1996
55 Section 29(2) ERA 1996
56 See *Mailway (Southern) Ltd* v *Willsher* (1978) IRLR 322
57 Section 29(3) ERA 1996; 'associated employer' is defined by section 231 ERA 1996
58 Section 29(4) ERA 1996
59 Section 29(5) ERA 1996
60 Section 30(1) ERA 1996
61 Section 30(2)–(4) ERA 1996
62 Section 31(1)–(3) ERA 1996
63 Section 34 ERel Act 1999
64 Section 32(2) ERA 1996
65 See *Cartwright* v *Clancey Ltd* (1983) IRLR 355
66 Section 32(3) ERA 1996
67 Section 34(3) ERA 1996
68 Section 35 ERA 1996
69 The rules are complex and this is merely a simple summary
70 See The Stakeholder Pension Scheme Regulations 2000 SI 2000/104
71 See *Mears* v *Safecar Security* (1982) IRLR 501
72 (1983) IRLR 139
73 (1997) IRLR 280
74 (1996) IRLR 521
75 See *Bainbridge* v *Circuit Foil UK Ltd* (1997) IRLR 305
76 (1998) IRLR 641
77 Section 155 SSCBA 1992 sets the entitlement limit at '28 times the appropriate weekly rate'
78 See section 157 SSCBA 1992
79 See Schedule 12 paragraph 2 SSCBA 1992
80 Section 151(2) SSCBA 1992
81 SSP Percentage Threshold Order 1995 SI 1995/512
82 Section 64(1) ERA 1996
83 Section 65 ERA 1996
84 See section 69(3) ERA 1996
85 See section 106(3) ERA 1996

Discrimination against Employees on the Grounds of Sex, Sexual Orientation or Race

OVERVIEW

Here we consider four important pieces of anti-discrimination legislation: the Equal Pay Act 1970, the Sex Discrimination Act 1975, the Race Relations Act 1976 and the Employment Equality (Sexual Orientation) Regulations 2003. Included in this is the important role played by the EU and decisions of the European Court of Justice. We begin with an explanation of the differences between direct and indirect discrimination and then look at those occasions when discrimination is lawful, eg when there is a genuine occupational qualification or requirement. There is an examination of issues raised by the Equal Pay Act and we look at the meaning of such terms as 'like work', 'work rated as equivalent' and 'work of equal value'.

THE SEX DISCRIMINATION ACT 1975, THE SEXUAL ORIENTATION REGULATIONS 2003 AND THE RACE RELATIONS ACT 1976

It is important to note that the titles of these measures do not fully reflect the matters that are covered. The Sex Discrimination Act 1975 (SDA 1975) outlaws, for example, discrimination against married (but not single) persons on the grounds of marital status.[1] "Sexual orientation" means an orientation towards persons of the same sex, the opposite sex or both sexes. It does not include sexual practices or preferences.[2] The Race Relations Act 1976 (RRA 1976) defines 'racial grounds' as meaning colour, race, nationality, national or ethnic origins.[3] A racial group that is defined by colour may include people of more than one ethnic origin.[4] In *Mandla* v *Lee*[5] the House of Lords held that 'ethnic origins' meant a group which was a segment of the population distinguished from others by a sufficient combination of shared customs, beliefs, traditions and characteristics derived from a common or presumed common past. This was so even if not drawn from what in biological terms was a common racial stock, in that it was that combination which gave them a historically determined social identity in their own eyes and in the eyes of those outside the group. In relation to 'national origins', it has been held that this concept is not limited to 'nationality' and thus to citizenship acquired at birth. A person can become a member of a racial group defined by reference to origins through adherence – for example, by marriage.[6] Although a racial group cannot be defined by language or religion alone,[7] it has been accepted that Sikhs, Jews and Gypsies all fall within the scope of the Race Relations Act 1976. In contrast, in *Dawkins* v *Department of the Environment*[8] it was accepted that Rastafarians are a separate group with identifiable characteristics, but the Court of Appeal concluded that they have not established a separate identity by reference to their ethnic origins and are therefore not protected by the 1976 Act.

In addition, Section 71(1) RRA 1976 requires the bodies or persons specified in Schedule 1A to carry out their functions having due regard to the need to:

- eliminate unlawful racial discrimination; and
- promote equality of opportunity and good relations between persons of different racial groups.

Currently Schedule 1A lists the larger public authorities.[9]

Both the Equal Opportunities Commission (EOC) and the Commission for Racial Equality (CRE) have issued Codes of Practice for the purpose of eliminating discrimination in employment.[10] A failure to observe any of the provisions of these codes does not render a person liable to legal proceedings but the Commissions' recommendations are admissible in evidence before employment tribunals.[11]

Both statutes recognise that discrimination can be either direct or indirect.

Direct discrimination

Direct discrimination occurs where on the grounds of sex, sexual orientation, marital status or race a person is treated less favourably than a person of the opposite sex, a single person or a person not of the same racial group would be treated.[12]

Section 1(1)(a) RRA 1976 and the EESO Regs 2003 cover all cases of discrimination on racial or sexual orientation grounds whether the characteristics in question are those of the person treated less favourably or some other person. Thus in *Weathersfield Ltd* v *Sargent*[13] it was held that a white European woman was unlawfully discriminated against on grounds of race when she resigned as a result of being given an unlawful instruction to discriminate on racial grounds against black and Asian people.

Section 1(2) RRA 1976 states that segregation on racial grounds amounts to less favourable treatment, although it has been decided that allowing members of a racial group to congregate voluntarily – eg in a particular department – will not render an employer liable.[14]

It appears that the phrase 'on the grounds of sex' does not refer to the alleged discriminator's reason or motive but to the intention to provide less favourable treatment. According to the House of Lords, the relevant question is: 'Would the complainant have received the same treatment but for his or her sex?'[15] Words or acts of discouragement can amount to less favourable treatment.[16]

Various amendments made to the SDA by the Sex Discrimination (Gender Reassignment) Regulations 1999[17] make discrimination against a transsexual for a reason related to gender reassignment unlawful although the Court of Appeal has ruled that a male to female transsexual had to be treated as female,[18] problems still remain in relation to the rights of pre-operative transsexuals, for example, in granting access to toilet facilities.[19]

Sexual and racial harassment

The phrase 'on the grounds of' covers cases of harassment and where the reason for the discrimination is a generalised assumption that people of a particular sex, marital status or race possess or lack certain characteristics.[20] Sexual harassment has been defined as 'unwanted conduct of a sexual nature, or other conduct based on sex affecting the dignity of women and men at work'.[21] In *Reed and Bull Information Systems* v *Stedman*[22] the EAT said that the essential characteristic of sexual harassment is that it is words or conduct which is unwelcome to the recipient. It is for the recipient themselves to decide what is acceptable and what is unwelcome or offensive. Provided that any reasonable person would understand him or her to be rejecting the conduct of which he or she is complaining, then a continuation of that conduct would generally be regarded as harassment. Tribunals should not make judgments as to the significance, if any, of individual incidents but should assess the impact of the totality of events.[23]

It is worth noting that both employment tribunals and the EAT are allowed to make a 'restricted reporting order' in cases where allegations of sexual misconduct are made. Whether such an order is made is up to the discretion of the tribunal, and its effect will be to prohibit the publication or broadcasting of anything likely to lead the public to identify either the person making the allegation or any person affected by it. This relates only to individuals, so tribunals do not have the ability to make a restricted reporting order protecting a corporate body.[24] Unless revoked earlier, an order will lapse when the tribunal makes its decision.[25]

The RRA 1976 and the EESO Regulations 2003 define harassment on the grounds of race, ethnic or national origins and sexual orientation as "unwanted conduct which has the purpose or effect of violating that other person's dignity, or creating an intimidating, histile, degrading, humiliating or offensive environment." However, conduct will only be regarded as having this effect if "having regard to all the circumstances, including in particular the peception of that other person, it should reasonably be considered as having that effect."[26] In *Jones* v *Tower Boot Co Ltd*[27] an employee whose mother was white and father black was held to have been racially harassed as a result of a number of incidents at work which included being called offensive names and having an arm burned with a hot screwdriver. The employer was held to be vicariously liable for the harassment because the acts were carried out 'during the course of employment'.[28] The definition of this term has been given a broad interpretation. It includes, for example, actions that take place during a social event held immediately after work and during a leaving party for a colleague.[29]

Section 1(1) of the Protection from Harassment Act 1997 declares that a person must not pursue a course of conduct which amounts to the harassment of another or which he or she knows, or ought to know, amounts to harassment of another. Section 2 makes such action a criminal offence, and section 3 provides for a civil remedy against the offender. The Act may be of limited use in the workplace because employees who suffer from harassment may see the solution to their problem to rest with the employer rather than with those individuals who are carrying out the harassment. It is additionally worth noting that it is also a criminal offence intentionally to cause another person harassment, alarm or distress. This applies not only to sexual and racial harassment but also to other grounds, for example sexual orientation or disability.[30]

Indirect discrimination

In relation to sex discrimination, a person can complain where a provision, criterion or practice which would apply equally to a person of the opposite sex (an unmarried person) would be to the detriment of a considerably larger proportion of people of the applicant's sex (married persons). As regards colour and nationality discrimination, an individual can complain where an employer applies a requirement or condition which would apply equally to a person not of the same racial group but which is such that the proportion of the applicant's racial group who can comply with it is considerably smaller than the proportion of persons not of the same racial group. The applicant must also show that he or she suffered a detriment as a result of being unable to comply with the requirement or condition (provision, criterion or practice). Employers can avoid liability by demonstrating that the requirement or condition (provision, criterion or practice) is 'justifiable' irrespective of the sex, marital status or colour or nationality of the person to whom it is applied.[31] In relation to race, ethnic or national origins and sexual orientation, indirect discrimination occurs where a provision, criterion or practice applies or would apply to persons not of the same race, ethnic or national origins or sexual orientation but such people would be put at a particular disadvantage and this cannot be shown to be a proportionate means of achieving a legitimate aim.[32] The legislation stipulates that when drawing comparisons the relevant circumstances must be the same or not materially different.[33]

Requirement or condition (provision, criterion or practice)

The term 'provision, criterion and practice' is not defined other than stating that it includes a 'requirement or condition'. However, it is likely to cover informal work practices. The words 'requirement or condition' are capable of including any obligation of service, for example an obligation to work full-time,[34] have a permanent contract,[35] or be mobile.[36] Indeed, the mere fact that the employer requires workers to perform the jobs they were employed to do may be regarded as 'applying a requirement'.[37] Similarly, the inclusion of a contractual term can amount to an application of a requirement or condition even though that term has not been invoked.[38] A requirement or condition can be discriminatory even if it is only expressed as being desirable, rather than essential. In *Falkirk Council* v *Whyte*[39] some prison officers failed to gain promotion because management training and supervisory experience were desirable before a promotion could be agreed. In practice this requirement turned out to be essential, and because most of the people in the basic grade posts were women, it was held to be discriminatory.

'Can comply'

The courts have interpreted the words 'can comply' to mean 'can in practice comply' rather than physically or theoretically comply.[40] Thus it has been held that an age-limit of 28 for recruitment could amount to indirect discrimination against women since they are less likely than men to be available for work below that age owing to child-bearing and -rearing.[41] However, the expression 'can comply' cannot be equated with 'may wish to comply'; ultimately it is a question of reasonableness, taking into account all the surrounding circumstances. In *Clarke and Powell* v *Eley (IMI) Kynoch Ltd*[42] the issue arose whether the words 'can comply' and 'cannot comply' include past opportunities to comply. The EAT decided that the date on which the detriment must be demonstrated was the date the discriminatory conduct operated so as to create the alleged detriment.

Proportion

As regards the relative proportion of persons who can comply, much will depend on the tribunal's own knowledge and experience and its selection of the appropriate section of the population for comparison. In *Jones* v *University of Manchester*,[43] for example, the Court of Appeal ruled that in finding that the requirement for a career adviser to be a graduate aged between 27 and 35 years had a disproportionate impact on women, the employment tribunal had erred in restricting the pool for comparison to mature students. According to the Court of Appeal, the appropriate pool was all men and women with the required qualifications not including the requirement complained of, in this case graduates with the necessary experience. The decision on what is a considerably smaller (or larger) proportion is a question of fact for the employment tribunal.[44]

Detriment

The words 'subjecting ... to any other detriment' are to be given their broad ordinary meaning, so it is clear that almost any discriminatory conduct by an employer is potentially unlawful.[45] Thus in *Garry* v *London Borough of Ealing*[46] the Court of Appeal accepted that the applicant had suffered a detriment when, for reasons connected with her ethnic origin, an investigation into her activities was continued longer than an ordinary investigation would have been, even though she was unaware that the investigation was continuing. For a detriment to occur, it must be shown that a reasonable worker would or might take the view that he or she had been disadvantaged in the circumstances that she or he had to work. However, it is not necessary to demonstrate some physical or economic consequence.[47] Finally, it should be noted that rules concerning appearance will not be discriminatory because their content is different for men and women so long as they enforce a common principle of smartness or conventionality and, taken as a whole, neither sex is treated less favourably in enforcing that principle.[48]

Justification

Where a *prima facie* case of indirect discrimination has been established, the employer will have to satisfy the tribunal that the discriminatory requirement or condition (provision, criterion or practice) was justifiable. Clearly, a nexus must be established between the function of the employer and the imposition of the requirement or condition (provision, criterion or practice). In addition, a tribunal must assess both the quantitative and the qualitative effects of the requirement or condition (provision, criterion or practice) on those affected by it.[49] In order to justify a requirement or condition (provision, criterion or practice) which has a disproportionate impact on one sex the employer must demonstrate that the requirement or condition (provision, criterion or practice) is designed to meet a legitimate objective and that the means chosen are appropriate and necessary to achieving that objective.[50] Finally, it should be noted that neither sex nor race discrimination can be justified on the basis of customer or union preferences.[51]

RECRUITMENT AND SELECTION

It is unlawful to discriminate on the prohibited grounds in the arrangements made for the purpose of determining who should be offered employment, in the terms on which employment is offered, or by 'refusing or deliberately omitting' to offer employment.[52] These arrangements can include the interviewing and assessing of candidates for a post. If racial grounds, for example, are the reason for the less favourable treatment resulting from the arrangements made, then direct discrimination is established. The reason for the discrimination is not relevant.[53] Harassment of an applicant for employment on the grounds of race, ethnic or national origins or sexual orientation is specifically covered by the legislation.[54]

'Employment' covers engagement under a contract of service or a contract personally to execute any work or labour.[55] According to the Court of Appeal, the legislation contemplates a contract of which the dominant purpose is that the party contracting to provide services under it personally performs the work or labour which constitutes the subject matter of the contract.[56] Both statutes aim to prevent the emergence or continuation of discriminatory practices, ie conduct which does not, in itself, amount to unlawful discrimination but which in fact results in discriminatory treatment.[57] Thus if it becomes common knowledge that Asians are unlikely to get jobs with a particular organisation because of the stringent English language tests it imposes, it may be possible to establish the existence of a discriminatory practice even though there is no applicant for a post.[58]

Advertisements must not indicate, or reasonably be understood as indicating, an intention to discriminate unlawfully; nor should they adopt a job title with a sexual connotation – eg waiter or stewardess – because this will be taken to indicate a discriminatory intent unless there is an indication to the contrary.[59] The word 'advertisement' is defined to include 'every form of advertisement, whether to the public or not'.[60]

It would seem to follow that human resource managers should ensure that application forms and interviewers ask only questions and insist on minimum qualifications that are relevant to the requirements of the job.[61] Thus a height requirement and certain conditions relating to past experience, eg having served an apprenticeship, might be difficult to justify under either Act. Clearly, word-of-mouth recruitment is suspect, and refusing to employ those who live in a particular geographical area could amount to indirect discrimination if there was a racial imbalance in the population residing there.[62] Employers also need to be aware that failure to provide a reference for an ex-employee might be construed as victimisation.[63] In *Coote* v *Granada Hospitality Ltd*[64] an ex-employee who had settled a complaint of sex discrimination was able to rely upon Article 6 of the Equal Treatment Directive[65] to show that the failure to provide the reference was victimisation.

LAWFUL DISCRIMINATION

Despite what has been stated above, discrimination may be lawful in certain circumstances:

1 *Genuine occupational qualifications or requirements*
The major exception, which is common to both statutes, is where sex, sexual orientation or race is a genuine occupational qualification (GOQ) or requirement. In the case of sex, this occurs where:[66]

- the essential nature of the job demands a particular physiology (excluding physical strength) or authenticity in entertainment
- the job needs to be held by a particular sex to preserve decency or privacy either because it is likely to involve physical contact in circumstances where members of the opposite sex might reasonably object to its being carried out (eg searching, for security purposes) or because

people are in a state of undress or are using sanitary facilities. In *Sisley v Britannia Security*[67] it was held that this exclusion covered all matters reasonably incidental to an employee's work and is not confined to cases where the job itself requires the holder to be in a state of undress

■ the nature or location of the employer's establishment makes it impracticable for the job-holder to live anywhere other than on the employer's premises and the premises are not equipped with separate sleeping accommodation and sanitary facilities for more than one sex and it is unreasonable to expect the employer to equip those premises with separate facilities or to provide separate premises (eg where the employment is on a remote site). The words 'to live in' involve the concept of residence (either permanent or temporary) and do not cover the situation where the employee is obliged to remain on the premises for a limited period eating or resting[68]

■ the nature of the establishment demands a person of a particular sex because it is an establishment for persons requiring special care or attention and those persons are all of a particular sex and it is reasonable, 'having regard to the essential character of the establishment', that the job should not be held by a person of the opposite sex[69]

■ the job-holder provides personal services which can most effectively be provided by a person of a particular sex (eg in a team of social workers)

■ the job is one of two to be held by a married couple

■ the job is likely to involve the holder's working or living in a private home and the job needs to be done by a member of one sex because objection might reasonably be taken to allowing someone of the other sex the degree of physical or social contact with a person living in the home or the knowledge of such a person's private affairs which the job is likely to entail

■ the job is likely to involve the performance of duties outside the UK in a country of which the laws or customs are such that the duties could not effectively be performed by a woman.

The only GOQs allowed for under the 1976 Act depend on authenticity in the provision of food and drink, in entertainment and modelling, and where the job-holder provides personal welfare services which can most effectively be provided by a person of a particular racial group. In relation to personal welfare services the Court of Appeal has ruled that the word 'personal' indicates that the identity of the giver and the recipient of the services is important and appears to contemplate direct contact between the giver and the recipient.[70]

The concept of a genuine occupational requirement was introduced in 2003. It applies where "having regard to the nature of the employment or the context in which it is carried out" being of a particular race, ethnic or national origin, or sexual orientation is a "genuine and determining occupational requirement." It must also be proportionate to apply the requirement and either the person to whom it is applied does not meet it or "the employer is not satisfied, and in all the circumstances it is not reasonable for him to be satisfied, that that person meets it."[71] GOQs apply even though they relate to only some of the job duties, and unless a duty is so trivial that it ought to be disregarded altogether, it is not for tribunals to assess its importance.[72] However, a GOQ will not provide a defence if the employer already has sufficient employees capable of carrying out those duties and whom it would be reasonable to employ in that way.[73] Although the GOQ defence is unavailable where there is a discriminatory dismissal, a genuine occupational requirement can be pleaded in relation to dismissal or other detriments suffered.

2 *It is lawful to discriminate if it is necessary to do so to comply with a requirement of an existing statutory provision of which the purpose is to protect women as regards pregnancy or maternity or other circumstances giving rise to risks specifically affecting women*[74]

It is also lawful to discriminate if it is necessary to do so to comply with a requirement of Part 1 HASAWA 1974 (see Chapter 9), or certain other health and safety legislation. For this exception to apply, the employer must demonstrate not only that the discriminatory act was necessary to comply with the statutory duty but also that it was done for the purpose of protecting the woman in relation to pregnancy, maternity or other circumstances giving rise to risks specifically affecting women. It should be noted that section 2(2) of SDA 1975 prevents men from complaining that special treatment has been afforded to women in connection with pregnancy or childbirth.

UNEQUAL TREATMENT IN EMPLOYMENT AND DISMISSALS

Turning our attention to unequal treatment in the course of employment and to discriminatory dismissals, it is unlawful for employers to discriminate:[75]

- (under the RRA 1976) in the terms of employment afforded[76]
- in the way they afford access to opportunities for promotion, transfer or training, or to any other benefits,[77] facilities or services, or by refusing or deliberately omitting to afford access to them
- by dismissing or subjecting the employee to any other detriment. In relation to dismissal the grounds of race, ethnic or national origins or sexual orientation, dismissal specifically includes the non-renewal of a limited term contract or a constructive dismissal.[78] Equally, where there has been a dismissal involving unlawful harassment or an act of discrimination on the grounds of race, ethnic or national origins, sex or sexual orientation, it is unlawful to inflict further harassment or discrimination on these grounds if it "arises out of and is closely connected to" the employment relationship.[79]
- by way of harassment on the grounds of race, ethnic or national origins or sexual orientation.

The following points should be noted:

- Positive action may be permissible in certain circumstances. The European Court of Justice has held that rules which allow women to be preferred for promotion over male colleagues are acceptable provided that the male and female candidates in question are equally qualified and that the sector in question is one in which women are under-represented.[80] Special arrangements can be made to train persons of a particular sex or racial group if it can be shown that within the previous 12 months only a small minority of that sex or racial group was performing a particular type of work.[81] In relation to sexual orientation, positive action can be taken if it "reasonably appears to the person doing the act that it prevents or compensates for disadvantages linked to sexual orientation suffered by persons of that sexual orientation doing that work or likely to take up that work."[82] A refusal to investigate complaints of unfair treatment may amount to a refusal of access to 'any other benefits, facilities or services'.[83]
- Occupational pensions schemes must contain an equal treatment rule which ensures that men and women are offered the same rights to join a scheme as well as being entitled to the same benefits.[84] However, equal treatment is enforceable only in relation to pensionable service after 17 May 1990. Enforcement is via the Equal Pay Act 1970 (see below) and actions can be brought against scheme trustees or managers.[85]
- Good motive cannot excuse discriminatory behaviour. Thus, despite the Court of Appeal's decision in Peake's case,[86] it is submitted that allowing one sex or racial group to arrive late or leave work early constitutes unlawful discrimination because those not specially favoured have been either denied access to a benefit or have suffered a detriment. The Court of Appeal has subsequently recognised that such arrangements cannot be condoned on the grounds of chivalry or administrative convenience and it is no trifling matter that an employer has introduced a sex-based scheme when the same objective could be achieved in a non-discriminatory fashion.
- When considering termination, it is automatically unfair to dismiss a woman, irrespective of her hours of work or length of service, if the reason for dismissal is that she is pregnant or if the reason is in any way connected with her pregnancy (see Chapter 8). The critical question is whether, on

an objective consideration of all the surrounding circumstances, the treatment complained of is on the ground of pregnancy or some other ground. This must be determined by an objective test of causal connection. The event or factor alleged to be causative of the matter complained of need not be the only or even the main cause of the result complained of. It is enough if it is an effective cause.[87] Thus in *Caruana* v *Manchester Airport plc*[88] it was held that there had been unlawful sex discrimination when the employee's fixed-term contract was not renewed because she would be unavailable for work at its commencement owing to pregnancy.

■ The dismissal of a woman on the ground of age when a man of that age in comparable circumstances would not have been dismissed, or vice versa, will be unlawful. However, there is nothing in the SDA 1975 which prevents an employer from having a variety of retiring ages for different jobs, provided there is no direct or indirect discrimination based on gender.[89] In *Marshall* v *Southampton and South West Hampshire AHA*[90] the European Court of Justice held that a policy of dismissing a woman solely because she had attained, or passed, the qualifying age for a state pension constituted discrimination on the ground of sex, contrary to the Equal Treatment Directive.[91] Article 5(1) of this Directive prohibits any discrimination on the grounds of sex with regard to working conditions, including conditions governing dismissal, and can now be relied on as against the state or an emanation of the state acting in its capacity as an employer.

■ Selection for redundancy on the grounds of sex will also be unlawful. However, suppose a woman was selected for redundancy on the grounds that although she had a longer period of *cumulative* service she had less *continuous* service than a man. It could be argued that because women are likely to have shorter periods of continuous service than men as a consequence of child-bearing and rearing, such a basis for selection constitutes indirect discrimination and would therefore need to be justified.[92] In *Clarke's* case[93] the EAT decided that redundancy selection criteria which resulted in the selection of part-timers first was unlawful because they had a disproportionate impact on women and could not be justified on the particular facts of the case. Dismissal on the grounds of sex or race cannot be excused simply because there was pressure from other employees.

■ A term in a contract or collective agreement is void[94] where its inclusion renders the making of the contract unlawful by virtue of the SDA 1975 or it provides for the doing of an act which would be unlawful under this legislation. This section also applies to the rules of employers, employers' associations, professional or qualifying bodies and trade unions. Employees (or job-seekers) can complain to an employment tribunal that a term of a collective agreement or a works rule is void. However, to do so they must believe that the term or rule may have some effect on them in the future, or that the term provides for the doing of an unlawful discriminatory act which might be done to them, and the collective agreement was made by or on behalf of the employer or an employers' organisation to which the employer belongs. It is interesting to note that tribunals have no power to amend the term so as to make it non-discriminatory. Where the victim of the discrimination is a party to the contract, the term is unenforceable against that person.[95]

■ In *Kowalska* v *Freie und Hansestadt Hamburg*[96] the ECJ declared that Article 119 EC (now Article 141 EC) precludes the application of a provision of a collective agreement under which part-timers are excluded from the benefit of severance pay when it is clear that a considerably smaller proportion of men than women work part-time, unless the employer shows that the provision is justified by objective factors unrelated to sex discrimination. Where there is indirect discrimination in a collective agreement, members of the group that is disadvantaged must be treated in the same way as other workers in proportion to the hours they work. Similarly, it would be unlawful for a collective agreement to provide for the service of full-timers to be fully taken into account for regrading purposes when only half of such service is taken into account in the case of part-timers, and the latter group comprise a considerably smaller percentage of men than women, unless the employer can prove that such a provision is objectively justified.[97]

LIABILITY

If the provisions of the anti-discrimination legislation are not complied with, both the employing body and named individuals may be sued. Individuals may be liable for instructing or putting pressure on someone to perform an unlawful act and for knowingly aiding another person to do an unlawful act.[98] In relation to aiding, it does not matter whether or not the help is substantial and productive provided it is not so insignificant as to be negligible.[99] Employers are liable for the acts of employees in the course of employment, whether or not they were done with the employer's knowledge or approval, unless it can be proved that the employer 'took such steps as were reasonably practicable to prevent the employee from doing that act'.[100] According to the EAT, tribunals should first identify whether the employer took any steps to prevent the employee from doing the act or acts complained of. Secondly, they should consider whether there were any further acts that the employer could have taken which were reasonably practicable.[101] Hence it is not sufficient to adopt an equal opportunities policy: it is also necessary to check that such a policy has been communicated to all staff, and has been understood and implemented. Additionally, employers should ensure that informal practices do not develop which could lead to an act of unlawful discrimination.[102]

The legislation permits individuals to bring complaints before an employment tribunal within three months of an 'act complained of' occurring.[103] For these purposes an act which extends over a period is to be treated as done at the end of that period. In *Owusu* v *London Fire Authority*[104] the EAT ruled that an act extends over a period if it takes the form of some policy, rule or practice in accordance with which decisions are taken from time to time.[105] Over the years the courts have struggled to distinguish a continuing act from a one-off act with a continuing consequence. The following have been held to constitute continuing acts: the refusal of a mortgage subsidy;[106] the failure to re-grade and give an employee the opportunity to act up when opportunities arose;[107] an employer's failure to implement promised remedial measures;[108] and a requirement to work on less favourable pension terms.[109] Although in *Sougrin* v *Haringey Health Authority*[110] the Court of Appeal thought that the placing of a black nurse at a lower grade than a white colleague and the rejection of her appeal was not a continuing act, it is difficult to see why the appeal itself could not constitute a separate 'act complained of'. According to the EAT, in determining when the 'act complained of was done' the question is whether the cause of action had crystallised on the relevant date, not whether the complainant felt that he or she had suffered discrimination on that date.[111] Out-of-time claims can be heard if it is just and equitable to do so,[112] and in this respect the strength of the employee's complaint may be a factor.[113]

Only the Equal Opportunities Commission or the Commission for Racial Equality can commence proceedings where there has been discriminatory advertising, a discriminatory practice, or where there have been instructions or pressure to discriminate.[114] However, there is nothing to prevent an individual from complaining that an advertisement led to discrimination in the arrangements made for determining who should be offered employment.[115]

'Evasive' replies from employers may imply unlawful discrimination

It is recognised that obtaining information can be particularly difficult where discrimination is alleged, and so Questions and Replies Orders were passed in 1975 (sex) and 1977 (race) to assist applicants in this respect. Although special forms are not necessary, an aggrieved person's questions and any reply by the employer are admissible in evidence. If there is a failure to reply within a reasonable period,[116] or an 'evasive or equivocal' response is received, the inference may be drawn that an unlawful act has been committed.[117] Thus, where an employer failed to answer all but one of nine questions asked by an unsuccessful job applicant, the reply was regarded as evasive and the inference drawn that the applicant had suffered unlawful discrimination in the selection arrangements.[118] Additionally the House of Lords has ruled that the contents of documents must be revealed if such disclosure is necessary to dispose fairly of the proceedings.[119] In this context 'fair disposal' means a disposal of the proceedings which is fair to the applicant.[120]

However, a tribunal is not empowered to order an employer to disclose information which is not available at the time.[121]

Both Acts allow the Commissions to devote resources to assisting actual or prospective complainants,[122] and if they think it desirable they can instigate formal investigations of anyone believed to be discriminating or harassing unlawfully.[123] However, the Commissions cannot embark on a 'named person' investigation in the absence of any belief that the person named might have committed an unlawful act.[124] The Commissions also have the power to require the production of documents, to make recommendations, and, if necessary, to issue non-discrimination notices.[125] As a last resort, either body may seek a county court injunction to prohibit discriminatory acts.

Discrimination and the burden of proof

The burden of proof is formally reversed in sex discrimination cases[126] and where harassment or discrimination on the grounds of race, ethnic or national origins, or sexual orientation is alleged.[127] However, where the discrimination is on the grounds of colour or nationality the following principles set out by the Court of Appeal in *King* v *GB-China Centre*[128] will apply:

- It is unusual to find direct evidence of discrimination.

- The outcome of a case will therefore usually depend on what inferences it is proper to draw from the facts found by the tribunal.[129]

- A finding of discrimination and of a difference in race (or sex) will often point to the possibility of discrimination. In such circumstances it will be for the employer to explain. If no explanation is offered or the tribunal considers the explanation to be unsatisfactory, it will be legitimate to infer that the discrimination was on racial (or sexual) grounds.

- It is unnecessary and unhelpful to introduce the concept of a shifting evidential burden of proof. Tribunals should reach a conclusion on the balance of probabilities, bearing in mind the difficulties which face a person who complains of unlawful discrimination and the fact that it is for the complainant to prove his or her case.

Evidence of events subsequent to the alleged act of discrimination can be taken into account if it provides proof of a relevant fact.[130]

If no settlement is reached,[131] and the complaint is held to be well-founded, three possible remedies are available:[132]

Compensation awards

- The tribunal can make a declaration of the complainant's rights.

- It can require the respondent to pay unlimited compensation.[133] In principle, successful complainants should be restored to the position they would have been in but for the unlawful conduct.[134] However, as regards unintentional indirect discrimination on the grounds of sex, sexual orientation or marital status, the tribunal can only award compensation if it has already made a declaration or recommendation (see below) and considers it just and equitable.[135] The RRA 1976 provides that in cases of indirect discrimination no compensation can be awarded if the employer shows that there was no intention to discriminate.[136] For these purposes the requisite intention is established if, at the time the relevant act is done, the employer (i) wants to bring about the state of affairs which constitutes the unfavourable treatment; and (ii) knows that this prohibited result will follow from the act. Complainants are entitled to compensation if they can show a direct causal link between an act of unlawful discrimination and their loss.[137] A tribunal can award compensation for both physical and psychological injury,[138] and a claim for hurt feelings is almost inevitable in discrimination cases.[139]

The Court of Appeal has acknowledged that feelings of upset and their degree of intensity are incapable of objective measurement in monetary terms. It has therefore suggested that there should be three broad bands of compensation for injury to feelings. A top band of between £15,000–£25,000; a middle band of £5,000–£15,000 and a bottom band of £500–£5,000 for the least serious cases.[140] Where there is high-handed, insulting or oppressive behaviour, aggravated damages can be awarded.[141] However, exemplary damages are unavailable.[142]

■ There may be a recommendation that the employer takes action within a specified period to reduce the effect of the discrimination which has taken place, such as by removing an age barrier to recruitment.[143] Where a recommendation is not complied with, the tribunal can award compensation or increase it.[144]

When the EA 2002 comes into force, if the relevant statutory procedure was not completed before the proceedings were commenced, and this was wholly or mainly attributable to a failure by the employer, the tribunal is required to increase the level of any award. Similarly, if the non-completion of the procedure was wholly or mainly caused by the employee's failure to comply with its requirements, or exercise a right of appeal under it, the tribunal must reduce the award.[145]

Finally, the anti-discrimination legislation outlaws the victimisation of people simply because they have given evidence in connection with proceedings, have brought proceedings or intend to do so against someone (eg some other employer) under the Equal Pay Act 1970, the SDA 1975, or the RRA 1976.[146] According to the House of Lords, in order to determine whether a person has suffered less favourable treatment there should be a simple comparison between the treatment afforded the complainant who has done a protected act and the treatment that was or would be afforded other employees who have not done the protected act.[147] Thus in *Commissioner of Inland Revenue* v *Morgan*,[148] the EAT held that a memorandum about Ms Morgan's case circulated by her head of department amounted to unlawful victimization in that it had an adverse effect on the attitude of her colleagues.

THE EQUAL PAY ACT 1970

According to the Equal Pay Act 1970, an equality clause operates when a person is employed on 'like work', work rated as equivalent or work of equal value to that of a person of the opposite sex in the same employment.[149] For these purposes men and women are to be treated as in the same employment if they are employed at the same establishment or at establishments in Great Britain which observe common terms and conditions of employment.[150] 'Common terms and conditions' means terms and conditions which are substantially comparable on a broad basis rather than the same terms and conditions.[151]

It should be noted that the class of comparators defined in Section 1(6) EPA 1970 is more restricted than applies under Article 141 EC (formerly Article 119 EC). Because Article 141 EC takes precedence, the crucial question is whether the applicant and the comparators are employed 'in the same establishment or service'. Thus the EAT has allowed a teacher employed by a Scottish local education authority to bring an equal pay claim comparing herself with a teacher employed by a different education authority in Scotland.[152] However, according to the European Court of Justice, a situation where the differences in pay of employees performing work of equal value cannot be attributed to a single source does not come within Article 141. This is because there is no body which is responsible for the inequality and which could restore equal treatment.[153]

The effect of the equality clause is that any term in a person's contract (whether concerned with pay or not) which is less favourable than in the contract of a person of the opposite sex is modified so as to be not less favourable. In *Evesham* v *North Hertfordshire Health Authority*[154] the EAT held that this meant being placed at the same point on an incremental scale as the comparator, not being placed on that scale at a level that was commensurate with her experience. It should also be noted that paragraph 2 of Article 141 EC states that 'pay' means 'the ordinary basic minimum wage or salary and any other consideration, whether in cash or in kind, which the worker receives, directly or indirectly, in respect of his employment from his employer'. According to the European Court of Justice, a benefit is pay if the worker is entitled to receive it from his or her employer by reason of the existence of the employment relationship. Thus Article 141 EC covers not only occupational retirement and survivors' pensions,[155] travel concessions on retirement, Christmas bonuses and statutory and contractual severance payments, but also paid leave or overtime for participation in training courses given by an employer under a statutory scheme.[156] Attention focuses on each aspect of remuneration rather than any general overall assessment of all the consideration paid to the workers.[157] Section 6 of the EPA 1970 provides that an equality clause does not operate where there are terms affording special treatment to women in connection with pregnancy or childbirth.[158]

What is 'like work'?

The concept of 'like work' focuses on the job rather than the person performing it. Once a person has shown that his or her work is of the same or broadly similar nature as that of a person of the opposite sex, unless the employer can prove that any differences are of practical importance in relation to terms and conditions of employment, that person is to be regarded as employed on 'like work'.[159] In comparing work, a broad approach should be taken and attention must be paid to the frequency with which any differences occur in practice as well as their nature and extent. Trivial differences or 'differences not likely in the real world to be reflected in terms and conditions of employment' are not to be taken into account.[160] Similarly, tribunals are required to investigate the actual work done rather than rely on theoretical contractual obligations. The performance of supervisory duties may constitute 'things done' of practical importance[161] but the time at which the work is done would seem to be irrelevant. In *Dugdale* v *Kraft Foods*[162] the men and women were employed on broadly similar work but only men worked the night shift. It was held that the hours at which the work was performed did not prevent equal basic rates being afforded because the men could be compensated for the night shift by an additional payment. Thus an equality clause will not result in equal pay if persons of one sex are remunerated for something which persons of the other sex do not do.[163] It is not permissible, however, to ignore part of the work which a person actually performs on the grounds that his or her pay includes an additional element in respect of that work,[164] although there might be an exception where part of the work is, in effect, a separate and distinct job. Finally, in determining whether differences are of practical importance a useful guide is whether the differences are such as to put the two employments in different categories or grades in an evaluation study.[165]

What is 'work rated as equivalent'?

According to section 1(5) EPA 1970, a person's work will only be regarded as rated as equivalent to that of a person of the opposite sex if it has been given equal value under a properly conducted job evaluation scheme, including the allocation to a grade or scale at the end of the evaluation process. Thus in *Springboard Trust* v *Robson*[166] it was accepted that the applicant was employed on work rated as equivalent, notwithstanding that the comparator's job scored different points, where the result of converting the points to grades provided for under the evaluation scheme was that the jobs were to be treated as in the same grade.

A valid job evaluation exercise will evaluate the job and not the person performing it, and if evaluation studies are to be relied on they must be analytical in the sense of dividing a physical or abstract whole into its constituent parts. It is clearly insufficient if bench-mark jobs have been evaluated using a system of job evaluation whereas the jobs of the applicant and comparators have not.[167] Employers are not prevented from using physical effort as a criterion if the tasks involved objectively require a certain level of physical strength, so long as the evaluation system as a whole precludes all sex discrimination by taking into account other criteria.[168] If the work has been rated as equivalent, a complainant does not have to show that the employees concerned have actually been paid in accordance with the evaluation scheme.[169]

Equal value claims

The House of Lords has ruled that an equal value claim can be pursued so long as the applicant's comparator is not engaged on like work or work rated as equivalent.[170] Where work has been given different ratings under a job evaluation study, however, an equal value claim cannot proceed unless a tribunal is satisfied that there are reasonable grounds for determining that the study was made 'on a system which discriminates on the grounds of sex.'[171] Section 2A(3) states that there is discrimination on the grounds of sex for these purposes where a 'difference, or coincidence, between values set by that system on different grounds under the same or different headings is not justifiable irrespective of the sex of the person on whom those demands are made'. This would appear to cover both direct and indirect discrimination.

The employer's defence

Where, for example, a woman can show that she is employed on like work, or work rated as equivalent, an employer can still defeat a claim for equal pay by proving on the balance of probabilities that the variation is 'genuinely due to a material difference (other than the difference of sex) between her case and his'.[172] If there is an equal value claim, the employer need only show that a variation between a woman's and a man's contract is genuinely due to a factor which is (a) material and (b) not the difference of sex. In this context 'material' means significant and relevant. The requirement for 'genuineness' is satisfied if the tribunal concludes that the reasons put forward were not a sham or pretence. An employer seeking to establish a material factor has to prove that: there were objective reasons for the difference unrelated to sex; that they corresponded to a real need on the part of the undertaking, were appropriate to achieve the objective pursued and were necessary to that end; that the difference conformed to the principle of proportionality and that that was the case throughout the period during which the differential existed.[173] According to the ECJ, the employer cannot rely on the fact that rates of pay have been set by collective bargaining even if the bargaining process is untainted by sex discrimination. In the same case the ECJ acknowledged that market forces cannot constitute a complete defence where they account only for part of the difference in pay.[174]

The objectively justified grounds need not be solely economic and could include administrative efficiency in appropriate cases.[175] It is worth noting that the following have been regarded as genuine material differences: the method of entering employment;[176] working in a different part of the country;[177] responsibility allowances;[178] financial constraints;[179] longer service[180]; physical effort and unpleasantness;[181] better academic qualifications; and higher productivity.

In *Jenkins v Kingsgate Clothing Ltd (No. 2)*[182] the question to be determined was whether a female part-timer was entitled to the same hourly rate as a full-time male employee. Having received no clear guidance from the European Court of Justice, the EAT chose to construe the EPA 1970 as requiring any difference in pay to be objectively justified. However, it is not unlawful to provide overtime payments only for hours worked in excess of the normal working hours for full-timers. Thus part-timers who work in excess of their contractual hours can be excluded from overtime payments if their total hours do not exceed the normal hours of full-timers.[183] According to the ECJ, a system for classifying part-time workers converting from job-sharing to full-time work comes within the concept of pay, and any rules which put part-timers at a disadvantage when changing by applying criteria based on length of service in the post is contrary to Article 141 EC because the great majority of job-sharers are women.[184] (On part-timers see also Chapter 4.)

In the *Danfoss* case[185] the Equal Pay Directive 75/117 was interpreted as meaning that where employees do not understand how the criteria for pay increments are applied, if a woman establishes that the average pay of females is lower than that of men, the burden of proof is on the employer to show that the pay system is not discriminatory. Thus where vocational training or flexibility operate to the disadvantage of women, the employer will have to justify their application. According to the European Court of Justice, vocational training can be justified as a criterion if the employer shows that such training is important for the performance of specific work tasks. Similarly, in so far as flexibility refers to adaptability to variable work schedules rather than to the quality of the work, it can be justified by demonstrating that such adaptability is of importance for the performance of specific job duties.

Piecework

In relation to piecework, the ECJ has ruled that where individual pay includes a variable element depending on each worker's output and it is impossible to identify the factors which determined how the variable element in pay was calculated, the burden of proving that the differences found are not the result of sex discrimination may shift to the employer. For these purposes any comparisons must cover a relatively large number of employees in order to ensure that the differences found are not purely fortuitous or differences in individual output.[186] As regards seniority, the ECJ has acknowledged that its objectivity depends on all the circumstances, notably on the relationship between the nature of the duties performed and the experience afforded by their performance after a certain number of working hours.[187]

Red-circling

The practice of drawing a circle around the names of those within a protected group – eg employees demoted through no fault of their own as the result of a reorganisation – is one device that needs to be scrutinised as a result of the EPA 1970. Such action may be perfectly lawful, eg where employees accept lower-paid work in a redundancy situation, but if the underlying reason for different treatment is sex-based it cannot be accepted as a defence.[188] Employers have to justify the inclusion of every employee in a red-circled group and must prove that at the time of admission to the circle the more favourable terms were related to a consideration other than sex.[189] Again, if a person's wages are protected on a transfer, perhaps because of age or illness, tribunals must be satisfied that this was not merely because of sex or that the new job was not one which was open only to one sex. The prolonged maintenance of a red circle may not only be contrary to industrial relations practice but may in all the circumstances give rise to a doubt as to whether the employers have discharged the statutory burden of proof imposed on them by section 1(3) EPA 1970. In their Code of Practice on Equal Pay, the EOC recommends an internal pay review as the most appropriate method of ensuring that a pay system delivers equal pay free from sex bias.[190]

Enforcement

Where there is a dispute as to the effect of an equality clause, both the employee and the employer can apply to an employment tribunal.[191] Equal pay claims must be lodged on or before a qualifying date. Normally, this will be six months after the last day on which the claimant was employed.[192] Similarly, where the proceedings relate to a period during which a stable employment relationship subsists, the qualifying date is six months after the day on which that stable employment relationship ended.[193] Arrears can be awarded back to the "arrears date" in respect of any time when there was unequal pay. Normally the arrears date will be six years before the date on which the claim is made.[194] Complainants must identify a comparable person of the opposite sex and cannot launch an application without some sort of *prima facie* case.[195] Although a comparison cannot be made with a hypothetical person, the ECJ has decided that Article 141 EC allows a complainant to compare himself or herself with a previous job incumbent.[196]

Under Section 7B(2)EPA 1970 the Secretary of State has prescribed forms by which an employee can question the employer on any matter that may be relevant to an equal pay claim. Similarly forms have been published by which the employer can reply.[197] If an employee asks the questions before a complaint is made or within 21 days of presentation the questions and replies may be used in evidence at a tribunal hearing, whether or not they were asked or answered in the prescribed form. If the employer, deliberately or without reasonable excuse, fails to answer the questions within eight weeks, or answers them evasively or equivocally, a tribunal may draw any inference it considers just and equitable, including an inference that the employer has contravened the provisions of the equality clause.[198]

Where an equal value claim is lodged, the employment tribunals must allow the parties to apply for an adjournment in order to reach a settlement.[199] A tribunal can reach a decision only if it is satisfied that there are reasonable grounds for determining that the work is of equal value, and it may ask for a report to be made by a member of the panel of independent experts.[200] An employment tribunal is not entitled to require an expert's report before deciding whether there are reasonable grounds.[201] However, it is entitled to hear evidence of a job evaluation scheme undertaken by the employer after the commencement of proceedings, provided it relates to facts and circumstances existing at the time the proceedings were initiated. Indeed, it is open to an employer to use such a scheme as evidence at any stage up to the final hearing.[202] The employer can ask the tribunal to hear the material factor defence before the matter is referred to an expert, but only in exceptional circumstances can this issue be raised again after the report has been submitted.[203] A minimum period of six weeks is allowed for the preparation of the report, and the parties have an opportunity to make representations before it is drawn up.[204] No method for comparing jobs is stipulated, although it is envisaged that this will involve evaluating factors such as effort, skill and decision. While there is a presumption in favour of admitting the report, it can be challenged on the following grounds:[205]

- the expert failed to follow the designated procedure
- the expert's conclusion was not reasonably reached
- for 'some other material reasons' (excluding simple disagreement with the expert's conclusion or reasoning) the report is unsatisfactory.

The expert may be obliged to attend the tribunal hearing as a witness and may be required to explain any matter contained in the report. Indeed, the tribunal is entitled to take into account the expert's oral evidence in deciding whether to admit the report.[206] Each party is entitled to call one witness to give evidence on the equal value question, but a tribunal has no power to require a complainant to be interviewed by an expert appointed by the employer.[207] The tribunal can hear factual evidence relating to a conclusion in the report only if it relates to the genuine material factor defence, or a party has failed to provide information or produce documents for the expert. Finally, it should be remembered that the decision on whether an equal value claim succeeds is that of the tribunal and not the expert. The current attitude of the EAT is that an independent expert appointed by a tribunal has no greater standing than an expert called by either side.[208]

KEY POINTS

- New Regulations on race, sexual orientation and equal pay have recently come into force and a statutory definition of harassment has been introduced.

- The Sex and Race Discrimination Acts cover more than their names suggest; the SDA 1975, for example, covers discrimination against married persons, while the RRA 1976 defines racial grounds as meaning colour, race, nationality, and national or ethnic origins.

- Direct discrimination occurs when on the grounds of sex, marital status or race a person is treated less favourably than a person of the opposite sex, a single person or a person not of the same racial group.

- Indirect sex discrimination occurs where a provision, criterion or practice which would apply equally to a person of the opposite sex (an unmarried person) would be to the detriment of a considerably larger proportion of people of the applicant's sex (married persons).

- Indirect discrimination on the grounds of colour or nationality occurs where an employer applies a requirement or condition which would apply equally to a person not of the same racial group but which is such that the proportion of the applicant's racial group who can comply with it is considerably smaller than the proportion of persons not of the same racial group.

- Indirect discrimination on the grounds of race, ethnic or national origins or sexual orientation occurs where a provision, criterion or practice applies or would apply to persons not of the same race, ethnic or national origins, or sexual orientation but such people would be put at a particular disadvantage and this cannot be shown to be a proportionate means of achieving a legitimate aim.

- There are occasions when it is lawful to discriminate; these include when there is a statutory requirement whose purpose is to protect women in relation to pregnancy or maternity provisions and when there is a genuine occupational qualification or requirement.

- The EPA 1970 inserts an equality clause into all contracts of employment when a person is employed on like work or work rated as equivalent or work of equal value to that of a person of the opposite sex in the same employment.

- An employer will need to show that any differences in pay between any two employees are the result of a genuine material difference not related to the sex of either employee.

NOTES

1 See *Chief Constable of Bedfordshire* v *Graham* (2002) IRLR 239
2 Regulation 2 EESO Regs 2003
3 Section 3(1) RRA 1976
4 See section 2(2) RRA 1976 and *London Borough of Lambeth* v *CRE* (1990) IRLR 231
5 (1983) IRLR 209
6 See *BBC* v *Souster* (2001) IRLR 150
7 See *Gwynedd CC* v *Jones* (1986) ICR 833; *Nyazi* v *Rymans Ltd* (1988) IRLIB 367
8 (1993) IRLR 284
9 See *The General Duty to Promote Racial Equality*, CRE, 2001
10 EOC Code of Practice for the elimination of discrimination on the grounds of sex and marriage and the promotion of equality of opportunity in employment 1985; CRE Code of Practice for the elimination of racial discrimination and the promotion of equality of opportunity in employment, 1983; see also CIPD Equal Opportunities Code
11 Section 56A(10) SDA 1975 and section 47(10) RRA 1976
12 On the use of actual and hypothetical comparators see *Balamoody* v *UKCC* (2002) IRLR 288
13 (1999) IRLR 94

14   See *FTAT* v *Modgill* (1980) IRLR 142

15   See *James* v *Eastleigh BC* (1990) IRLR 288

16   See *Tower Hamlets* v *Rabin* (1989) ICR 693

17   SI 1999/1102

18   See *A* v *Chief Constable of West Yorkshire Police* (2003) IRLR 32

19   See *Croft* v *Consignia plc* (2003) IRLR 592

20   See *Coleman* v *Skyrail Oceanic* (1981) IRLR 398; *Hurley* v *Mustoe* (1981) IRLR 208 and EOC Code para 13(a)

21   See European Commission Recommendation 91/131 on the protection of the dignity of women and men at work; see also CIPD statement on harassment at work and *Chief Constable of Lincolnshire Police* v *Stubbs* (1999) IRLR 81

22   (1999) IRLR 299

23   See *Driskell* v *Peninsular Business Services* (2000) IRLR 151

24   See *Leicester University* v *A* (1999) IRLR 352

25   Sections 11 and 13 ETA 1996; see also *Chief Constable of West Yorkshire* v *A* (2000) IRLR 465

26   Section 3A RRA 1976 and Regulation 5 EESO Regulations 2003

27   (1997) IRLR 168

28   Section 32 RRA 1976 and section 41 SDA 1975

29   *Chief Constable of Lincolnshire Police* v *Stubbs* (note 21)

30   Section 4A Public Order Act 1986

31   Section 1(2) and 3(1) SDA 1975 and section 1(1) RRA 1976

32   Section 1A RRA 1976 and Reg 3(1)(6) EESO Regs 2003

33   Section 5(3) SDA 1975, section 3(4) RRA 1976 and Regulation 3(2) EESO Regulations 2003; see *Shamoon* v *RUC* (2001) IRLR 520 and *Wakeman* v *Quick Corporation* (1998) IRLR 424

34   *Allonby* v *Accrington and Rossendale College* (2001) IRLR 364

35   *Whiffen* v *Milham Ford Girls School* (2001) IRLR 468

36   *Meade-Hill* v *British Council* (1995) IRLR 478

37   See *Briggs* v *North Eastern Education and Library Board* (1990) IRLR 181

38   See *Meade-Hill* v *British Council* (note 36)

39   (1997) IRLR 560

40   See *Coker* v *Lord Chancellor* (2002) IRLR 80

41   *Price* v *Civil Service Commission* (1978) IRLR 3

42   (1982) IRLR 482

43   (1993) IRLR 218

44   *London Underground* v *Edwards* (1998) IRLR 364

45   See *Barclays Bank* v *Kapur* (1991) IRLR 136. However, Section 76 RRA 1976 specifies that "detriment" does not include conduct which constitutes harassment under Section 3A RRA 1976

46   (2001) IRLR 681

47   *Shamoon* v *RUC* (2003) IRLR 285

48   See *Smith* v *Safeway plc* (1996) IRLR 456 and CRE Code para 1.24; on possible human rights issues relating to appearance see Chapter 17

49   See *Jones* v *University of Manchester* (note 43)

50   See *Allonby* v *Accrington and Rossendale College* (2001) IRLR 364 (note 34).

51   Section 40 SDA 1975 and section 31 RRA 1976 deal with inducement or attempted inducement to perform an unlawful act

52   Section 6(1) SDA 1975 and section 4(1) RRA 1976; *Brennan* v *Dewhurst Ltd* (1983) IRLR 357

53   See *Nagarajan* v *London Regional Transport* (1999) IRLR 572

54   See Section 4(2A) RRA 1976 and Regulation 6(3) EESO Regulations 2003

55   See section 82(1) SDA 1975 and section 78(1) RRA 1976; on employment wholly outside Great Britain see section 10 SDA 1975 and section 8 RRA 1976

56 See *Mirror Group Ltd* v *Gunning* (1986) IRLR 27; section 9 SDA 1975 and section 7 RRA 1976 outlaw discrimination against contract workers: see *Allonby* v *Accrington and Rossendale College* (2001) IRLR 364

57 Section 37 SDA 1975 and section 28 RRA 1976

58 On language qualifications see *Raval* v *DHSS* (1985) IRLR 370; on language training see CRE Code 1.26–27

59 Section 38 SDA 1975 and section 29 RRA 1976

60 Section 82(1) SDA 1975 and section 78(1) RRA 1976

61 See EOC Code para 23; CRE Code 1.13–14 and CIPD Recruitment Code; see also *Martins* v *Marks & Spencer* (1998) IRLR 326

62 See EOC Code para 19; CRE Code 1.13–14 and CIPD Recruitment Code

63 Section 4 SDA 1975

64 (1999) IRLR 452

65 Directive 76/207

66 Section 7 SDA 1975

67 (1983) IRLR 404

68 *Sisley* v *Britannia Security* (note 67)

69 See *Lasertop Ltd* v *Webster* (1997) IRLR 498

70 See *Lambeth BC* v *CRE* (note 4)

71 Section 4A(2) RRA 1976 and Regulation 7(2) EESO Regulations 2003. On sexual orientation and employment for the purposes of organized religion see also Regulation 7(3) EESO Regulations 2003

72 See *Tottenham Green Under-fives* v *Marshall* (No.2) (1991) IRLR 161

73 See *Etam plc* v *Rowan* (1989) IRLR 150

74 Section 51(1)(2) SDA 1975; compare section 41 RRA 1976 and *Hampson* v *DES* (1990) 3 WLR 42

75 Section 6(2) SDA 1975; section 4(2)(2A) RRA 1976; Regulation 6 EESO Regulations 2003; EOC Code paras 25, 28, 32 and CRE Code paras 1.1–17, 1.2–1 on employment for the purposes of a private household see Section 4(3) RRA 1976

76 Section 4(2)a RRA 1976; in relation to sex, the EPA 1970 deals with discrimination in contractual matters

77 Regulation 25 EESO Regulations 2003 provides an exception for benefits dependent on martial status

78 See Section 4(4A) RRA 1976 and Regulation 6(5) EESO Regulations 2003

79 See Section 27A RRA 1976, Regulation 21 EESO Regulations 2003 and Section 20A SDA 1975. Also *Rhys-Harper* v *Relaxion* (2003) IRLR 484

80 *Marschall* v *Land Nordrhein-Westfalen* (1998) IRLR 39; *EFTA Surveillance Authority* v *Norway* (2003) IRLR 318

81 Section 47 SDA 1975 and section 37 RRA 1976

82 Regulation 26 EESO Regulations 2003

83 See *Eke* v *Commissioners of Customs and Excise* (1981) IRLR 384; EOC Code para 31 and CRE Code para 1.22

84 See sections 62–66 Pensions Act 1995. Section 64 deals with exclusions, for example, in relation to bridging pensions and actuarial factors

85 See Occupational Pension Schemes (Equal Treatment) Regulations 1995 SI 1995/3183; on the possible impact of Article 141 on access to a statutory scheme see *Allonby* v *Accrington and Rossendale College* (2001) IRLR 364

86 *Peake* v *Automotive Products* (1977) IRLR 365

87 See *O'Neill* v *Governors of St Thomas More School* (1996) IRLR 372

88 (1996) IRLR 378; see also *Tele Danmark* case (2001) IRLR 853

89 See *Bullock* v *Alice Ottley School* (1992) IRLR 564

90   (1986) IRLR 140

91   Directive 76/207

92   On indirect discrimination see *Whiffen* v *Milham Ford Girls School* (2001) IRLR 468 and *Allonby* v *Accrington and Rossendale College* (2001) IRLR 364

93   See note 42

94   Section 77 SDA 1975. On colour and nationality see Section 72 RRA 1976 and on race, ethnic or national origins see Section 72A RRA 1976.

95   See *Meade-Hill* v *British Council* (note 36)

96   Case 33/89 (1990) IRLR 447

97   Case 184/89 *Nimz* v *Freie und Hansestadt Hamburg* (1991) IRLR 222

98   Sections 30–40, 42 SDA 1975; sections 30–31, 33 RRA 1976; Regulations 22–3 EESO Regulations 2003. See *Yeboah* v *Crofton* (2002) IRLR 634

99   See *Anyanwu* v *South Bank University* (2001) IRLR 305

100   Section 41 SDA 1975 and section 32 RRA 1976

101   *Canniffe* v *East Riding Council* (2000) IRLR 555

102   See EOC Code paras 33–40; CRE Code paras 1.33–43

103   When Section 32 EA 2002 comes into force, employees wishing to complain under this legislation must first submit a statement of grievance to their employer: See paragraphs 6 and 9 Schedule 2 EA 2002

104   (1995) IRLR 574; see also *Tyagi* v *BBC World Service* (2001) IRLR 465

105   See *Hendricks* v *Commissioner of Police for the Metropolis* (2003) IRLR 96

106   *Calder* v *Finlay* (1989) IRLR 55

107   *Owusu* v *London Fire Authority* (note 104)

108   *Littlewoods* v *Traynor* (1993) IRLR 54

109   *Barclays Bank* v *Kapur* (1991) IRLR 136

110   (1992) IRLR 416

111   See *Clarke* v *Hampshire Electro-Plating* (1991) IRLR 491

112   Section 76 SDA 1975 and section 68 RRA 1976; see *Apelogen-Gabriels* v *London Borough of Lambeth* (2002) IRLR 116 and *Afolabi* v *London Borough of Southwark* (2003) IRLR 220

113   See *Foster* v *South Glamorgan HA* (1988) IRLR 277

114   Section 72(4) SDA 1975 and section 63(4) RRA 1976; see *Cardiff Women's Aid* v *Hartup* (1994) IRLR 390

115   See *Brindley* v *Tayside Health Board* (1976) IRLR 364

116   Where the questions relate to discrimination on the grounds of race, ethnic or national origins, or sexual orientation, the period is eight weeks: see Section 65(2)(6) RRA 1976 and Regulation 33(2)(6) EESO Regulations 2003

117   Section 74 SDA 1975 and section 65 RRA 1976

118   See *Virdee* v *ECC Quarries* (1978) IRLR 295

119   See *Nasse* v *Science Research Council* (1979) IRLR 465

120   See *British Library* v *Palyza* (1984) IRLR 307

121   See *Carrington* v *Helix Ltd* (1990) IRLR 6

122   Section 75 SDA 1975 and section 66 RRA 1976

123   Sections 57–8 SDA 1975 and sections 48–9 RRA 1976

124   See *Re Prestige plc* (1984) IRLR 166

125   Sections 59–60, 67 SDA 1975 and sections 50–51, 58 RRA 1976; see *R* v *CRE ex parte Westminster CC* (1985) IRLR 426

126   Section 63A(2) SDA 1975. See *Barton* v *Investec Ltd* (2003) IRLR 332

127   Section 54A RRA 1976 and Regulation 29 EESO Regulations 2003.

128   (1991) IRLR 513

129   See *Law Society* v *Bahl* (2003) IRLR 640

130 See *Eke's* case (note 83) and *Chattopadhyay* v *Headmaster of Holloway School* (1981) IRLR 487

131 On conciliation see *Livingstone* v *Hepworth Refractories* (1992) IRLR 63

132 Section 65 SDA 1975 and section 56 RRA 1976

133 See Employment Tribunals (Interest on Awards in Discrimination Cases) Regulations 1996 SI No.2803, which gave tribunals discretion to include interest on sums awarded

134 See *MOD* v *Cannock* (1994) IRLR 509

135 Section 65(1B) SDA 1975 and Regulation 30(2) EESO Regulations 2003

136 Section 57(3) RRA 1976

137 See *Essa* v *Laing Ltd* (2003) IRLR 346

138 See *Sheriff* v *Klyne Tugs* (1999) IRLR 481

139 See *Orlando* v *Didcot Social Club* (1996) IRLR 262

140 See *Ventco* v *Chief Constable of West Yorkshire* (2003) IRLR 102

141 *HM Prison Service* v *Salmon* (2001) IRLR 425. This can also apply to the conduct of proceedings: see *Zarwalla & Co* v *Walia* (2002) IRLR 697

142 *MOD* v *Meredith* (1995) IRLR 539

143 See *Noone* v *North West Thames RHA* (1988) IRLR 530

144 Section 65(3) SDA, Section 56(4) RRA, Regulation 30(3) EESO Regulations 2003

145 Section 31 and Schedule 3 EA 2002

146 Section 4 SDA 1975 and section 2 RRA 1976

147 *Chief Constable of West Yorkshire* v *Khan* (2001) IRLR 830

148 (2002) IRLR 776

149 Section 1(2) EPA 1970; on work of greater value see *Murphy* v *Bord Telecom Eirann* (1988) IRLR 267

150 See section 1(6) EPA 1970

151 *British Coal* v *Smith* (1996) IRLR 404

152 *South Ayrshire Council* v *Morton* (2002) IRLR 256; see also *South Ayrshire Council* v *Milligan* (2002) IRLR 153 and *Allonby* v *Accrington and Rossendale College* (2001) IRLR 364

153 *Lawrence* v *Regent Office Care Ltd* (2002) IRLR 822

154 (1999) IRLR 155

155 See *Ten Oever's* case (1993) IRLR 601

156 See *Botel's* case (1992) IRLR 423

157 See *Brunnhofer* v *Bank der Österreichischen AG* (2001) IRLR 571

158 See *Abdoulaye* v *Renault* (1999) IRLR 811 on lump sum maternity payments

159 Section 1(4) EPA 1970

160 See *Capper Pass Ltd* v *Lowton* (1976) IRLR 366

161 See *Eaton* v *Nuttall* (1977) IRLR 71

162 (1976) IRLR 368

163 See *Thomas* v *NCB* (1987) IRLR 451 and *Calder* v *Rowntree Mackintosh* (1993) IRLR 212

164 See *Maidment* v *Cooper & Co* (1978) IRLR 462

165 See *British Leyland* v *Powell* (1978) IRLR 57

166 (1992) IRLR 261

167 See *Bromley* v *Quick Ltd* (1988) IRLR 249

168 See *Rummler* v *Dato-Druck GmbH* (1987) IRLR 32; on job evaluation generally see ACAS advisory booklet entitled *Job Evaluation: An introduction*

169 See *O'Brien* v *Sim-Chem Ltd* (1980) IRLR 373

170 See *Pickstone* v *Freemans plc* (1988) IRLR 357

171 Section 2A (1–2) EPA 1970

172 See *Financial Times* v *Byrne* (No.2) (1992) IRLR 163

173 See *Barton* v *Investec Ltd* (2003) IRLR 332

174   *Enderby* v *Frenchay Health Authority* (1993) IRLR 591

175   See *Rainey* v *Greater Glasgow HB* (1987) IRLR 26

176   *Rainey* v *Greater Glasgow HB* (note 175)

177   *NAAFI* v *Varley* (1976) IRLR 408

178   *Avon and Somerset Police Authority* v *Emery* (1981) ICR 229

179   *Beneviste* v *University of Southampton* (1989) IRLR 122

180   *Health and Safety Executive* v *Cadman* (2003) EAT 0947/02

181   *Christie* v *Haith Ltd* (2003) IRLR 670

182   (1981) IRLR 388

183   See *Stadt Lengerich* v *Angelica Helmig* (1996) IRLR 35

184   See *Hill and Stapleton* v *Revenue Commissioners* (1998) IRLR 466

185   (1989) IRLR 532

186   See the *Dansk Industrie* case (1995) IRLR 648

187   See *Nimz* v *Freie und Hansestadt Hamburg* (1991) IRLR 222

188   See *Snoxell* v *Vauxhall Motors* (1997) IRLR 123

189   See *Methuen* v *Cow Industrial Polymers* (1980) IRLR 289

190   EOC 2003

191   When Section 32 EA 2002 comes into force, an employee wishing to complain under the legislation must first submit a statement of grievance to their employer see paragraphs 6 and 9 Schedule 2 EA 2002

192   See Section 2(4) EPA 1970

193   Section 2ZA EPA 1970

194   Section 2ZB EPA 1970

195   See *Clwydd CC* v *Leverton* (1985) IRLR 197

196   See *Kells* v *Pilkington plc* (2002) IRLR 693

197   See Equal Pay (Questions and Replies) Order 2003 S.I. No. 722

198   Section 7B(4)(6)

199   Rule 13 Schedule 2 Employment Tribunal (Constitution and Rules of Procedure) Regulations 1993 SI 1993/2687

200   Section 2A(1)(4) EPA 1970; see Sex Discrimination and Equal Pay (Miscellaneous Amendments) Regulations 1996 SI 1996/438

201   See *Sheffield MDC* v *Siberry* (1989) ICR 208

202   *Dibro Ltd* v *Hore* (1990) IRLR 129

203   See Rule 9 Schedule 2 Employment Tribunal Regulations 1993 and Employment Tribunals (Constitution and Rules of Procedure) Amendment Regulations 1994 SI 1994/536

204   Rule 8A Schedule 2 Employment Tribunal Regulations 1993

205   See *Tennant's Textiles* v *Todd* (1989) IRLR 3

206   See *Aldridge* v *British Telecom* (1990) IRLR 10

207   See *Lloyds Bank* v *Fox* (1989) IRLR 103

208   See *Dibro Ltd* v *Hore* (note 202)

Discrimination on the Grounds of Disability, Religion or Belief and Age

CHAPTER 7

OVERVIEW

This chapter deals with discrimination by employers on the grounds of disability, religion or belief and age. The Disability Discrimination Act 1995 makes it unlawful to discriminate against current or prospective employees for a reason relating to their disability. We examine how the Act defines disability and the duties of the employer to take such steps as are reasonable in the circumstances to stop any physical or other arrangements' placing a disabled person at a disadvantage. We look at two of the measures arising from EU Directive 2000/78/EC on Equal Treatment in Employment. Firstly the issues and measures related to discrimination on the grounds of an individual's religion or beliefs. Secondly on measures that will make age discrimination in employment unlawful from October 2006.

DISABILITY

The Disability Discrimination Act 1995 (DDA 1995) makes it unlawful for employers to discriminate against existing or prospective staff for a reason relating to their disability.[1] People are also protected if they have recovered from a disability that is covered by this Act.[2] The DDA 1995 covers employees and contract workers, apprentices and those working under a contract to do any work.

Discrimination and harassment

The DDA 1995 is substantially amended by the Disability Discrimination Act (Amendment) Regulations 2003 (DDAA Regulations) with effect from October 1 2004. Amongst other matters these Regulations strengthen the definition of discrimination in the employment field, as well as making harassment of disabled persons unlawful.

A person discriminates against a disabled person if he or she, for a reason related to the disabled person's disability,

   (a) treats the disabled person less favourably than he or she would treat others to whom that reasons does not apply
   (b) cannot show that the treatment in question is justified.[3]

Less favourable treatment can only be justified if it meets two tests. The reasons for the treatment must be both material to the circumstances and must be substantial. If the treatment amounts to direct discrimination against the disabled person then it cannot be justified at all. Direct discrimination means treating the disabled person less favourably than a person who does not have the particular disability, but whose relevant circumstances (including his or her abilities) are the same as, or similar to, those of the disabled person.[4]

In *Clark v Novacold*[5] the Court of Appeal concluded that the test of less favourable treatment is based on the reason for the treatment of the disabled person and not on the fact of the disability. The employer must establish that the reasons given satisfy the statutory requirements. The employment tribunal may assess the evidence on which the employer's decision was made, but cannot substitute its own views. The approach to be taken is similar to that taken in unfair dismissal cases when the 'range of reasonable responses' test is used with regard to the employer's actions (see Chapter 13). In disability discrimination cases the test is whether the reasons for the employer's response were both 'material and substantial'.[6]

Harassment is defined in a similar way to the provisions contained in the Regulations concerning discrimination on the grounds of sexual orientation (see Chapter 6) and religion or belief (see below). Here harassment occurs when a person subjects a disabled person, for a reason related to the person's disability, to unwanted conduct whose purpose is to

(a) violate the disabled person's dignity, or

(b) to create an intimidating, hostile, degrading, humiliating or offensive environment for the disabled person.[7]

Defining disability

According to section 1(1) DDA 1995, a person has a disability 'if he has a physical or mental impairment which has a substantial and long-term adverse effect on his ability to carry out normal day-to-day activities'. The definition covers impairments affecting the senses such as hearing and sight, together with learning difficulties or a mental illness that is clinically well-recognised. However, addictions, tattoos and body-piercing are all excluded from the protection of the Act.[8] For these purposes an impairment has a long-term effect only if it has lasted for at least 12 months, is likely to do so, or is likely to last for the rest of the life of the person affected. Long-term effects include those that are likely to recur.[9]

Day-to-day activities are normal activities carried out on a regular basis and must involve one of the following:

- mobility
- manual dexterity (this covers the ability to use hands and fingers with precision)
- physical co-ordination
- continence
- the ability to lift, carry or move everyday objects
- speech, hearing or eyesight
- memory or ability to concentrate, learn or understand
- perception of the risk of physical danger.

However, severe disfigurements are treated as disabilities although they have no effect on a person's ability to carry out normal day-to-day activities.[10]

Impairments with a 'substantial effect'

Medication or equipment is not taken into account when assessing whether an impairment has a substantial effect. One exception to this is when people wear glasses or contact lenses.[11] Where a progressive condition has resulted in an impairment that has affected a person's day-to-day activities but the effect is not yet substantial, it is to be treated as having a substantial effect if that is the likely prognosis. The examples given of progressive conditions are: cancer, multiple sclerosis, muscular dystrophy and HIV infection.[12] 'In *Mowat-Brown v University of Surrey*[13], however, an individual with multiple sclerosis was held not to have fallen within the definition of a 'progressive condition'. It was not enough for an individual to show that he or she has a progressive condition and that it has had an effect on day to day activities. It needs to be shown that, on the balance of probabilities, the impairment will have in the future a substantial effect on the individual's ability to carry out day to day activities.' It should be noted that the DDA 1995 does not cover those with a latent genetic predisposition to disability – for example, Huntington's chorea – unless the disability develops.

Who has a disability?

The proper approach to the question of whether a person has a disability, within the meaning of the Act, was considered in *Goodwin* v *The Patent Office*.[14] The EAT concluded that a tribunal should look at the evidence by reference to four different conditions:

1 *the impairment condition*

   Does the applicant have an impairment which is either physical or mental? The term impairment should carry its ordinary and natural meaning. It can be the result of an illness or be the illness itself. The onus is on the applicant to prove the impairment, on the balance of probabilities.[15] How the illness or impairment was caused is not relevant. Thus a person suffering liver damage as a result of alcohol abuse may come within the ambit of the DDA 1995, even though addiction to alcohol itself is expressly excluded from being treated as an impairment under the Act.[16] If there is any doubt whether the impairment condition is fulfilled in a mental illness case, reference should be made to the World Health Organisation International Classification of Diseases.

2 *the adverse effect condition*

   Does the impairment affect the applicant's ability to carry out normal day-to-day activities as set out in paragraph 4(1) of Schedule 1 to the Act (see below)? This condition is concerned with the ability to carry out normal day-to-day activities whether at work or at home[17] – eg a person may be able to cook, but only to do so with the greatest difficulty. When an employment tribunal considers whether an impairment affects the ability to carry out these day-to-day activities, it should focus on the list in para 4(1) and ask whether the ability to carry out any of these has been affected. If the answer is yes, then there is likely to have been an adverse effect on the person's abilities.[18] It is not necessarily appropriate to examine each individual's normal day-to-day activity. In *Abadeh* v *British Telecommunications plc*,[19] for example, the employment tribunal had found that travelling by Underground was not a normal day-to-day activity, because the applicant did not live or work in London. It also found that flying was not such an activity because the applicant's work did not involve plane travel. The EAT held that it was inappropriate to examine each form of transport, but to look at transport as a whole, when deciding whether a person's ability to carry out normal activities had been impaired.

3 *the substantial condition*

   Is the adverse condition substantial? The tribunal will need to look at how the person's abilities were affected at the material time while receiving treatment, and then try to deduce what he or she would have been like without this treatment. This treatment can include counselling for someone suffering from a form of depression.[20] The question is then whether the actual or deduced effects on the applicant's ability to carry out normal day-to day activities is more than trivial. In *Leonard* v *Southern Derbyshire Chamber of Commerce*[21] a management adviser was dismissed on the grounds of capability after being away from work for some time with clinical depression. The EAT upheld her complaint of disability discrimination. It held that the employment tribunal should concentrate, in deciding whether the adverse effect was substantial, on what the individual could not do, rather than on what she was still able to do. In this case account had to be taken of the serious tiredness which affected the employee's ability to sustain an activity over a period of time.

   As stated above, if a person has a progressive condition (such as cancer, multiple sclerosis, muscular dystrophy or infection by the AIDS virus) and, as a result, has an impairment which has, or had, an adverse effect on the ability to carry out day-to-day duties, then the person is to be taken as having an impairment with a substantial adverse effect.[22] Consideration of whether a condition is as a result of an impairment should not be done too narrowly. In *Kirton v Tetrosyl Ltd*[23] a person had an operation for prostate cancer which resulted in urinary incontinence. The Court of Appeal held that the urinary impairment should be taken as being as a result of the prostate cancer and not just of the surgical treatment, which was a common one for such complaints. As a result it was correct to conclude that the impairment resulted from the progressive condition.

4 *the long-term condition*

Is the adverse condition long-term? In *Cruickshank* v *Vaw Ltd*[23A] the EAT held that the material time at which to assess a person's disability is at the time of the alleged discriminatory act.

The duty to make adjustments
Steps for employers to take

According to Section 6, and prior to the coming into effect of the DDAA Regulations 2003 where any of the employer's arrangements or any physical feature of the premises place a disabled person at substantial disadvantage, the employer must take such steps as are reasonable in all the circumstances to prevent the arrangements or feature having that effect. The following are examples of steps that an employer may have to take in order to comply with this obligation:

- making adjustments to premises
- allocating some of the disabled person's duties to another
- transferring the disabled person to fill an existing vacancy
- altering the disabled person's working hours
- assigning him or her to a different place of work
- allowing him or her to be absent during working hours for rehabilitation, assessment or treatment
- training or arranging for training to be given to him or her
- acquiring or modifying equipment
- modifying instructions or reference manuals
- modifying procedures for testing or assessment
- providing a reader or interpreter
- providing supervision.[24]

In deciding whether it is reasonable for an employer to take a particular step, regard will be had, in particular, to:

- the extent to which taking the step would prevent the particular effect in question
- the extent to which it is practicable for the employer to take the step
- the financial and other costs which would be incurred and the extent to which taking it would disrupt the employer's activities
- the extent of the employer's financial and other resources
- the availability to the employer of financial and other assistance in making the adjustment.

According to the EAT the test under section 6 DDA is an objective one. The question to be asked is whether the employer has taken such steps as were reasonable in the circumstances to prevent the arrangements made by the employer from placing the disabled person at a substantial disadvantage in comparison with others who are not disabled. The test of whether it was reasonable for the employer to have to take a particular step does not relate to what the employer considered, but to what the employer did and did not do.[25] This includes making an assessment of what is required to eliminate a disabled person's disadvantage. In *Mid Staffordshire General Hospitals NHS Trust* v *Cambridge*[26] an employer failed to do this assessment when an employee became ill and was absent from work for a long period of time. She was only able to work for short hours and was adversely affected by the office conditions in which she was required to work. She was eventually dismissed on the grounds of incapacity due to ill health. In this case the duty required by section 6(1) DDA to make adjustments also included a duty to make an assessment of her condition and prognosis, the effect of the disability on her and her ability to perform the duties of her post as well as what steps might be taken to remove or reduce the disadvantages to which she was subject. The EAT held that the making of this assessment could not be separated from the duty to actually make the adjustments and so a failure to make the assessment was a breach of section 6(1) DDA. There is a limit to the adjustments that an employer is required to make. They do not include the provision of personal carer services for a person who might need such help. They might, however, include the accommodation of such a carer if provided by others.[27]

The DDAA Regulations also make it very clear that a failure by an employer to comply with the duty to make reasonable adjustments in relation to the disabled person will amount to discrimination.[28]

After October 1 2004, the rule is that where an employer applies

(a) a provision, criterion or practice or
(b) any physical feature of the employer's premises

which places the disabled person at a substantial disadvantage compared to someone who is not disabled, then the employer has a duty to take such steps as are reasonable in order to prevent the provision, criterion, practice or physical feature having that effect.[29] The duty concerning provisions, criterion or practice applies to applicants as well as employees of the employer.

These rules will also apply to contract workers, where the duty to make adjustments rests with the Principal who is providing work for the disabled contract worker, unless the disabled worker has an employer with whom the duty rests.

From October 1 2004 the DDAA Regulation 2003 provide that the employer needs knowledge of the disability. If the employer did not know, or could not reasonably be expected to know, then the provisions relating to the duty to make adjustments do not arise.

Unlawful discrimination
It is unlawful for employers to discriminate against disabled people:

- in the arrangements made for determining who should be offered employment[30]
- in the terms on which employment is offered
- by refusing or deliberately not offering employment.

It is also unlawful to discriminate against disabled employees:

- in the terms of employment
- in the opportunities afforded for promotion, training, transfer or receiving any other benefit
- by refusing to afford or deliberately not affording any such opportunity
- by dismissing or subjecting the disabled person to any other detriment.[31]

Disability and redundancy

With reference to the last point, in *British Sugar plc v Kirker*,[32] for example, an individual selected for redundancy claimed that he had been discriminated against because of a visual impairment suffered since birth. The employers had carried out an assessment exercise in order to select those to be dismissed. This had consisted of marking employees against a set of factors. The complainant claimed that the marks attributed to him were the result of a subjective view arising out of the disability. The employee had scored 0 for promotion potential and 0 out of 10 for performance and competence. The EAT observed that such marks would indicate that the employee did not always achieve the required standard of performance and required close supervision. Yet the employee had never been criticised for poor performance and was not subject to any supervision. There was no need to consider the scores of other employees because the DDA did not require comparisons. It was clear that this individual had been undermarked by reason of his disability. The fact that many of the relevant events took place before the coming into force of the DDA did not stop the employment tribunal from looking at them in order to help draw inferences about the employer's conduct.[33] There have been conflicting decisions in the EAT about whether the DDA 1995 applies to constructive dismissal. In *Catherall v Michelin Tyre plc*[34] a manager, suffering from rheumatoid arthritis, was given a choice between his post being made redundant or taking early retirement on medical grounds. Although he opted for the latter, he complained that the employer's action in only giving him these two choices amounted to constructive dismissal. In this case the EAT concluded that dismissal under the DDA 1995 could include constructive dismissal. The DDAA 2003 inserts new section 4(5) into the DDA, from October 1 2004, which make it clear that constructive dismissal is included.

Section 68(1) DDA 1995 defines the term 'employment' as being employment under either a contract of service or a contract to personally do any work. The EAT has interpreted this to mean that the dominant purpose of the contract was the execution of personal work or labour. Thus, for example, a subpostmaster who, though answerable to the Post Office, was not obliged to carry out the work in person, was unable to claim discrimination on the grounds of a disability.[35]

Discrimination against contract workers

Similar provisions apply to contract workers.[36] It is unlawful for a 'principal', in relation to contract work, to discriminate against a disabled person. In *Abbey Life Assurance Co Ltd v Tansell*[37] the principal was described as the 'end-user' in a situation where a contract computer person was employed by his own limited liability company which had a contract with a consultancy who supplied services to the end-user. Taking a purposive approach to the statute, the Court of Appeal concluded that it was the end-user who should be the target for the complaint since the agency would simply justify their actions by reference to their instructions.

Lodging a complaint under the DDA

Claims that the DDA 1995 has been infringed must normally be lodged with an employment tribunal within three months of the act complained of. As with other tribunal proceedings, ACAS conciliation officers will make their services available in order to assist the parties to reach a settlement. There is an obligation upon the tribunal to enquire about what steps the employer has taken and whether they were reasonable.[38] If, however, a tribunal finds that a complaint is well-founded, it may provide any of the following remedies it considers just and equitable:

- a declaration as to the rights of the parties
- an order for compensation to be paid to the complainant
- a recommendation that the employer takes action within a specified period for the purpose of obviating or reducing the adverse effect on the complainant of any matter to which the complaint relates.[39]

It is made clear that compensation is available for injury to feelings, and there is no limit on the amount of money that can be awarded.[40]

Recruitment advertisements and the disabled

Where an advertisement might reasonably be understood to have indicated that a person might not get the job because of a disability or that an employer is unwilling to make adjustments for disabled people, and a disabled person who was not offered the post complains, the employment tribunal must take the advertisement into account. Unless it can be proved otherwise, the tribunal will assume that the reason the complainant did not get the job related to his or her disability.[41] It should be noted that, apart from section 6, employers are not obliged to treat disabled persons more favourably than others, although such discrimination in itself will not necessarily be unlawful.[42] Equally, there is nothing in this statute which prevents positive discrimination.

Victimising those seeking the protection of the DDA

Section 55 makes it unlawful for a person to victimise another for:

- bringing proceedings under the DDA 1995
- giving evidence or information in connection with such proceedings
- doing anything under the DDA 1995
- alleging that another person contravened the DDA 1995 (unless the allegation was false and not made in good faith).

The DDAA Regulations make clear, that, from October 1 2004, the rules regarding discrimination also apply to those whose relationship has come to an end. Thus it will be unlawful to discriminate against, or subject to harassment, any ex employee where the discrimination or harassment arises out of, or is closely connected to, the previous employment relationship. This includes terminations that took place before the DDAA Regulations come into force, but where the actions take place after that date.[43]

Employer liability under the DDA

As with sex and race discrimination, anything done by a person in the course of employment is treated as also done by the employer, whether or not it was done with the employer's approval. However, employers will not be liable if they can show that they took such steps as were reasonably practicable to prevent the employee's action.[44] Similarly, section 57 provides that anyone who knowingly aids another to perform an unlawful act is to be treated as having committed the same unlawful act.

The Disability Rights Commission[45] advises the government on ways to eliminate and reduce discrimination and on the operation of the Act generally. The Commission produces Codes of Practice and carries out formal investigations in particular sectors or where it is concerned that the law is not being followed. The Secretary of State can also produce Codes of Practice and has the power to appoint people to advise him or her on matters relating to the employment of disabled persons.[46]

RELIGION OR BELIEF

The Equal Treatment in Employment Directive requires Member States to introduce measures to make unlawful discrimination on the basis of religion or belief in the field of employment. The Employment Equality (Religion or Belief) Regulations (the RB Regulations) implemented this in the United Kingdom from December 2 2003.[47]

Religious discrimination can be closely linked to racial discrimination. A good example was the case *Ahmad v ILEA*.[48] This concerned a Muslim school teacher who required a short time off on Friday afternoons to attend prayers at a nearby Mosque. He resigned and claimed unfair dismissal when his employers refused him paid time off. They had offered him a part-time position working 4½ days per week. The United Kingdom had not at the time incorporated the European Convention on Human Rights into national law, but, as Lord Denning stated in this case, 'we will do our best to see that our decisions are in conformity with it'. In this case it still meant rejecting the claim as it would give the Muslim community 'preferential treatment'. The court held that Article 9(2) of the Convention did not give an employee the right to absent him or her self from work in breach of the contract of employment. Lord Scarman dissented stating that the issue began, but did not end, with the law of contract. The judgment would mean that any Muslim, who took their religious duties seriously, could never be employed on a full-time contract as a teacher. This is an old case and one must doubt whether the same decision would be reached to day, even without the new Regulations. It does, however, illustrate how it is possible to penalise someone for carrying out the activities and ritual connected to their religious beliefs.

The 2001 census illustrated the religious diversity that exists when it asked a question about religion. It was a voluntary question and over 4 million people did not answer it. Of those who did, their professed religious loyalty was as follows:

Religious affiliations 2001 census

Religion	Numbers
Christian	42,079,417
Muslim	1,591,126
Hindu	558,810
Sikh	336,149
Jewish	266,740
Buddhist	151,816
Other	178,837
No religion /religion not stated	13,626,299

Regulation 2(1) provides a very limited definition of religion or belief. These words are defined as meaning 'any religion, religious belief, or similar philosophical belief'. This implies that not any philosophical belief will do, but only those which are similar to a religion or religious belief. It has been a deliberate choice of the Government to effectively not define the words 'religion' or 'belief', but to leave it to the courts to interpret them. The Guidance to the Regulations suggests that the courts might take into account such factors as collective worship, a clear belief system or a profound belief affecting the individual's way of life or view of the world.

Discrimination and harassment

A person discriminates against another person if, on the grounds of religion or belief, he or she treats the person less favourably than another. This definition of direct discrimination is the same as that adopted in section 1 of the Sex Discrimination Act 1975 and the Race Relations Act 1976 (see Chapter 6).Regulation 3 also defines indirect discrimination as when

'A applies to B a provision, criterion or practice, which he applies or would apply equally to persons not of the same religion or belief as B, but

(i) which puts or would put persons of the same religion or belief as B at a particular disadvantage when compared with other persons,

(ii) which puts B at that disadvantage, and

(iii) which A cannot show to be a proportionate means of achieving a legitimate aim.'

The RB Regulations also provide for discrimination by way of victimisation.[49] In this case A discriminates against B if B is treated less favourably than other persons because B has

(a) brought proceedings against A under the Regulations

(b) given evidence or information in connection with proceedings brought against A

(c) done anything under the Regulations in relation to A or anyone else

(d) alleged that A or someone else has contravened the RB Regulations.

Harassment is defined in a similar way to the provisions contained in the Regulations concerning discrimination on the grounds of sexual orientation (see Chapter 6) and disability (see above). Harassment occurs when a person subjects a person, for a reason related to the person's religion or belief, to unwanted conduct whose purpose is to

(a) violate the person's dignity, or

(b) to create an intimidating, hostile, degrading, humiliating or offensive environment for the person.[50] As with other discrimination regulations, people are protected from being subject to detriment or harassment when an employment or other relationship has come to an end when these arise out of that relationship.[51]

Part II of the Regulations is concerned with the employment field and applies the Regulations to a wide variety of events. This includes making it unlawful for an employer to discriminate against a person, on the grounds of religion or belief,

■ in the arrangements made for deciding who should be offered employment

■ in the terms on which employment is offered

■ by refusing to offer, or deliberately not offering, employment

■ in the opportunities offered for promotion or training

■ by dismissing the person or subjecting him or her to any detriment.[52]

An important issue for these Regulations, which will undoubtedly be the source of future litigation, is the 'genuine occupational requirement' exception. There are two aspects to this which are recognised in Regulation 7, which relates to exceptions for genuine occupational requirements.

The first concerns an exception where

(a) being of a particular religion or belief is genuine and determining occupational requirement and

(b) it is proportionate to apply that requirement in the particular case.

According to the Guidance, a determining occupational requirement is where the need for a religion or belief is a decisive factor in selecting someone for the particular job. In this case it applies whether or not the employer has an ethos based on a particular religion or belief.

The second aspect concerns the situation where the employer does have an ethos based upon religion or belief. In this case the test is broader and less demanding in that the test is where 'being of a particular religion or belief is a genuine occupational requirement for the job', i.e. not a determining or decisive requirement. This approach derives from the Equal Treatment in Employment Directive which, in Article 4(2) provides for 'churches and other public or private organisations whose ethos is based upon religion or belief'. Such organisations may be permitted to recruit staff on the basis of their religion or belief, subject, of course to there being a genuine occupational requirement 'having regard to the organisation's ethos'.

This religious organisations exception is likely to cause problems. Some religious organisations may, for example, refuse to employ gay people. An example of an exception where employers may discriminate on these grounds is with school teachers employed by 'schools with a religious character'. The Independent Schools Regulations 2003 provide that schools which are designated as having a religious character will be permitted to give preference to teachers

- whose religious opinions are in accordance with the tenets of the religion or the religious denomination of the school
- who attend religious worship in accordance with those tenets
- who give, or are willing to give, religious education at the school in accordance with those tenets[53]

The RB Regulations do not attempt to define which organisations are likely to be treated as having an ethos based upon religion or belief. This is to be left to the courts to decide, although the burden of proof will rest with the employer.

Regulation 25 RB Regulations does provide for some exceptions for positive action. Thus the Regulations will not make unlawful any act which

(a) affords persons of a particular religion or belief access to facilities for training which would help them fit for particular work, or
(b) encourages persons of a particular religion or belief to take advantage of opportunities for doing particular work

where it appears that this will prevent or compensate for any disadvantages suffered by people of a particular religion or belief.[54]

Complaints are to be made to an Employment Tribunal. The Tribunal, if it finds the complaint well-founded, may

- make an order declaring the rights of the complainant
- require the respondent to pay compensation
- recommend that the respondent take action, within a specified time, to obviate or reduce the adverse effects on the complainant of any act of discrimination or harassment

Unreasonably failing to comply with the recommendation within a specified time may lead to increased compensation being awarded.[55]

AGE DISCRIMINATION IN EMPLOYMENT

People of all ages can suffer from age discrimination, but it manifests itself mostly in discrimination against older people and young people. Article 1 of the Equal Treatment in Employment and Occupation Directive[56] provides that the Directive's purpose is to lay down a general framework for combating discrimination in relation to a number of grounds including that of age. This is to be, according to Article 3, in relation to conditions for access to employment, access to vocational training, employment and working conditions and membership of employers' or workers' organisations. The Directive was due to be transposed into national law by December 2003, but there was a provision, in Article 18, for Member States to have an additional period of three years. Not surprisingly, the United Kingdom took advantage of this flexibility and plans to transpose the Directive, in relation to age, by the end of 2006.

Over the 25 year period between 1996 and 2021 the proportion of people, in the United Kingdom, over the age of 44 years will increase from 38% to 46%; the 45 to 59 age group will increase by almost one quarter; the 60 to 74 age group will increase by over one third and the 75 years and over group will increase by 28%. In contrast the 16 to 29 years age group will fall by 5.7%. This process is a Europe wide one, although the speed of the process is variable. The number of people in the European Union aged between 50 and 64 years is projected to increase by 6.5 million during the next ten years.

The relevance of these statistics is that whilst the population is ageing and the proportion of older workers is increasing, there is also a decrease in the proportion of people who are economically active in the older age groups.

In 1999 the government introduced a Code of Practice on Age Diversity in Employment. The Code has no statutory basis and is entirely voluntary, but is intended to encourage employers to stop using age as a criterion in human resource policies.

The purpose of the Code, according to its introduction, was to help employers 'to improve people management in their organisations and be better able' to:

- recruit and retain staff
- eliminate unfair and short-sighted age discrimination
- introduce good practice
- understand how to make that good practice work within their organisation
- recognise the business benefits of an age-diverse workforce.

The government has identified six stages in the employment process in which good practice is required to create an age-diverse workforce and reduce discrimination. These are:

- recruitment
- selection
- promotion
- training and development
- redundancy
- retirement.

Section 156 of the ERA 1996 deprives employees of any rights to redundancy payments if they continue working after normal retirement age. *Secretary of State* v *Levy*[57] concerned a female employee who had worked a few months past her retirement age. Despite the fact that she had 18 years' service with the employer, she was not paid any compensation for her dismissal through redundancy (her employer had become insolvent and she made a claim against the Redundancy Fund). The Employment Appeal Tribunal stated that:

> The logic of choosing pensionable ages for the purpose of disentitlement ... must be that after retirement there can be no redundancy. The employee may cease to work, but the job may not cease to exist, and in any event there would be no dismissal caused by redundancy.

Retirement and loss of redundancy rights

The implication of this is that every employee who reaches normal or the state retirement age is deemed to have retired, regardless of whether they continue to work. This means that if the normal retirement age in an organisation is 55 years, then after this age a worker will have lost all his or her rights to redundancy payments and, indeed, rights to protection against unfair dismissal, unless there is a contractual obligation to the contrary. Such workers are likely to be working entirely at their employer's discretion, who may dispose of their services without any fear of costs arising out of redundancy or unfair dismissal claims.

In *Secretary of State for Scotland* v *Taylor*[58] the Scottish Prison Service was held to have 'embarked on a policy with regard to retirement of older employees in order to achieve a workforce generally of younger persons who could, as a consequence, be paid less'. Mr Taylor argued that the organisation's equal opportunities policy, which included age discrimination, had become incorporated into the contract of employment, and therefore the insistence on a lower actual retirement age (of 55 years), and his own consequent replacement by a younger person, was in breach of that contractual term. He won his case at the employment tribunal, but on appeal the Employment Appeal Tribunal distinguished between the period before retirement and the period following it. The EAT stated that:

> In the final analysis, it is our decision that the protection in this case in respect of age discrimination subsisted in the contract to the benefit of the employee so long as he was working within the currency of the contract up to normal retirement age. Thereafter, the issue of age discrimination per se, whatever else may be the rights of an employee working after his retirement age at the discretion of the employer, simply disappears.

In other words, there was agreement that the equal opportunities policy was incorporated into the contract of employment, but that contract of employment disappeared when the employee reached retirement age. The age discrimination aspects of the equal opportunities policy applied only to those under retirement age (55 years) and ended when that age was reached. This decision was then upheld on appeal to the Court of Session.

In *Nash* v *Mash*[59] an applicant was dismissed from his post as a warehouse manager at the age of 69 years. He sought to claim unfair dismissal and a redundancy payment. His case was that sections 109 (which deprives people over normal retirement age of the right to claim unfair dismissal) and 156 of the Employment Rights Act 1996 are indirectly discriminatory against men, contrary to Article 119 EC (now Article 141 EC). Figures were produced which showed that in 1991 6.8 per cent of the male population aged 65 to 74 years were economically active, compared with 3.9 per cent of females. Figures from the Equal Opportunities Commission showed that 7.5 per cent of men over the age of 65 years were economically active whereas 3.1 per cent of women were also active. The employment tribunal concluded that the relevant sections of the Act were incompatible with Article 141 (previously Article 119 EC) of the EC Treaty. They were not willing to await the outcome of other judgments from the European Court of Justice because of the time they would take and with respect to the complainant's age.

A different and perhaps, more significant approach has been taken in *Rutherford* v *Towncircle Ltd.*[60] Mr Rutherford was told that he was to be dismissed on the grounds of redundancy. At the time he was 67 years old. He argued that the upper age limit in sections 109 and 156 of the Employment Rights Act 1996 was indirectly discriminatory against men. The court considered all the factors, including the statistics, which showed that a greater proportion of men over 65 continued to work than the proportion of females who continued to do so. The conclusion was that the resources were, therefore, indirectly discriminatory against men. Having also concluded that the State failed to show objective justification for the measures, the court allowed Mr Rutherford to go ahead with his claims.

Proposed measures

The approach in the Equal Treatment in Employment Directive to age is the same as other measures in relation to disability, sexual orientation, religion or belief. The Directive aims to introduce the 'principle of equal treatment' into all these areas. This means that there shall be no direct or indirect discrimination (Article 2.2). Harassment is also deemed to be a form of discrimination.

Article 4 provides for the possibility that a difference of treatment may be justified where there is 'a genuine and determining occupational requirement, provided that the objective is legitimate and the requirement is proportionate'.

Article 6 refers to the justification of differences of treatment on the grounds of age. Differences in treatment on the basis of age may be justified if 'they are objectively and reasonably justified by a legitimate aim including legitimate employment policy, labour market and vocational treatment'. Examples given of such differences are

- the setting of special conditions for access to employment and training, including dismissal and remuneration for young people, older workers and persons with caring responsibilities in order to promote their integration into the workforce;
- the fixing of minimum conditions of age, professional experience or seniority for access to employment or certain advantages linked to employment;
- the fixing of a maximum age for recruitment which is based either on the training needs of a post, or the need for a reasonable period before retirement.

It is interesting that it was felt necessary to spell out these exceptions to age discrimination in the Directive. It is perhaps symptomatic of the way that age discrimination is treated differently from other forms of discrimination. These provisions effectively state that some age discrimination is benign. There appears to be an economic or business imperative that suggests that more harm will be done if discrimination does not take place, rather than an imperative that states that age discrimination is wrong and can only be justified in exceptional circumstances. Effectively widespread discrimination is not to be allowed to continue except those forms which are held to be for the economic good of business.

Direct Discrimination takes place when a decision is made on the basis of a person's chronological or perceived age; unless it can be justified.

Article 6 of the Directive (see above) is interpreted as allowing Member States to justify direct discrimination where it can be objectively justified by reference to specific aims and are appropriate and necessary. The sort of specific aims which might justify differences in treatment are given in Government proposals as:

- health, welfare and safety; e.g. the protection of young workers
- facilitation of employment planning; e.g. where a business has a number of people approaching retirement age at the same time
- the particular training requirements of the post in question; e.g. air traffic controllers, who have to undertake 18 months theoretical and practical training at the College of Air Traffic Control, followed by further on the job training
- encouraging and rewarding loyalty

- the need for a reasonable period of employment before retirement

The Government proposes that there will be an opportunity for employers to justify specific practices in relation to retirement age, pay and non-pay benefits and age limits for recruitment, selection and promotion Indirect Discrimination is said to arise when

- employers or others with obligations apply an apparently neutral provision equally to employees or prospective employees or others protected by the Directive
- it puts people of a particular age at a disadvantage, and
- an individual can show that he/she has suffered a disadvantage

The Government plans to use the same approach as in new regulations on sexual orientation, religion or belief, including the rules on victimisation and harassment.

Age rules in UK legislation

There are current rules in UK legislation which permit discrimination on the basis of age and which will be reviewed as part of the new Regulations. Some of these are

(a) National minimum wage – lower rates for young workers can be justified.

(b) Working time – different rules for young workers

(c) Unfair dismissal – section 109 ERA 1996 currently provides for an upper age limit for those entitled to the right not to be unfairly dismissed

(d) Statutory redundancy payments – section 156 ERA 1996 currently provides for an upper age limit for those entitled to a redundancy payment.

(e) Basic award for unfair dismissal and redundancy payments are age related

Perhaps the most dramatic change is likely to be the ending of the mandatory retirement age. Traditional reasons for having a fixed retirement age are

- occupational pensions have a normal retirement date
- older workers make way for young ones
- younger workers have a higher level of productivity

The Government proposes that the State Pension Age is to remain as at present, to be equalised at 65 years. Occupational pension schemes will continue to operate on a normal retirement age basis. This is important because it is these factors which will limit the effect of abolishing or changing the mandatory contractual retirement age.

KEY POINTS

- It is unlawful for employers with 15 or more employees to discriminate against employees or applicants for reasons related to their disability.
- A disability, within the meaning of the Act, is a physical or mental impairment which has a substantial and long-term adverse effect on the ability to carry out normal day-to-day activities.
- A tribunal needs to approach the question of whether a person has a disability by reference to the impairment condition, the adverse effect condition, the substantial condition and the long-term condition.
- An employer has a duty to take steps and make adjustments in order not to place a disabled person at a substantial disadvantage.
- It is unlawful to discriminate in employment matters on the basis of religion or belief, but it is to be left to the courts to decide what is meant by these terms.
- Employers with an ethos of religion or belief may be able to select on the basis of religion or belief provided it is a genuine occupational requirement.
- Regulations on age discrimination in employment will not come into effect until the end of October 2006.

NOTES

1 Regulation 7 DDAA Regulations 2003, a small firm exemption of firms with 15 or fewer employees is removed by October 1 2004
2 See section 2 and Schedule 1 paragraph 2(2)
3 Section 3A(1) DDA as amended
4 Section 3A(4) and (5) DDA as amended
5 (1999) IRLR 318
6 *Jones* v *Post Office* (2001) IRLR 384
7 Section 4 DDA as amended
8 See the Disability Discrimination (Meaning of Disability) Regulations 1996 SI 1996/1455
9 See Schedule 1 paragraph 2 DDA 1995
10 Schedule 1 paragraphs 3 and 4 DDA 1995
11 Schedule 1 paragraph 6 DDA 1995
12 Schedule 1 paragraph 8 DDA 1995
13 (2002) IRLR 235
14 (1999) IRLR 4
15 See *McNicol* v *Balfour Beatty Rail Maintenance Ltd* (2002) IRLR 711
16 See *Power* v *Panasonic UK Ltd* (2002) IRLR 153
17 See *Cruickshank* v *Vaw Ltd* (2002) IRLR 24
18 See *Ekpe* v *Commissioner of Police* (2001) IRLR 605
19 (2001) IRLR 23
20 See *Kapadia* v *London Borough of Lambeth* (2000) IRLR 699
21 (2001) IRLR 19
22 Schedule 1 DDA 1995
23 (2003) IRLR 353
23A (2002) IRLR 24
24 See Code of Practice for the elimination of disability discrimination in employment 1996
25 See *British Gas Services Ltd* v *McCaull* (2001) IRLR 60
26 (2003) IRLR 566
27 See *Kenny* v *Hampshire Constabulary* (1999) IRLR 76

28 Regulation 3A(2) DDAA Regulations 2003
29 Section 4A DDA 1995 inserted by Regulation 5 DDAA Regulations 2003, with effect from October 1 2004
30 The Code of Practice makes helpful suggestions about job specifications and interviews (note 24)
31 Section 4 DDA 1995.
32 (1998) IRLR 624
33 See also *Kent County Council* v *Mingo* (2000) IRLR 90 where a redeployment policy that gave preference to redundant or potentially redundant employees, in preference to those with a disability amounted to discrimination in accordance with sections 5(1) and 5(2) DDA 1995
34 (2003) IRLR 61
35 *Sheehan* v *Post office Counters Ltd* (1999) ICR 734
36 Section 12 DDA 1995
37 (2000) IRLR 387
38 See *Morse* v *Wiltshire County Council* (1998) IRLR 352
39 The Employment Tribunals (Constitution and Rules of Procedure) (Amendment) Regulations 1998 SI 1996/1757 oblige tribunals to give extended reasons for their decisions and enable them to make restricted reporting orders in DDA 1995 cases.
40 Section 8 and Schedule 3 DDA 1995
41 Section 11 DDA 1995
42 See *Clark* v *Novacold Ltd* (note 19). Section 6(7) DDA 1995 states that 'nothing in this part is to be taken to require an employer to treat a disabled person more favourably than he treats or would treat others'.
43 New section 16A DDA 1995
44 Section 58 DDA 1995
45 Disability Rights Commission Act 1999
46 See sections 53 and 60 DDA 1995
47 SI 2003/1660
48 [1977] ICR 490
49 Regulation 4 RB Regulations 2003
50 Regulation 5 RB Regulations
51 Regulation 21 RB Regulations 2003
52 Regulation 7(2) RB Regulations
53 The Independent Schools (Employment of Teachers in Schools with a Religious Character) Regulations 2003 SI 2003/2037
54 Regulation 26 RB Regulations 2003 also make special provisions for Sikhs and the wearing of protective headgear
55 Regulations 28–30 RB Regulations 2003
56 Directive 2000/78/EC
57 (1989) IRLR 469
58 (1999) IRLR 362
59 (1998) IRLR 168
60 *Rutherford* v *Towncircle Ltd* t/a Harvest (No 2) (2002) IRLR 768

Parental Rights

CHAPTER 8

> ## OVERVIEW
>
> This chapter discusses the rights of parents in certain circumstances. In particular the rights of pregnant women and those who have recently given birth together with the right to ordinary, compulsory and additional maternity leave. Other rights examined here are the rules associated with parental leave, adoption leave and paternity leave. We then consider the rights of parents for time off to deal with emergencies and the right to ask for more flexible working arrangements.

TIME OFF FOR ANTENATAL CARE

Irrespective of the length of service or the number of hours she works, a pregnant woman who, on the advice of a registered medical practitioner, midwife or health visitor, has made an appointment to receive antenatal care has the right not to be unreasonably refused time off during working hours to enable her to keep the appointment. Apart from the first appointment, the woman may be required to produce a certificate and some documentary evidence of the appointment for the employer's inspection. A woman who is permitted such time off is entitled to be paid for her absence at the appropriate hourly rate.[1]

If time off is refused or the employer has failed to pay the whole or part of any amount to which she feels she is entitled, a woman can complain to an employment tribunal. Unless the 'time-limit escape clause' applies, her claim must be presented within three months of the date of the appointment concerned.[2] Where a tribunal finds that the complaint is well-founded, it must make a declaration to that effect, and if time off has been unreasonably refused, the employer will be ordered to pay a sum equal to that which she would have been entitled to had the time off not been refused. If the complaint is that the employer failed to pay the amount to which she was entitled, the employer must pay the amount that the tribunal finds due to her. Any contractual remuneration paid to a woman in respect of a period of time off under this section, however, goes towards discharging any statutory liability to pay that arises. Conversely, any payment made as a result of this section goes towards discharging any contractual liability to pay for the period of time off.[3]

MATERNITY LEAVE

Article 8 of the Pregnant Workers Directive[4] provides that pregnant workers, or those who have recently given birth, have a right to a period of maternity leave of at least 14 weeks, which must include a compulsory period of at least two weeks before and/or after confinement. Community law and the European Court of Justice have played an important part in developing rules that protect women during their pregnancy and maternity leave period. The ECJ has regarded discrimination against pregnant women as acts of sex discrimination which are in breach of Article 141, the Equal Treatment Directive[5] and the Equal Pay Directive.[6]

In *Pedersen*,[7] for example, the ECJ held that a policy which stated that workers who are unfit for work because of illness would receive full pay, but that pregnant women off sick from work for an illness related to the pregnancy would not, was in breach of Article 141 EC and the Equal Pay Directive. This developed further the view of the ECJ as expressed in *Brown* v *Rentokil*,[8] in which the Court of Justice held that the dismissal of a woman at any time during her pregnancy for absences caused by illness resulting from that pregnancy is direct discrimination on the grounds of sex contrary to the EC Equal Treatment Directive.[9] Thus, in *Patefield* v *Belfast City Council*,[10] the replacement of a pregnant temporary agency worker with a permanent employee while the temporary worker was on maternity leave amounted to discrimination on the grounds of sex. The employer could have lawfully replaced her with a permanent replacement at any time before she went on leave. Replacing her while she was unavailable for work, because of her pregnancy, was to treat her less favourably than a man (who would not have become unavailable for work because of pregnancy) would have been treated. Similarly, in *GUS Home Shopping Ltd* v *Green and McLaughlin*,[11] not paying employees a loyalty bonus because they were absent from work owing to pregnancy was also held to amount to unlawful sex discrimination.

Part VIII of the ERA 1996 contains provisions for maternity rights and is more generous than the minimum requirements in the EU Directive. The provisions are further detailed in the Maternity and Parental Leave Regulations 1999[12], which were substantially amended by the Maternity and Parental Leave (Amendment) Regulations 2001[13] and 2002.[14] All references that follow are to the amended Regulations (the MPL Regulations).

The ordinary maternity leave period

The dates of maternity leave are calculated as being periods before or after the 'expected week of child-birth'. This is defined as the week, beginning with midnight between Saturday and Sunday, in which it is expected that childbirth will occur.[15]

Regulation 2 of the MPL Regulations defines childbirth as 'the birth of a living child or the birth of a child whether living or dead after 24 weeks of pregnancy'. This means that a woman who gives birth to a still-born child after 24 weeks of pregnancy will be entitled to the same leave as a person who gave birth to a live child.

The MPL Regulations state that an employee is entitled to ordinary maternity leave if she satisfies certain conditions. These are[16]:

- that no later than the 15th week before her expected week of childbirth she notifies her employer of her pregnancy and the date on which she intends to start her ordinary maternity leave. If it is not reasonably practicable to inform the employer by this time, then the requirement is that notice must be provided as soon as is reasonably practicable. The employee may subsequently vary the date, provided that does so at least 28 days before the date to be varied or the new date, whichever is earlier.
- that the employee must give these notices in writing if the employer so requests
- that the employer is able to request, for inspection, a certificate from a registered medical practitioner or a registered midwife stating the expected week of childbirth. Failure to provide such a certificate, if requested, will remove the employee's entitlement to ordinary maternity leave.

Regulation 5 MPL Regulations 1999 provides that if the ordinary maternity leave has not commenced:

- by the first day after the beginning of the fourth week before the expected week of childbirth on which the employee is absent from work wholly or partly because of pregnancy, or
- by the day on which childbirth occurs,

then the ordinary maternity leave will be deemed to have commenced on that day, provided that the employee notifies her employer, in writing if requested, as soon as reasonably practicable. Failure to provide this notification may result in the employee's losing her entitlement to ordinary maternity leave.[17]

Ordinary maternity leave continues for a period of 26 weeks from its commencement, or until the end of the compulsory maternity leave period, whichever is later.[18] This period can be extended if there is a statutory provision that prohibits the employee from working after the end of the ordinary maternity leave period, for a reason related to the fact that she had recently given birth.

Contractual rights during ordinary maternity leave

Section 71(4) ERA 1996 states that an employee on ordinary maternity leave is:

- entitled to the benefit of the terms and conditions of employment which would have applied had she not been absent. This does not include terms and conditions relating to remuneration[19]
- bound by obligations arising under those terms and conditions
- entitled to return from leave to the job in which she was employed before her absence, with her seniority, pension and similar rights as if she had not been absent. She is also to return on terms and conditions not less favourable than those which would have applied if she had not been absent.

The compulsory maternity leave period

An employer may not permit an employee to work during her compulsory maternity leave period. An employer who allows an employee to work during this period will be subject to a fine.[20] This compulsory period will not be less than two weeks in length, commencing with the day on which childbirth occurs, and it is included in the ordinary leave period (see above).[21]

The additional maternity leave period

An employee who is entitled to ordinary maternity leave and has, at the beginning of the fourteenth week before the expected week of childbirth, been continuously employed for a period of not less than 26 weeks is also entitled to additional maternity leave.[22] This additional maternity leave period commences on the day after the last day of the ordinary maternity leave period and continues for 26 weeks from the day on which it commenced.[23]

The date of the return to work

To avoid confusion, an employer who has been notified under Regulation 4 about when an employee's ordinary maternity leave will commence, or has commenced, has an obligation to notify the employee of the date on which the ordinary maternity leave will end and, if relevant, the date on which her additional maternity leave will end. This must be done within 28 days of the date on which the employer received notification of the commencement.[24]

If the employee wishes to return early and not take her full entitlement of maternity leave, then she must give 28 days' notice, in writing, of her intended return date. If she does not give the required notice, the employer may delay her return for up to 28 days.[25]

Where the employer has engaged a replacement for the absent woman, provided that person has been informed in writing that his or her employment will be terminated on the woman's return to work, the dismissal of the replacement will be regarded as having been for a substantial reason (see Chapter 13). This does not mean that such a dismissal will always be fair, because a tribunal will have to be satisfied that it was reasonable to dismiss in the circumstances. For instance, it might be unfair to dismiss if the employer had a vacancy that the replacement could have filled.

If during ordinary or additional maternity leave it becomes clear that the employer cannot continue to employ the employee under her existing contract of employment by reason of redundancy, the employee is entitled to be offered any other suitable employment which may be available. The work to be done must be both suitable and appropriate in the circumstances, and its provisions as to the capacity and place of work and other terms and conditions to be not substantially less favourable than if she had continued to be employed under the previous contract.[26]

PARENTAL LEAVE

An employee who has been continuously employed for a period of not less than one year and who has, or expects to have, responsibility for a child[27] is entitled to be absent from work on parental leave for the purposes of caring for that child.[28]

The entitlement to parental leave is in respect of a child who is less than five years old. When the child reaches his or her fifth birthday, the entitlement ceases. There are three exceptions to this:

- when a child is adopted or placed for adoption with an employee. In such cases the entitlement ceases on the fifth anniversary of the date on which the placement began and the upper age limit, therefore, cannot apply. The Regulations place an absolute upper age limit of the date of the child's eighteenth birthday.
- when a child is in receipt of, or entitled to, a disability living allowance. In this case the upper age limit of 18 years applies.
- when the employer exercises his or her right to delay parental leave (see below) and this results in the child passing the fifth birthday. The entitlement can still be taken at the end of the period for which leave has been postponed, even though the child will now be over five years old.

An employee is entitled to 13 weeks leave in respect of any individual child.[29] The leave entitlement is for 'any individual child', so that an employee/parent of multiple-birth children will be entitled to 13 weeks leave in respect of each child. This figure is increased to 18 weeks for those with responsibility for a child who is entitled to a disability living allowance.[30]

Notice provisions

Before employees can exercise their rights to parental leave, they must, unless otherwise stipulated by collective or workforce agreements (see Chapter 2):

- comply with any request from the employer to produce for inspection evidence of the employee's responsibility or expected responsibility for the child as well as evidence of the child's age
- give the employer notice of the period of leave that is proposed. This notice must specify the dates on which the leave is to begin and end and be given at least 21 days before the date upon which the leave is to start. Where the leave to be taken is in respect of a child to be adopted and the leave is to begin on the date of the placement, then the notice must specify the week in which the placement is expected to occur and the period of leave. The notice is to be given to the employer at least 21 days before the beginning of that week, or if that is not reasonably practicable, as soon as it is so. These rules also apply to a situation where the employee is the father of the child and the leave is to be taken when the child is born (but see below on paternity leave).
- ensure that the employer has not postponed the leave in accordance with the MPL Regulations (see below).

Postponing parental leave[31]

An employer may postpone a period of parental leave, subject to any collective or workforce agreements, where:

- the employee has applied and given the necessary notice, and
- the operation of the employer's business would be unduly disrupted if the employee took leave during the period identified in the notice, and
- the employer permits the employee to take a period of leave of the same length that had been requested within six months of the date on which it was due to begin, and
- the employer gives notice in writing of the postponement stating the reasons for it and specifying the dates on which the employee may take parental leave. This notice must be given to the employee not later than seven days after the employee's notice was given to the employer.

An employee may complain to an employment tribunal if the employer has unreasonably postponed a period of parental leave or attempted to prevent the employee from taking it.[32] The tribunal may award such compensation that it considers 'just and equitable'.

Terms and conditions during periods of additional maternity leave and parental leave

Section 73(4) ERA 1996 declares that an employee who takes additional maternity leave is:

- entitled to the benefit of the terms and conditions of employment which would have occurred had she not been absent. This does not include terms and conditions relating to remuneration[33]
- bound by obligations arising under those terms and conditions
- entitled to return to a job of a prescribed kind (see below).

Sections 77(1) to (4) ERA 1996 make the same provisions for those on parental leave. In addition, Regulation 17 MPL Regulations 1999 states that employees on additional maternity leave and parental leave are:

- entitled to the benefit of the employer's implied obligation of trust and confidence (see Chapter 3) and any terms of employment relating to
  - notice of the termination of the employment contract by the employer
  - compensation in the event of redundancy
  - disciplinary and grievance procedures
- bound by an implied obligation of good faith to the employer and any terms and conditions of employment relating to
  - notice of the termination of the employment contract by the employee
  - the disclosure of confidential information
  - the acceptance of gifts or other benefits, or
  - the employee's participation in any other business.

The right to return to work after maternity leave or parental leave

The Regulations distinguish between those employees who take shorter periods of leave from those who take longer periods. Thus, if an employee is returning to work after a period of ordinary maternity leave or of parental leave of less than four weeks duration, then that employee will be entitled to return to the job in which she was employed before her absence. This is provided that the period of leave was an isolated one or that it was the last of two consecutive periods of statutory leave which did not include any periods of additional maternity or adoptive leave, or parental leave of more than four weeks.[34]

Unless subject to dismissal through redundancy, an employee who takes additional maternity leave or parental leave of more than four weeks is entitled to return from that leave to the job in which he or she was employed prior to the absence. If this is not reasonably practicable, the employer must permit the employee to return to another job which is both suitable and appropriate in the circumstances.[35] This right to return to work is a right to return:

- on terms and conditions, relating to remuneration, not less favourable than those that would have applied had he or she not been absent from work since the beginning of ordinary maternity leave or the beginning of parental leave, as appropriate
- with seniority, pension and similar rights preserved as if there had been continuous employment
- on terms and conditions otherwise not less favourable than those that would have applied had there been no absence on additional maternity leave or parental leave.

PATERNITY LEAVE

The provisions relating to paternity leave, introduced by the Employment Act 2002[36] and the Paternity and Adoption Leave Regulations 2002 (the PAL Regulations)[37] only had effect in relation to children born, or matched or placed for adoption after April 6 2003. Entitlement to paternity leave is, according to Regulation 4(1) for the purpose of caring for a child or supporting the child's mother. In order to qualify for paternity leave an individual must meet certain conditions and comply with the notice requirements.[38] The conditions are:

- that the employee has been continuously employed for a period of at least 26 weeks ending with the week immediately preceding the 14th week before the expected week of childbirth
- that the employee is the father of the child or, if not the father, then married to, or partner of, the child's mother
- that, if he is the father, he has, or expects to have, responsibility for bringing up the child; if he is not the father, but the partner of the mother, then has, or expects to have, the main responsibility (apart from any responsibility of the mother) for bringing up the child

There are a number of complications to this simple formula, which are dealt with by the Regulations. These are, firstly, that if the child is born earlier than expected, then the original date is still used in order to calculate whether the employee has 26 weeks service before the 14th week preceding the expected week of childbirth. Secondly, if the child's mother dies, then her partner or husband would still be assumed to be married to or the partner of the mother. Thirdly, an employee will be assumed to have responsibility for bringing up the child, even if the child is stillborn after 24 weeks of pregnancy or dies. All these measures are aimed at ensuring that the employee will still be entitled to paternity leave when these issues arise.

The notice and evidence requirements are[39]:

- an employee must give his employer notice of his intention to take paternity leave, specifying the expected week of childbirth, the length of the period of leave (see below) and the date on which the employee has chosen that his period of leave will begin
- this notice must be given to the employer in or before the 15th week before the expected week of childbirth, or if it was not reasonably practicable to do so, then as soon as it is so

- if the employer requests it, the employee must give a signed declaration stating that the purpose of the leave is either for caring for the child or supporting the child's mother and that he satisfies the conditions of entitlement listed above.

Unlike parental leave, multiple births from the same pregnancy do not have any effect on the amount of paternity leave the father is entitled to.[40] An employee may take one or two week's leave in respect of the child (or children). This leave must be taken between the date of the birth and a date 56 days after that. It is for the employee to choose whether he takes the leave commencing with the date of the birth or at some time after that, within the 56 day period.[41] Partly because the dates of birth are not entirely predictable, there are opportunities for the employee to vary the start date for the leave, providing that the employee gives the employer 28 days notice or, if this is not reasonably practicable, then as soon as it is reasonably practicable.

Employees who are married to, or the partner of, an adopter have the same entitlement to paternity leave. They need to meet similar conditions and abide by similar notice rules. The important date is that on which the child is placed with the adopter, as this is the date from which the critical 56 day period commences.[42]

Other rules relating to paternity leave are identical to those connected with maternity leave. There is the same right to return to the job in which employed before the absence, in a case where the paternity leave is an isolated period of leave or the last of two consecutive periods of statutory leave not including additional maternity leave or a period of parental leave of more than four weeks. Where other combinations of leave occur, there is the right to return to the same job or, if that is not reasonably, practicable, then to one that is similar and appropriate in the circumstances. The employee will return with his seniority, pension and other rights as if he had not been absent.[43]

ADOPTION LEAVE

The right to adoption leave was introduced by the Employment Act 2002 and the PAL Regulations 2002.[44] An employee who meets the necessary conditions and complies with the notice and evidential requirements is entitled to adoption leave. As with maternity leave this is divided into ordinary and additional adoption leave, although there is no equivalent of compulsory maternity leave.

An employee is entitled to adoption leave if the employee[45]

- is the child's adopter
- has been continuously employed for a period of not less than 26 weeks ending with the week in which the employee was notified of being matched with the child, and
- has notified the agency that he agrees that the child should be placed with him on the date of placement

An employee's entitlement to adoption leave is not affected by the placement for adoption of more than one child as part of the same arrangement.

Ordinary adoption leave

An employee may choose between two options when deciding when ordinary adoption leave starts. The choices are between the date on which the child is placed for adoption, or some other predetermined date which is no more than 14 days before the date on which the child is expected to be placed, and no later than this date. Thus the notice and evidential requirements are[46]

- an employee must give the employer notice of intention to take ordinary adoption leave, specifying the date on which the child is expected to be placed for adoption and the date on which the employee has chosen when the period of leave should begin

- the notice must be given to the employer no more than seven days after the date on which the employee has been notified of having been matched with a child or, if this was not reasonably practicable, then as soon as it is so

- where the employer requests it, the employee must provide evidence, in the form of documents issued by the adoption agency, of the name and address of the agency, the name and birth date of the child, the date on which the employee was notified of the match and the date on which the agency expects to place the child with the employee.

Within 28 days of the receipt of the employee's notification, the employer must give the employee notice of when the period of additional adoption leave, if there is an entitlement, will end. There are also provisions for the employee to vary the start date, subject to notice to the employer.

Additional adoption leave

An employee is entitled to additional adoption leave if

- the child was placed with the employee for adoption
- the employee took ordinary adoption leave
- the ordinary adoption leave did not end prematurely (see below)

The leave begins on the day after the last day of ordinary adoption leave.[47]

Premature ending

Ordinary adoption leave and additional adoption leave will normally last for 26 weeks each. It may be less, of course, if the employee were dismissed before the end of this period.[48] It may also end early if the placement is disrupted.[49] The circumstances where this applies are

- where the adoption leave commences prior to the placement and the employee is subsequently notified that he placement will not take place
- if the child dies
- if the child is returned to the adoption agency under section 30(3) of the Adoption Act 1976

Unless the employee has less than eight weeks to go before their leave comes to an end, the adoption leave, in these circumstances, will end after a period of eight weeks after the week in which the employee was informed that the placement will not be made, or the child dies, or the child is returned.

Other issues

The other matters concerning adoption leave are identical to those concerning maternity leave, which are outlined earlier in this chapter. These matters concern the right to return to work[50], notice periods for early return[51] and matters concerning terms and conditions during adoption leave.[52]

TIME OFF FOR DEPENDANTS

Section 57A ERA 1996 states that an employee is entitled to be permitted by the employer to take a reasonable amount of time off during the employee's working hours, in order to take action which is necessary:

- to provide assistance on an occasion when a dependant falls ill, gives birth or is injured or assaulted
- to make arrangements for the provision of care for a dependant who is ill or injured

- in consequence of the death of a dependant

- because of the unexpected disruption or termination of arrangements for the care of a dependant, or

- to deal with an incident which involves a child of the employee and which occurs unexpectedly in a period during which an educational establishment which the child attends is responsible for him or her.

There is an obligation on the employee to inform the employer of the reason for absence and of its duration as soon as reasonably practicable. The time off is limited to incidents involving a dependant, who is defined as:[53]

- a spouse

- a child

- a parent

- a person who lives in the same household as the employee but who is not an employee, tenant, lodger or boarder

- any person who reasonably relies on the employee for assistance if he or she is ill or assaulted[54]

- any person who reasonably relies on the employee to make arrangements for the provision of care in the event of illness or injury.[55] The references to illness or injury include mental illness or injury.[56]

Section 57B ERA 1996 asserts that an employee may apply to an employment tribunal to complain about a failure to be allowed time off. A tribunal may make a declaration and award compensation which the tribunal considers 'just and equitable in the circumstances'.

In *Qua v John Ford Morrison Solicitors*[57] the EAT considered a situation where a single mother with a child who had medical problems was dismissed after taking time off on 17 different days. The EAT held that the right to time off did not enable employees to take time off for themselves to look after a sick child, except for enabling the parent to deal with an immediate crisis. Such longer term care would be covered by the employee's parental leave entitlement. The right to time off is the right to a 'reasonable' amount of time in order to take action that is 'necessary'. The decision as to whether it was necessary depended upon a number of factors, including, for example:

- the nature of the incident that has occurred

- the closeness of the relationship between the employee and the dependant, and

- the extent to which anyone else was available to help out.

All of this would depend upon the individual circumstances. An employee is not, however, entitled to unlimited amounts of time off and the employer may take into account the number and length of previous absences, as well as the dates on which they occurred when deciding whether the time off sought for a subsequent occasion is reasonable. The time off is to deal with unforeseen circumstances. Thus if a child were known to suffer regular relapses needing attention, then time off for dealing with these illnesses would not come within the terms of Section 57A ERA 1996.

In determining the reasonableness of the amount of time taken off, the disruption to an employer's business by the employee's absence cannot be taken into account. This, unfortunately perhaps for an employer, is not a relevant factor.

FLEXIBLE WORKING

Section 47 of the Employment Act 2002 inserted sections 80F to 80I into the ERA 1996, concerned with flexible working. There are also two sets of Regulations spelling out the details of employee rights. These are the Flexible Working (Eligibility, Complaints and Remedies) Regulations 2002[58] and the Flexible Working (Procedural Requirements) Regulations 2002.[59]

A qualifying employee may make an application to the employer to vary his or her contractual terms in relation to hours of work, times when required to work or place of work. The purpose of the application is to enable the employee to care for a child.

A qualifying employee is an individual who

- has been continually employed for a period of not less than 26 weeks; and
- is the mother, father, adopter, guardian or foster parent of the child; or is married to, or partner of, the child's mother, father, adopter, guardian or foster parent; and
- has, or expects to have, responsibility for the upbringing of the child.

The application must be made by 14 days before the child reaches the age of 6 or, if disabled, 18 years. The application must be in writing.

The employer must hold a meeting with the employee within 28 days from the date when the application is made, unless the contract variation is agreed to and the employee is notified accordingly.

Where the meeting is held, the employer must give notice, in writing, of the decision within 14 days of the meeting. The notice must consist of

- either the employer's agreement, and the date on which the change becomes effective, or
- notice of the employer's decision to refuse the application, together with the reasons and details of an appeals procedure.

An employee is entitled to appeal, in writing, against the employer's decision within a further 14 days. The appeal meeting itself must take place within 14 days of the date of the appeal notice and the employer then has a further 14 days in which to give written notice of the decision. This can be either agreement and the date on which the change will come into effect, or refusal with reasons.

All these periods of time can be extended by agreement between the employer and the employee.

The times and dates of the meetings must be convenient for both parties and the employee has the right to be accompanied by a single companion. The employee may complain to an employment tribunal and obtain an award of up to 2 weeks pay if the employer fails to allow and make provision for the employee to be accompanied.

The employer may only refuse the application for one of these reasons:

- burden of additional costs
- detrimental effect on the ability to meet customer demand
- inability to re-organise work among existing staff
- inability to recruit additional staff

- detrimental impact on quality
- detrimental impact on performance
- insufficiency of work during the periods the employee proposes to work
- planned structural changes
- such other grounds as the Secretary of State may specify

An employee may complain to an employment tribunal that his/her employer has failed to comply with the duty under section 80G, or that a decision to reject the application was based upon incorrect facts. Failure to comply with the duty includes a failure to hold the required meeting, or a failure to notify a decision. The maximum amount of compensation that can be awarded is 8 weeks pay.

PROTECTION FROM DETRIMENT[60]

An employee is entitled not to be subjected to any detriment by any act, or failure to act, on the part of the employer for one of the following reasons:

- that she is pregnant or has given birth to a child
- that the employee is subject to a relevant requirement or a relevant recommendation as defined by section 66(2) ERA 1996
- that she took paternity leave, ordinary maternity or ordinary adoption leave or availed herself of the benefits of her terms and conditions of employment during such leave
- that the employee took additional maternity leave, parental leave, additional adoption leave or time off under section 57A ERA 1996
- that the employee declined to sign a workforce agreement for the purposes of the MPL Regulations 1999
- that the employee was a representative of the workforce, a candidate for election as a representative or performed any activities or functions related to being a representative or a candidate.

UNFAIR DISMISSAL[61]

It is automatically unfair to dismiss an employee, irrespective of the length of service, if:

- the reason or principal reason for dismissal is that she is pregnant or is in any way connected with her pregnancy
- she is dismissed during her maternity leave period and the reason or principal reason for dismissal is that she has given birth or is connected with her having given birth[62]
- she is dismissed after the end of her maternity leave period and the reason or principal reason for dismissal is that she took, or availed herself of the benefits of, ordinary maternity leave, ordinary adoptive leave or paternity leave
- the reason or principal reason for dismissal is a requirement or recommendation referred to in section 66 ERA 1996 (suspension on maternity grounds)
- she is dismissed during the maternity or adoption leave period and the principal reason for dismissal is that she is redundant and the employer has not offered her any suitable alternative vacancy
- the employee failed to return to work after additional maternity or adoption leave and the employer had failed to notify the employee of the date on which the period would end and the employee reasonably believed that the period had not ended; or the employer had given the employee less

than 28 days notice of the date on which the period would end, and it was not reasonably practicable for the employee to return on that date[63]

■ the employee took time off for additional maternity leave, additional adoption leave, parental leave or time off for dependants in accordance with section 57A of the ERA 1996

■ the employee refused to sign a workforce agreement for the purposes of the MPL Regulations 1999

■ the reason is that, for the purposes of the MPL Regulations, the employee was a representative of the workforce, stood for election as a representative or performed any of the functions or activities of such a representative or a candidate for such representation.

Where an employee is dismissed while she is pregnant or during her ordinary or additional maternity leave period, she is entitled to written reasons for her dismissal. This right does not depend on any qualifying period of service and the woman does not need formally to request the reasons.[64]

There are exceptions to the application of these automatically unfair dismissal rules. They do not apply if:

■ before the end of the additional maternity or additional adoption leave period or dismissal, the number of employees employed by the employer together with associated[65] employers does not exceed five; and if it is not reasonably practicable for the employer or associated employer(s) to offer her a suitable and appropriate job to return to

■ it is not reasonably practicable for an employer to offer a suitable position, but an associated employer does offer such a job and the employee accepts or unreasonably refuses that offer.

The onus for showing that these provisions are satisfied rests on the employer.

RISK ASSESSMENT

Where an employee is pregnant, has given birth within the past six months or is breast-feeding, the employer must assess the special risks which the woman faces in the workplace and take measures to avoid them.[66] If preventive action is impossible or would be inadequate to avoid the risk, the employee's working conditions or hours of work must be altered. If that would be unreasonable or would not avoid the risk, the employer must offer suitable alternative work, or where none is available, suspend her from work on full pay.[67] Alternative work will be suitable if it is both suitable in relation to the employee and appropriate for her to do in the circumstances. The terms and conditions applicable must not be substantially less favourable than those which apply to her normal work. An employment tribunal may award compensation to a woman if her employer fails to offer suitable alternative employment.[68] An example of this can be seen in *British Airways* v *Moore and Botterill*.[69] The case concerned two cabin crew employees who became grounded, by agreement, after their sixteenth week of pregnancy. They were given alternative duties and continued to receive their normal levels of pay less the allowances that they had previously received while flying. Despite the fact that these arrangements were in accord with a collective agreement, the EAT held that the reduction in pay was enough to show that the employees concerned had not been offered suitable alternative employment.

A woman who is suspended on maternity grounds is entitled to be paid by her employer during the suspension. However, this right is lost if she unreasonably refuses an offer of suitable alternative work. The remuneration payable is a week's wage for each week of suspension and *pro rata* for any part of a week of entitlement. Any contractual remuneration paid goes towards discharging the employer's liability. Conversely, any suspension payment goes towards discharging any contractual obligation the employer may have. Where an employer fails to pay all or any of the amount due, an employment tribunal will order the employer to pay the remuneration owed.[70]

KEY POINTS

- A pregnant woman is entitled to paid time off for ante natal care
- The maternity leave period is divided into ordinary, compulsory and additional leave periods; adoptive leave is divided into ordinary and additional leave periods
- An employee has the right to return to his or her job under the original contract of employment and on terms and conditions not less favourable than those which would have applied if the employee had not taken maternity, adoption, parental or paternity leave; if this is not practicable then the right is to be offered a suitable and appropriate alternative position
- Where an employee is pregnant, has given birth within the last six months, or is breast feeding, the employer must assess the special risks faced by the woman in the workplace and take measures to avoid those risks
- It is automatically unfair, regardless of length of service, to dismiss an employee for reasons connected with pregnancy or the taking of maternity, adoption, parental or paternity leave
- Parents with child responsibilities are entitled to time off for parental leave for a maximum of 13 weeks or 18 weeks for a child in receipt of invalidity benefit
- Employees are entitled to time off to provide assistance to dependants in certain circumstances
- A qualifying employee may make an application to the employer to vary his or her contractual terms in relation to hours of work, times when required to work or place of work. The purpose of the application is to enable the employee to care for a child.

NOTES

1   See section 56(1) ERA 1996
2   Section 57 ERA 1996
3   Section 56(6) ERA 1996
4   Directive 92/85/EEC of 19 October 1992
5   Directive 76/207/EEC, amended by Directive 2002/37/EC
6   Directive 75/117/EEC
7   *Handels og Kontorfunktionærernes Forbund i Danmark acting on behalf of Pedersen* v *Fællesføreningen før Danmarks Brugsføreninger acting on behalf of Kvicklyskive (C-66/96)* (1999) IRLR 55, ECJ
8   Case 394/96 (1998) IRLR 445
9   See also *Caledonia Bureau Investment and Property* v *Caffrey* (1998) IRLR 110
10 (2000) IRLR 664
11 (2001) IRLR 75
12 SI 1999/3312
13 SI 2001/4010
14 SI 2002/2789
15 Regulation 2(1) MPL Regulations 1999
16 Regulation 4 MPL Regulations 1999
17 Regulation 3(4)(b) MPL Regulations 1999
18 Regulation 7 MPL Regulations 1999
19 See Regulation 9; remuneration is defined as 'sums payable by wages or salary'
20 Section 72(5) ERA 1996
21 Section 72(3) ERA 1996 and Regulation 8 MPL Regulations 1999
22 Regulation 5 MPL Regulations 1999
23 Regulation 7(4) MPL Regulations 1999

24   Regulation 7(6) MPL Regulations 1999
25   Regulation 11 MPL Regulations 1999
26   Regulation 10 MPL Regulations 1999
27   Responsibility for a child means having or acquiring parental responsibility under the provisions of the Children Act 1989 or being registered as the child's father in accordance with the provisions of the Births and Deaths Registration Act 1953
28   Regulation 13(1) MPL 1999
29   Regulation 14 MPL Regulations 1999
30   Regulation 14(1)(A) MPL Regulations 1999
31   Schedule 2 section 6 MPL Regulations 1999
32   Section 80 ERA 1996
33   Section 73(5) ERA 1996
34   Regulation 18(1) MPL Regulations 1999
35   Regulation 18 MPL Regulations 1999
36   Now contained in sections 80A–80D ERA 1996 and sections 171ZA–171ZK Social Security Contributions and Benefits Act 1992
37   SI 2002/2788
38   Regulation 4(1) PAL Regulations 2002
39   Regulation 6 PAL Regulations 2002
40   Regulation 4(6) PAL Regulations 2002
41   Regulation 5 PAL Regulations 2002
42   See Regulations 8–11 PAL Regulations 2002
43   See Regulations 12–14 PAL Regulations 2002
44   Now contained in sections 75A–75D ERA 1996 and sections 171ZL–171ZT Social Security Contributions and Benefits Act 1992
45   Regulation 15 PAL Regulations 2002
46   Regulation 17 PAL Regulations 2002
47   Regulation 20 PAL Regulations 2002
48   Regulation 24 PAL Regulations 2002
49   Regulation 22 PAL Regulations 2002
50   Regulation 26 PAL Regulations 2002
51   Regulation 25 PAL Regulations 2002
52   Regulation 21 PAL Regulations 2002
53   Section 57A(3) ERA 1996
54   Section 57A(4)(a) ERA 1996
55   Section 57A(4)(b) ERA 1996
56   Section 57B ERA 1996
57   (2003) IRLR 184
58   SI 2002/3236
59   SI 2002/3207
60   Regulation 19 MPL Regulations 1999 and section 47C ERA 1996
61   See Regulation 20 MPL Regulations 1999
62   In *Rees* v *Apollo Watch Repairs* (1996) ICR 467 it was held that a woman was unfairly dismissed during her maternity leave after the employers hired a replacement whom they found to be more efficient
63   Regulation 4 MPL Regulations 1999 and Regulation 29 PAL Regulations 2002
64   Section 92(4) ERA 1996
65   Associated employer is defined by Regulation 2 MPL Regulations 1999
66   See the revised ACOP issued with the 1999 Health and Safety (Miscellaneous Modifications) Regulations; the revised ACOP refers employers to HSE guidance entitled *New and Expectant Mothers at Work: A guide for employers*

67 Regulation 16 of the Management of Health and Safety at Work Regulations 1999 SI 1999/3242
68 Sections 66–67 ERA 1996
69 *British Airways (European Operations at Gatwick) Ltd* v *Moore and Botterill* (2000) IRLR 296
70 Sections 68–70 ERA 1996

Health and Safety at Work

CHAPTER 9

OVERVIEW

In this chapter we examine some aspects of health and safety legislation. We look briefly at guidance, approved codes of practice and regulations issued by the Health and Safety Executive and the Health and Safety Commission. Consideration is then given to the Health and Safety at Work Act 1974 and the duties of employers to ensure the health, safety and welfare of their employees and others, and their duty to issue written statements. There is then an examination of the Management of Health and Safety at Work Regulations 1999 and the COSHH Regulations 2002.

Scope of the current legislation

An important feature of the Health and Safety at Work Act 1974 (HASAWA 1974) and the Management of Health and Safety at Work Regulations 1999 (MHSW Regulations)[1] is that they apply to people rather than premises and, with certain exceptions, all employed persons are covered. The Act sets out the general duties which employers have towards employees and members of the public, and which employees have towards themselves and each other.

The MHSW Regulations generally make more explicit what employers are required to do to manage health and safety under the Act. Like the HASAWA 1974 the MHSW Regulations apply to every work activity. They also seek to protect persons other than those at work against risks to their health and safety arising out of, or in connection with, work activities. While a breach of HASAWA 1974 or regulations issued under it amounts to a criminal offence, civil liability arises only if there is a failure to comply with regulations.[2] Where the Health and Safety Commission (HSC) or Executive (HSE) consider action is necessary, they have three main options. They can issue:

1 *guidance*, which has three purposes. It is intended firstly to help people understand the law by inter-preting it; secondly, to help people comply with the law; and thirdly, to provide technical advice

2 *approved codes of practice* (ACOP), which offer practical examples of good practice. They also give practical advice on how to comply with the law. A failure to observe any provision of an approved code of practice does not of itself render a person liable to any civil or criminal proceedings. However, such a code is admissible in evidence, and proof of a failure to meet its requirements will be sufficient to establish a contravention of a statutory provision, unless a court is satisfied that the provision was complied with in some other way.[3] According to the HSC, a duty-holder who has complied with an ACOP will have done enough to satisfy the law on the specific issues addressed by the code.

3 *regulations*, which are made under the HASAWA 1974. Regulations identify specific risks and set out particular actions that need to be taken.[4]

HEALTH AND SAFETY AT WORK ACT 1974

According to section 2(1) HASAWA 1974, 'It shall be the duty of every employer to ensure, so far as is reasonably practicable, the health, safety and welfare at work of all his employees.' The matters to which this duty extends include:[5]

- the provision and maintenance of plant[6] and systems of work that are, so far as is reasonably practicable, safe and without risks to health

- arrangements for ensuring, so far as is reasonably practicable, safety and absence of risks to health in connection with the use, handling, storage and transport of articles and substances[7]

- the provision of such information, instructions, training and supervision as is necessary to ensure, so far as is reasonably practicable, the health and safety at work of employees

- so far as is reasonably practicable as regards any place of work under the employer's control, the maintenance of it in a condition which is safe and without risks to health and the provision and maintenance of means of access to and egress from it that are safe and without such risks

- the provision and maintenance of a working environment for his employees that is, so far as is reasonably practicable, safe, without risks to health, and adequate as regards facilities and arrangements for their welfare at work.[8] (On working time see Chapter 10.)

The responsibility under section 2(1) HASAWA 1974 is not confined to the employer centrally. In *R v Gateway Foodmarkets Ltd*[9] the employer, at head office level, had instituted procedures for the maintenance of lifts in its stores throughout the country, but failings at store management level led to the death of an employee. As a result the company was held to be in breach of its duties under section 2(1) HASAWA 1974.

It could be argued that these duties merely enact the employer's common-law obligations. Although this is largely true, the extent to which detailed requirements are spelled out is of considerable consequence. The words 'reasonably practicable' do not mean that the employer must do everything that is physically possible to safeguard employees, only that the risks be weighed against the trouble and expense of eliminating or reducing them.[10] Employers are to be judged according to the knowledge they had or ought to have had at the time, and in any legal proceedings the accused has to prove that it was not reasonably practicable to do more than was in fact done.[11] The existence of a universal practice is evidence which goes to the question whether any other method was reasonably practicable but it does not necessarily discharge the onus on the employer.[12] Additionally, the employer may need to have regard to any particular issues relating to an employee's background. In *Tasci v Pekalp of London Ltd*[13] a Kurdish refugee, who spoke little English, was employed as a wood machinist. He was given training to operate a bench-mounted circular saw and where to stand when he did so. He was also given seven specific safety instructions. Initially there were regular checks on his operation of the machine. Three weeks later he was injured, partly through not obeying correct operating instructions. The Court of Appeal held that, given the claimant's background and the degree of instruction and supervision after the initial instructions, the system of work operated by the employer fell short of that which was required by the relevant safety regulations and the employer's common-law duty of care.

Stress

One aspect of the duty of care owed by employers to their employees is related to the issue of stress at work and any possible subsequent psychiatric harm. Stress is the second biggest cause of work-related illness in the United Kingdom with one in five workers reporting they have been affected by it. About half a million people experience work-related stress at a level they believe was making them ill and up to five million people in the United Kingdom feel "very" or "extremely" stressed by their work. Work-related stress costs society between £3.7 billion and £3.8 billion every year.[14]

Young v Post Office[15] concerned a workshop manager with the Post Office. This was a fairly stressful job and was becoming more so with the introduction of new technology. Mr Young showed increasing signs of stress and, as a result, eventually suffered a nervous breakdown. During his absence his management seemed very constructive and agreed to help him return to work on a flexible basis, choosing the hours he wanted and leaving when he wanted. Promises by management to visit him regularly after his return were, however, not kept. Within seven weeks he was back running the workshop and subsequently suffered a recurrence of his psychiatric illness. The Court of Appeal held that the employers were in breach of their common law duty of care. It was perfectly foreseeable that, where an employee has already suffered from psychiatric illness resulting from occupational stress, that there might be a recurrence if the appropriate steps were not taken prior to the employee's return to work. He had returned to his old job which had caused the stress in the first place and the management had not visited him regularly as promised.

Under normal circumstances an employer is entitled to assume that someone returning to work, unless there has been some disclosure, is fit to return to work. To initiate the duty to take steps to safeguard an employee from impending harm it needs to be plain enough to the reasonable employer to realise that something needed to be done. The employer's duty of care is towards each individual and whether an illness was foreseeable depended upon each individual's situation. The employer will be in breach of the duty of care if there is a failure to take the steps that are reasonable in the circumstances. Some possible steps suggested by the Court of Appeal include giving a sabbatical, transferring to other work, giving extra help, arranging treatment or counselling and providing a 'buddying' or mentoring scheme to encourage confidence. What steps are reasonable for an employer to take will depend upon the employer's size and the scope of the employer's operation.[16]

Written statements

Except where fewer than five employees are employed at any one time in an undertaking,[17] every employer must:

> Prepare and, as often as may be appropriate, revise a written statement of his general policy with respect to the health and safety at work of his employees, and the organisation and arrangements for the time being in force for carrying out that policy, and bring the statement and any revision of it to the notice of all of his employees.[18]

The Act does not give any further indication of what the statement should contain, but advice and guidance notes, which are not legally enforceable, are available from the HSE. Clearly, it is intended that employers will seek solutions to their own particular safety problems and it will not be sufficient simply to adopt a model scheme drawn up by some other body. As an absolute minimum the safety policy should deal with the various responsibilities of all employees, from the board of directors down to the shop floor. Indeed, the statement may be used as evidence if a prosecution is launched under section 37 HASAWA 1974 (see below). It should also deal with general safety precautions, mechanisms for dealing with special hazards, routine inspections, emergency procedures, training and arrangements for consulting the workforce.

In industrial relations terms it is obviously desirable to reach agreement with employee representatives on the contents of the written statement, but this is not a legal requirement. No guidance is given as to how the statement should be brought to the notice of employees, although ideally a copy should be supplied to each person. Special precautions may have to be taken in relation to those who have language difficulties.

Persons other than employees

Section 3 HASAWA 1974 imposes a duty on employers and self-employed persons to conduct their undertakings in such a way as to ensure, so far as is reasonably practicable, that persons not in their employment who may be affected thereby are not exposed to risks to their health and safety. More specifically,

Regulation 12 of the MHSW Regulations 1999 obliges employers and self-employed people to supply any person working in their undertaking who is not their employee with comprehensible information and instruction on any risks which arise out of the conduct of the undertaking. It is clear that the word 'risk' should be given its ordinary meaning of denoting the possibility of danger rather than actual danger.[19] This may apply to subcontractors working on the employer's premises.

The question of employer control

Employers cannot delegate their duty under Section 3 HASAWA 1974 and criminal liability is not limited to the acts of the 'directing mind' or senior management of a company.[20] In *R* v *Associated Octel*[21] the House of Lords held that the cleaning, repair and maintenance necessary for the carrying out of the employer's business is part of the conduct of the undertaking so as to impose a duty of care with regard to persons not in its employment, whether it is done by the employer's own employees or by independent contractors. It is unnecessary to show that the employer has some actual control over how the work is done. Nevertheless, as far as operations carried out by independent contractors are concerned, the question of control may be very relevant in that, in most cases, the employer has no control over how a competent contractor does the work and it may not be reasonably practicable to do other than rely on the contractor. Of course, there will be situations where it is reasonably practicable for the employer to give instructions.

The case of *R* v *Nelson Group Services (Maintenance) Ltd*[22] further considered the liability of employers for negligent work by employees. The company employed 800 fitters whose work was installing and maintaining gas installations. A small number of fitters had left appliances in an unsafe condition, thus exposing householders to risks to their health and safety. The question was to what extent the employer was responsible for this negligence. The obligation upon the employer, in section 3(1) HASAWA 1974, is to ensure that the business is conducted in such a way as not to expose persons not in its employment to such risks, as far as is reasonably practicable. The organisation had its own training centre, and the Court of Appeal concluded that an employer could establish a defence against being held liable for its employees' carelessness if it had done everything that was reasonably practicable to discharge its duty under the HASAWA 1974. The Court did not think it necessary, in order to safeguard the public, that an employer should always be held liable for a one-off piece of negligence by an employee. It was enough that the employer had shown that it had done everything that was reasonably practicable to ensure that the employee was trained, had a safe system of work, and was adequately supervised.

Safe premises

Section 4 HASAWA 1974 provides that a person who has control of non-domestic premises used as a place of work must take such measures as are reasonably practicable to ensure that the means of access and egress and any plant or substance in the premises is safe and without risks to health. According to the House of Lords, once it is proved that:

- the premises made available for use by others are unsafe and constitute a risk to health
- the employer had a degree of control over those premises, and
- having regard to the employer's degree of control and knowledge of the likely use, it would have been reasonable to take measures to ensure that the premises were safe,

then the employer must demonstrate that, weighing the risk to health against the means (including cost) of eliminating it, it was not reasonably practicable to take those measures. However, if the premises are not a reasonably foreseeable cause of danger to people using them in the circumstances that might reasonably be expected to occur, it is not reasonable to require further measures to be taken.[23]

Employee duties

Section 7 of HASAWA 1974 imposes two general duties on employees while they are at work:[24]

- to take reasonable care of the health and safety of themselves and of others who may be affected by their acts or omissions
- as regards any duty imposed on employers or any other person by any of the relevant statutory provisions, to co-operate with them so far as is necessary to enable that duty to be performed.

THE MHSW REGULATIONS

Regulation 4 of the Management of Health and Safety at Work Regulations 1999 requires an employer to implement preventive and protective measures on the basis of certain general principles of prevention set out in the EC Framework Directive on Health and Safety.[25] These general principles are:

- avoiding risks
- evaluating the risks which cannot be avoided
- combating the risks at source
- adapting the work to the individual, both with regard to the design of workplaces and the choice of work equipment, and working and production methods with regard to reducing the effects on health of monotonous work and work at a pre-determined work rate
- adapting to technical progress
- replacing the dangerous by the non-dangerous or less dangerous
- developing a coherent overall prevention policy which covers technology, organisation of work, working conditions, social relationships and factors related to the work environment
- giving collective protective measures priority over individual protective measures
- giving appropriate instructions to employees.

Risk assessment

The MHSW Regulations impose a duty on all employers and the self-employed to conduct a risk assessment. This assessment must be both suitable and sufficient and must consider the risk to the health and safety of all employees and other persons arising from the conduct of the undertaking.[26] The purpose of the assessment is to identify the measures that need to be taken to ensure compliance with the relevant statutory provisions. These provisions are specified in the Approved Code of Practice and include the duties under HASAWA 1974. The risk assessment must be reviewed if there is reason to suspect that it is no longer valid or there has been a significant change in the matters to which it relates. An employer is specifically forbidden from employing a young person (someone under the age of 18 years[27]) unless a review has occurred which takes particular account of certain special characteristics such as the inexperience, lack of awareness of risks and the immaturity of young persons.[28] Regulation 19 provides employers with a particular duty to ensure that young employees are protected from risks to their health and safety arising out of their inexperience. If there are any women of child-bearing age working in an undertaking, then there is a special obligation, in Regulation 16, to assess any potential risk that might affect the health and safety of a new or expectant mother.

Regulation 5 requires employers to give effect to appropriate arrangements for the effective planning, organisation, control, monitoring and review of the measures they need to take as a result of the risk assessment. Again, such arrangements must be recorded if the employer has five or more employees. Regulation 6 obliges employers to provide appropriate health surveillance for their employees.

Defining and appointing 'competent persons'

Under Regulation 7 employers must appoint one or more 'competent persons' to assist them in implementing the measures they need in order to comply with the relevant statutory provisions. The number of people appointed, the time available for them to fulfil their functions, and the means at their disposal must be adequate, having regard to the size of the undertaking and the risks to which employees are exposed. A 'competent person' is defined as someone who has sufficient training and experience or knowledge to enable him or her to assist properly in the undertaking.[29] In the amended Regulations, however, there is a requirement for the employer to give preference to the appointment of a 'competent person' in their employment over one from outside.[30]

Regulation 8 obliges an employer to establish appropriate procedures to be followed in the event of 'serious and imminent danger to persons at work in his undertaking'. Employers must nominate a sufficient number of competent persons to implement these procedures and to be sure that employees are unable to enter dangerous areas without having received adequate health and safety instruction. It is made clear that this Regulation requires both the provision of information and procedures which enable employees to leave their work immediately in the event of 'serious and imminent danger'.[31]

COSHH

Each year, approximately 16,000 to 25,000 people become ill as a result of exposure to substances hazardous to health at work, e.g. respiratory disease, dermatitis etc. This includes an estimated 3,000 to 12,000 cancer deaths mostly related to chemicals, including asbestos.[32]

The Control of Substances Hazardous to Health Regulations (COSHH) originally came into force in October 1989 but have been amended and replaced several times. The most recent version came into effect in November 2002.[33]

According to the Health and Safety Executive (HSE) hazardous substances are anything that can harm your health when you work with them if they are not properly controlled e.g. by using adequate ventilation. They can include:

- substances used directly in work activities eg glues, paints, cleaning agents
- substances generated during work activities eg fumes from soldering and welding
- naturally occurring substances eg grain dust, blood, bacteria

For the vast majority of commercial chemicals, the presence (or not) of a warning label will indicate whether COSHH is relevant. For example, household washing up liquid doesn't have a warning label but bleach does – so COSHH applies to bleach but not washing up liquid when used at work.[34]

COSHH provides employers with a general duty to prevent or adequately control the exposure of their employees and others who may be affected to hazardous substances. In addition there are a number of specific duties:

1. Risk assessment – an employer must not carry out work which is liable to expose any employees to any substance hazardous to health unless the employer has carried out an assessment of the risk to the health of employees and the steps that need to be taken to meet the requirements of the Regulations.[35] The risk assessment is to be reviewed regularly and appropriate changes made as a result of these reviews. All but the smallest of employers (those employing less than five employees) must record the 'significant' findings of the risk assessment and the steps which have been taken as a result.

2. Prevention or control of exposure – every employer must ensure that the exposure of his employees to substances hazardous to health is either prevented or, where this is not reasonably practicable, adequately controlled.[36] Substitution of the hazardous substance is preferred, but if this is not reasonably practicable then the employer needs to comply with this duty by applying protection measures, such as adequate ventilation, using appropriate work processes and the provision of suitable protective equipment.

3. Maintenance, examination and testing – all employers who provide control measures must ensure, where relevant, that they are maintained in an efficient state, in efficient working order, in good repair and in a clean condition.[37] A suitable record of the examinations and tests plus any subsequent repairs carried out must be kept and made available for at least five years after it was made.

Where employees are, or liable to be, exposed to a hazardous substance, then those employees must be kept under suitable health surveillance. The employer should ensure that a health record is kept in respect of each of these employees and must make sure that it is kept and available for forty years from the date it was made. Employees, and the Health and Safety Executive, have a right of access to their own records.[38] The employer also has a duty to ensure that all employees who may be exposed to hazardous substances are provided with suitable information, instruction and training. This will include details about the substances, maximum exposure limits, findings of the risk assessment and the precautions and actions that need to be taken by the employee to safeguard him or herself and others at the workplace.[39]

The Regulations are supported by an Approved Code of Practice which gives detailed practical advice on compliance. The ACOP includes appendices dealing with carcinogens, biological agents and substances that cause occupational asthma.

Dugmore v Swansea NHS Trust[40] concerned a nurse who developed an allergy to latex protein as a result of using powdered latex gloves in the course of her work. She was given vinyl gloves to use instead, but still came into contact with the latex ones and suffered an illness which stopped her returning to work as a nurse. She claimed damages from her employers, alleging, amongst other matters, a breach of Regulation 7(1) of the COSHH Regulations (see point 2 above). The Court of Appeal held that the purpose of the COSHH Regulations was protective and preventive. Lady Justice Hale stated that they did not simply rely on criminal sanctions or civil liability to induce good practice. They involved positive obligations to seek out the risks and take precautions. In this case the employer had a duty to ensure that exposure is adequately controlled. The Court suggested that it would have been a simple matter to change the latex gloves to vinyl ones and the onus was on the employer to show that they were unable to do this. They failed to do so and the Court allowed Ms Dugmore's claim.

REPORTING INJURIES

The Reporting of Injuries, Diseases and Dangerous Occurrences Regulations 1995[41] (RIDDOR 1995) apply to events which arise 'out of or in connection with work'[42] activities covered by HASAWA 1974. Whenever any of the following arises it must be reported to the enforcing authority in writing and a record kept.[43] If any of (a)–(d) happens, the enforcing authority must first be notified by the quickest practicable means:

(a) the death of any person as a result of an accident, whether or not he or she is at work

(b) someone at work suffers a major injury as the result of an accident[44]

(c) someone who is not at work suffers an injury as the result of an accident and is taken to a hospital for treatment

(d) one of a list of specified dangerous occurrences takes place[45]

(e) someone is unable to do his or her normal work for more than three days as the result of an injury caused by an accident at work

(f) the death of an employee, if this occurs after a reportable injury which led to the employee's death, but not more than one year afterwards

(g) a person at work suffers a specified disease, provided that a doctor diagnoses the disease and the person's job involves a specified work activity.[46]

The duty to report the events listed above is imposed on the 'responsible person'.[47] Regulation 13 gives the HSE a limited power to grant exemptions from the requirements imposed by RIDDOR 1995.

OFFENCES

Apart from the Crown, any person or body corporate can be prosecuted for an offence under HASAWA 1974. However, if an offence is proved to have been committed with the consent or connivance of, or to have been attributable to neglect on the part of, any director, manager, secretary or other similar officer, then that person as well as the body corporate may be found guilty of an offence.[48] Thus in *Armour* v *Skeen*[49] a local authority director of roads was prosecuted for failing to prepare and carry out a sound safety policy. His neglect led to breaches of safety provisions that resulted in the death of a council employee.

Where the commission of an offence by any person is due to the act or default of some other person, that other person may be charged whether or not proceedings are taken against the first-mentioned person.[50] Crown servants may be prosecuted despite the immunity of the Crown itself. Proceedings under this Act can be brought only by an inspector or with the consent of the Director of Public Prosecutions.

The normal maximum penalty for a person found guilty of an offence on summary conviction (ie in a magistrate's court) is a fine not exceeding level 5 on the standard scale. However, where there is a breach of sections 2–6 of HASAWA 1974, or of an improvement or prohibition notice, a fine of up to £20,000 can be imposed. If there is a breach of a notice or a court order under section 42 HASAWA 1974 (see below), an offender may receive a sentence of up to six months' imprisonment. When proceedings are brought on indictment (in a Crown court) there is the possibility of an unlimited fine and, in specified circumstances, up to two years' imprisonment.[51]

In deciding on the level of the fine to be imposed the court will take into account the ability of the company to pay. Generally, fines will not be so large as to endanger the earnings of employees or create a risk of bankruptcy, unless the offence is so serious that the firm should not be in business.[52] The questions to be asked, according to the Court of Appeal, which should guide courts in assessing fines were:

- What financial penalty does the offence merit?
- What financial penalty can a defendant reasonably be ordered to meet, and over what period? A longer period might be acceptable in the case of a company as opposed to an individual.[53]

In reaching a decision on the fine the aggravating features to be taken into account will include:

- whether the company has failed to heed warnings
- whether the defendant deliberately profited financially from the failure to take the necessary health and safety measures.

Conversely, the features which might be taken in mitigation include:

- prompt admission of responsibility and a timely plea of guilty
- steps to remedy the deficiencies once they have been drawn to the defendant's attention
- a good safety record.

Where people are convicted of offences in respect of any matters that appear to the court to be within their power to remedy, the court may, in addition to or instead of imposing any punishment, order them to take such steps as may be specified to remedy those matters.[54]

ENFORCING THE ACT

The HASAWA 1974 established two bodies, the HSC and the HSE. The HSC is appointed by the Secretary of State and consists of a chairperson together with three members appointed following consultations with employers' organisations, three members appointed after consultation with trade unions and three others appointed after local authorities and other appropriate organisations have been consulted. Apart from its general duty to 'do such things and make such arrangements as it considers appropriate', the HSC is required to:

- assist and encourage persons concerned with matters relevant to any of the general purposes of the Act to further those purposes
- make arrangements for carrying out research, provide information and training, and encourage others to perform these functions
- make arrangements for providing an information and advisory service
- submit proposed regulations.[55]

Except for the enforcement responsibilities of local authorities, HASAWA 1974 is enforced by the HSE, whose director is appointed by the HSC with the approval of the Secretary of State. Although the HSE is to give effect to any directions issued by the HSC, the former cannot be *directed* to enforce a statutory provision in a particular case.

Inspectors' powers
The enforcing authorities appoint inspectors who may exercise the following powers:[56]

(a) at any reasonable time (or, if there is a dangerous situation, at any time) to enter premises

(b) to take with them a police officer, if they have reasonable cause to be apprehensive of any serious obstruction in the execution of their duty

(c) to take with them any other authorised person and any equipment or materials required

(d) to make such examination and investigation as may be necessary

(e) to direct that the premises be left undisturbed for so long as is reasonably necessary for the purpose of examination or investigation

(f) to take such measurements, photographs and readings as they consider necessary

(g) to take samples of any articles or substances found in any premises and of the atmosphere in, or in the vicinity of, any such premises[57]

(h) in the case of an article or substance which appears to have caused or to be likely to cause danger, to dismantle it or subject it to any process or test. The article or substance may be damaged or destroyed if it is thought necessary in the circumstances. However, if they are so requested by a person who is present and has responsibilities in relation to those premises, this power must be exercised in that person's presence unless the inspector considers that to do so would be prejudicial to the safety of the state

(i)   in the case of an article or substance which appears to have caused or to be likely to cause danger, to take possession of it and detain it for so long as is necessary in order to examine it, to ensure that it is not tampered with before the examination is completed, and to ensure that it is available for use as evidence in any proceedings for an offence or any proceedings relating to a notice under section 21 or 22 HASAWA 1974 (see below). An inspector must leave a notice giving particulars of the article or substance stating that he or she has taken possession of it and, if it is practicable, he or she should give a sample of it to a responsible person at the premises.[58]

(j)   if carrying out examinations or investigations under (d), to require persons whom they have reasonable cause to believe to be able to give any information to answer such questions as the inspector thinks fit to ask and to sign a declaration of the truth of their answers

(k)   to require the production of, inspect and take copies of an entry in, any books or documents which are required to be kept and any other books or documents which it is necessary for them to see for the purpose of any examination or investigation under (d) above

(l)   to require any persons to afford them such facilities and assistance with respect to any matters within that person's control or responsibilities as are necessary for the inspectors to exercise their powers

(m) any other power which is necessary for the purpose of carrying into effect the statutory provisions.

Improvement notices

Where an inspector is of the opinion that a person is contravening or has contravened a relevant statutory provision in circumstances that make it likely that the contravention will continue or be repeated, he or she may serve an 'improvement notice' stating that opinion. The notice must specify the provision, give particulars of the reasons why he or she is of that opinion and will require that person to remedy the contravention within such period as may be specified in the notice.[59] This period must not be less than the time allowed for appealing against the notice, ie 21 days.[60]

Prohibition notices

In respect of an activity covered by a relevant statutory provision, if any inspector believes that activities are being carried on or are about to be carried on which will involve a risk of serious personal injury, the inspector may serve a 'prohibition notice'. Such a notice will state the inspector's opinion, specify the matters which give rise to the risk, and direct that the activities to which the notice relates must not be carried on by or under the control of the person on whom the notice is served (unless the matters specified in the notice have been remedied). A prohibition notice will normally take effect immediately. Both types of notice may (but need not) include directions as to the measures to be taken to remedy the contravention or the matter to which the notice relates. Where a notice which is not to take immediate effect has been served, that notice may be withdrawn by the inspector within 21 days. Similarly, the period specified for rectification may be extended by an inspector at any time when an appeal against the notice is not pending.

A person on whom a notice is served may appeal to an employment tribunal, which has the power to cancel or affirm the notice or affirm it in a modified form.[61] For the purpose of hearing such appeals the tribunal may include specially appointed assessors. Bringing an appeal against an improvement notice has the effect of suspending the operation of that notice until the appeal is disposed of. Lodging an appeal against a prohibition notice suspends it only if the tribunal so directs and then only from the time when the direction is given.[62] Failure to comply with a notice is an offence.[63]

Because it is not possible to bring a prosecution against the Crown,[64] it is equally impossible to enforce improvement and prohibition notices against Crown bodies. However, the HSE has been prepared to issue 'Crown notices' where, in its opinion, an improvement or prohibition notice would have been appropriate. Such notices have no legal effect but may be of some value in so far as they put moral pressure on the employing body. Of course, trade union representatives who receive copies of these notices may be in a position to apply industrial pressure.

KEY POINTS

- The HASAWA 1974 sets out the general duties which employers have towards employees and members of the public, and which employees have towards themselves and each other.
- The HSC and HSE have the option to propose and issue guidance, ACOPs or regulations.
- Every employer with five employees or more must prepare and revise a written statement of their general policy on health and safety at work, and the organisation and arrangements for carrying out that policy.
- The HASAWA 1974 also places an obligation on employers to have regard for the health and safety of persons not in their employment.
- All employers have an obligation to conduct a risk assessment. The purpose of this assessment is to identify the measures that need to be taken to ensure compliance with the statutory provisions contained in the ACOP and the HASAWA 1974.
- There is a duty on employers to provide information and consult employees and their representatives who are either trade-union-appointed or directly elected.
- One aspect of the duty of care owed by employers to their employees is related to the issue of stress at work and any possible subsequent psychiatric harm
- COSHH provides employers with a general duty to prevent or adequately   control the exposure of their employees and others who may be affected to hazardous substances.

NOTES

1   SI 1999/3242; see also Management of Health and Safety at Work Regulations 1999 Approved Code of Practice and Guidance, HSE 2000
2   Except in so far as the regulations provide otherwise. See section 47(2) HASAWA 1974 and Regulation 15 MHSW Regulations 1992
3   Section 17 HASAWA 1974
4   The website of the Health and Safety Executive contains a large amount of free information about various regulatory requirements
5   Section 2(2) HASAWA 1974
6   Defined in section 53 HASAWA 1974 as including any machinery, equipment or appliance
7   Defined in section 54 HASAWA 1974 as 'any natural or artificial substance whether in solid or liquid form of a gas or vapour'
8   See *Pickford* v *ICI* (1998) IRLR 435 on the problems associated with caring for employees who carry out a large amount of typing
9   (1997) IRLR 189
10   See *West Bromwich Building Society* v *Townsend* (1983) IRLR 147
11   Section 40 HASAWA 1974
12   See *Martin* v *Boulton & Paul Ltd* (1982) ICR 366
13   (2001) ICR 633
14   Information from the Health and Safety Executive web site

15   (2002) IRLR 660
16   See *Sutherland* v *St Thomas Becket RC High School* (2002) IRLR 263
17   An 'undertaking' is not statutorily defined for these purposes, but is likely to cover all enterprises or businesses
18   Section 2(3) HASAWA 1974
19   See *R* v *Trustees of the Science Museum* (1993) 3 All ER 853
20   See *R* v *British Steel* (1995) IRLR 310
21   (1997) IRLR 123
22   (1998) 4 All ER 331
23   See *Inspector of Factories* v *Austin Rover* (1989) IRLR 404
24   On the meaning of 'at work' see section 52(1) HASAWA 1974
25   Directive 89/391/EEC
26   See HSE Leaflet *A Guide to Risk Assessment Requirements*, HSE 2001
27   Regulation 1(2) MHSW Regulations 1999
28   Regulation 3(5) MHSW Regulations 1999
29   See Regulation 6(5)
30   Regulation 6(8) 1999 Regulations
31   See Regulation7(2)
32   Information from the Health and Safety Executive web site
33   The Control of Substances Hazardous to Health Regulations 2002 SI 2002/2677
34   See HSE web site
35   Regulation 6 COSHH Regulations 2002
36   Regulation 7 COSHH Regulations 2002
37   Regulation 9 COSHH Regulations 2002
38   Regulation 11 COSHH Regulations 2002
39   Regulation 12 COSHH Regulations 2002
40   (2003) IRLR 164
41   SI 1995/3163
42   Defined by Regulation 2(2)c RIDDOR 1995
43   Regulation 7 RIDDOR 1995
44   Major injuries are listed in Schedule 1 RIDDOR 1995
45   Dangerous occurrences are listed in Schedule 2 RIDDOR 1995
46   The specified diseases and corresponding work activities are listed in Schedule 3 RIDDOR 1995
47   Defined in Regulation 2
48   Section 37 HASAWA 1974. Directors who are convicted of an offence can be disqualified from office under the Directors Disqualification Act 1986
49   (1977) IRLR 310. See also *R* v *Boal* (1992) IRLR 420
50   Section 36 HASAWA 1974
51   Section 33(2)(5) HASAWA 1974 (as amended)
52   See *R* v *F Howe & Son* (1999) IRLR 434
53   See *R* v *Rollco Screw Co Ltd* (1999) IRLR 439
54   Section 42(1) HASAWA 1974
55   Section 11(1)(2) and section 50(3)
56   Section 20 HASAWA 1974
57   See *Laws* v *Keane* (1982) IRLR 500
58   See also section 25 HASAWA 1974 on the power to deal with an imminent cause of danger
59   See *West Bromwich Building Society* v *Townsend* (note 10)
60   Rule 2 Schedule 4 Employment Tribunal (Constitution and Rules of Procedure) Regulations 1993 SI 1993/2687

61 Section 24(2) HASAWA 1974. Section 82(1)(c) defines 'modifications' as including additions, omissions and amendments. See *British Airways* v *Henderson* (1979) ICR 77

62 Section 24(3) HASAWA 1974

63 See section 33(1)(g) HASAWA 1974 and *Deary* v *Mansion Hide Upholstery Ltd* (1983) IRLR 195

64 Section 48 HASAWA 1974

The Regulation of Working Time

CHAPTER 10

OVERVIEW

This chapter is concerned with the Working Time Regulations 1998 and those occasions when there is a statutory right to time off work. (Issues relating to parental rights, including maternity leave, parental leave and time off for dependants, are dealt with in Chapter 8.) There is an examination of the contents of the Regulations. This is followed by a consideration of the rights of trade unionists for time off to take part in trade union duties and activities. Finally we look at other rights to time off, including time off for carrying out public duties.

THE WORKING TIME REGULATIONS 1998

The Working Time Regulations[1] (WT Regulations) implement the Working Time Directive[2] and provisions of the Young Workers Directive.[3] The preamble to the Working Time Directive states that 'in order to ensure the safety and health of Community workers, the latter must be granted minimum daily, weekly and annual periods of rest and adequate breaks' and that 'it is necessary in this context to place a maximum limit on working time'. Thus the legal basis for the Directive was Article 118a EC (now Article 137 EC) relating to health and safety. This was the subject of an unsuccessful challenge by the United Kingdom[4] which claimed that this was the wrong legal basis and that the regulation of working time was a matter for Member States and not a health and safety matter to be dealt with at Community level.

Exclusions from the WT Regulations

Certain activities and certain sectors were excluded from the scope of the WT Regulations, although these exclusions have been modified as a result of the Working Time (Amendment) Regulations 2003.[5] One of the problems with excluding whole sectors from the application of the Regulations is that all workers are affected. There may be special problems associated with limiting the number of hours of mobile workers, such as long-distance lorry drivers and those at sea, but a blanket exclusion includes non-mobile workers who perhaps should be included. This was the issue in *Bowden* v *Tuffnel Parcels Express Ltd*.[6] In this case three clerical workers employed in the road transport industry failed to receive paid holidays. The European Court of Justice held that the exclusion provisions of the Directive applied to all workers within an excluded sector. Thus the administrative workers were to be treated no differently than the travelling workers in any such sector.

The effect of the 2003 Regulations was to distinguish between mobile workers and others[7] Mobile workers are defined as 'any worker employed as a member of the travelling or flying personnel by an undertaking which operates transport services for passengers or goods by rail or air'.[8] Thus it is these mobile workers who are excluded from the WT Regulations and for whom special arrangements are made to cope with the special nature of the work. Specifically excluded groups include seafarers and those that work on board both sea going ships and on ships or hovercraft operating on inland waterways; mobile road transport workers; mobile workers in aviation and those in the armed or civil forces, such as the army or police, whose duties would inevitably conflict with the requirements of the WT Regulations. Also excluded are jobs in domestic service.[9] There are special transition arrangements for doctors in training,[10] whose maximum working week is due to reduce to 56 hours by 2007.

Defining 'workers'

Regulation 2 defines a 'worker' as an individual who has entered into, or works under, a contract of employment or 'any other contract, whether express or implied and (if it is express) whether oral or in writing, whereby the individual undertakes to do or perform personally any work or services for another party to the contract whose status is not by virtue of the contract that of a client or customer of any professional or business undertaking carried out by the individual'. A young worker is defined as an individual who is at least 15 years of age, over the compulsory school leaving age and who has not yet attained the age of 18 years. This does not include children who are covered by other legislation. Thus, in *Addison v Ashby*[11] a 15-year-old paperboy could not be classified as a worker, within the definition of the WT Regulations, because he was not over the compulsory school leaving age. Regulation 36 deals with agency workers, who are not otherwise workers, by deeming the agency or principal to be the employer depending upon who is responsible for paying the worker. Labour only sub-contractors were held to be workers within the definition of worker in the WT Regulations.[12] This was despite the fact that their contracts allowed them to appoint substitutes in their place in certain circumstances. The sub-contractors spent most of their working personally and they were to be distinguished, according to the EAT, from others who might be seen as running a business undertaking, such as in *Commissioners of Inland Revenue v Post Office Ltd*[13] where a number of sub-postmasters and mistresses claimed that they were workers for the purposes of the WT Regulations. Their claim failed because, the EAT held, they were carrying on a business undertaking with the Post Office being a client of their business. This was despite the fact that they gave undertakings to work personally for at least 18 hours per week in their sub-post offices (see Chapter 2).

Working time, in relation to the worker, is defined[14] as:

- any period during which the worker is working, at the employer's disposal and carrying out the worker's activity or duties
- any period during which the worker is receiving relevant training
- any additional period which is to be treated as working time for the purpose of these Regulations under a relevant agreement (see below).

One issue concerning the WT Regulations has been the position of people who are on call, but not necessarily working all the time that they are required to be available. An example of this is a hospital doctor who is required to be on call and, inevitably, also be available in the hospital. The European Court of Justice[15] considered one case where a doctor spent three quarters of his working hours on call, sometimes for periods up to 25 hours. He was provided with a room where he could sleep when his services were not required. The Court decided that all his hours on call should be counted as working time. The crucial point was that he was required to be present at the place decided by the employer.

The maximum working week

Regulation 4 provides that working time, including overtime, must not exceed 48 hours per week (seven days) averaged over a reference period of 17 weeks, unless the worker has first agreed in writing to perform such work. The employer is unable to insist that the employee works longer hours. In *Barber v RJB Mining (UK) Ltd*[16] the employees were granted a declaration by the High Court that, having worked in excess of the permitted hours during the reference period, they need not work again until such time as their average working time fell within the limits specified in Regulation 4(1).

The Regulations supply a formula for calculating the average hours over the reference period.[17] The formula is:

$$A + B \backslash C$$

where A is the total number of hours comprised in the worker's working time during the reference period; B is the total number of hours comprised in the working time during the course of the period immediately after the end of the reference period and ending when the number of days in that subsequent period on which he or she has worked equals the number of excluded days during the reference period; and C is the number of weeks in the reference period. The excluded days in B are periods including annual leave, sick and maternity leave and periods in which an individual opting-out agreement is in effect. For new employees the reference period is the number of weeks actually worked.

Regulations 4 and 5 allow a worker to effectively opt out of the maximum working week provided that the agreement:

- is in writing
- relates either to a specified period or applies indefinitely
- may be terminable by the worker on seven days' notice, unless a different notice period is specified (subject to a maximum of three months); and
- requires the employer keeps up-to-date records of all the workers who have agreed to opt out.[18]

The Regulations set a maximum working time for young workers of eight hours per day or 40 hours per week.[19] There are wide some exceptions to this rule. These are where

- the young worker's employer requires him or her to undertake work necessary to maintain continuity of service or production, or to help cope with a surge in demand
- no adult worker is available to perform the work
- performing the work would not adversely affect the young worker's education or training.[20]

Night work

Regulation 2 defines 'night-time' as a period which is not less than 7 hours in length and includes the hours of 12 midnight to 5 am. A 'night-worker' is a worker who, as a normal course, works at least 3 hours of working time during 'night-time'[21] or is a worker who is likely, during 'night-time', to work a certain proportion of his or her annual working time as defined by a collective or workforce agreement (see below). In *R v Attorney General for Northern Ireland*[22] the meaning of the term 'normal course' was considered. The employee in the case had been asked to change to a shift system which meant working a night shift, between 9 pm and 7 am, one week in three. The court held that the definition which requires an individual to work at least three hours during night-time as a 'normal course' meant no more than that this should be a regular feature of the individual's work. It would be wrong to confine the protection only to those who work night shifts exclusively or predominantly.

Regulation 6 states that a night-worker's normal hours of work must not exceed, in a reference period, an average of 8 in any 24-hour period. A night-worker's average normal hours of work for each 24 hours during a reference period are calculated by the formula:

$$A \backslash B - C$$

where A is the number of hours during the reference period which are the normal working hours for that worker; B is the number of days during the reference period; and C is the total number of hours during the reference period spent in rest periods (see below) divided by 24.

There is an obligation upon the employer to ensure that no night-worker whose work involves special hazards or heavy physical or mental strain works for more than 8 hours in any 24-hour period during which night work is performed.[23] Such hazards or strain can be identified in a collective or workforce agreement or as a result of a risk assessment carried out in accordance with Regulation 3 of the Management of Health and Safety at Work Regulations 1999 (see Chapter 9). Night-workers are also entitled to a free health assessment prior to taking up night work and at regular intervals thereafter.[24] Regulation 7(6) also stipulates that where a medical practitioner informs the employer that a worker is suffering from health problems connected with working night work, the employer should, if it is possible, transfer the worker to more suitable work or work which is not night work. The employer also has an obligation to provide adequate rest breaks where the pattern of work is likely to cause health problems, such as where there is monotonous work or a predetermined work-rate.[25] Regulation 9 also ensures that employers keep adequate records for a period of at least two years.

A restricted period for working is also introduced. This period is between 10 pm and 6 a.m., or if a worker's contract provides for him or her to work after 10 p.m., then the restricted period is between 11 p.m. and 7 a.m. The significance of this restricted period is that employers must ensure that no young worker works during these hours.[26] This effective ban on night work for young workers is also qualified. The rule does not apply to work in hospitals or similar establishments and does not apply in connection with cultural, artistic, sporting or advertising activities. The restricted period is reduced to the hours between midnight and 4 a.m. for young workers in a number of businesses such as agriculture, retail trading, postal or newspaper deliveries, catering, hotels and bakeries.[27]

Rest periods and rest breaks

According to Regulation 10, adult workers are entitled to a rest period of at least 11 consecutive hours in each 24-hour period. For young workers this period constitutes at least 12 consecutive hours. The rest period can be interrupted in the case of activities which involve periods of work that are split up over the day or are of short duration. In addition,[28] adult workers are entitled to an uninterrupted weekly rest period of at least 24 hours in each seven-day period. The employer may change this to two uninterrupted rest periods of 24 hours in each 14 days or one uninterrupted rest period of 48 hours every 14 days. Young workers are entitled to an uninterrupted 48-hour rest period every seven days, although this may be interrupted in cases of activities which involve periods of work that are split up over the day or are of short duration, or where there are technical or organisational reasons for reducing it.[29]

Regulation 12 provides that where an adult worker's daily working time is more than six hours, the worker is entitled to a rest break. The details of this rest break can be in accordance with a workforce or collective agreement, provided that it is for at least 20 minutes and the worker is entitled to spend it away from the work station. Young workers are entitled to a break where their working time is more than four and a half hours. Their break is to be for at least 30 minutes and can be spent away from the work station. There is an additional complication for employers in Regulation 12(5), which states that where a young worker is employed by more than one employer, then the daily working time is the total number of hours that the young worker has worked.

Annual leave

In any leave year a worker is entitled to four weeks' paid leave,[30] although it is clear that public and other state holidays are included within this total. Unless there is a relevant agreement for another date, the worker's leave year begins on the date employment commenced and every anniversary thereafter. If the worker commences employment on a date that is different from the date agreed for the commencement of a leave year, he or she is entitled to a proportion for that first year. The leave may be taken during the year, but there is only an entitlement to the amount that has accrued so far. This is calculated on the basis of one-twelfth of the four-week entitlement for each month of service.[31] A worker is deemed to have been continuously employed if his or her relations with the employer have been governed by a contract during the whole or part of each of those weeks. The leave may only be taken in the leave year in respect of which it was due and cannot be replaced by a payment in lieu, unless the employment is terminated.[32] The correct approach to calculating the appropriate daily rate when working out what is owed to an employee is to divide the annual salary by the number of working days in the year, rather than the number of calendar days.[33] If an employee's employment is terminated and he or she has taken in excess of the entitlement calculated on a pro rata basis, there is no opportunity for the employer to claw back any of the overpayment unless there is in existence a relevant agreement, such as a collective or workforce agreement, allowing this to be done.[34]

A worker may give the employer notice of when he or she wishes to take the leave.[35] This notice must be given by a date which is equivalent to twice the amount of leave the worker is proposing to take. An employer can, however, stipulate when holidays can be taken by giving the worker concerned notice using the same formula. Regulation 16 provides that in respect of annual leave workers are entitled to be paid a sum equivalent to a week's pay for each week of leave.[36]

The entitlement to paid annual leave arises if an individual has been a worker during all or part of a leave year. There is no rule which states that the individual will actually have to be at work or do work. Thus individuals on long-term sick leave are entitled to claim holiday pay under the WT Regulations for the periods when away on sick leave. This was the situation in *Kigass Aero Components v Brown*[37] where Mr Brown had been away from work, following a traffic accident, since October 1998. He successfully applied for holiday pay for the leave year beginning January 1999.

In *Gridquest Ltd v Blackburn*[38] a number of agency workers had been paid an hourly rate which included an element of holiday pay. The workers concerned stated that they did not know of this and had not agreed to a part of their pay being for this purpose. The Court of Appeal held that the weekly pay can only be assumed to include some other element, such as holiday pay, if that has been agreed with the employees. If this was so agreed then a 'rolled up rate' would be possible. This, however, seems to be in contrast to another decision in *MPB Structure Ltd v Munro*[39], where the Court of Sessions held that part of the purpose of the WT Regulations was to provide funds so that workers could take the leave to which they were entitled. They were to be paid at the time of taking the holiday regardless of any contractual agreement. The EAT, in *Marshalls Clay Products*[40], observed that to lessen the risk of 'rolled up' holiday pay not counting towards an employer's obligation to give holiday pay a number of steps should be taken. These were:

(i)   the rolled up holiday pay must be clearly shown in the contract of employment which had been agreed;

(ii) the allocation of the amount or percentage of pay which is for holiday pay must be clearly identified;

(iii) it must be a true addition to the normal contractual pay;

(iv) records of holidays taken must be kept;

(v) reasonable practicable steps must be taken to ensure that workers take their holiday before the expiry of the holiday year.

In other words employers should adopt a good practice approach to identifying and paying the holiday pay entitlement.

Records

There is an obligation, in Regulation 9, for employers to keep records in respect of the maximum weekly working time (in respect of those workers who have agreed to opt out of the 48-hour limit), night work and health assessment checks for night-workers. These records must be adequate to show that the relevant time-limits are being complied with in the case of each worker employed. Such records must be retained for a period of two years.

The right not to suffer detriment

Workers have the right not to be subjected to any detriment by any act, or failure to act, on the part of the employer on the grounds that the worker:

- refused, or proposed to refuse, to comply with any requirement in contravention of the WT Regulations
- refused, or proposed to refuse, to give up a right conferred by the WT Regulations
- failed to sign a workforce agreement (see below) or vary any other agreement with the employer which is provided for by the WT Regulations
- was a workforce representative or a candidate in an election for such representatives
- alleged that the employer had infringed the worker's rights under the WT Regulations
- was bringing proceedings to enforce rights under the WT Regulations.

The worker will be entitled to such compensation as the tribunal considers is just and equitable in all the circumstances, taking into account the default of the employer and the loss suffered by the worker.[41] If the detriment amounts to a dismissal for one of the above reasons, then an employee may bring a complaint of unfair dismissal in accordance with Part X ERA 1996.[42] Any compensation awarded to a worker who is not an employee will be limited to that which an employee could claim under the unfair dismissal provisions.[43]

Derogation by agreement

Apart from the individual's ability to opt out of the maximum working week (see above), the WT Regulations allow derogations, in some instances, by agreement between the employer and representatives of the employees. The types of agreement are:

1 *collective agreements*
   which, according to Regulation 2, are defined in section 178 TULRCA. They are agreements between employers and independent trade unions recognised for collective bargaining purposes, which allow agreement to be reached on
   - extension of the reference period for averaging the 48-hour week from 17 weeks up to a maximum of 52 weeks[44]
   - modifying or excluding the application of the regulations concerning the length of night work, health assessments, daily and weekly rest periods and daily rest breaks[45]

2 *workforce agreements*
   which, according to schedule 1 to the Regulations, are valid if the following conditions are met:
   - the agreement is in writing
   - it has effect for a specified period not exceeding five years
   - it applies to all the relevant members of the workforce or to a particular group within the relevant workforce
   - the agreement is signed by representatives of the workforce or group
   - before the agreement is signed, the employer provides all the workers concerned with a copy plus any necessary guidance.

If the employer has fewer than 20 workers, a workforce agreement can be reached either by representatives of that workforce or by obtaining the support of the majority of the workforce. Representatives of the workforce are the elected representatives of the workforce concerned. A workforce agreement will allow the same derogations as those for collective agreement.

Regulation 2 also contains a definition of a relevant agreement. It is an agreement which can be a provision of a collective agreement which forms part of a contract between the worker and the employer, or a work-force agreement, or any other agreement in writing that is legally enforceable as between employer and worker.

TIME OFF FOR TRADE UNION DUTIES AND ACTIVITIES

No minimum period of service is required before trade unionists can claim time off.

Trade union duties

According to section 168 TULRCA 1992, employers must permit employees who are officials of independent trade unions recognised by them to take reasonable time off with pay during working hours to enable them to:

(a) carry out their duties which are concerned with negotiations with the employer that are related to or connected with any of the matters specified in section 178(2) TULRCA and in relation to which the employer recognises the union

(b) carry out any other duties which are concerned with the performance of any functions that are related to or connected with any matters listed in section 178(2) TULRCA 1992 and that the employer has agreed may be performed by the union – this includes accompanying workers, at their request, to disciplinary and grievance hearings[46]

(c) receive information from the employer and be consulted under section 188 TULRCA 1992 or the Transfer Regulations 1981

(d) undergo training in aspects of industrial relations which is both relevant to the carrying out of any of the duties mentioned in (a) and approved by their trade union or the TUC.

An official is defined as someone who is an officer of the union or branch of it, or someone who is elected or appointed in accordance with the rules to be a representative of its members or some of them[47] (see Chapter 19 on the meaning of 'independence' and recognition).

The amount of time off allowed, together with the purpose for which, the occasions on which, and any conditions subject to which, time off may be taken, depends on what is reasonable in all the circumstances having regard to any relevant provisions in the ACAS Code of Practice.[48] The Code does not lay down any fixed amount of time that employers should permit officials to take off. Its main theme is that employers and trade unions should reach agreements on arrangements for handling time off in ways appropriate to their situations.

Pay for permitted time off

Officials who are permitted time off should receive normal remuneration as if they had worked. Where the remuneration varies with the work done, average hourly earnings should be paid.[49] No claim can be made for overtime which would normally have been worked unless that overtime was contractually required, and there is no entitlement to be paid for time spent on trade union duties outside working hours.[50] It follows that an employee on the night shift who attends a works committee meeting during the day will not be entitled to a payment, whereas a day shift worker would. Nevertheless, employees may reasonably require paid time off during working hours to enable them to undertake the relevant duties or training – for example, to travel to or return from a training course.[51] Two further points should be noted. First, the 'set-off formula' applies here.[52] Second, employers who give their part-time employees paid time off only up to the limit of their normal working hours may be discriminating contrary to Article 141 EC. In *Davies* v *Neath Port Talbot Borough Council*[53] the employee concerned worked a 22-hour week. The individual was a health and safety representative and was given time off to attend two five-day courses run by the union. The employer agreed to pay for the usual working hours, not the actual time spent on the courses. The employee made an equal pay claim under Article 119 (now Article 141) of the EC Treaty. The EAT agreed that part-time workers had a right to be paid on the same basis as full-timers when attending such courses and that to do otherwise would amount to indirect sex discrimination.

Legitimate reasons for time off

The Code of Practice recommends that officials of recognised trade unions should be allowed reasonable time off for duties concerned with negotiations related to or connected with:[54]

- terms and conditions of employment, or the conditions in which employees are required to work – eg pay, hours of work, holiday pay and entitlement, sick pay arrangements, pensions, vocational training, equal opportunities, notice periods, the working environment and the utilisation of machinery and other equipment

- engagement or non-engagement, or termination or suspension of employment or the duties of employment, of one or more workers – eg recruitment and selection policies, human resource planning, redundancy and dismissal arrangements

- allocation of work, or the duties of employment as between workers or groups of workers – eg job grading, job evaluation, job descriptions and flexible working practices

- matters of discipline – eg disciplinary procedures, arrangements for representing trade union members at internal interviews, arrangements for appearing on behalf of trade union members, or as witnesses before agreed outside appeal bodies or employment tribunals

- trade union membership or non-membership – eg representational agreements, any union involvement in the induction of new workers

- facilities for officials of trade unions – eg accommodation, equipment, names of new workers to the union

- machinery for negotiation and consultation and other procedures – eg arrangements for collective bargaining, grievance procedures, joint consultation, communicating with members, communicating with other union officials also concerned with collective bargaining with the employer.

The Code states that where an official is not taking part in industrial action but represents members who are, normal arrangements for time off with pay should apply. Additionally, the code suggests that management should make available the facilities necessary for officials to perform their duties efficiently and to communicate effectively with members. The items mentioned are accommodation for meetings, access to a telephone, notice-boards and the use of office facilities.[55]

Preparatory and explanatory work by officials may well be in fulfilment of duties concerned with any of the matters listed in section 178(2) TULRCA 1992.[56] What has to be demonstrated is that there is a sufficient connection between the collective bargaining and the duty for which leave is sought.[57] Employment tribunals will have to decide whether the preparatory work is directly relevant to one of the matters specified in section 178(2), and if the employer does not negotiate on the issue, the employer's agreement to the performance of the duty will have to be demonstrated.[58] It also seems that the recognised union must, expressly or impliedly, require the performance of the duty; otherwise, it would be impossible to hold that the individual was 'carrying out those duties … as such an official'.[59] If no agreement on time off is reached in advance of a meeting, a sensible approach might be to determine claims for payment on the basis of what the minutes disclosed. Where only a proportion of the time was spent on section 168 TULRCA 1992 matters, a tribunal will probably find that only a proportion of the time should reasonably be paid for.

As regards industrial relations training, again no fixed amount of time is specified but the code recommends that officials should be permitted paid time off for initial basic training as soon as possible after their election or appointment. Time off should be allowed for further training where the official has special responsibilities or where it is necessary to meet changed industrial relations circumstances.[60] In determining whether a course meets the requirement of relevance to the specified duties, the description of people attending the course by those responsible for it will be pertinent.[61] Indeed, as a general principle it would seem wise for employers to insist on being shown a copy of course prospectuses.

Trade union activities

An employer must also permit a member of a recognised independent trade union to take reasonable time off during working hours for trade union activities and to represent the union. However, in the absence of any contractual term to the contrary, an employer does not have to pay for such time off. Trade union activities are not statutorily defined, although the code gives the following examples of the activities of a member:

- attending workplace meetings to discuss and vote on the outcome of negotiations with the employer
- meeting full-time officials to discuss issues relevant to the workplace
- voting in properly conducted ballots on industrial action
- voting in union elections.[62]

Paragraph 22 of the Code gives examples of activities where the member is acting as a representative of a union:

- branch, area or regional meetings of the union where the business of the union is under discussion
- meetings of official policy-making bodies such as the executive committee or annual conference
- meetings with full-time officials to discuss issues relevant to the workplace.

Section 170(2) TULRCA expressly excludes activities which consist of industrial action, although paragraph 39 of the code recommends that time off should be provided for the use of agreed procedures. Finally, in *Wignall v British Gas*[63] the EAT rejected the argument that the statute requires each proposed activity on the part of the employee in the service of his or her union to be weighed and tested on its own merits without regard to any other activities or duties on the union's behalf for which the employee might be taking time off. Thus every application for time off under section 170 should be looked at on its merits in the particular circumstances.

Employees wishing to complain of failure to permit time off or to pay the amount required by section 169 TULRCA 1992 must apply to an employment tribunal within three months of the date when the failure occurred.[64] According to the EAT, a complainant must establish on the balance of probabilities that a request for time off was made, that it came to the notice of the employer's appropriate representative, and that he or she refused it, ignored it or failed to respond to it.[65] If the tribunal finds that the claim is well-founded, it must make a declaration to that effect and may make an award of compensation of such amount as it considers 'just and equitable in all the circumstances having regard to the employer's default' ... and to any loss sustained by the employee which is attributable to the matters complained of'.[66]

TIME OFF FOR PUBLIC DUTIES

Section 50 EPA 1996 permits employees who are:

- members of a local authority[67]

- members of any statutory tribunal
- members of a health authority, NHS trust or a Health Board
- members of a relevant education body[68]
- members of a police authority[69]
- part of the Service Authority of the National Crime Squad or the National Criminal Intelligence Service
- members of a board of prison visitors or a prison visiting committee[70]
- members of the Environment Agency or the Scottish Environment Protection Agency

to take time off during working hours for the purpose of performing any of the duties of their office or as members. Employees are eligible for time off irrespective of their length of service, but are not entitled to a payment from their employer by virtue of this section.

The duties referred to are attendance at meetings of the body (or its committees or sub-committees) and 'the doing of any other thing approved by the body' for the purpose of discharging its functions. The amount of time off which is to be allowed and the occasions on which and conditions subject to which it may be taken are those that are reasonable in the circumstances. No code of practice exists for these purposes but regard must be had to the following matters:[71]

- how much time off is required for the performance of the public duty as a whole and how much is required for the particular duty
- how much time off has already been permitted for trade union duties and activities (see above)
- the circumstances of the employer's business and the effect of the employee's absence on the running of it.

The EAT has commented that an employee who undertakes a variety of public and other duties may have some responsibility to plan the absences from work, and to scale down the level of commitment which such public duties involve, so as to produce a pattern which can be regarded as reasonable in the circumstances.[72] A complaint that an employer has failed to permit time off in accordance with the above provisions must be lodged in the same way as a claim that the employer has not complied with sections 168 or 170 TURLCA 1992, and the remedies available are identical. However, two observations may be helpful at this stage. First, rearranging employees' hours of work but requiring them to perform the same duties does not constitute giving time off. Second, it is not the function of employment tribunals to stipulate what amounts of, or conditions for, time off would be appropriate in the future.[73]

TIME OFF FOR EMPLOYEE REPRESENTATIVES[74] AND EMPLOYEE TRUSTEES OF PENSION FUNDS

A person who is an employee representative for the purposes of consultation over redundancies or the transfer of undertakings (see Chapter 13), or a candidate in an election to be such a representative, is entitled to reasonable time off during working hours to perform the functions of such a representative or candidate.[75] Employees who are permitted time off are entitled to be paid at the appropriate rate.[76] Those who feel that their rights have been infringed can use the enforcement mechanisms available in relation to time off for antenatal care.[77]

Section 58 (1) ERA 1996 allows employee trustees of a pension fund reasonable time off during working hours for the purpose of performing any of their duties as a trustee or undergoing training relevant to those duties. In ascertaining what is reasonable in all the circumstances regard must be had to:

- how much time off is required for the performance of the trustee's duties and undergoing relevant training, and how much time off is needed for undertaking the particular duty or training, and

- the circumstances of the employer's business and the effect of the employee's absence on the running of it.[78]

Employees who feel that this right has been infringed must normally complain to an employment tribunal within three months. The remedies available are identical to those that apply to time off for trade union duties (see above).[79]

It should also be noted that employee representatives (or candidates in an election) and trustees of pension funds have the right not to be subjected to any detriment on the ground that they performed (or proposed to perform) their functions or activities.[80] Claims must be lodged within three months of the act (or failure to act) complained of, and the remedies available are the same as for the right not to be subject to detriment on trade union grounds (see above).[81]

TIME OFF FOR STUDY OR TRAINING

Section 63A of the ERA 1996 permits certain young employees to have time off for study or training. The employees concerned are those who:

- are aged 16 or 17 years, and
- are not receiving full-time or further education, and
- have not attained such standard of achievement as is prescribed by regulations made by the Secretary of State.[82]

These standards of achievement are set out in the Right to Time Off for Study or Training Regulations 2001[83] (RTOST Regulations). Examples of the standards of achievement are: grades A–C in five subjects at GCSE or one intermediate level GNVQ or one GSVQ at level 2.[84]

In addition young employees who:

- are aged 18 years
- are undertaking training or study leading to a relevant qualification
- began that study before reaching the age of 18 years

are also entitled to time off during working hours.

The amount of time off permitted must be reasonable, taking into account the requirements of the employee's study or training and the circumstances of the employer's business and the effect of the time taken off on that business.[85] An employee who has the right to take time off for study and training also has the right to be paid remuneration by the employer at the normal hourly rate.[86] If an employee has been unreasonably refused permission for time off or has not been paid correctly for that time off, he or she may make a complaint to an employment tribunal.[87] The complaint needs to be made within three months, unless not reasonably practicable, beginning with the day that the time off was taken or should have been taken. If the complaint is well-founded, the tribunal may make a declaration to that effect or order the employer to pay compensation equal to the amount of remuneration to which the employee would have been entitled.

TIME OFF TO LOOK FOR WORK

A person who has been continuously employed for two years or more and is under notice of dismissal by reason of redundancy is entitled to reasonable time off during working hours to look for new employment or make arrangements for training for future employment.[88] Such an employee should be paid at the appropriate hourly rate for the period of absence. This is one week's pay divided by the number of normal weekly hours, or, where the number of working hours varies, the average of such hours.[89]

A complaint that an employer has unreasonably refused time off or has failed to pay the whole or any part of any amount to which the employee is entitled must be presented to an employment tribunal, if reasonably practicable, within three months of the day on which it is alleged that the time off should have been allowed or paid for.[90] If the complaint is well-founded, the tribunal must make a declaration to that effect and order the employer to pay the amount which it finds due to the employee. Curiously, although the employee is entitled to be paid 'an amount equal to the remuneration to which he would have been entitled if he had been allowed the time off', the maximum that a tribunal can award is two-fifths of a week's pay. In *Dutton v Hawker Siddeley Aviation Ltd*[91] the EAT rejected the argument that employees had to give details of any appointments or interviews for which they wished to take time off.

KEY POINTS

- The WT Regulations implement the WT Directive and parts of the Young Workers Directive.
- The Regulations provide for a maximum 48-hour week during a 17-week reference period and provide rules on night work, rest periods and annual leave.
- The individual is able to agree to opt out of the 48-hour week and there are provisions for determining the rules by collective and workforce agreements.
- No minimum period of service is required before trade unionists can claim time off.
- Employers must permit employees who are officials of independent trade unions recognised by them to take reasonable time off with pay.
- Members of a recognised independent trade union are entitled to reasonable time off during working hours for trade union activities and to represent the union.
- Employees are to be permitted time off, without pay, for a variety of public duties such as being a justice of the peace or a member of a local authority.
- Young employees who are not receiving full-time education are entitled to time off to study and train for certain qualifications.
- A person who has been continuously employed for two years or more and is under notice of dismissal for redundancy is entitled to reasonable time off, during working hours, to look for new work.

NOTES

1 SI 1998/1833
2 Directive 93/104 concerning certain aspects of the organisation of working time
3 Directive 94/33 on the protection of young people at work
4 *UK* v *Council of the European Union* (1997) ICR 443
5 SI 2003/1684
6 (2001) IRLR 838
7 See amended Regulation 18 WT Regulations 1998
8 Amended Regulation 2 WT Regulations 1998

9 Regulation 20 WT Regulations 2003
10 Regulation 25A WT Regulations 2003
11 (2003) IRLR 211
12 *Byrne Brothers Ltd* v *Baird* (2002) IRLR 96
13 (2003) IRLR 199
14 See Regulation 2 WT Regulations 1998
15 *Landeshauptstadt Kiel* v *Jaeger* (2003) IRLR 804
16 (1999) IRLR 308
17 Regulation 4(6) WT Regulations 1998
18 This requirement was introduced by the Working Time Regulations 1999 SI 1999/3372. It had the effect of simplifying the records that needed to be kept, thus making it easier for such opt-out agreements to be reached
19 Regulation 5A WT Regulations 1998
20 Regulation 27A WT Regulations 1998
21 See *R* v *Attorney General for Northern Ireland* (1999) IRLR 315
22 (1999) IRLR 315
23 Regulation 6(7) WT Regulations 1998
24 Regulation 7 WT Regulations 1998
25 Regulation 8 WT Regulations 1998
26 Regulation 6A WT Regulations 1998
27 Regulation 27A(3) WT Regulations 1998
28 Regulation 11 WT Regulations 1998; Regulation 11(7) states that the weekly rest period may not be in addition to the daily rest period 'where this is justified by objective or technical reasons or reasons concerning the organisation of work'
29 Regulation 11(8) WT Regulations 1998; the rest period may not be less than 36 consecutive hours
30 Regulation 13 WT Regulations 1998; see also *Gibson* v *East Riding of Yorkshire* (2000) IRLR 598, where a local authority employee tried unsuccessfully to rely on the Working Time Directive being directly effective to claim four weeks' holiday
31 Regulation 15A, inserted by The Working Time (Amendment) Regulations 2001 SI 2001/3256. These Regulations also removed a requirement for an employee to have 13 weeks' continuous service before there was an entitlement to annual leave
32 In which case the worker is entitled to a proportionate payment in lieu; see Regulation 14
33 *Leisure Leagues UK Ltd* v *Maconnachie* (2002) IRLR 600
34 *Hill* v *Chapell* (2002) IRLR 19
35 Regulation 15 WT Regulations 1998
36 A week's pay is defined in sections 221–224 ERA 1996. See *Davies* v *MJ Wyatt (Decorators) Ltd* (2000) IRLR 759, where the EAT held that an employer could not unilaterally reduce an employee's contractual pay in order to provide for holiday pay
37 (2002) IRLR 312
38 *Gridquest Ltd (t/a Select Employment)* v *Blackburn* (2002) IRLR 604
39 (2003) IRLR 350
40 *Marshalls Clay Products* v *Caulfield* (2003) IRLR 552
41 Regulation 30 WT Regulations 1998
42 Section 101A ERA 1996
43 Section 49(5A) ERA 1996
44 Regulation 23(b) WT Regulations 1998
45 Regulation 23(a) WT Regulations 1998, although Regulation 24 allows for compensatory rest periods and rest breaks
46 Section 10(7) ERel Act 1999

47 Section 119 TULRCA 1992
48 ACAS Code of Practice on Time off for Trade Union Duties and Activities 1997
49 Section 169(3) TULRCA 1992
50 Working hours are defined in the same way as section 146(2) TULRCA 1992
51 See *Hairsine* v *Hull City Council* (1992) IRLR 211
52 Section 169(4) TULRCA 1992
53 (1999) IRLR 769
54 Paragraph 12
55 Paragraph 28
56 See paragraph 13
57 See *London Ambulance Service* v *Charlton* (1992) IRLR 510
58 See *British Bakeries* v *Adlington* (1989) IRLR 218
59 See *Ashley* v *Ministry of Defence* (1984) IRLR 57
60 Paragraph 18
61 See *Ministry of Defence* v *Crook* (1982) IRLR 488
62 Paragraph 21
63 (1984) IRLR 493
64 Unless the 'time-lapse escape clause' applies; section 171 TULRCA 1992
65 *Ryford Ltd* v *Drinkwater* (1995) IRLR 16
66 Section 172 TULRCA 1992
67 Defined in section 50(5) ERA 1996
68 Defined in section 50(9) ERA 1996
69 Defined in section 50(6) ERA 1996
70 Defined in section 50(7) ERA 1996
71 Section 50(4) ERA 1996
72 *Borders Regional Council* v *Maule* (1993) IRLR 199
73 See *Corner* v *Buckinghamshire Council* (1978) IRLR 320
74 Workers must be permitted to take time off during working hours for the purpose of accompanying another worker at a disciplinary or grievance hearing: section 10 ERel Act 1999
75 Section 168(1) TULRCA 1992 and section 61(1) ERA 1996
76 See section 62 ERA 1996
77 Section 63 ERA 1996
78 See section 58(2) ERA 1996
79 Section 60(3)(4) ERA 1996
80 See sections 47 and 46 ERA 1996 respectively. Dismissal on these grounds is unfair (see Chapter 14)
81 Sections 48–49 ERA 1996
82 Section 63A(1)(a)–(c) ERA 1996
83 SI 2001/2801
84 Regulation 3 RTOST Regulations 2001; the awarding bodies that are recognised for these purposes are listed in the schedule to the Regulations
85 Section 63A(5) ERA 1996
86 See section 63B(1) ERA 1996
87 Section 63C ERA 1996
88 Section 52 ERA 1996
89 Section 53 ERA 1996
90 Section 54 ERA 1996
91 (1978) IRLR 390

Variation, Breach and Termination of the Contract of Employment at Common Law

CHAPTER 11

OVERVIEW

This chapter deals with various issues raised by the common-law approach to the variation and ending of contracts of employment. To begin with we look at the consequences of unilateral variation of the contract by the employer. We then examine the options open when a breach of contract takes place by studying, firstly, the innocent party's choice in accepting the breach or not, and secondly, the principal remedies for a breach. The issues concerned with frustration of the contract and summary dismissal are considered. Finally we look at the consequences of termination without notice and the remedies for wrongful dismissal.

VARIATION

Theoretically, neither employer nor employee can unilaterally alter the terms and conditions of employment, for these can be varied only by mutual agreement.[1] It follows that an employer cannot lawfully vary a contract simply by giving 'notice to vary'. Such a notice will have legal effect only if it terminates the existing contract and offers a new contract on revised terms.[2] Consent to change may be obtained through individual or collective negotiation or may be implied from the conduct of the parties. Thus if employees remain at work for a considerable period of time after revised terms have been imposed, they may be deemed to have accepted the changes.[3] Where the individual continues in employment but works 'under protest', it is a question of fact whether or not the variation has been accepted. In *WPM Retail* v *Lang*[4] it was held that the employer's obligation to pay a bonus in accordance with the terms when the employee was promoted remained in force until the employment was terminated three years later, notwithstanding that the bonus had been paid only in the first month after promotion and the employee had carried on working thereafter. As a general rule, courts and tribunals will be reluctant to find that there has been a consensual variation 'where the employee has been faced with the alternative of dismissal and where the variation has been adverse to his interest'.[5]

A unilateral variation which is not accepted will constitute a breach and could amount to a repudiation of the contract. However, there is no law that any breach which an employee is entitled to treat as repudiatory brings the contract to an end automatically.[6] Where there is repudiatory conduct by the employer, the employee has the choice of affirming the contract (by continuing in employment) or accepting the repudiation as bringing the contract to an end. If the latter option is exercised and the employee resigns within a short period, there will be a constructive dismissal for statutory purposes (see Chapter 12). In practice, developments in the law of unfair dismissal make it very difficult for an employee to resist a unilateral variation. Suffice to say at this stage that employers can offer, as a fair reason for dismissal, the fact that there was a sound business reason for insisting on changes being put into effect. So long as a minimum amount of consultation has taken place, it is relatively easy to satisfy a tribunal, particularly where the majority of employees has been prepared to go along with the employer's proposals, that an employer has acted reasonably in treating a refusal to accept a variation as a sufficient reason for dismissing.[7]

BREACH OF CONTRACT

Employers' options: disciplinary and legal

The options open to an innocent party will depend on whether the breach is of a minor or serious nature. An innocent party may choose to continue with the contract as if nothing had happened (ie waive the breach), may sue for damages, or, in the case of a serious or fundamental breach, may regard the contract as at an end (ie accept the other party's repudiation of it).[8] Although the employer could sue or possibly dismiss for breach of contract, there are a number of reasons why disciplinary rather than legal action is preferred. First, the potential defendant may be unable to pay any damages awarded. Second, the amount likely to be obtained may not be worth the time and effort involved. Third, taking legal rather than disciplinary action against in-dividual employees is not conducive to harmonious industrial relations.

What options are open to employers when employees refuse to carry out all or part of their contractual obligations? Apart from the measures outlined in the previous paragraph, the employer may withhold pay on the grounds that employees who are not ready and willing to render the services required by their con-tracts are not entitled to be paid.[9] In *Wiluszynski* v *London Borough of Tower Hamlets*[10] the employee refused to perform the full range of his duties and had been told by the employer that until he did he would not be required for work or be paid. Although he went to work and performed a substantial part of his duties, the Court of Appeal held that the local authority was entitled to withhold the whole of his remu-neration. Clearly, employees are not entitled to pick and choose what work they will do under their con-tracts, but if employers are prepared to accept part-performance, they will be required to pay for such work as is agreed.

The principal remedies for breach of contract are an injunction (an order restraining a particular type of action), a declaration of the rights of the parties, and damages. An account of profits may be additionally ordered in exceptional circumstances.[11] Traditionally, great emphasis was placed on the personal nature of the contract of employment, and courts were extremely reluctant to order a party to continue to perform the contract. However, in recent years the courts have been more willing to grant injunctions against employ-ers who act in breach of contract.[12] Nevertheless, they need to be satisfied not only that it would be just to make such an order but also that it would be workable.[13] The mere fact that the employer and employee are in dispute does not mean that mutual confidence has evaporated.[14] The position remains that an employee cannot be compelled to return to work,[15] although a tribunal has the power to order the re-employment of someone who has been unfairly dismissed and seeks this remedy (see Chapter 15). Those who seek damages can be compensated for the direct and likely consequences of the breach, although nothing can be recovered for the manner of the breach or for the mental stress, frustration or annoyance caused.[16] However, in *Gogay* v *Hertfordshire County Council*[17] the Court of Appeal confirmed that damages could be awarded for a psychological disorder brought on by an unlawful suspension. Compensation will not be recoverable for damage to an existing reputation unless pecuniary loss was sustained as a fore-seeable consequence of the breach.[18]

The jurisdiction of employment tribunals extends to breach of contract claims which have arisen or are out-standing at the end of employment.[19] Under section 3(2) ETA 1996 the claim must be for:

- damages for breach of a contract of employment or any other contract connected with the employ-ment; however, this does not include the loss of an opportunity to claim unfair dismissal through being sacked prior to satisfying the requirement of having one year's service.[20]
- a sum due under such a contract
- the recovery of a sum in pursuance of any enactment relating to the terms or performance of such a contract.

Certain claims are excluded – for example, personal injury, breach of confidence and restrictive covenant cases. Employers can bring proceedings (counterclaims) only if an employee has made a claim first, but the employer's claim can then continue even if the employee is unable to continue with the claim.[21]

An employee's claim must normally be brought within three months of the effective date of termination[22] and an employer's counterclaim must be presented within six weeks of receiving a copy of the originating application. A case is heard by a chairperson sitting alone unless it is decided that a full tribunal should hear it. Although ACAS's services are available, the parties can reach their own agreement without any need for a conciliated settlement or compromise agreement.

AUTOMATIC TERMINATION: FRUSTRATION

A contract is said to have been frustrated where events make it physically impossible or unlawful for the contract to be performed, or where there has been a change such as to radically alter the purpose of the contract. Once a contract has come to an end by reason of frustration, it cannot be treated by the parties as still subsisting. If the parties come to an arrangement to continue the employment relationship, then this may constitute a new contract or some other arrangement. It will not be a continuation of the original contract which has been frustrated.[23] A contract that is still capable of being performed but becomes subject to an unforeseen risk is not frustrated.[24] As long as the frustrating event is not self-induced, there is an automatic termination of the contract – ie there is no dismissal.[25] This being so, it was not uncommon for an employer to resist a claim for unfair dismissal by alleging that the contract had been frustrated, eg on grounds of sickness. Although the EAT thought that the concept of frustration should normally come into play only where the contract is for a long term that cannot be determined by notice, the Court of Appeal has allowed this doctrine to be applied to contracts of employment that can be terminated by short periods of notice.[26]

Frustration of the contract through illness

The following principles are relevant to the application of the doctrine of frustration in the event of illness.[27] First, the courts must guard against too easy an application of the doctrine. Second, an attempt to decide the date that frustration occurred may help to decide whether it is a true frustration situation. Third, the factors below may help to decide the issue:

- length of previous employment
- how long the employment was expected to continue
- the nature of the job
- the nature, length and effect of the illness or disabling event[28]
- the employer's need for the work to be done and the need for a replacement employee
- whether wages have continued to be paid
- the acts and statements of the employer in relation to the employment. In *Hart* v *Marshall & Sons*[29] the EAT held that the employer's acceptance of sick notes did not prevent a tribunal from finding that the contract had been frustrated
- whether in all the circumstances a reasonable employer could have been expected to wait any longer
- the terms of the contract as to sick pay, if any
- a consideration of the prospects of recovery.

A prison sentence is a potentially frustrating event, but the circumstances of each case have to be examined to discover whether such a sentence has in fact operated to frustrate the contract or whether its termination was due to some other cause.[30]

TERMINATION WITHOUT NOTICE: SUMMARY DISMISSAL

A summary dismissal occurs where the employer terminates the contract of employment without notice. It must be distinguished from an instant dismissal, which has no legal meaning but normally refers to a dismissal without investigation or inquiry. Whereas an instant dismissal is likely to be procedurally defective in unfair dismissal terms (see Chapter 13), a summary dismissal may be lawful under both common law and statute.

In order to justify summary dismissal the employee must be in breach of an important express or implied term of the contract, ie be guilty of gross misconduct. Although certain terms are always regarded as important – for example, the duty not to steal or damage the employer's property, the duty to obey lawful orders and not to engage in industrial action – the significance of other terms will depend on the nature of the employer's business and the employee's position in it. Thus smoking may not normally be viewed as an act of gross misconduct, but if it occurs at a gas-bottling plant it is likely to be so regarded! If an employer feels that a particular act or omission would warrant summary dismissal, this fact should be communicated clearly to all employees.[31]

One consequence of the contractual approach is that everything hinges upon the facts in the particular case and previous decisions usually have little bearing. Nevertheless, a number of general principles can be discerned:

- single acts of misconduct are less likely to give rise to a right of summary dismissal than a persistent pattern
- it is the nature of the act rather than its consequences which is relevant
- an employer is more likely to be entitled to dismiss summarily for misconduct within the workplace than outside it
- a refusal to obey instructions can still amount to repudiation even though the employee has mistakenly proceeded in the *bona fide* belief that the work which he or she had been instructed to do fell outside the scope of the contract.[32]

If employers do not invoke the right to end the contract within a reasonable period, they will be taken to have waived their rights and can only seek damages. What is a reasonable period will depend on the facts of the particular case. In *Allders International* v *Parkins*[33] it was held that nine days was too long a period to be allowed to pass in relation to an allegation of stealing before deciding what to do about the alleged repudiatory conduct. In *Gunton* v *London Borough of Richmond*[34] the Court of Appeal decided that the general doctrine that repudiation by one party does not terminate a contract applies to employment law. An unlawful summary dismissal thus does not terminate a contract of employment until the employee has accepted the employer's repudiation, and certain contractual rights and obligations will survive until that time – eg in relation to a disciplinary procedure (see Chapter 12 on the effective date of termination for statutory purposes). Nevertheless, in the absence of special circumstances a court will easily infer that the repudiation has been accepted.[35] Finally, at common law an employer is not required to supply a reason for dismissal, although this is now qualified by statute[36] (see Chapter 13).

TERMINATION WITH NOTICE

Usually, either party is entitled to terminate a contract of employment by giving notice,[37] and once notice has been given it cannot be unilaterally withdrawn.[38] (Of course, an employer who makes a mistake could offer to re-employ.) The courts have consistently ruled that for notice to be effective it must be possible to ascertain the date of termination, and not infrequently employees have confused an advanced warning of closure with notice of dismissal.[39] The length of the notice will be determined by the express or implied terms of the contract, and if no term can be identified, both parties are required to give a reasonable period of notice. What is reasonable will depend on the circumstances of the relationship – eg the employee's position and length of service. Thus in *Hill* v *C. A. Parsons & Co. Ltd* [40] a 63-year-old engineer with 35 years' service was held to be entitled to at least six months' notice.

Apart from the situation where individuals are disentitled to notice by reason of their conduct,[41] section 86(1) ERA 1996 provides that certain minimum periods of notice must be given. After a month's service an employee is entitled to a week's notice and this applies until the employment has lasted for two years. At this point two weeks' notice is owed and from then on the employee must receive an extra week's notice for each year of service up to a maximum of 12 weeks. According to section 86(2) ERA 1996, an employee with a month's service or more need give only one week's notice to terminate, but there is nothing to prevent the parties from agreeing that both should receive more than the statutory minimum.

Although the statute does not prevent an employee from accepting a payment in lieu of notice, strictly speaking an employer must have contractual authority for insisting on such a payment. Without such authority a payment in lieu of notice will be construed as damages for the failure to provide proper notice.[42] Thus a payment in lieu can properly terminate a contract of employment if the contract provides for such a payment or the parties agree that the employee will accept a payment in lieu, provided the payment relates to a period no shorter than that of the notice to which the employee would be entitled either under the contract of employment or section 86(1) ERA 1996.[43] The date of termination at common law is the day notice expires or the day wages in lieu are accepted. Except where the notice to be given by the employer is at least one week more than the statutory minimum, an employee is entitled to be paid during the period of notice even if:

- no work is provided by the employer
- the employee is incapable of work because of sickness or injury
- the employee is absent from work wholly or partly because of pregnancy or childbirth
- the employee is absent in accordance with the terms of his or her employment relating to holidays.[44]

Any payments by the employer by way of sick pay, maternity pay, holiday pay or otherwise go towards meeting this liability.[45] If employees take part in a strike after they have been given notice, payment is due for the period when they were not on strike. However, where employees give notice and then go on strike, they do not qualify for any payment under section 88 or 89 ERA 1996.[46]

REMEDIES FOR WRONGFUL DISMISSAL

Basically a wrongful dismissal is a dismissal without notice or with inadequate notice in circumstances where proper notice should have been given. The expression also covers dismissals which are in breach of agreed procedures. Thus where there is a contractual disciplinary procedure, an employee may be able to obtain an injunction or declaration from the courts so as to prevent a dismissal or declare a dismissal void if the procedure has not been followed.[47] However, an injunction will only be granted if the court is convinced that the employer's repudiation has not been accepted, that the employer has sufficient trust and confidence in the employee, and that damages would not be an adequate remedy.[48]

Judicial review is available where an issue of public law is involved, although employment by a public authority does not by itself inject any element of public law.[49] Indeed, where an alternative remedy is available, judicial review will only be exercised in exceptional circumstances. Factors to be taken into account in considering whether the circumstances are exceptional include the speed of the alternative procedure, whether it was as convenient, and whether the matter depended on some particular knowledge available to the appellate body.[50]

For the reason mentioned earlier the courts are reluctant to enforce a contract of employment, so in the vast majority of cases the employee's remedy will lie in damages for breach of contract. A person who suffers a wrongful dismissal is entitled to be compensated for such loss as arises naturally from the breach and for any loss which was reasonably foreseeable by the parties as being likely to arise from it. Hence an employee will normally recover only the amount of wages lost between the date of the wrongful dismissal and the date when the contract could lawfully have been terminated.[51] Examples of compensation that have been awarded include the following:

- an employee was allowed to keep share options, even though the terms of the share option scheme provided that the option to purchase lapsed on termination as a result of disciplinary action[52]

- a senior employee with a contract that allowed for a 10 per cent per annum salary increase and substantial annual bonuses during a three-year notice period was entitled to the benefit of those payments even though they were at the discretion of the board; for the board to exercise its discretion to reduce these payments to nil would have been capricious and a breach of contract[53]

- an employee was entitled to damages in respect of enhanced pension rights which he lost when his employment was terminated without due notice 12 days before his 55th birthday. For these purposes there is no difference in principle between lost pension rights and lost pay.[54]

Damages are not available for hurt feelings or the manner in which the dismissal took place, even though the manner might have made it more difficult to obtain other employment.[55]

Except where employees have a contractual right to a payment in lieu of notice,[56] or are entitled to their full payments during a contractual notice period[57] they have a duty to mitigate their loss, which means in effect that they are obliged to look for another job. Where there is a failure to mitigate, the court will deduct a sum it feels the employee might reasonably have been expected to earn. As regards state benefits, it would appear that any benefit received by the dismissed employee should be deducted only where not to do so would result in a net gain to the employee.[58] Finally, the first £30,000 of damages is to be awarded net of tax, but any amount above this figure will be awarded gross since it is taxable in the hands of the recipient.

KEY POINTS

- Theoretically, neither employer nor employee can unilaterally alter the terms and conditions of employment.
- A unilateral variation which is not accepted will constitute a breach and, if serious, could amount to a repudiation of the contract.
- An innocent party to a breach of contract may choose to continue, sue for damages or, in serious cases, accept the repudiation and regard the contract as being at an end.
- Frustration of a contract occurs when it is physically impossible or unlawful for the contract to continue to be performed.
- In order to justify summary dismissal the employee needs to be in breach of an important express or implied term of the contract.
- Once notice to terminate has been given it cannot be unilaterally withdrawn.
- For notice of termination to be effective, it must be possible to ascertain the date of termination.
- Wrongful dismissal is a dismissal without notice or with inadequate notice in circumstances where proper notice should have been given or where dismissals have been in breach of agreed procedures.

NOTES

1   See *Security and Facilities Division* v *Hayes* (2001) IRLR 81
2   *Alexander* v *STC Ltd* (1991) IRLR 286
3   *Aparau* v *Iceland Frozen Foods* (1996) IRLR 286
4   (1978) IRLR 343
5   See *Sheet Metal Components Ltd* v *Plumridge* (1979) IRLR 86
6   See *Boyo* v *Lambeth Borough Council* (1995) IRLR 50
7   See *Hollister* v *National Farmers Union* (1979) IRLR 238
8   See *Macari* v *Celtic Football Club* (1999) IRLR 787
9   See *Ticehurst* v *British Telecom* (1992) IRLR 219; section 14(5) ERA 1996 allows deductions to be made in respect of participation in industrial action
10 (1989) IRLR 279
11 See *Attorney-General* v *Blake* (2001) IRLR 37
12 See *Peace* v *City of Edinburgh* (1999) IRLR 417
13 See *Robb* v *London Borough of Hammersmith* (1991) IRLR 72
14 See *Hughes* v *London Borough of Southwark* (1988) IRLR 55
15 Section 236 TULRCA 1992
16 See *Bliss* v *South East Thames Regional Health Authority* (1988) IRLR 308
17 (2000) IRLR 703
18 See *Malik* v *BCCI* (1997) IRLR 462 and *BCCI* v *Ali* (No.3) (1999) IRLR 508
19 See *Miller Ltd* v *Johnston* and *Peninsular Ltd* v *Sweeney* (2004) IRLR 49 (2002) IRLR 386
20 See *Virgin Net Ltd* v *Harper (2003)* IRLR 831
21 See *Patel* v *RCMS Ltd* (1999) IRLR 161
22 See *Capek* v *Lincolnshire County Council* (2000) IRLR 590
23 See *GF Sharp & Co Ltd* v *McMillan* (1998) IRLR 632
24 See *Convefoam Ltd* v *Bell* (1981) IRLR 195
25 Where an employer dies or the business is destroyed, a dismissal is deemed to occur for the purpose of safeguarding an employee's right to a redundancy payment; section 174 ERA 1996
26 See *Nottcutt* v *Universal Equipment Ltd* (1986) I WLR 641
27 See *Williams* v *Watsons Ltd* (1990) IRLR 164
28 Employers need to be aware of the possible implications of the DDA 1995; see Chapter 7 and *Goodwin* v *The Patent Office* (1999) IRLR 4 on when a person is considered to have a disability
29 (1977) IRLR 61
30 See *F Shepherd* v *Jerrom* (1986) IRLR 358
31 See ACAS Code of Practice on Disciplinary and Grievance Procedures 2000, paragraph 7
32 See *Blyth* v *Scottish Liberal Club* (1983) IRLR 245
33 (1981) IRLR 68
34 (1980) IRLR 321
35 See *Boyo* v *Lambeth Borough Council* (note 6)
36 Section 92 ERA 1996
37 A contract of apprenticeship is for a fixed term and the ordinary law relating to dismissal does not apply; see *Wallace* v *CA Roofing Ltd* (1996) IRLR 435
38 See *Harris & Russell Ltd* v *Slingsby* (1973) IRLR 221
39 See *ICL* v *Kennedy* (1981) IRLR 28
40 (1971) 3 WLR 995
41 See section 86(6) ERA 1996
42 See *Cerberus Ltd* v *Rowley* (2001) IRLR 160
43 See *Ginsberg Ltd* v *Parker* (1988) IRLR 483
44 Section 88(1) ERA 1996
45 Section 88(2) ERA 1996

46 Section 91(2) ERA 1996
47 See *Jones* v *Gwent County Council* (1992) IRLR 521
48 See *Dietman* v *London Borough of Brent* (1988) IRLR 299 and *Wall* v *STC* (1990) IRLR 55
49 See *R* v *East Berkshire Health Authority ex parte Walsh* (1984) IRLR 278 and *McLaren* v *Home Office* (1990) IRLR 338
50 See *R* v *Chief Constable of Merseyside Police ex parte Calveley* (1986) 2 WLR 144 and *R* v *Broxtowe Borough Council ex parte Bradford* (2000) IRLR 329
51 See *Marsh* v *National Autistic Society* (1993) ICR 453
52 See *Lovett* v *Biotrace International Ltd* (1999) IRLR 375
53 *Clark* v *BET plc* (1997) IRLR 348; see also *Clark* v *Nomura plc* (2000) IRLR766
54 See *Silvey* v *Pendragon plc* (2001) IRLR 685
55 See *Johnson* v *Unisys Ltd* (2001) IRLR 716
56 See *Abrahams* v *Performing Rights Society* (1995) IRLR 486
57 See *Gregory* v *Wallace* (1998) IRLR 387
58 See *Westwood* v *Secretary of State* (1984) IRLR 209

Unfair Dismissal (1)

CHAPTER 12

OVERVIEW

Here we are concerned with the meaning of dismissal for statutory purposes and with the various qualifications that need to be achieved before an employee is entitled to protection against unfair dismissal. We start by looking at the hurdles to be overcome, such as the need to be below normal retirement age and have continuous service of one year for unfair dismissal protection. The ways in which a contract of employment can be ended are considered, such as termination with or without notice, by mutual agreement or by constructive dismissal. We then look at the importance of establishing the effective date of termination.

EXCLUSIONS AND QUALIFICATIONS

Every employee has the right not to be unfairly dismissed,[1] although there are a number of general exclusions and qualifications. Certain share fishers cannot lodge a complaint, but Crown employees are covered.[2]

Age limits[3]

No claim can be made if on or before the effective date of termination (see below) the individual had attained the normal retiring age for an employee in his or her position or was 65 years old.[4] However, there is no age limit if the reason or principal reason for dismissal is 'inadmissible' (see Chapter 13).[5] In *Secretary of State for Scotland* v *Taylor*[6] the Scottish Prison service was challenged after changing the retirement age of its employees to 55 years in order to save money, despite having an equal opportunities policy that excluded discrimination on the basis of age. The Court of Appeal accepted that this policy had become incorporated into the contract of employment, but that any retirement age was likely to have an age discrimination content and that this could not fetter the employer's discretion. In *Nothman* v *London Borough of Barnet*[7] the House of Lords ruled that there was one upper age-limit per person and that the 65 years restriction only applied when there is no normal retiring age fixed by the contract of employment. 'Normal retirement age' is the age at which employees in a group[8] can reasonably expect to be compelled to retire unless there is some special reason in a particular case for a different age to apply. In *Barclays Bank* v *O'Brien*[9] the Court of Appeal regarded a departure from the normal retirement age of 60 as being for a special reason. The exception was limited in time and was made for a relatively small category of employees in response to representations made on their behalf on the grounds of hardship.

Retirement at a variety of ages

The contractual retirement age does not conclusively fix the normal retirement age. Where there is a contractual retirement age there is a presumption that that age is the normal retirement age, but this presumption can be rebutted by evidence that there is in practice some higher age at which employees are regularly retired and which they have reasonably come to regard as their normal retirement age. According to the EAT, an employer cannot reduce the normal retirement age below the contractual age of retirement.[10] If the contractual retirement age is regularly departed from it is irrelevant that employment beyond that age was at management's discretion or that continued employment was subject to regular review.[11] Where there is evidence that employees retire at a variety of ages, there will be no normal retirement age and the statutory alternative applies. If there is no contractual retirement age, the correct approach is to consider whether there is evidence of a practice which establishes a normal retirement age.[12]

According to the Court of Appeal, in determining normal retirement age it is necessary to establish what, at the effective date of the termination of the employee's employment (see below), and on the basis of the facts then known, the age was at which employees of all ages in the employee's position could reasonably regard as the normal retirement age applicable to the group.[13] Thus the expectation is that of the group as a whole and need not be the universal expectation of each and every member of it.[14] Finally, it should be noted that the normal retirement age must be a definite age rather than an age-band.[15]

Continuous service

In order to complain of unfair dismissal one year's continuous service is required. This qualification does not apply if the reason or principal reason for dismissal was 'inadmissible' (see Chapter 13). Continuity is to be calculated up to the effective date of termination in accordance with sections 210–219 ERA 1996 (see Chapter 16). Employees who are wrongfully deprived of their statutory minimum entitlement to notice or receive a payment in lieu can add on that period of notice in ascertaining their length of service.[16] Longer contractual notice cannot be added, and it should be remembered that employees who are guilty of gross misconduct forfeit their entitlement to notice.[17] Two other exceptions should be noted. First, if an employee is dismissed rather than suspended on medical grounds, only one month's service is required.[18] Second, where unlawful discrimination is being alleged, no minimum period of service is needed because the case will be brought under the relevant anti-discrimination legislation rather than ERA 1996.

Contracting out

It is possible to contract out of the unfair dismissal and redundancy payment provisions in the following ways:

- An employee will be excluded if a dismissal procedures agreement has been designated by the Secretary of State as exempting those covered by it. An application must be made jointly by all the parties to the agreement and the Secretary of State must be satisfied about the matters listed in section 110(3) ERA 1996.

- An agreement to refrain from presenting a complaint will be binding if it has been reached after the involvement of a conciliation officer or satisfies the conditions regulating 'compromise agreements' (see Chapter 15).[19]

THE MEANING OF DISMISSAL

Apart from the lay-off and short-time provisions, an employee is to be treated as dismissed if:[20]

- the contract under which he or she is employed is terminated by the employer with or without notice, or
- a limited-term contract terminates by virtue of the limiting event without being renewed under the same contract, or
- the employee terminates the contract with or without notice in circumstances such that he or she is entitled to terminate it without notice by reason of the employer's conduct.

For redundancy purposes section 174 ERA 1996 provides that a contract is terminated by the employer's death unless the business is carried on by the personal representatives of the deceased. Similarly, if the employee dies after being given notice of dismissal, he or she is to be treated as dismissed.[21] Finally, a court order for the compulsory winding up of a company, the appointment of a receiver by a court and a major split in a partnership can all constitute a termination by the employer.

Termination by the employer with or without notice

It is vitally important not to confuse a warning of impending dismissal – for example, through the announcement of a plant closure – with an individual notice to terminate.[22] For the giving of notice to constitute a dismissal at law the actual date of termination must be ascertainable. Where an employer has given notice to terminate, an employee who gives counter-notice indicating that he or she wishes to leave before the employer's notice has expired is still to be regarded as dismissed.[23] However, in the case of redundancy this counter-notice must be given within the 'obligatory period' of the employer's notice. This 'obligatory period' is the minimum period which the employer is required to give by virtue of section 86(1) ERA 1996 (see Chapter 15) or the contract of employment.[24] Before the counter-notice is due to expire the employer can write to the employee and ask for it to be withdrawn, stating that unless this is done liability to make a redundancy payment will be contested.[25] If employees do not accede to such a request, a tribunal is empowered to determine whether they should receive the whole or part of the payment to which they would have been entitled. Tribunals decide what is just and equitable 'having regard to the reason for which the employee seeks to leave the employment and those for which the employer requires him to continue in it'.[26] Another possibility is that an employee leaves before the expiry of the employer's notice of termination for reasons of redundancy by mutual consent. This will not affect entitlement to a redundancy payment.[27]

Mutually agreed termination

A mutually agreed termination does not amount to a dismissal at law, although as a matter of policy tribunals will not find an agreement to terminate unless it is proved that the employee really did agree with full knowledge of the implications. Thus in *Hellyer Bros* v *Atkinson*[28] it was held that the employee was merely accepting the fact of his dismissal rather than agreeing to terminate his employment.

Whether a mutual agreement is void because of duress is a matter for the employment tribunal.[29] Moreover, where a provision for automatic termination is introduced by way of a variation to a subsisting contract, it may be declared void if its effect is to exclude or limit the operation of ERA 1996.[30] It is possible to have a mutual determination of a contract in a redundancy situation, and in *Birch and Humber* v *University of Liverpool*[31] the Court of Appeal held that there was no dismissal when the employer accepted the employees' applications for premature retirement. However, where an employer seeks volunteers for redundancy, those who are dismissed will be eligible for a payment despite their willingness to leave.[32]

Obviously, if people resign of their own volition there is no dismissal at law – yet if pressure has been applied, the situation is different, eg where the employee is given the choice of resigning or being dismissed. However, an invitation to resign must not be too imprecise, and in *Haseltine Lake & Co.* v *Dowler*[33] it was held that there was no dismissal when the employee was told that if he did not find a job elsewhere his employment would eventually be terminated. It would also appear that there is no dismissal when an employee resigns on terms offered by an employer's disciplinary subcommittee. In *Staffordshire County Council* v *Donovan*[34] the EAT stated:

> It seems to us that it would be most unfortunate if, in a situation where the parties are seeking to negotiate in the course of disciplinary proceedings and an agreed form of resignation is worked out by the parties, one of the parties should be able to say subsequently that the fact that the agreement was reached in the course of disciplinary proceedings entitles the employee thereafter to say that there was a dismissal.

The importance of the actual words used in resigning/dismissing

Problems can arise in determining whether the words used by an employee can properly be regarded as amounting to a resignation. Normally, where the words are unequivocal and are understood by the employer as a resignation, it cannot be said that there was no resignation because a reasonable employer would not have so understood the words. However, exceptions may be made in the case of immature employees, or of decisions taken in the heat of the moment or under pressure exerted by an employer.[35] An objective test of whether the employee intended to resign applies only where the language used is ambiguous or where it is not plain how the employer understood the words. In *Southern* v *Franks Charlesly*[36] the Court of Appeal decided that the words 'I am resigning' were unambiguous and indicated a present intention of resigning. Equally, doubts can arise in relation to expressions used by an employer, and in *Tanner* v *Kean*[37] it was decided that the words 'You're finished with me' were merely spoken in annoyance and amounted to a reprimand rather than a dismissal. The EAT has advised tribunals that in deciding whether the employer's words constituted a dismissal in law they should consider all the circumstances of the case to determine whether the words were intended to bring the contract to an end.

Where a limited-term contract terminates

According to section 235(2A), a limited term contract is one which terminates by virtue of a limiting event. There are three categories of limiting event: the expiry of a fixed term (see Chapter 4); the performance of a specific task; or the occurrence of an event or failure of an even to occur.[38]

Constructive dismissal

The situation in which an employee terminates the contract with or without notice in circumstances such that he or she is entitled to terminate it without notice by reason of the employer's conduct is commonly referred to as a 'constructive' dismissal. In these circumstances the employer's behaviour constitutes a repudiation of the contract and the employee accepts that repudiation by resigning.

Employees are entitled to treat themselves as constructively dismissed only if the employer is guilty of conduct which is a significant breach going to the root of the contract or which shows that the employer no longer intends to be bound by one or more of its essential terms. Thus a finding that there has been conduct which amounts to a breach of the implied term of trust and confidence will mean inevitably that the employee is entitled to claim constructive dismissal.[39] Whether the repudiatory conduct of a supervisor binds the employer depends on whether the acts were done in the course of the supervisor's employment.[40]

If employees continue for any length of time without leaving, they will be regarded as having elected to affirm the contract and will lose the right to treat themselves as discharged.[41] However, provided that employees make clear their objection to what is being done, they are not to be taken to have affirmed the contract by continuing to work and draw pay for a limited period of time.[42] Where the employer has allowed the employee time to make up his or her mind there is no need expressly to reserve the right to accept repudiation.[43] Even though a repudiatory breach of an express term has been waived it could still form part of a series of acts which cumulatively amounted to a breach of the employer's implied duty to show trust and confidence.[44] If there is merely a threat to repudiate, the employee is not to be treated as constructively dismissed unless there has been unequivocal acceptance of the repudiation before the threat is withdrawn.[45]

Breach of contract is a question of fact

It is not necessary to show that the employer intended to repudiate the contract. The tribunal's function is to look at the employer's conduct as a whole and determine whether its cumulative effect judged reasonably and sensibly is such that the employee cannot reasonably be expected to tolerate it. The mere fact that a party to a contract takes a view of its construction that is ultimately shown to be wrong does not of itself constitute repudiatory conduct. It has to be shown that he or she did not intend to be bound by the contract as properly construed.[46] According to the Court of Appeal, whether or not there is a fundamental breach of contract is a question of fact, so the EAT cannot substitute its decision for that of an employment tribunal unless the latter misdirected itself in law or the decision was one which no reasonable tribunal could reach.[47]

Demotion and change of duties

A physical assault, demotion, or significant change in job duties or place of work[48] can amount to a constructive dismissal. In relation to the place of work, it is now established that even an express right to transfer may be subject to an implied right to reasonable notice, because employers must not exercise their discretion in such a way as to prevent employees from being able to carry out their part of the contract.[49] However, this does not mean that an employer repudiates a contract simply by introducing a general rule with which a particular employee is unable to comply – for example, a no-smoking policy.[50]

In *Millbrook Furnishing Ltd* v *McIntosh*[51] the EAT accepted that 'if an employer, under the stresses of the requirements of his business, directs an employee to transfer to other suitable work on a purely temporary basis and at no diminution in wages, that may, in the ordinary case, not constitute a breach of contract'. Nevertheless, the EAT has also held that for a breach to go to the root of the contract it need not involve a substantial alteration to terms and conditions on a permanent basis. A substantial alteration is sufficient by itself.[52] As regards demotion, even where this is provided for within a disciplinary procedure it may amount to repudiation if it can be said that the punishment was grossly out of proportion to the offence.[53] Similarly issuing a final written warning in respect of a relatively minor incident could amount to a constructive dismissal.[54]

Issues of pay

It is clear that an employer is not entitled to alter the formula whereby wages are calculated, but whether a unilateral reduction in additional pay or fringe benefits is of sufficient materiality as to entitle the employee to resign is a matter of degree.[55] A failure to pay an employee's salary or wage is likely to constitute a fundamental breach if it is a deliberate act on the part of an employer rather than a mere breakdown in technology.[56] In *Gardner Ltd* v *Beresford*,[57] where the employee resigned because she had not received a pay increase for two years while others had, the EAT accepted that in most circumstances it would be reasonable to infer a term that the employer will not treat employees arbitrarily, capriciously or inequitably in the matter of remuneration. However, if a contract makes no reference at all to pay increases, it is impossible to say that there is an implied term that there will always be a pay rise.[58]

Many cases have been decided on the basis that the employer failed to display sufficient trust and confidence in the employee (see Chapter 3).[59] Thus unjustified accusations of theft, foul language or a refusal to act reasonably in dealing with grievances, matters of safety or incidents of harassment could all give rise to a claim of constructive dismissal. According to the EAT, whatever the respective actions of employer and employee at the time of termination, the relevant question is: who really terminated the contract? So when an employer falsely inveigled an employee to resign and take another job with the express purpose of avoiding liability for redundancy it was held that there was a dismissal at law.[60] Similarly, where an employer unilaterally imposes radically different terms of employment, these will be a dismissal under section 95(I)(a) or section 136(1)(a) ERA 1996 if, on an objective construction of the employer's conduct, there is a removal or withdrawal of the old contract. This was held to be the case in *Alcan Extrusions* v *Yates*[61] where the employer imposed a continuous rolling shift system in place of the traditional shifts provided for in contracts of employment.

THE EFFECTIVE AND RELEVANT DATE OF TERMINATION

Whether a person is qualified to complain of unfair dismissal or has presented a claim within the prescribed time period (see Chapter 15) must be answered by reference to the effective date of termination. Similarly, entitlement to a redundancy payment and the computation of it, together with the time-limit for submitting a claim, all depend on ascertaining the 'relevant date' of dismissal. Thus, as a matter of policy, employers should ensure that there is no doubt as to what constitutes the effective or relevant date. Sections 97 and 145 ERA 1996 provide that:

- where the contract is terminated by notice, the effective or relevant date is the date on which the notice expires even though the employee does not work out that notice.[62] Where the employee gives counter-notice, the effective date is when the employee ceased working in accordance with that notice.[63] If the employee has given counter-notice in accordance with section 136(3) ERA 1996, the 'relevant date' is the date the counter-notice expires. However, once an employee has been given notice of redundancy to take effect on a specified date, there is nothing to prevent the employer and employee from altering that date by mutual agreement.[64] In *West* v *Kneels Ltd*[65] the EAT concluded that oral notice starts to run the day after it is given. Logically, the same should be true of notice in writing

- where the contract is determined without notice, the effective or relevant date is the date on which the termination takes effect,[66] although there is no reason the date cannot be agreed between the parties, even if it is a date that is prior to the agreement itself.[67] The date of termination of people dismissed with payments in lieu of notice is the date on which they are told they are dismissed.[68] According to the Court of Appeal, where an employee is summarily dismissed during the course of a working day, and no question arises as to whether that dismissal constitutes a repudiation which the employee has not accepted, both the contract of employment and the status of employee cease at the moment when the dismissal is communicated to the employee.[69] Where employees are given notice of dismissal and told to work it, but the employer subsequently requires them to leave immediately, the effective or relevant date is the date when they stop working[70]

- where a limited-term contract terminates by virtue of the limiting event without being renewed under the same contract, the effective or relevant date is the date on which the termination takes effect

- where under the redundancy provisions a statutory trial period has been served, for the purpose of submitting a claim in time the relevant date is the day that the new or renewed contract terminated. This is to be assessed in accordance with the three points above.

It is worth noting that the form P45 has nothing to do with the date on which employment terminates.[71]

Whether in a particular case the words of dismissal evince an intention to terminate the contract at once or an intention to terminate it only at a future date depends on the construction of those words. Such construction should not be technical but reflect what an ordinary, reasonable employee would understand by the language used. Moreover, words should be construed in the light of the facts known to the employee at the time of notification.[72] If the language used is ambiguous, it is likely that tribunals will apply the principle that words should be interpreted most strongly against the person who uses them.[73] It should also be observed that where a dismissal has been communicated by letter, the contract of employment does not terminate until the employee has actually read the letter or had a reasonable opportunity of reading it.[74] What is the effective (or relevant) date where there is an appeal against dismissal? According to the House of Lords, unless there is a contractual provision to the contrary, the date of termination is to be ascertained in accordance with the above formula and is not the date on which the employee was informed that his or her appeal had failed.[75]

KEY POINTS

- Every employee has the right not to be unfairly dismissed, although there are a number of exclusions and qualifications, such as the need to be under normal retirement age and have one year's continuous service.

- An employee is to be treated as dismissed if his or her contract of employment is terminated by the employer with or without notice, a limited-term contract expires without renewal, or the employee terminates it as a result of the employer's conduct.

- Employees are entitled to treat themselves as constructively dismissed if the employer is guilty of conduct which is a significant breach going to the root of the contract of employment, or which shows that the employer no longer intends to be bound by one or more of its essential terms.

- In order to complain of unfair dismissal, one year's continuous service is required, unless the dismissal is for an inadmissible reason.

- Whether a person is qualified to complain of unfair dismissal or claim a redundancy payment must be answered by reference to the effective date of termination which, in the case of termination by notice, is the date on which notice expires, or otherwise the date on which termination takes effect.

NOTES

1   Section 94 ERA 1996
2   See sections 199(2) and 191 ERA 1996 respectively
3   See *Rutherford* v *Harvest Towncircle Ltd* (No 2) (2002) IRLR 768 (No. 2) (2003) IRLR 858 on possible indirect discrimination against men, and Chapter 7 for issues related to age discrimination in employment
4   Section 109(1) ERA 1996; 'Position' is defined in section 235(1) ERA 1996 as meaning the following matters taken as a whole: status, the nature of the work, and the terms and conditions of employment. See *Brookes* v *British Telecom* (1992) IRLR 67
5   See section 109(2) ERA 1996 and section 154 TULRCA 1992; for issues about whether the upper age-limit is discriminatory against men, see Chapter 7
6   (1999) IRLR 362
7   (1979) IRLR 35
8   See *Barber* v *Thames TV* (1992) IRLR 410
9   (1994) IRLR 580
10 See *Bratko* v *Walmsley* (1995) IRLR 629
11 See *Whittle* v *MSC* (1987) IRLR 441
12 See *Waite* v *GCHQ* (1983) IRLR 341
13 See *Brookes* v *British Telecom* (note 4); on identifying the particular group see *Barber* v *Thames TV* (note 8)
14 See *Barclays Bank* v *O'Brien* (1994) IRLR 580
15 See *Swaine* v *HSE* (1986) IRLR 205
16 Sections 97(2) and 213(1) ERA 1996; see *Staffordshire CC* v *Secretary of State* (1989) IRLR 117
17 See *Lanton Leisure* v *White* (1987) IRLR 119
18 Section 108(2) ERA 1996
19 Section 203(2)(e) and (f) ERA 1996
20 Sections 95 and 136 ERA 1996
21 See section 176 ERA 1996
22 See *Doble* v *Firestone Tyre* (1981) IRLR 300
23 Section 95(2) ERA 1996 and *Ready Case Ltd* v *Jackson* (1981) IRLR 312
24 Section 136(4) ERA 1996
25 Section 142(2) ERA 1996
26 Section 142(3) ERA 1996

27 See *CPS Recruitment Ltd* v *Bowen* (1982) IRLR 54
28 (1994) IRLR 88
29 See *Logan Salton* v *Durham CC* (1989) IRLR 99
30 See *Igbo* v *Johnson Matthey* (1986) IRLR 215
31 (1985) IRLR 165; see also *Scott* v *Coalite* (1988) IRLR 131
32 *Lassman* v *De Vere Hotel* (2003) ICR 44
33 (1981) IRLR 25
34 (1981) IRLR 108; see also *Logan Salton* v *Durham CC* (note 30)
35 See *Kwik-Fit* v *Lineham* (1992) IRLR 156
36 (1981) IRLR 278
37 (1978) IRLR 110
38 Section 235 (2B) ERA 1996
39 See *Morrow* v *Safeway Stores* (2002) IRLR 9
40 See *Hilton Hotels* v *Protopapa* (1990) IRLR 316
41 See *Wilton* v *Cornwall Health Authority* (1993) IRLR 482
42 See *Cantor Fitzgerald* v *Bird* (2002) IRLR 867
43 See *Bliss* v *South East Thames Regional Health Authority* (1985) IRLR 308
44 See *Lewis* v *Motorworld Garages* (1985) IRLR 465
45 See *Harrison* v *Norwest Holst* (1985) IRLR 240
46 See *Brown* v *JBD Engineering Ltd* (1993) IRLR 568
47 See *Martin* v *MBS Fastenings* (1983) IRLR 198
48 See *Aparau* v *Iceland Frozen Foods* (1996) IRLR 119
49 See *White* v *Reflecting Roadstuds* (1991) IRLR 332
50 See *Dryden* v *Greater Glasgow Health Board* (1992) IRLR 469
51 (1981) IRLR 309
52 See *McNeil* v *Crimin Ltd* (1984) IRLR 179
53 See *Cawley* v *South Wales Electricity Board* (1985) IRLR 89
54 *Cole Ltd* v *Sheridan* (2003) IRLR 52
55 See *Rigby* v *Ferodo Ltd* (note 49)
56 See *Cantor Fitzgerald International* v *Callaghan* (1999) IRLR 234
57 (1978) IRLR 63
58 See *Murco Petroleum* v *Forge* (1987) IRLR 50
59 See *Morrow* v *Safeway Stores plc* (2002) IRLR 9
60 *Caledonian Mining Ltd* v *Bassett* (1987) IRLR 165; on possible fraudulent misrepresentation see *Post Office* v *Sanhotra* (2000) IRLR 866
61 (1996) IRLR 327
62 See *TBA Industrial Products Ltd* v *Morland* (1982) IRLR 331
63 See *Thompson* v *GEC Avionics* (1991) IRLR 448
64 See *Mowlem Ltd* v *Watson* (1990) IRLR 500
65 (1986) IRLR 430
66 This principle was applied to a constructive dismissal in *BMK Ltd* v *Logue* (1993) ICR 601
67 See *Lambert* v *Croydon College* (1999) IRLR 346
68 See *R. Cort & Son Ltd* v *Charman* (1981) IRLR 437
69 See *Octavius Atkinson Ltd* v *Morris* (1989) IRLR 158
70 See *Stapp* v *Shaftesbury Society* (1982) IRLR 326
71 See *Leech* v *Preston BC* (1985) IRLR 337
72 See *London Borough of Newham* v *Ward* (1985) IRLR 509
73 See *Chapman* v *Letheby & Christopher Ltd* (1981) IRLR 440
74 See *McMaster* v *Manchester Airport plc* (1998) IRLR 112
75 *West Midlands Co-op Ltd* v *Tipton* (1986) IRLR 112; see also *Drage* v *Governors of Greenford High School* (2000) IRLR 314

Unfair Dismissal (2)

CHAPTER 13

OVERVIEW

We continue our examination of the rules concerning unfair dismissal by looking at the procedures to be followed after an employee has established that he or she qualifies to make a claim. We begin by looking at the burden on employers to show the reason for dismissal, and then consider those reasons that are automatically unfair. We study the potentially fair reasons of capability or qualifications, conduct, statutory ban and some other substantial reason. We consider the particular rules that apply to dismissals during industrial action and the amendments made by the Employment Relations Act 1999. We look at the ACAS Code of Practice on Disciplinary and Grievance Procedures as well as the advisory handbook on discipline and grievances at work. Finally, we outline the statutory dismissal and disciplinary procedures introduced by the EA 2002.

GIVING A REASON FOR DISMISSAL

Once employees have proved that they were dismissed, the burden shifts to the employer to show the reason, or, if there was more than one, the principal reason, for the dismissal and that it falls within one of the following categories.[1]

- It relates to the capacity or qualifications of the employee for performing work of the kind which he or she was employed to do.
- It relates to the conduct of the employee.
- The employee was redundant.
- The employee could not continue to work in the position held without contravention, either on the employee's part or that of the employer, of a duty or restriction imposed by or under a statute.
- There was some other substantial reason of such a kind as to justify the dismissal of an employee holding the position which the employee held.

Several points need to be made at this stage:

- Where no reason is given by the employer, a dismissal will be unfair simply because the statutory burden has not been discharged. Equally, if a reason is engineered in order to effect dismissal because the real reason would not be acceptable, the employer will fail because the underlying principal reason is not within section 98(1) or (2) ERA 1996.[2]
- The fact that an employer has inaccurately described the reason for dismissal is not necessarily fatal, for it is the tribunal's task to discover what reason actually motivated the employer at the time of dismissal.[3] That the correct approach is the subjective one has been confirmed by the Court of Appeal: 'A reason for the dismissal of an employee is a set of facts known to the employer, or it may be of beliefs held by him, which causes him to dismiss the employee.'[4] Subsequently the Court of Appeal has been prepared to attribute a reason for dismissal even where the employers had argued throughout the case that they had not dismissed but the employee had resigned.[5]

- The reason for dismissal must have existed and been known to the employer at the time of dismissal, which makes it impossible, for example, to rely on subsequently discovered misconduct.[6] The reason itself may be an anticipated event. For example, if an employee is subject to a long period of notice, it is possible to give notice in anticipation of a decision, giving what the employer expects to happen as a reason for the decision.[7]

- Section 107 ERA 1996 provides that in determining the reason for dismissal, or whether it was sufficient to dismiss, a tribunal cannot take account of any pressure, in the form of industrial action or a threat of it, which was exercised on the employer to secure the employee's dismissal. It is not necessary that those exerting the pressure explicitly sought the dismissal of the employee: the test is whether it could be foreseen that the pressure would be likely to result in dismissal.[8]

Employers' duty to provide a statement of reasons for dismissal

According to section 92 ERA 1996, a person who has been continuously employed for one year[9] and has been dismissed or is under notice of dismissal has the right to be supplied with a written statement giving particulars of the reasons for dismissal. The employer must provide the statement within 14 days of a specific request being made. In *Gilham* v *Kent County Council*[10] the Court of Appeal held that the Council had responded adequately by referring the employee's legal representative to two previous letters in which the reasons for dismissal were fully set out, enclosing copies of those letters and stating that their contents contained the reasons for dismissal. A claim may be presented to an employment tribunal on the grounds that the employer unreasonably failed to provide such a statement or that the particulars given were inadequate or untrue. However, section 92 merely obliges employers to indicate truthfully the reasons they were relying on when they dismissed. Only if an unfair dismissal claim is brought will a tribunal have to examine whether the reasons given justify dismissal.[11] The same time-limit applies as for unfair dismissal claims (see Chapter 15).

The test for determining the reasonableness of an employer's failure is objective. Thus, where the employer maintains that there was no dismissal in law but the tribunal finds that there was, it must then decide whether there was an unreasonable failure to supply a statement.[12] If the complaint is well-founded, a tribunal may make a declaration as to what it finds the employer's reasons were for dismissing and must order that the employee receive two weeks' pay from the employer.[13] Perhaps the most important aspect of this section is that such a statement is admissible in evidence in any proceedings. This means that an employee who detects any inconsistency between the particulars given and the reasons offered as a defence to an unfair dismissal claim – eg on the employer's 'notice of appearance' – can exploit the situation to the full.

AUTOMATICALLY UNFAIR DISMISSAL

In certain circumstances a dismissal will be unfair because the reason for it was 'inadmissible'. A dismissal is thus automatically unfair if the reason for it related to any of the following:

- the assertion of a statutory right (see below)
- trade union membership or activities, or non-union membership (see Chapter 20)
- pregnancy or maternity (see Chapter 9)
- certain health and safety grounds (see below)
- certain shop workers and betting workers who refuse to work on a Sunday[14]
- workers dismissed for refusing to comply with a requirement which is in contravention of the WT Regulations 1998 (see Chapter 10)[15]
- the reason, or the principal reason, for the dismissal is that the employee made a protected disclosure (see Chapter 3)[16]

- the employee is dismissed for trying to enforce the national minimum wage[17]

- the proposed or actual performance of any of the functions of an employee trustee of a pension scheme[18]

- the proposed or actual performance of any functions or activities as an employee representative or candidate[19]

- the dismissal of a worker for exercising rights in relation to the statutory recognition of a trade union (see Chapter 19)

- the dismissal of a worker within eight weeks of taking part in protected industrial action (see below)

- the application of the Tax Credit Act 1999.[20]

- the exercise of a right to request a contract variation (see chapter 8 on flexible working).[21]

- the exercise of rights under the Part-Time Workers Regulations 2000 and Fixed-term Employees Regulations 2002[22]

- (when Section 98A ERA 1996 comes into force) a statutory dismissal and disciplinary procedure has not been completed and this is wholly or mainly attributable to the failure by the employer to comply with its requirements

Additionally, if any of the above 'inadmissible' reasons was used to select a person for redundancy, dismissal will also be unfair (see below). Other unfair reasons for dismissal are those connected to transfers of undertakings (see Chapter 16); to the anti-discrimination provisions, which stipulate that it is unlawful to discriminate on the prohibited grounds by way of dismissal (see Chapter 6); to the Rehabilitation of Offenders Act 1974, which states that 'a conviction which has become spent ... shall not be a proper ground for dismissing';[23] and finally to section 4(2) of the Disability Discrimination Act 1995, which states that it is unlawful to discriminate against disabled persons by dismissing them (see Chapter 7).

Asserting statutory rights

As regards the assertion of statutory rights, employees are protected if they have brought proceedings against the employer to enforce a 'relevant' statutory right and have alleged that the employer has infringed such a right. The 'relevant' statutory rights are:

- any right conferred by ERA 1996 which may be the subject of a complaint to an employment tribunal

- minimum notice rights under section 86 ERA 1996

- certain rights relating to the unlawful deduction of union contributions from pay, action short of dismissal on union membership grounds, time off for union duties and activities and union learning representatives

- rights afforded by the WT Regulations 1998[21a]

- rights afforded by the TULRCA 1992 in relation to statutory recognition of trade unions.

It should be noted that employees are protected irrespective of whether they qualify for the right that has been asserted or whether the right was actually infringed. All that has to be demonstrated is that the employee's claim was made in good faith.[24]

Health and safety

In relation to health and safety, section 100 ERA 1996 provides that a dismissal is unfair if the reason for it was that the employee:

- carried out, or proposed to carry out, activities designated by the employer in connection with preventing or reducing risks to the health and safety of employees

- performed, or proposed to perform, any of his or her functions as a safety representative or a member of a safety committee

- took part or proposed to take part in consultation with the employer pursuant to the HSCE Regulations 1996 (see Chapter 9) or in an election of representatives of employee safety within the meaning of those Regulations

- where there was no safety representative or committee or it was not reasonably practicable to raise the matter in that way, brought to the employer's attention, by reasonable means, circumstances connected with his or her work which he or she reasonably believed were harmful or potentially harmful to health and safety[25]

- left or proposed to leave, or refused to return to (while the danger persisted), his or her place of work or any dangerous part of the workplace, in circumstances of danger which he or she reasonably believed to be serious and imminent and which he or she could not reasonably have been expected to avert

- took, or proposed to take, appropriate steps to protect himself or herself or other persons, in circumstances of danger which he or she reasonably believed to be serious and imminent. Whether those steps were 'appropriate' must be judged by reference to all the circumstances, including the employee's knowledge and the facilities and advice available at the time. A dismissal will not be regarded as unfair if the employer can show that it was, or would have been, so negligent for the employee to take the steps which he or she took, or proposed to take, that a reasonable employer might have dismissed on these grounds.

POTENTIALLY FAIR REASONS FOR DISMISSAL

Capability or qualifications

According to section 98(3) ERA 1996, 'capability' is to be assessed by reference to 'skill, aptitude, health or any other physical or mental quality', and it has been held that an employee's inflexibility or lack of adaptability came within his or her aptitude and mental qualities.[26] 'Qualifications' means 'any degree, diploma, or other academic, technical or professional qualification relevant to the position which the employee held'. In *Blue Star Ltd* v *Williams*[27] it was held that a mere licence, permit or authorisation is not such a qualification unless it is substantially concerned with the aptitude or ability of the person to do the job.

For our purposes it is convenient to consider capability in terms of competence and ill health. As regards competence, the ACAS advisory handbook *Discipline and Grievances at Work*[28] recommends that the following principles should be observed when employment commences:

- The standard of work required should be explained and employees left in no doubt about what is expected of them. Special attention should be paid to ensuring that standards are understood by employees whose English is limited and by young persons with little experience of working life.

- Where job descriptions are prepared they should accurately convey the main purpose and scope of each job and the tasks involved.

- Employees should be made aware of the conditions which attach to any probation period.

- The consequences of any failure to meet the required standards should be explained.

- Where an employee is promoted, the consequences of failing to 'make the grade' in the new job should be explained.

It almost goes without saying that proper training and supervision are essential to the achievement of satisfactory performance and that performance should be discussed regularly with employees. Paragraphs 22–25 of the ACAS Code of Practice on Disciplinary and Grievance Procedures make the following recommendations about dealing with poor performance:

> 22. Individuals have a contractual responsibility to perform to a satisfactory level and should be given every help and encouragement to do so. Employers have a responsibility for setting realistic and measurable standards of performance and for explaining these standards carefully to employees.
>
> 23. Where workers are found to be failing to perform to the required standard the matter should be investigated before any action is taken. Where the reason for substandard performance is found to be a lack of the required skills the worker should, wherever practicable, be assisted through training or coaching and given reasonable time to reach the required standard. Where the substandard performance is due to negligence or lack of application on the part of the worker, some form of disciplinary action will normally be appropriate. Failures to perform to the required standard can be dealt with either through the normal disciplinary procedure or through a separate capability procedure.
>
> 24. A worker should not normally be dismissed because of a failure to perform to the required standard unless warnings and an opportunity to improve (with reasonable targets and time scales) have been given. However, where a worker commits a single error due to negligence and the actual or potential consequences of that error are, or could be, extremely serious, warnings may not be appropriate. The disciplinary or capability procedure should indicate that summary dismissal action may be taken in such circumstances.
>
> 25. Employers may need to have special arrangements for dealing with poor performance of workers on short-term contracts or new workers during their probationary period.

Paragraphs 19–21 of the same Code of Practice make the following recommendations about dealing with absence:

> 19. When dealing with absence a distinction should always be made between absences on grounds of medically certificated illness, both physical and mental, and those which may call for disciplinary action. All unexpected absences should be investigated promptly and the worker asked to give an explanation. If, after investigation, it appears that there were no acceptable reasons for the absence the matter should be treated as a conduct issue and be dealt with under the disciplinary procedure. It

is important that the worker is told what improvement in attendance is expected and warned of the likely consequences if this does not happen.

20. Where the absence is due to medically certificated illness the issue becomes one of capability and employers should take a sympathetic and considerate approach to these sorts of absences. In deciding what action to take in these cases employers will need to take into account the likelihood of an improvement in health and subsequent attendance (based where appropriate on professional medical advice), the availability of suitable alternative work, the effect of past and likely future absences on the organisation, how similar situations have been handled in the past and whether the illness is a result of a disability as defined in the Disability Discrimination Act 1995. Even though employers may have a separate procedure for dealing with illness any hearing which could result in a formal warning or some other action will attract the statutory right of accompaniment.

21. In cases of extended sick leave both statutory and contractual issues will need to be addressed and specialist advice may be necessary.

Where an employee is absent owing to long-term illness the ACAS advisory handbook recommends that the following procedure be invoked.

- the employee should be contacted periodically and in turn should maintain regular contact with the employer[29]
- the employee should be kept fully informed if employment is at risk
- before applying to an employee's doctor for a medical report, the employee must notify the employee in writing that it is proposed to make the application, and secure the employee's consent in writing
- on the basis of the GP's report the employer should consider whether alternative work is available
- the employer is not expected to create a special job for the employee concerned, nor to be a medical expert, but to take action on the basis of the medical evidence
- where there is reasonable doubt about the nature of the illness or injury, the employee should be asked if he or she would agree to be examined by a doctor to be appointed by the company
- where an employee refuses to co-operate in providing medical evidence or to undergo an independent medical examination, the employee should be told in writing that a decision will be taken on the basis of the information available and that it could result in dismissal
- where the employee is allergic to a product used in the workplace, the employer should consider remedial action or a transfer to alternative work

- where the employee's job can no longer be kept open and no suitable alternative work is available, the employee should be informed of the likelihood of dismissal

- where dismissal action is taken, the employee should be given the period of notice to which he or she is entitled and informed of any right of appeal.

Medical evidence of ill health is not always required

In cases of intermittent absences owing to ill health, there is no obligation on an employer to call medical evidence. According to the EAT, an employer has to have regard to the whole history of employment and to take into account a range of factors including: the nature of the illness and the likelihood of its recurrence; the lengths of absences compared with the intervals of good health; the employer's need for that particular employee; the impact of the absences on the rest of the workforce; and the extent to which the employee was made aware of his or her position. There is no principle that the mere fact that the employee is fit at the time of dismissal makes that dismissal unfair.[30]

In deciding whether an employer acted fairly in dismissing, tribunals must determine as a matter of fact what consultation, if any, was necessary or desirable in the known circumstances; what consultation took place; and whether that consultation process was adequate in the circumstances.[31] Thus in *Eclipse Blinds v Wright*[32] the Court of Appeal ruled that it was not unfair to dismiss without consultation where the employer was genuinely concerned about giving the employee information about her health of which she seemed unaware.

Four further points need to be made:

- An employee's incapability need only 'relate to' the performance of contractual duties; there is no requirement to show that the performance of all those duties has been affected.[33]

- Although employees who are sick will hope to remain employed at least until their contractual sick pay entitlement (if any) is exhausted, this does not mean that a person cannot be dismissed before the period of sick pay has elapsed. Equally, it will be unfair to dismiss simply because the sick pay period has expired.

- If the employer's treatment of the employee has caused the unfitness to work, there could be a finding of unfair dismissal.[34]

- An employee who has become incapable of work may have to be treated as a person with a disability within the meaning of section 1 of the Disability Discrimination Act 1995 (see Chapter 7).

Conduct

It is the function of tribunals to decide not whether misconduct is gross or criminal but whether the employer has, in the circumstances of the case, acted reasonably in dismissing. Thus in *John Lewis plc v Coyne*[35] it was held that the employer had acted unfairly in dismissing the employee for using the company telephone for making personal calls without investigating the seriousness of the offence. There is no necessary inference that because an employee is guilty of gross misconduct in relation to his or her actual employment, he or she must necessarily be considered unsuitable for any employment whatsoever.[36] Clearly there will be cases where the misconduct is sufficiently serious that an employee can be dismissed without warning, and paragraph 7 of the ACAS Code of Practice on Disciplinary and Grievance Procedures (2000) advocates that employees should be given 'a clear indication of the type of conduct which may warrant summary dismissal'.

Employers must clarify what conduct leads to summary dismissal

According to the EAT, disciplinary rules which fail to follow the ACAS Code in specifying those offences that constitute gross misconduct and justify dismissal at the first breach will be defective. In *Lock v Cardiff*

Railway Company Ltd[37] a train conductor was dismissed for gross misconduct when he asked a 16-year-old to leave the train because he did not have a valid ticket or sufficient money to pay the excess fare. The employer's disciplinary code did not specify which offences would be regarded as gross misconduct that would result in dismissal for the first offence. As a result the EAT held that no reasonable tribunal properly directing itself could have concluded that the dismissal was fair.

Fighting is an example of an area where it is not necessary to state that such behaviour will be regarded very gravely, since the courts have decided that whether or not to dismiss for this reason is essentially a matter for the employer. The test is what would be the reaction of a reasonable employer in the circumstances. Thus if without proper inquiry an employer implements a policy of dismissing any employee who struck another, there could be a finding of unfairness.[38] Similarly, false clocking or claims in respect of hours done are serious offences which can justify dismissal without a warning if the employer has had due regard to all the circumstances.[39]

Disobedience: when it is and is not 'reasonable'

As a general rule, if an order is lawful, a refusal to obey it will be a breach of contract and amount to misconduct even though similar refusals have been condoned in the past. Nevertheless, in disobedience cases the primary factor to be considered is whether the employee is acting reasonably in refusing to carry out an instruction.[40] Acknowledging that employers are obliged to issue instructions in order to ensure compliance with health and safety legislation, tribunals have readily accepted that non-compliance with safety rules or procedures constitute sufficient grounds for dismissal.

Dismissal arising from issues of competition

The intention to set up in competition with the employer is not in itself a breach of the implied duty of loyalty. Unless the employer has reasonable grounds for believing that the employee has done or is about to do some wrongful act, dismissal will not be justified.[41] Thus in *Marshall* v *Industrial Systems Ltd*[42] the EAT held that it was reasonable to dismiss a managing director after discovering that with another manager he was planning to set up in competition and take away the business of their best client, and that he tried to induce another key employee to join them in that venture.

Suspicion of dishonesty

Theft of an employer's property will amount to a fair reason for dismissal; far more difficult to handle are cases of *suspected* dishonesty. According to the Court of Appeal, fairness demands that serious allegations of dishonesty be put with sufficient formality and at an early enough stage to provide a full opportunity for answer.[43] The same court has approved of the approach taken in *British Home Stores* v *Burchell*,[44] where it was stated that tribunals had to decide whether the employer entertained a reasonable suspicion amounting to a belief in the guilt of the employee at that time. There are three elements to this:

- the employer must establish the fact of that belief
- the employer must show that there were reasonable grounds upon which to sustain that belief
- at the stage at which the belief was formed the employer must have carried out as much investigation into the matter as was reasonable in the circumstances.

Thus the question to be determined is not whether, by an objective standard, the employer's belief that the employee was guilty of the misconduct was well-founded but whether the employer believed that the employee was guilty and was entitled so to believe having regard to the investigation conducted.[45] If these requirements are met, it is irrelevant that the employee is acquitted of criminal charges or that they are dropped.

Where there is a reasonable suspicion that one or more employees within a group have acted dishonestly, it is not necessary for the employer to identify which of them acted dishonestly.[46] Thus, provided certain conditions are satisfied, an employer who cannot identify which member of a group was responsible for an act can fairly dismiss the whole group, even where it is probable that not all were guilty of the act. These conditions are:

- the act must be such that if committed by an identified individual it would justify dismissal
- the employer had made a sufficiently thorough investigation with appropriate procedures
- as a result of that investigation the employer reasonably believed that more than one person could have committed the act
- the employer had acted reasonably in identifying the group of employees who could have committed the act and each member of the group was individually capable of doing so
- between the members of the group the employer could not reasonably identify the individual perpetrator.

The fact that one or more of the group is not dismissed does not necessarily render the dismissal of the remainder unfair, provided the employer is able to show solid and sensible grounds for differentiating between members of the group.[47]

In certain cases it will be reasonable to rely on the results of extensive police investigation rather than carry out independent inquiries.[48] Similarly, where an employee admits dishonesty there is little scope for the kind of investigation referred to in *Burchell*'s case. Where the probability of guilt is less apparent, the safer course may be to suspend until any criminal proceedings have been completed.[49] Whether a conviction forms an adequate basis for dismissal will depend to some extent on the nature of the crime. Clearly, there may be cases where the offence is trivial and dismissal would be unreasonable.[50]

Employers' contact with employees under criminal investigation

The fact that employees have been charged with a criminal offence does not prevent the employer communicating with them or their representatives to discuss the matter. What needs to be discussed is not so much the alleged offence as the action the employer is proposing to take. If the employee chooses not to give a statement to the employer, the latter is entitled to consider whether the evidence available is strong enough to justify dismissal.[51] However, it will not always be wrong to dismiss before a belief in guilt has been established, because involvement in an alleged criminal offence often involves a serious breach of duty or discipline. Even when charged by the police with a criminal offence, failure to give employees an opportunity to explain themselves may render the dismissal unfair.[52]

Offences committed outside the workplace

In the context of unfair dismissal, conduct may mean actions of such a nature, whether done in the course of employment or outside, that reflect in some way on the employer–employee relationship.[53] Thus it may cover the wilful concealment of convictions which are not 'spent', criminal offences outside employment, such as stealing or gross indecency, or even 'moonlighting'. Finally, in an appropriate case it may be unfair to dismiss without first considering whether the employee could be offered some other job.[54]

Statutory ban

Section 98(2)(d) ERA 1996 states that if it would be unlawful to continue to work in the position which the employee held, there is a valid reason for dismissing. In *Bouchaala* v *Trust House Forte*[55] the EAT held that the absence of the words 'related to' in this section were significant, and that a genuine but erroneous belief is insufficient for these purposes. Again, a tribunal must be satisfied that the requirements of section 98(4)

ERA 1996 have been met. Thus the loss of a permit or licence may fall within section 98(2)(d) ERA 1996, but in deciding what is reasonable, attention will focus on whether the legal ban is permanent or temporary. If the former, an employer might be expected to consider the feasibility of redeployment, and if the latter, short-term alternative work might be offered. Whether such measures should be taken will depend on the type of business and the employee's work record. Of course, in some circumstances it may be possible for employees to continue in their normal job by making special arrangements – eg a sales representative who has been disqualified from driving may be prepared to hire a driver at his or her own expense in order to remain in employment.

Some other substantial reason

Section 98(1)(b) ERA 1996 was included in the legislative scheme so as to give tribunals the discretion to accept as a fair reason for dismissal something that would not conveniently fit into any of the other categories. It covers such diverse matters as dismissal for having been sentenced to imprisonment,[56] being dismissed as manager of a public house because a partner had resigned from jointly holding the position,[57] dismissal for refusing to sign an undertaking not to compete,[58] or dismissal because the employer's best customer was unwilling to accept the particular individual.[59] However, in *Wadley* v *Eager Electrical*[60] the EAT decided that an employee's dismissal on the grounds that there had been breaches of trust by his wife during her employment with the employer did not amount to a substantial reason.

According to the Court of Appeal, tribunals have to decide whether the reason established by the employer falls within the category of reasons which *could* justify the dismissal of an employee holding the position that the employee held.[61] Employers cannot claim that a reason for dismissal is substantial if it is whimsical or capricious. Nevertheless, if they can show that they genuinely believed a reason to be fair and that they had it in mind at the time of dismissal,[62] this would bring the case within section 98(1)(b) ERA 1996. It may be held that the reason was substantial even though more sophisticated opinion can be adduced to demonstrate that the belief had no scientific foundation.[63] The notion of genuine belief has also been invoked to assist employers who are unable to rely on any other reasons for dismissal owing to an error of fact. Thus this subsection could be relied on where an employee was dismissed as a result of the employer's mistaken belief that a work permit was needed.[64]

Dismissal for refusing new terms arising from a business reorganisation

'Some other substantial reason' has frequently provided a convenient context in which employees have been dismissed as a result of a re-organisation of the business. The Court of Appeal has taken the view that it is not necessary for an employer to show that in the absence of a reorganisation there would be a total business disaster. It is sufficient if there is a sound business reason, which means only that there is a reason which management thinks on reasonable grounds is sound.[65] If the employer can satisfy a tribunal that a certain policy has evolved which was thought to have discernible advantages, then dismissal in accordance with that policy can be said to be for 'some other substantial reason'.

Where an employee refuses to agree changes consequent upon a re-organisation, the test to be applied by tribunals is not simply whether the terms offered were those which a reasonable employer could offer. Looking at the employer's offer alone would exclude from scrutiny everything that happened between the time the offer was made and the dismissal – eg a potentially significant factor is whether other employees accepted the offer.[66] Equally, there is no principle of law that if new contractual terms are much less favourable to an employee than the previous ones, dismissal for refusing to accept them will be unfair unless the business reasons are so pressing that it is vital for the survival of the business that the revised terms are accepted. In *Farrant* v *The Woodroffe School*[67] an employee was dismissed for refusing to accept organisational changes. The employer mistakenly believed that the employee was obliged to accept a new job description and that the dismissal was therefore lawful. The EAT held that dismissal for refusing to obey an unlawful order was not necessarily unfair. Of importance was not the lawfulness or otherwise of the employer's instructions but the overall question of reasonableness. In this case it was not unreasonable for the employer to act on professional advice, even if that advice was wrong. Tribunals will examine an employer's motive for introducing changes in order to ensure that they are not being imposed arbitrarily.[68] The reasonable employer will explore all the alternatives to dismissal, but – like consultation with trade unions and the individual concerned – such a consideration is only one of the factors that must be taken into account under section 98(4) ERA 1996 (see below).

INDUSTRIAL ACTION AND LACK OF JURISDICTION

Protected industrial action

Section 238A TULRCA states that a dismissal will be unfair if the reason is that the employee took part in protected industrial action[69] and one of three situations applies:

- the dismissal takes place within a period of eight weeks from the day on which the employee first took part in the protected industrial action
- the dismissal takes place after that eight-week period and the employee had ceased to take part in protected industrial action before the end of that period
- the dismissal takes place after the end of the period and the employee has not ceased to take part in the protected industrial action before the end of that period and the employer has not taken such procedural steps as would have been reasonable for the purpose of resolving the dispute to which the action relates.

In deciding whether an employer has taken those steps mentioned in the last point above, tribunals will look at whether the employer or union:[70]

1 has followed procedures established by a collective agreement
2 had offered or agreed to start or resume negotiations after the start of the protected industrial action
3 unreasonably refused a request that conciliation services be used
4 unreasonably refused a request that mediation services be used.

The fact that employees are in breach of their duty to attend work is relevant to the question of whether they are taking part in a strike but it is not an essential ingredient. Thus employees who are off sick or on holiday could be held to be taking part in a strike if they associated themselves with it – for example, by attending a picket line.[71] By way of contrast, if sick employees merely wish their colleagues well, this may be regarded as supportive but would not amount to taking part in industrial action.[72]

An offer of re-engagement refers to an offer (made either by the employer, a successor or an associated employer) to re-engage either in the job which the employee held immediately before the date of dismissal, or in a different job which would be 'reasonably suitable in his case'.[73] In *Williams* v *National Theatre*[74] it was decided that treating employees who had been on strike as having received a second warning nevertheless constituted an offer to re-engage in the same job. However, a job may have conditions attached to it which are so disadvantageous compared to the position before the dismissal that it cannot realistically be suggested that the employee is being offered re-employment.

Unofficial action

The ERel Act 1999 did not change the position with regard to those taking part in unofficial action. By virtue of section 237 TULRCA 1992 employees cannot complain of unfair dismissal if at the time of dismissal they were taking part in an unofficial strike or other unofficial industrial action. For these purposes, a strike or other industrial action will be treated as unofficial unless the employee:

- is a union member and the action is authorised or endorsed by that union, or
- is not a union member but there are among those taking part in the industrial action members of a union by which the action has been authorised or endorsed within the meaning of section 20(2) TULRCA 1992 (see Chapter 21).

A strike or other industrial action will not be regarded as unofficial if none of those taking part in it is a union member. However, employees who were union members when they began to take industrial action will continue to be treated as such even if they have subsequently ceased to be union members.[75]

Section 237(4) states that the issue of whether or not the action is unofficial is to be determined by reference to the facts at the time of the dismissal. Nevertheless, where the action is repudiated in accordance with section 21 TULRCA 1992 (see Chapter 21), the industrial action is not to be treated as unofficial before the end of the next working day after the repudiation has taken place. According to the EAT, this means midnight on the following working day.[76] On the absence of statutory immunity for acts in support of those dismissed for taking unofficial action see Chapter 21.

REASONABLENESS IN THE CIRCUMSTANCES

Where the employer has given a valid reason for dismissal, the determination of the question whether the dismissal was fair or unfair:

- depends on whether in the circumstances (including the size and administrative resources of the employer's undertaking) the employer acted reasonably or unreasonably in treating it as a sufficient reason for dismissing the employee, and
- will be in accordance with equity and the substantial merits of the case.[77]

However, when section 98A ERA 1996 comes into force, if the requirements of the statutory dismissal procedure have been met, the failure to follow a more sophisticated procedure will not be treated "as by itself making the employer's action unreasonable if he shows that he would have dismissed the employee if he had followed the procedure".

As a matter of law, a reason cannot be treated as sufficient where it has not been established as true or that there were reasonable grounds on which the employer could have concluded that it was true.[78] Under section 98(4) ERA 1996, tribunals must take account of the wider circumstances. In addition to the employer's business needs, attention must be paid to the personal attributes of the employee – for example, seniority and previous work record. Thus when all the relevant facts are considered, a dismissal may be deemed unfair notwithstanding the fact that the disciplinary rules specified that such behaviour would result in immediate dismissal.[79] Conversely, employers may act reasonably in dismissing even though they have breached an employee's contract.[80]

In appropriate cases the test of fairness must be interpreted, so far as possible, compatibly with the European Convention on Human Rights.[81]

Employers will be expected to treat employees in similar circumstances in a similar way. The requirement that the employer must act consistently between all employees means that an employer should consider truly comparable cases which were known about or ought to have been known about. Nevertheless, the overriding principle seems to be that each case must be considered on its own facts and with the freedom to consider both aggravating factors and mitigating circumstances.[82] The words 'equity and the substantial merits' also allow tribunals to apply their knowledge of good industrial relations practice and to ensure that there has been procedural fairness (see below).[83]

According to the Court of Appeal, employment tribunals should not ask themselves whether they would have done what the employer did in the circumstances. Their function is merely to assess the employer's decision to dismiss and decide if it falls within a range of responses that a reasonable employer could have taken.[84] Even so, the 'range of reasonable responses' test does not mean that such a high degree of unreasonableness must be shown so that nothing short of a perverse decision to dismiss can be held unfair.[85] Finally, it would seem that in determining the reasonableness of a dismissal tribunals are not barred from taking into account events which occurred between the giving of notice and its expiry – for example, if alternative work becomes available after redundancy notices have been issued.[86]

THE CODE OF PRACTICE AND PROCEDURAL FAIRNESS

The ACAS Code of Practice of Disciplinary and Grievance Procedures does not have the force of law, so failure to comply with it does not make a dismissal automatically unfair. It will, however, weigh heavily against the employer if not followed.[87]

Situations in which the Code may be ignored

In certain circumstances there may be a good excuse for not following the Code. For example, if the inadequacy of the employee's performance is extreme or the actual or potential consequences of a mistake are grave, warnings may not be necessary.[88] Although it is management's responsibility to ensure that there are adequate disciplinary rules and procedures, the Code mentions the desirability of union involvement in agreeing procedural arrangements.[89] Naturally, tribunals tend to pay greater attention to agreed rather than unilaterally-imposed procedures. The rules required will again depend on the nature of the employment but they should be reasonable in themselves, consistently enforced, and reviewed in the light of legal developments and organisational needs. Employees should know and understand the rules and be made aware of the likely consequences of breaking them.[90]

Outline of a disciplinary procedure according to the Code

The essential features of a disciplinary procedure are outlined in paragraph 9 of the Code. They should:

- be in writing
- specify to whom they apply
- be non-discriminatory
- provide for matters to be dealt with without undue delay[91]
- provide for proceedings, witness statements and records to be kept confidential
- indicate the disciplinary actions which may be taken
- specify the levels of management which have the authority to take the various forms of disciplinary action
- provide for individuals to be informed of the complaints against them and where possible to be made aware of all relevant evidence before any hearing
- provide workers with an opportunity to state their case before decisions are reached
- afford individuals the right to be accompanied
- ensure that, except for gross misconduct, no employees are dismissed for a first breach of discipline
- ensure that disciplinary action is not taken until the case has been carefully investigated
- ensure that workers are given an explanation for any penalty imposed

■   provide a right of appeal – normally to a more senior manager – and specify the procedure to be followed.[92]

Fairness and natural justice

It is clear from the above that natural justice is an important element in such procedures. Fairness requires that accused persons should know the case to be met; should hear or be told the important points of the evidence in support of that case; should have an opportunity to criticise or dispute that evidence and to adduce their own evidence and argue their case.[93] However, natural justice in this context does not include the automatic right to be present throughout a disciplinary hearing if the employee's interests are safeguarded by a representative. Similarly, employers are not required to conduct a quasi-judicial investigation, with cross-examination and confrontation of witnesses.[94]

Schedule 2 EA 2002, which is expected to come into force towards the end of 2004, provides two different procedures which may apply when an employer is considering disciplining or dismissing: a standard procedure and a modified procedure.

The standard dismissal and disciplinary procedure will normally apply when an employer wishes to dismiss or take "relevant disciplinary action".[95] The modified procedure will apply where a dismissal results from circumstances outside the employer's control or there is immediate dismissal for gross misconduct. It is important to note that adhering to the relevant procedure will not necessarily be sufficient to ensure that the dismissal is fair because the ACAS Code of Practice must also be complied with.[96] However, it is proposed that neither party will be required to follow the statutory procedures when one of the following exists:[97]

■   the other party is violent, abusive or behaves in an unacceptable way;
■   factors beyond the control of either party make it effectively impossible for the procedure to be gone through
■   in circumstances where the modified procedure would apply, the employee makes a tribunal complaint about the dismissal before the employer has issued the Step One letter;
■   the issue is being discussed collectively;
■   the employee applies for interim relief (see chapter 15 below); or
■   to do so would require the disclosure of information contrary to the interests of national security.

Statutory dismissal and disciplinary procedures

Employee representation

According to the section 10 ERel Act 1999, workers have the right to make a reasonable request to be accompanied during a disciplinary or grievance hearing.[98] For these purposes a disciplinary hearing is one which could result in the administration of a formal warning, the taking of some other action or the confirmation of previous actions.[99] According to the EAT, a disciplinary warning becomes a "formal warning" if it becomes part of the employee's disciplinary record.[100] A grievance hearing is one which concerns the performance of an employer's duty in relation to a worker.[101]

A worker may be accompanied by a single companion who:

■   is chosen by the worker
■   is to be permitted to address the hearing
■   is not to answer questions on behalf of the worker
■   is to be allowed to confer with the worker during the hearing.

Such a person can be an official of a trade union or another of the employer's workers.[102] A worker may propose an alternative time for the hearing if his or her chosen companion is unavailable at the time proposed by the employer. The employer must postpone the hearing to the time proposed by the worker, provided that the alternative time is reasonable and falls within a period of five working days beginning with the first working day after the day on which the worker was informed of the time by the employer.[103] An employer must permit a worker to take time off during working hours in order to accompany another of the employer's workers. Section 11 ERel Act 1999 provides that an employer who infringes these rights is liable to pay up to two weeks' pay. In addition, section 12 protects workers who are subjected to a detriment on the ground that they have exercised a right under section 10 or sought to accompany another worker pursuant to a request under that section.

Protecting informants

If allegations are made by an informant, a careful balance must be maintained between the desirability of protecting informants who are genuinely in fear and providing a fair hearing of the issues for employees who are accused.[104] In *Rowe* v *Radio Rentals*[105] the EAT decided that the employer's appeal procedure did not conflict with the rules of natural justice because the person hearing the appeal had been informed of the decision to dismiss before it took place and the person who took that decision was also present throughout the appeal hearing. It was recognised as inevitable that those involved in the original decision to dismiss will be in daily contact with their supervisors who will be responsible for deciding the appeal. However, if it is not necessary for the same person to act as both witness and judge in the procedure leading to dismissal, there may be a finding of unfairness.[106]

'Rectifiable' and 'final' warnings

Warnings are particularly appropriate in cases of misconduct but may also be useful in dealing with other types of case. Basically, there are two types of warning that must be distinguished: a 'rectifiable' warning means that the employee will be dismissed unless an existing situation is resolved, whereas a 'final' warning indicates that the employee will be dismissed if further unacceptable behaviour occurs. Warnings are dealt with in paragraph 15 of the Code of Practice, where it is recommended that written warnings should set out the nature of the offence and the likely consequences of it being repeated. Because an ambiguous warning will be construed strictly against the employer who drafted it, the date and time on which a warning is to commence and expire should be specified clearly.[107]

According to the Court of Appeal, provided a formal disciplinary warning has been given on adequate evidence, and not for an oblique or improper motive, it is a relevant consideration to which an employment tribunal should have regard in deciding whether the dismissal was unfair, even where the warning was under appeal and the appeal had not been determined at the time of the dismissal.[108] It follows that systematic records will have to be kept by employers, although it is suggested in paragraph 15 of the Code of Practice that written warnings 'should be disregarded for disciplinary purposes after a specified period (eg 12 months)'.

Where dismissal may still be unfair

As regards appeal procedures, the House of Lords has confirmed that a dismissal is unfair if the employer unreasonably treats the reason for dismissal as a sufficient one, either when the original decision to dismiss is made or when that decision is maintained at the conclusion of an internal appeal.[109] Indeed, a dismissal may also be unfair if the employer refuses to entertain an appeal or to comply with the full requirements of the appeal procedure.[110] Where two employees are dismissed for the same incident, and one is successful on appeal and the other is not, in determining the fairness of the latter's dismissal the question is whether the appeal panel's decision was so irrational that no employer could reasonably have accepted it.[111] Whether procedural defects can be rectified on appeal will depend on the degree of unfairness at the original hearing. If there is to be a correction by the appeal, then that appeal must be of a comprehensive nature – in essence a rehearing and not merely a review.

Finally, paragraph 26 of the Code of Practice urges that special consideration be given to the way in which disciplinary procedures operate in exceptional cases. Three examples are given:

- workers to whom the full procedure is not immediately available
- trade union officials
- criminal charges or convictions outside employment.

KEY POINTS

- Once employees have proved that they were dismissed, the employer must show the reason for the dismissal.
- The employer must demonstrate that the reason for the dismissal relates to capability or qualifications, conduct, a statutory ban or some other substantial reason of a kind to justify the dismissal.
- There are certain reasons which are automatically unfair, such as those relating to trade union membership or activities or to pregnancy and maternity.
- Employees cannot claim unfair dismissal if they are dismissed while taking part in unofficial industrial action.
- Capability is assessed by reference to 'skill, aptitude, health or any other physical or mental ability'.
- Misconduct is a potentially fair reason for dismissal, but the employment tribunal will decide whether dismissal was a reasonable course of action, taking into account all the circumstances.
- 'Some other substantial reason' is a category which gives tribunals the discretion to accept as fair reasons that have not been defined by statute, such as reasons arising out of the reorganisation of a business.
- An employer must act reasonably in treating a reason as sufficient for dismissal. It should be guided by the ACAS Code of Practice and the ACAS advisory handbook *Discipline and Grievances at Work* and must follow the statutory dismissal and disciplinary procedures when they come into force.

NOTES

1 Sections 98(1) and (2) ERA 1996
2 See *Maund v Penwith District Council* (1984) IRLR 24
3 See *Wilson v Post Office* (2000) IRLR 834
4 See *Abernathy v Mott, Hay and Anderson* (1974) IRLR 213
5 See *Ely v YKK Ltd* (1993) IRLR 500
6 See *Devis & Sons Ltd v Atkins* (1977) IRLR 314
7 See *Parkinson v March Consulting* (1997) IRLR 308
8 See *Ford Motor Co v Hudson* (1978) IRLR 66
9 No service qualification applies if a dismissal is on the grounds of pregnancy or maternity; see Chapter 8
10 (1985) IRLR 16
11 See *Harvard Securities v Younghusband* (1990) IRLR 17
12 See *Bromsgrove v Eagle Alexander* (1981) IRLR 127
13 Section 93(2) ERA 1996
14 Section 101 ERA 1996
15 Section 101A ERA 1996
16 Section 103A ERA 1996
17 Section 104A ERA 1996
18 Section 102 ERA 1996
19 Section 103 ERA 1996

20   Section 104B ERA 1996

21   Section 104C ERA 1996

21A *See Armstrong* v *Walter Scott Motors Ltd* (2003) IRLB 724

22   Regulation 7 Part-time Workers Regulations 2000 and Regulation 6 fixed-term Employees Regulations 2002 respectively

23   Section 4(3)b Rehabilitation of Offenders Act 1974; see *Wood* v *Coverage Care Ltd* (1996) IRLR 264

24   Section 104 ERA 1996; see also *Mennell* v *Newell & Wright Ltd* (1997) IRLR 519

25   See *Balfour Kilpatrick Ltd* v *Acheson* (2003) IRLR 683

26   See *Abernathy* v *Mott, Hay and Anderson* (note 4)

27   (1979) IRLR 16

28   November 2001

29   See *Mitchell* v *Arkwood Plastics* (1993) ICR 471

30   See *Cereal Packaging Ltd* v *Lyncock* (1998) IRLR 510

31   See *Links A & Co Ltd* v *Rose* (1991) IRLR 353

32   (1992) IRLR 133

33   See *Shook* v *London Borough of Ealing* (1986) IRLR 46

34   See Frewin v Consignia plc (2003) IRLB 726

35   (2001) IRLR 139

36   See *Hamilton* v *Argyll and Clyde Health Authority* (1993) IRLR 99

37   (1998) IRLR 358

38   See *Taylor* v *Parsons Peebles Ltd* (1981) IRLR 199 where the employee concerned had a good conduct record extending over 20 years

39   See also *United Distillers* v *Conlin* (1992) IRLR 503

40   See *UCATT* v *Brain* (1981) IRLR 224

41   See *Laughton* v *Bapp Industrial Ltd* (1986) IRLR 245

42   (1992) IRLR 294; see also *Adamson* v *B&L Cleaning Ltd* (1995) IRLR 193

43   See *Panama* v *London Borough of Hackney* (2003) IRLR 278

44   (1978) IRLR 379

45   *Scottish Midland Co-op* v *Cullion* (1991) IRLR 261. See also *Sainsburys Ltd* v *Hitt* (2003) IRLR 23

46   See *Parr* v *Whitbread plc* (1990) IRLR 39

47   *Frames Snooker* v *Boyce* (1992) IRLR 472

48   See *Parker* v *Dunn Ltd* (1979) IRLR 56

49   On suspension see ACAS Code of Practice paragraph 13

50   See *Secretary of State* v *Campbell* (1992) IRLR 263

51   See *Harris* v *Courage Ltd* (1982) IRLR 509

52   *Lovie Ltd* v *Anderson* (1999) IRLR 164

53   See *Thomson* v *Alloa Motor Co* (1983) IRLR 403

54   See *P* v *Nottingham County Council* (1992) IRLR 362

55   (1980) IRLR 382

56   See *Kingston* v *British Rail* (1984) IRLR 146

57   *Alboni* v *Ind Coope Retail Ltd* (1998) IRLR 131

58   See *RS Components Ltd* v *Irwin* (1973) IRLR 239

59   See *Scottpacking Ltd* v *Paterson* (1978) IRLR 166

60   (1986) IRLR 93

61   See *Dobie* v *Burns International* (1984) IRLR 329

62   See *Ely* v *YKK Ltd* (note 5)

63   See *Saunders* v *National Scottish Camps Association* (1981) IRLR 277

64   See *Bouchaala* v *Trust House Forte* (1980) IRLR 382

65   See *Hollister* v *National Farmers Union* (1979) IRLR 238

66   See *St John of God Ltd* v *Brooks* (1992) IRLR 546

67 (1998) IRLR 176

68 See *Catamaran Cruisers* v *Williams* (1994) IRLR 386

69 'Protected industrial action' consists of acts that are not actionable in tort; see section 219 TULRCA 1992

70 Section 238A(6) TULRCA 1992

71 See *Bolton Roadways Ltd* v *Edwards* (1987) IRLR 392

72 See *Rogers* v *Chloride Systems* (1992) ICR 198

73 Section 238(4) TULRCA 1992

74 (1982) IRLR 377

75 Section 237(6) TULRCA 1992

76 *Balfour Kilpatrick* v *Acheson* (2003) IRLR 683

77 Section 98(4) ERA 1996

78 See *Smith* v *City of Glasgow DC* (1987) IRLR 326

79 See *Ladbroke Racing* v *Arnott* (1983) IRLR 154

80 See *Brandon* v *Murphy Bros* (1983) IRLR 54

81 See *X* v *Y* (2003) IRLR 561 on Article 8 and respect for private life

82 See *London Borough of Harrow* v *Cunningham* (1996) IRLR 256

83 See *Whitbread plc* v *Hall* (2001) IRLR 275

84 See *Sainsburys Ltd* v *Hitt* (2000) IRLR 23

85 See *Rentokil Ltd* v *Mackin* (1989) IRLR 286

86 See *Stacey* v *Babcock Power Ltd* (1986) IRLR 3

87 See *Lock* v *Cardiff Railway Company* (1998) IRLR 358

88 See *Alidair Ltd* v *Taylor* (1978) IRLR 82

89 See Code of Practice paragraph 4

90 See Code of Practice paragraphs 6 and 7

91 See *RSPCA* v *Cruden* (1986) IRLR 83

92 See *Vauxhall Motors Ltd* v *Ghafoor* (1993) ICR 376

93 See *Spink* v *Express Foods* (1990) IRLR 320; on the possible impact of Article 6 of the European Convention on Human Rights see *R* v *Securities and Futures Authority ex parte Fleurose* (2001) IRLR 764

94 See *Santamera* v *Express Cargo Ltd* (2003) IRLR 273

95 "Relevant disciplinary action" is defined as action short of dismissal "on the grounds of conduct or capability, other than suspension or the issuing of warnings either oral or written": draft Regulation 2 Employment Act 2002 (Dispute Resolution) Regulations

96 This Code of Practice is due to be updated in October 2004

97 See draft Regulations 5–8 Employment Act 2002 (Dispute Resolution) Regulations

98 On reasonable requests see paragraph 56 ACAS Code of Practice

99 Section 13(4) E Rel Act 1999

100 See *Harding* v *London Underground* (2003) IRLR 252

101 See Section 13(5) E Rel Act 1999

102 Paragraphs 57–61 of the ACAS Code concern the accompanying person

103 Paragraphs 62–64 of the ACAS Code concern the operation of the right to be accompanied

104 See *Linfood Cash and Carry* v *Thomson* (1989) IRLR 235

105 (1982) IRLR 177

106 See *Byrne* v *BOC Ltd* (1992) IRLR 505

107 See *Bevan Ashford* v *Malin* (1995) IRLR 360

108 See *Tower Hamlets Health Authority* v *Anthony* (1989) IRLR 394

109 See *West Midlands Co-op Ltd* v *Tipton* (1986) IRLR 112

110 See *Westminster City Council* v *Cabaj* (1996) IRLR 399 and the ACAS Code of Practice paragraphs 27–31

111 See *Securicor Ltd* v *Smith* (1989) IRLR 356

Redundancy

CHAPTER 14

OVERVIEW

In this chapter we consider the meaning of dismissal as a result of redundancy. We begin by looking at the statutory definition and then consider the rules concerning offers of alternative employment and the opportunity for the employee to make a decision about them. Finally, there is an examination of possible unfairness in the redundancy process.

QUALIFICATIONS AND EXCLUSIONS

In order to qualify for a right to a redundancy payment an employee must have been continuously employed for two years at the relevant date.[1] It is, of course, only employees who have a right to redundancy payments. As with the right to claim unfair dismissal there is an upper age limit. The right to a redundancy payment ends at the age of 65 years or at normal retirement age if that is earlier.[2] In addition there are a number of situations in which employees lose their right to a redundancy payment:

- employees who are dismissed with or without notice for reasons connected to their conduct[3]

- employees who give notice to the employer terminating the employment with effect from a date prior to the date upon which the employer's notice of redundancy is due to expire; in such a case employees may lose their right to a redundancy payment, although if the employees leave early by mutual consent the redundancy payment will not be affected[4]

- an employee whose contract of employment is renewed, or who is re-engaged under a new contract of employment, provided that the renewal or re-engagement takes place within four weeks of the ending of the employment[5]

- an employee who takes part in strike action after having received notice of termination. In such a case the employer is entitled to issue a notice of extension. This notice, which must be in writing and indicate the employer's reasons, may request the employee to extend the contract of employment beyond the termination date by a period equivalent to the number of days lost through strike action. Failure by the employee to agree to this extension, unless he or she has good reasons such as sickness or injury, may enable the employer to challenge the right to a redundancy payment[6]

- section 158 ERA 1996 enables the Secretary of State to exclude those receiving a pension from the right to redundancy payments. Those employees who have a right or a claim to periodical payments or lump sums resulting from pensions, gratuities or superannuation allowances, which are paid with reference to the employment or on the leaving of the particular employment, can be excluded

- certain specifically excluded categories of employee, such as public-office-holders and civil servants.[7]

The ending of a limited-term contract is a dismissal and may be a dismissal for reasons of redundancy. Thus employees such as college lecturers in *Pfaffinger* v *City of Liverpool Community College*,[8] who were employed during each academic year only, were dismissed for redundancy at the end of each academic term.

THE DEFINITION OF REDUNDANCY

According to 139(1) ERA 1996, employees[9] are to be regarded as being redundant if their dismissals are attributable wholly or mainly to:

- the fact that the employer has ceased, or intends to cease, to carry on the business[10] for the purposes for which the employees were employed, or
- the fact that the employer has ceased, or intends to cease, to carry on that business in the place where the employees were so employed, or
- the fact that the requirement of that business for employees to carry out work of a particular kind, or for employees to carry out work of a particular kind in the place where they were so employed, has ceased or diminished or is expected to cease or diminish.

In this context 'cease' or 'diminish' mean either permanently or temporarily and from whatever cause.[11] The House of Lords has held[12] that the definition of redundancy requires two questions of fact to be answered. These are:

- Have the requirements of the employer's business for employees to carry out work of a particular kind ceased or diminished, or were they expected to cease or diminish?
- Was the dismissal of the employee attributable, wholly or mainly, to this state of affairs?

This means looking at the employer's overall requirements to decide whether there has been a diminution of need for employees irrespective of the terms of the individual's contract or of the function that each performed. The House of Lords approved the approach of the EAT[13] in deciding that 'bumping' could give rise to a redundancy payment. 'Bumping' is where an individual's job may continue, but there is a reduction in requirement for the same number of people to carry out the work, and that individual is made redundant.

Determining what constitutes the place of employment

For these purposes, the place where an employee was employed does not extend to any place where he or she could contractually be required to work. The question of what is the place of employment concerns the extent or area of a single place, not the transfer from one place to another.[14] If there is no express term relating to mobility, a tribunal will have to examine all the evidence to see if a term should be inferred.[15] However, even though an employee may be contractually justified in declining to move, a request to do so may have to be considered as an offer of suitable alternative employment (see below).

Determining what constitutes 'work of a particular kind'

One of the most onerous tasks of tribunals is to determine what constitutes 'work of a particular kind'. It is clear that a change in the time when the work is to be performed will not give rise to a redundancy payment,[16] nor will a reduction of overtime if the work to be done remains the same. Thus in *Lesney Products Ltd* v *Nolan*[17] the Court of Appeal held that the company's reorganisation by which one long day shift plus overtime was changed into two day shifts was done in the interests of efficiency and was not the result of any diminution in the employer's requirements for employees to carry out work of a particular kind.[18] However, both the work that the employee actually carried out and the work that the employee was required to do by his or her contract will be considerations when an employment tribunal needs to decide on this issue.[19]

Three further points need to be made:

■ Employees will be entitled to a payment notwithstanding that it could be seen from the commencement of the contract that they would be dismissed for redundancy. The fact that the contract was temporary and short term makes no difference in this respect.[20]

■ The statutory definition of redundancy focuses on the employer's requirements rather than needs. Thus – even where there is still a need for the work to be done – if, owing to lack of funds, the requirement for the employee's service has ceased, the employee is redundant.[21]

■ Section 163(2) ERA 1996 states that an employee who is dismissed is presumed to have been dismissed by reason of redundancy unless the contrary is proved.[22]

OFFERS OF ALTERNATIVE EMPLOYMENT

If, before the ending of a person's employment, the employer or an associated employer makes an offer, in writing or not, to renew the contract or to re-engage under a new contract which is to take effect either on the ending of the old one or within four weeks thereafter, then section 141 ERA 1996 has the following effect:

■ if the provisions of the new or renewed contract as to the capacity and place in which the person would be employed, together with the other terms and conditions, do not differ from the corresponding terms of the previous contract, or

■ the terms and conditions differ, wholly or in part, but the offer constitutes an offer of suitable employment, and

■ in either case the employee unreasonably refuses that offer, then he or she will not be entitled to a redundancy payment.

The burden is on an employer to prove both the suitability of the offer and the unreasonableness of the employee's refusal.[23] Offers do not have to be formal, nor do they have to contain all the conditions which are ultimately agreed.[24] However, supplying details of vacancies is not the same as an offer of employment.[25] Clearly, sufficient information must be provided to enable the employee to take a realistic decision.[26]

The suitability of the alternative work must be assessed objectively by comparing the terms on offer with those previously enjoyed. A convenient test has been whether the proposed employment will be 'substantially equivalent' to that which has ceased.[27] Merely offering the same salary will not be sufficient,[28] but short-term employment could be suitable if it is full-time.[29] The fact that the employment will be at a different location does not necessarily mean that it will be regarded as unsuitable.

'Reasonable' refusal by employees of alternative employment

By way of contrast, in adjudicating upon the reasonableness of an employee's refusal, subjective considerations can be taken into account – eg domestic responsibilities. In *Spencer* v *Gloucestershire County Council*[30] the employees had refused offers of suitable employment on the grounds that they would not be able to do their work to a satisfactory standard in the reduced hours and with reduced staffing levels. The Court of Appeal held that it was for employers to set the standard of work they wanted carried out but it was a different question whether it was reasonable for a particular employee, in all the circumstances, to refuse to work to the standard which the employer set. This is a question of fact for the tribunal. Similarly, it might be reasonable for an employee to refuse an offer of employment which, although suitable, involved loss of status.[31] Although in theory the questions of suitability and the reasonableness of refusal are distinct, they are often run together in practice.

Trial periods for new or renewed contracts

To allow an employee to make a rational decision about any alternative employment offered, section 138(3)

ERA 1996 states that if the terms and conditions differ, wholly or in part, from those of the previous contract, a trial period may be invoked. Such a period commences when the employee starts work under the new or renewed contract and ends four calendar weeks later[32] unless a longer period has been agreed for the purpose of retraining. Any such agreement must be made before the employee starts work under the new or renewed contract; it must be in writing, and specify the date the trial period ends, and the terms and conditions which will apply afterwards.[33] In order to have an agreement, an employee must do something to indicate acceptance. However, it is not necessary for the employer to provide all the information required by section 1 ERA 1996; the agreement need embody only important matters such as remuneration, status and job description.[34] If, during the trial period, the employee for any reason terminates or gives notice to terminate the contract, or the employer terminates or gives notice to terminate it for any reason connected with or arising out of the change, the employee is to be treated, for redundancy payment purposes, as having been dismissed on the date the previous contract ended. Of course, the employee's contract may be renewed again, or he or she may be re-engaged under a new contract in circumstances which give rise to another trial period.[35] Indeed, the termination of a trial period could lead to a finding of unfair dismissal.[36]

The statutory trial period applies to those who have been dismissed by their employer and have unconditionally accepted a new or renewed contract. However, at common law if the employer is guilty of repudiating the contract, employees are allowed a reasonable period within which to decide whether or not to regard themselves as constructively dismissed (see above) or to carry on with the contract. In these circumstances the statutory trial period will not commence until after the expiry of the common-law period, so the employee gets the benefit of both.[37] Among the circumstances to be considered in determining the length of the common-law period are the steps taken by the employer to enquire what the employee is going to do. If the employer makes no such enquiries, the period continues until either the employee has announced a decision or a period expires which is long enough for it to be said that it would be unreasonable to consider the trial to be subsisting.[38]

UNFAIR REDUNDANCY

It is possible for a dismissed employee to claim both a redundancy payment and unfair dismissal, although double compensation cannot be obtained.[39] For unfair dismissal purposes the statutory presumption of redundancy does not apply, so it is up to the employer to establish this as the reason, or principal reason, for dismissal. However, tribunals will not investigate the background which led to the redundancy or require the employer to justify redundancies in economic terms. According to the EAT, employers do not have to show that their requirements for employees to carry out work of a particular kind have diminished in relation to *any* work that the employees could have been asked to do under their contracts. Thus where an employee is hired to perform a particular trade, it is that basic obligation which has to be looked at when deciding whether the employer's requirements have ceased or diminished, rather than any work that the employee could be required to carry out in accordance with a contractual flexibility clause.[40]

A dismissal on grounds of redundancy will be unfair if it is shown that 'the circumstances constituting the redundancy applied equally to one or more other employees in the same undertaking who held positions similar' and either the reason, or principal reason, for which the employee was selected was inadmissible (see Chapter 13).[41] A situation where a number of employees at a similar level are made to apply for a reduced number of jobs at that level may still result in a dismissal on the grounds of redundancy which is fair, even though the work of that particular employee still continues to be done.[42]

The involvement of trade unions
Because section 105 ERA 1996 is concerned purely with selection on grounds that are not permissible, a failure to comply with a procedural requirement to consult trade unions and to consider volunteers will not automatically be unfair.[43] Nevertheless section 98(4) ERA 1996 can still have a considerable impact on

dismissals for redundancy, a point which has been emphasised by the decision in *Williams* v *Compair Maxam*.[44] In this case it was held that it is not enough to show that it was reasonable to dismiss *an* employee, a tribunal must be satisfied that the employer acted reasonably in treating redundancy as 'sufficient reason for dismissing *the* employee'. According to the EAT, where employees are represented by a recognised independent trade union, reasonable employers will seek to act in accordance with the following principles:

■ The employer will seek to give as much warning as possible of impending redundancies so as to enable the union and employees who may be affected to take early steps to inform themselves of the relevant facts, consider possible alternative solutions, and, if necessary, find alternative employment in the undertaking or elsewhere.

■ The employer will consult the union as to the best means by which the desired management result can be achieved fairly and with as little hardship to the employees as possible.[45] In particular, the employer will seek to agree with the union the criteria to be applied in selecting the employees to be made redundant.[46] When a selection has been made the employer will consider with the union whether the selection has been made in accordance with those criteria.[47]

■ Whether or not an agreement as to the criteria to be adopted has been agreed with the union, the employer will seek to establish criteria for selection which so far as possible do not depend solely upon the opinion of the person making the selection but can be checked objectively against such things as attendance record, efficiency at the job or length of service.

■ The employer will seek to ensure that the selection is made fairly in accordance with these criteria and will consider any representations the union may make as to such selection.

■ The employer will seek to see whether instead of dismissing, an employee could be offered alternative employment.

Fair application of selection criteria

In selecting employees for redundancy a senior manager is entitled to rely on the assessments of employees made by those who have direct knowledge of their work. Employers may need to show, however, that their method of selection was fair and applied reasonably. An absence of adequate consultation with the employees concerned or their representatives might affect their ability to do this[48] (consultation issues are considered below). It will not always be possible to call evidence subsequently to show that adequate consultation would not have made a difference to the decision on those selected for redundancy. If the flaws in the process were procedural, it might be possible to reconstruct what might have happened if the correct procedures had been followed. If, however, the tribunal decides that the flaws were more substantive, such a reconstruction may not be possible.[49] In practice many employers have established redundancy appeal procedures to deal with complaints that selection criteria have been unfairly applied.

Alternatives to compulsory redundancy

It is now well established that employers have a duty to consider the alternatives to compulsory redundancy. Indeed, ACAS suggests the following methods of avoiding such redundancies:

■ natural wastage
■ restrictions on recruitment
■ the retirement of employees who are beyond normal retiring age and the seeking of applicants for early retirement or voluntary redundancy (see chapter 7 on age discrimination)
■ reductions in overtime
■ short-time working
■ retraining and redeployment to other parts of the organisation

■ termination of the employment of temporary or contract staff.[50]

'Last-in, first-out' is frequently used as a criterion for selection and it is assumed to be based on periods of continuous rather than cumulative service.[51] Arguably, this form of selection indirectly discriminates against women and needs to be justified. Selecting employees on part-time and/or fixed-term contracts may also be potentially discriminatory. In *Whiffen* v *Milham Ford Girls School*[52] those employees not employed under a permanent contract of employment were the first to be selected in a redundancy exercise. This was held to be a case of indirect discrimination because a smaller proportion of women than comparable men were able to satisfy this condition (see Chapter 6).

As regards alternative employment, 'the size and administrative resources' of the employer will be a relevant consideration here. However, if a vacancy exists, an employer would be advised to offer it rather than speculate about the likelihood of the employee accepting it. This is so even if the new job entails demotion or other radical changes in the terms and conditions of employment. Nevertheless, only in very rare cases will a tribunal accept that a reasonable employer would have created a job by dismissing someone else. Finally, employers should consider establishing both redundancy counselling services – which would provide information on alternative employment, training, occupational and state benefits – and hardship committees, which would seek to alleviate 'undue hardship'.[53]

CONSULTATION

An important requirement in redundancy situations is the need for consultation (see chapter 18 for specific requirements in relation to collective redundancies). Consultation may be directly with the employees concerned or with their representatives. In *Mugford* v *Midland Bank plc*[54] the EAT held that a dismissal on the grounds of redundancy was not unfair because no consultation had taken place with the employee individually, only with the recognised trade union. The EAT described the position with regard to consultation as follows:

■ Where no consultation about redundancy has taken place with either the trade union or the employee, the dismissal will normally be unfair, unless the reasonable employer would have concluded that the consultation would be an utterly futile exercise.

■ Consultation with the trade union over the selection criteria does not of itself release the employer from considering with the employee individually his being identified for redundancy.

■ It will be a question of fact and degree for the tribunal to consider whether the consultation with the individual and/or the trade union was so inadequate as to render the dismissal unfair.

The overall picture must be viewed at the time of termination for the tribunal to decide whether the employer acted reasonably or not. The consultation must be fair and proper, which means that there must be:

■ consultation when the proposals are still at a formative stage

■ adequate information and adequate time to respond

■ a conscientious consideration by the employer of the response to consultation.[55]

Although proper consultation may be regarded as a procedural matter, it might have a direct bearing on the substantive decision to select a particular employee, since a different employee might have been selected if, following proper consultation, different criteria had been adopted. It is not normally permissible for an employer to argue that a failure to consult or warn would have made no difference to the outcome in the particular case. It is what the employer did that is to be judged, not what might have been done. Nevertheless, if the employer could reasonably have concluded in the light of the circumstances known at the time of dismissal that consultation or warning would be 'utterly useless', he or she might well have acted reasonably.[56] While the size of an undertaking might affect the nature or formality of the consultation, it cannot excuse lack of any consultation at all.[57] Finally, it should be noted that the EAT has taken the view that warning and consultation are part of the same single process of consultation, which should commence with a warning that the employee is at risk.[58]

KEY POINTS

- Employees are to be regarded as redundant if the employer has ceased or intends to cease carrying on the business for the purposes for which the employees were employed, or in the place where they are employed there has been, or will be, a diminution in the need for work of a particular kind.
- If there is no express term relating to mobility in the contract of employment, the tribunal will have to examine the evidence to consider whether one should be inferred.
- The burden of proof is on the employer to show that any offer of alternative employment was suitable and that any refusal by the employee was unreasonable.
- A trial period may be invoked to consider offers of alternative employment if there is likely to be a difference in terms and conditions of employment.
- The employer should give as much warning as possible of impending redundancies to enable the union and the affected employees to take early steps to consider alternative solutions or possibly find alternative work in the undertaking or elsewhere.

NOTES

1 Section 155 ERA 1996
2 Section 156 ERA 1996
3 See Section 140 ERA 1996
4 See *CPS Recruitment Ltd* v *Bowen* (1982) IRLR 54
5 Section 138(1) ERA 1996
6 Sections 143–144 ERA 1996
7 See sections 159 and 191 ERA 1996
8 (1996) IRLR 508
9 It is for the tribunal to decide if a person is an employee by considering the facts and concluding that there is a genuine contractual relationship of employer/employee; see *Secretary of State* v *Bottrill* (1999) IRLR 326
10 'Business' is defined in section 235(1) ERA 1996
11 Section 139(6) ERA 1996
12 See *Murray* v *Foyle Meats Ltd* (1999) IRLR 562
13 *Safeway Stores* v *Burrell* (1997) IRLR 200
14 See *Bass Leisure* v *Thomas* (1994) IRLR 104; also *High Table Ltd* v *Horst* (1997) IRLR 514
15 See *Aparau* v *Iceland Frozen Foods* (1996) IRLR 119
16 See *Johnson* v *Nottingham Police Authority* (1974) ICR 170
17 (1977) IRLR 77
18 See also *Shawkat* v *Nottingham City Hospital NHS Trust (No.2)* (2001) IRLR 555
19 See *Shawkat* v *Nottingham City Hospital NHS Trust (No. 2)* (2001) IRLR 555
20 See *Pfaffinger* v *City of Liverpool Community College* (1996) IRLR 508
21 See *AUT* v *Newcastle University* (1987) ICR 317
22 See *Wilcox* v *Hastings* (1987) IRLR 299
23 See *Jones* v *Aston Cabinet Ltd* (1973) ICR 292
24 See *Singer Co.* v *Ferrier* (1980) IRLR 300
25 See *Curling* v *Securicor Ltd* (1992) IRLR 549

26 See *Modern Injection Moulds Ltd* v *Price* (1976) IRLR 172

27 See *Hindes* v *Supersine Ltd* (1979) IRLR 343

28 See *Taylor* v *Kent County Council* (1969) 2 QB 560

29 See *Morganite Crucible* v *Street* (1972) ICR 110

30 (1985) IRLR 393

31 See *Cambridge and District Co-op* v *Ruse* (1993) IRLR 156

32 See *Benton* v *Sanderson Kayser* (1989) IRLR 299

33 Section 138(6) ERA 1996

34 See *McKindley* v *W. Hill Ltd* (1985) IRLR 492

35 Section 138(5) ERA 1996

36 See *Hempell* v *WH Smith & Sons Ltd* (1986) IRLR 95

37 See *Turvey* v *Cheyney Ltd* (1979) IRLR 105

38 See *Air Canada* v *Lee* (1978) IRLR 392

39 Section 122(4) ERA 1996

40 See *Johnson* v *Peabody Trust* (1996) IRLR 387

41 Section 105 ERA 1996; 'undertaking' is not defined in this context; 'position' is defined in note 4 Chapter 12; on 'positions similar' see *Powers and Villiers* v *A. Clarke & Co.* (1981) IRLR 483

42 See *Safeway Stores plc* v *Burrell* (1997) IRLR 200

43 See *McDowell* v *Eastern BRS Ltd* (1981) IRLR 482

44 (1982) IRLR 83

45 See *Hough* v *Leyland DAF* (1991) IRLR 194

46 See *Rolls Royce Ltd* v *Price* (1993) IRLR 203

47 See *John Brown Engineering Ltd* v *Brown* (1997) IRLR 90

48 See *King* v *Eaton* (1996) IRLR 199

49 See *King* v *Eaton (No. 2)* (1998) IRLR 686

50 Advisory booklet No.12 page 7

51 See *International Paint Co* v *Cameron* (1979) IRLR 62

52 (2001) IRLR 468

53 See generally ACAS advisory booklet No.12 *Redundancy Handling*

54 (1997) IRLR 208

55 *King* v *Eaton Ltd* (1996) IRLR 199

56 See *Mugford* v *Midland Bank* (1997) IRLR 208

57 See *De Grasse* v *Stockwell Tools* (1992) IRLR 269

58 See *Elkouil* v *Coney Island Ltd* (2002) IRLR 174

Unfair Dismissal and Redundancy Claims

OVERVIEW

This chapter looks at the rules concerning making a claim for unfair dismissal or a redundancy payment. We begin by discussing the time-limits for making a complaint to an employment tribunal and then look at the making of conciliation and compromise agreements or using arbitration as an alternative to presenting a complaint to the tribunal. We go on to examine the remedies for unfair dismissal, which consist of reinstatement, re-engagement or compensation. There is then a consideration of how levels of compensation are arrived at and the method for calculating redundancy payments. The chapter concludes by outlining the rights of employees if the employer becomes insolvent.

MAKING A CLAIM

Unfair dismissal

When Section 32 EA 2002 comes into force, an employee wishing to complain of unfair dismissal must first submit a statement of grievance to their employer.[1] Unless the 'time-limit escape clause' applies,[2] claims must normally arrive at an employment tribunal within three months of the effective date of termination. However, where employees dismissed for taking part in industrial action allege that they should have been offered re-engagement, a complaint must be lodged within six months of the date of dismissal.[3] A time-limit expires at midnight on the last day of the stipulated period even when that is a non-working day.[4] A complaint can also be presented before the effective date of termination provided it is lodged after notice has been given. This includes notice given by an employee who is alleging constructive dismissal.[5] What is or is not reasonably practicable is a question of fact, and the onus is on the employee to prove that it was not reasonably practicable to claim in time. The meaning of 'reasonably practicable' lies somewhere between reasonable and reasonably capable of physically being done.[6] The tribunal will look at this issue of reasonableness against all the surrounding circumstances. Sickness may be taken into account, but will be more important if it falls within the critical latter part of the three-month period, rather than at the beginning.[7]

The courts have dealt with this jurisdictional point on several occasions and have taken the view that since the unfair dismissal provisions have been in force for many years tribunals should be fairly strict in enforcing the time-limit.[8] Nevertheless, the issue of reasonable practicability depends upon the awareness of specific grounds for complaint, not upon the right to complain at all. Thus there is nothing to prevent an employee who is precluded by lapse of time from claiming under one ground of complaint from proceeding with a second complaint under another ground raised within a reasonable period. According to the Court of Appeal, if employers want to protect themselves from late claims presented on the basis of newly discovered information they should ensure that the fullest information is made available to the employee at the time of dismissal.[9]

Delaying an application through ignorance or mistaken belief

The fact that an internal appeal or criminal action is pending does not by itself provide a sufficient excuse for delaying an application.[10] The correct procedure is for employees to submit their applications, known as originating applications, and request that they be held in abeyance. It is a general principle of English law that ignorance does not afford an excuse. Nevertheless in *Wall's Meat Co. Ltd* v *Khan*[11] it was decided that ignorance or mistaken belief can be grounds for holding that it was not reasonably practicable if it could be shown that the ignorance or mistaken belief was itself reasonable. Thus in *Churchill* v *Yeates Ltd*[12] the EAT held that it was not reasonably practicable for an employee to bring a complaint until he or she had knowledge of a fundamental fact which rendered the dismissal unfair. In this case, after the three-month period had elapsed an employee who had been dismissed on the grounds of redundancy discovered that he had been replaced. Ignorance or mistaken belief will not be reasonable if it arises from the fault of complainants in not making such inquiries as they reasonably should have in the circumstances. However, the failure by an adviser – such as a trade union official, Citizen's Advice Bureau worker or solicitor – to give correct advice about a time-limit will not necessarily prevent an employee from arguing that it was not reasonably practicable to claim in time.[13]

The correct way to calculate the period of three months beginning with the effective date of termination is to take the day before the effective date and go forward three months. If there is no corresponding date (31st or 30th) in that month, the last day of the month is taken.[14] Where an application is posted within three months but arrives after the period has expired, the question to be determined is whether the claimant could reasonably have expected the application to be delivered in time in the ordinary course of the post.[15] The unexplained failure of an application to reach the tribunal is insufficient to satisfy the statutory test unless all reasonable steps were taken to confirm that the application was duly received.[16]

Redundancy

Employees who have not received a redundancy payment will normally be entitled to make a claim only if within six months of the relevant date they have:

- given written notice to the employer that they want a payment, or
- referred a question as to their right to a payment, or its amount, to a tribunal, or
- presented a complaint of unfair dismissal to a tribunal.[17]

The written notice to the employer does not have to be in a particular form. The test is whether it is of such a character that the recipient would reasonably understand in all the circumstances that it was the employee's intention to seek a payment.[18] In this context the words 'presented' and 'referred' seem to have the same meaning – ie an application must have been received by the employment tribunal within the six-month period.[19] Nevertheless, if any of the above steps are taken outside this period but within 12 months of the relevant date, a tribunal has the discretion to award a payment if it thinks that it would be just and equitable to do so. In such a case a tribunal must have regard to the employee's reasons for failing to take any of the steps within the normal time-limit.[20]

CONCILIATION AND COMPROMISE AGREEMENTS

Copies of unfair dismissal applications and redundancy claims, and subsequent correspondence are sent to an ACAS conciliation officer who has the duty to promote a settlement of the complaint:

- if requested to do so by the complainant and the employer (known as the respondent), or
- if, in the absence of any such request, the conciliation officer considers that he or she could act with a reasonable prospect of success.

In *Moore* v *Duport Furniture*[21] the House of Lords decided that the expression 'promote a settlement' should be given a liberal construction capable of covering whatever action by way of such promotion is appropriate in the circumstances. Where the complainant had ceased to be employed, the conciliation officer must seek to promote that person's re-employment (ie reinstatement or re-engagement) on terms that appear to be equitable. If the complainant does not wish to be re-employed, or this is not practicable, the conciliation officer must seek to promote agreement on compensation.[22] In addition, section 18(3) ETA 1996 requires conciliation officers to make their services available before a complaint has been presented if requested to do so by either a potential applicant or a respondent. However, conciliation officers have no statutory duty to explain to employees what their statutory rights are.[23]

Where appropriate, a conciliation officer is to 'have regard to the desirability of encouraging the use of other procedures available for the settlement of grievances', and anything communicated to a conciliation officer in connection with the performance of the above functions is not admissible in evidence in any proceedings before a tribunal except with the consent of the person who communicated it.[24] It should be noted that an agreement to refrain from lodging a tribunal complaint is subject to all the qualifications by which an agreement can be avoided at common law – for example, on grounds of economic duress.[25] Where a representative holds himself or herself out as having authority to reach a settlement, in the absence of any notice to the contrary the other party is entitled to assume that the representative does in fact have such authority. In such circumstances the agreement is binding on the client whether or not the adviser had any authority to enter into it.[26] A conciliated settlement will be binding even though it is not in writing[27] and the employee will be prevented from bringing the case before a tribunal.[28]

Formerly, an agreement purporting to preclude a person from bringing an employment tribunal complaint was void unless action had been taken by a conciliation officer in accordance with the above provisions. However, an agreement to refrain from bringing certain tribunal proceedings will not be void if it satisfies the conditions governing 'compromise agreements'. These conditions are that:

- the agreement must be in writing and must relate to the particular complaint
- the employee must have received independent legal advice from a relevant independent adviser[29] as to the terms and effect of the proposed agreement and, in particular, its effect on the employee's ability to pursue his or her rights before a tribunal
- at the time the adviser gives the advice there must be in force an insurance policy covering the risk of a claim by the employee in respect of loss arising in consequence of the advice
- the agreement must identify the adviser and state that the conditions regulating compromise agreements under the relevant Act are satisfied.[30]

According to the EAT, an employment tribunal has jurisdiction to enforce a compromise agreement relating to the terms on which employment is to terminate.[31]

ARBITRATION

ACAS has prepared an arbitration scheme as an alternative to an employment tribunal hearing for the resolution of unfair dismissal claims. The central feature of the scheme is that it is 'designed to be free of legalism'.[32] The arbitrator will decide on procedural and evidential matters and appeals will be allowed against awards only where EU law or the Human Rights Act 1998 are relevant. Hearings will be conducted in an inquisitorial manner, rather than an adversarial one, and the parties must comply with any instruction given by the arbitrator. Entry to the scheme is to be entirely voluntary, but the parties will opt for arbitration on the understanding that they accept the arbitrator's decision as final. The arbitrator will decide whether the dismissal was fair or unfair, and in doing so will have regard to the ACAS Code of Practice on Disciplinary and Grievance Procedures, and the ACAS handbook *Discipline and Grievances at Work*. Where the dismissal is found to be unfair, the arbitrator may award reinstatement, re-engagement or compensation. Hearings will take place in a location convenient to all the parties, and all the parties will be responsible for their own expenses.

THE REMEDIES FOR UNFAIR DISMISSAL

Re-employment

When applicants are found to have been unfairly dismissed, tribunals must explain their power to order reinstatement or re-engagement and ask employees if they wish such an order to be made.[33] Only if such a wish is expressed can an order be made, and if no order is made, the tribunal must turn to the question of compensation.[34] Where re-employment is sought, a tribunal must first consider whether reinstatement is appropriate, and in so doing must take into account the following matters:

- whether the complainant wishes to be reinstated
- whether it is practicable for the employer to comply with an order for reinstatement
- where the complainant caused or contributed to some extent to the dismissal, whether it would be just to order reinstatement.[35]

If reinstatement is not ordered, the tribunal must then decide whether to make an order for re-engagement, and if so, on what terms. At this stage the tribunal must take into account the following considerations:

- any wish expressed by the complainant as to the nature of the order to be made
- whether it is practicable for the employer or, as the case may be, a successor or associated employer to comply with an order for re-engagement
- where the complainant caused or contributed to some extent to the dismissal, whether it would be just to order re-engagement, and if so, on what terms.

Except in a case where the tribunal takes into account contributory fault under the last point above, if it orders re-engagement it will do so in terms that are, so far as is reasonably practicable, as favourable as an order for reinstatement.[36] However, it would seem that tribunals cannot order that employees be re-engaged on significantly more favourable terms than they would have enjoyed had they been reinstated in their former jobs.[37] According to the Court of Appeal, a tribunal could approach the question of whether it would be practicable to order re-employment in two stages. The first stage would be before any order had been made, when a provisional decision could be taken. The second stage would arise if such an order was made but not complied with.[38]

If at least seven days before the hearing the employee has expressed a wish to be re-employed but it becomes necessary to postpone or adjourn the hearing because the employer does not, without special reason, adduce reasonable evidence about the availability of the job from which the employee was dismissed, the employer will be required to pay the costs of the adjournment or postponement.[39] In addition, section 116(5) ERA 1996 states that where an employer has taken on a permanent replacement, this shall not be taken into account unless the employer shows either:

- that it was not practicable to arrange for the dismissed employee's work to be done without engaging a permanent replacement, or
- that a replacement was engaged after the lapse of a reasonable period without having heard from the dismissed employee that he or she wished to be reinstated or re-engaged, and that when the employer engaged the replacement it was no longer reasonable to arrange for the dismissed employee's work to be done except by a permanent replacement.

The practicability of reinstating employees

Practicability is a question of fact for each tribunal. In *Boots plc* v *Lees*[40] the EAT agreed that it was practicable to reinstate notwithstanding that the employee's ultimate superior remained convinced that he was guilty of theft. In contrast, in *Wood Group Heavy Industrial Turbines Ltd* v *Crossan*,[41] the EAT held that an employer's genuine belief that an employee was dealing in drugs made re-engagement impracticable. In addition, the following arguments have been used to prevent an order being made: that the employee was unable to perform the work; that a redundancy situation arose subsequent to the dismissal; and that other employees were hostile to the complainant's return to work. It has also been suggested by the EAT that in a small concern where a close personal relationship exists reinstatement will be appropriate only in exceptional circumstances.[42]

For these purposes reinstatement is defined as treating the complainant 'in all respects as if he had not been dismissed', and on making an order the tribunal must specify:

- any amount payable by the employer in respect of any benefit which the complainant might reasonably be expected to have had but for the dismissal, including arrears of pay, for the period between the date of termination and the date of reinstatement
- any rights and privileges, including seniority and pension rights, which must be restored to the employee
- the date by which the order must be complied with.[43]

The complainant also benefits from any improvements that have been made to the terms and conditions of employment since dismissal.[44]

The terms that a tribunal must set out for re-engagement

An order for re-engagement may be on such terms as the tribunal decides, and the complainant may be engaged by the employer, a successor or an associated employer in comparable or suitable employment. On making such an order the tribunal must set out the terms, including: the identity of the employer, the nature of the employment and the remuneration payable, together with the matters listed above in relation to reinstatement.[45]

Redress for non-compliance with a tribunal order to re-engage

Where a person is reinstated or re-engaged as the result of a tribunal order but the terms are not fully complied with,[46] a tribunal must make an additional award of compensation of such amount as it thinks fit, having regard to the loss sustained by the complainant in consequence of the failure to comply fully with the terms of the order.[47] It is a matter for speculation how long re-employment must last for it to be said that an order has been complied with. If a complainant is not re-employed in accordance with a tribunal order, he or she is entitled to enforce the monetary element at the employment tribunal.[48] Compensation will be awarded together with an additional award unless the employer satisfies the tribunal that it was not practicable to comply with the order.[49] According to the Court of Appeal, a re-engagement order does not however place a duty on an employer to search for a job for the dismissed employee irrespective of the vacancies that arise.[50]

The additional award will be of between 26 and 52 weeks' pay.[51] The employment tribunal has discretion as to where, within this range, the additional compensation should fall, but it must be exercised on the basis of a proper assessment of the factors involved. One factor would ordinarily be the view taken of the employer's conduct in refusing to comply with the order.[52] Conversely, employees who unreasonably prevent an order being complied with will be regarded as having failed to mitigate their loss.

Finally, when Section 112(5)(6) ERA 1996 come into force, if the employer has failed to complete a statutory dismissal procedure, an award of four weeks' pay must be included in a re-employment order unless this would cause injustice.

AWARDS OF COMPENSATION

Compensation for unfair dismissal will usually consist of a basic award and a compensatory award. It should be noted that if an award is not paid within 42 days of the tribunal's decision being recorded, it will attract interest.

Basic award

Normally, this will be calculated in the same way as a redundancy payment and will be reduced by the amount of any redundancy payment received.[53] However, persons below the age of 20 are also entitled to a basic award, and the basic award is reduced for both men and women above the age of 64. Where the reason or principal reason for dismissal is related to union membership or the employee's health and safety responsibilities there is a minimum award of £3,500 (in 2003), subject to any deduction on the grounds stated below.[54] Similarly, when Section 120(1A) ERA 1996 comes into force, a minimum basic award of four weeks' pay will be made against an employer who fails to complete a statutory dismissals procedure (unless this would result in injustice).

The basic award can be reduced by such proportion as the tribunal considers just and equitable on two grounds:[55]

- the complainant unreasonably refused an offer of reinstatement. Such an offer could have been made before any finding of unfairness
- any conduct of the complainant before the dismissal, or before notice was given.[56] This does not apply where the reason for dismissal was redundancy unless the dismissal was regarded as unfair by virtue of section 100(1)(a) or (b), 101A(d), 102(1) or 103 ERA 1996. In that event the reduction will apply only to that part of the award payable because of section 120 ERA 1996. An award of two weeks' pay will be made to employees who were redundant but unable to obtain a redundancy pay-ment in either of the following circumstances:
  - they are not to be treated as dismissed by virtue of section 138 ERA 1996, which deals with the renewal of a contract or re-engagement under a new one, or
  - hey are not entitled to a payment because of the operation of section 141 ERA 1996, which is concerned with offers of alternative employment.[57]

Compensatory award

The amount of this award is that which a tribunal 'considers just and equitable in all the circumstances having regard to the loss sustained by the complainant in consequence of the dismissal insofar as that loss is attributable to action taken by the employer'.[58] This may include losses resulting from subsequent employment or unemployment if those losses can be attributed to the dismissal. In *Dench v Flynn & Partners*[59] an assistant solicitor was able to claim compensation for unemployment after a subsequent short-term job because it was attributable to the original dismissal. However, the mere fact that the employer could have dismissed fairly on another ground arising out of the same factual situation does not render it unjust or inequitable to award compensation.[60]

Section 123(3) ERA 1996 specifically mentions that an individual whose redundancy entitlement would have exceeded the basic award can be compensated for the difference, while a redundancy payment received in excess of the basic award payable goes to reduce the compensatory award. The compensatory award can be reduced in two other circumstances: where the employee's action caused or contributed to the dismissal, and where the employee failed to mitigate his or her loss. Before reducing an award on the ground that the complainant caused or contributed to the dismissal, a tribunal must be satisfied that the employee's conduct was culpable or blameworthy – ie foolish, perverse or unreasonable in the circumstances.[61] Thus there could be a finding of contributory fault in a case of constructive dismissal on the basis that there was a causal link between the employee's conduct and the employer's repudiatory breach of contract.[62] However, compensation in respect of discriminatory non-re-engagement following dismissal while taking part in industrial action will not normally be reduced on the grounds of contributory conduct.[63]

Reductions to compensatory awards

In determining whether to reduce compensation the tribunal must take into account the conduct of the complainant and not what happened to some other employee – for example, one who was treated more leniently.[64] Not all unreasonable conduct will necessarily be culpable or blameworthy; it will depend on the degree of unreasonableness. Although ill-health cases will rarely give rise to a reduction in compensation on grounds of contributory fault, it is clear that an award may be reduced under the overriding 'just and equitable' provisions.[65] Having found that an employee was to blame, a tribunal must reduce the award to some extent, although the proportion of culpability is a matter for the tribunal.[66] According to the Court of Appeal, tribunals should first assess the amount which it is just and equitable to award because this may have a very significant bearing on what reduction to make for contributory conduct.[67] The percentage amount of reduction is to be taken from the total awarded to the employee before other deductions such as offsetting what has already been paid by the employer, because this would be fairer to the employer.[68]

Clearly, complainants are obliged to look for work, but there are stages that the tribunal must go through before it can decide what amount to deduct for an employee's failure to find work.[69] These are:

- to identify what steps should have been taken by the applicant to mitigate loss
- to find the date on which such steps would have produced an alternative income
- thereafter, to reduce the amount of compensation by the amount of income which would have been earned.

The onus is on the employer to prove that there was such a failure. While acknowledging that the employee has a duty to act reasonably, the EAT has concluded that this standard is not high in view of the fact that the employer is the wrongdoer.[70]

When the EA 2002 comes into force, if the relevant statutory dismissal procedure was not completed before the unfair dismissal proceedings were commenced, and this was wholly or mainly attributable to a failure by the employer, the tribunal is required to increase the level of the compensatory award. Similarly, if the non-completion of the procedure was wholly or mainly caused by the employee's failure to comply with its requirements, or exercise a right of appeal under it, the tribunal must reduce the award.[71]

No account is to be taken of any pressure that was exercised on the employer to dismiss the employee,[72] and according to section 155 TULRCA 1992 compensation cannot be reduced on the grounds that the complainant:

- was in breach of or proposed to breach a requirement that he or she must be, or become, a member of a particular trade union or one of a number of trade unions; ceases to be, or refrains from becoming a member of any trade union or of a particular trade union or of one of a number of particular trade unions; or would not take part in the activities of any trade union, of a particular trade union or of one of a number of particular trade unions
- refused, or proposed to refuse, to comply with a requirement of a kind mentioned in section 152(3)(a) TULRCA 1992
- objected, or proposed to object, to the operation of a provision of a kind mentioned in section 152(3)(b).

Nevertheless, this section permits a distinction to be drawn between what was done by the complainant and the way in which it was done.[73]

The maximum compensatory award is £53,500 in 2003, but it should be noted that this figure is linked to the retail price index. The limit applies only after credit has been given for any payments made by the employer and any deductions have been made,[74] but any 'excess' payments made by the employer over that which is required are deducted after the amount of the compensatory award has been fixed.[75] As regards deductions, normally an employer is to be given credit for all payments made to an employee in respect of claims for wages and other benefits. Thus payments in lieu of notice and *ex gratia* payments can be deducted.[76] Where an employee has suffered discrimination as well as unfair dismissal, section 126 ERA 1996 prevents double compensation for the same loss.

It is the duty of tribunals to inquire into the various grounds for damages, but it is the responsibility of the aggrieved person to prove the loss. The legislation aims to reimburse the employee rather than to punish the employer. Hence employees who appear to have lost nothing – eg where it can be said that, irrespective of the procedural unfairness which occurred, they would have been dismissed anyway – do not qualify for a compensatory award. However, if the employee puts forward an arguable case that dismissal was not inevitable, the evidential burden shifts to the employer to show that dismissal was likely to have occurred in any event.[77] Additionally, a nil or nominal award may be thought just and equitable in a case where misconduct was discovered subsequently to the dismissal.[78]

The possible grounds (heads) of loss have been divided into the following categories:

1 Loss incurred up to the date of the hearing
   Here attention focuses on the employee's actual loss of income, which makes it necessary to ascertain the employee's take-home pay. Thus, tax and National Insurance contributions are to be deducted, but overtime earnings and tips can be taken into account. Similarly, any sickness or invalidity benefits received may be taken into account.[79] It should also be noted that the loss sustained should be based on what the employee was entitled to, whether or not he or she was receiving it at the time of dismissal.[80] As well as lost wages, section 123(2) ERA 1996 enables an individual to claim compensation for the loss of other benefits – eg a company car or other perks. Similarly, 'expenses reasonably incurred' are mentioned in the statute – so, for example, employees will be able to recover the cost of looking for a new job or setting up their own business. However, complainants cannot be reimbursed for the cost of pursuing their unfair dismissal claims.

2 *Loss flowing from the manner of dismissal*
   Compensation can be awarded only if the manner of dismissal has made the individual less acceptable to potential employers. There is nothing for non-economic loss, for example, hurt feelings. The EAT has stated that economic loss may arise where the person is not fit to take up alternative employment as early as he or she would otherwise have done (or ever); or that by virtue of stigma damage, loss of reputation or embarrassment no suitable employer was prepared to engage him or her, at any rate on terms that would not cause continuing loss.[81]

3 *Loss of accrued rights*
   This head of loss is intended to compensate the employee for the loss of rights dependent on a period of continuous service, but because the basic award reflects lost redundancy entitlement, sums awarded on these grounds have tended to be nominal. Nevertheless, tribunals should include a sum to reflect the fact that dismissed employees lose the statutory minimum notice protection that they have built up.[82]

4 *Loss of pension rights*
   Undoubtedly this presents the most complex problems of computation. Basically, there are two

types of loss: the loss of the present pension position and the loss of the opportunity to improve one's pension position with the dismissing employer. When an employee is close to retirement, the cost of an annuity which will provide a sum equal to the likely pension can be calculated. In other cases the starting-point will be the contributions already paid into the scheme, and in addition to having their own contributions returned, employees can claim an interest in their employer's contributions, except in cases of transferred or deferred pensions. However, in assessing future loss the tribunal must take into account a number of possibilities – for example, future dismissal or resignation, early death, and the fact that a capital sum is being paid sooner than would have been expected. Although employment tribunals have been given actuarial guidelines on loss of pension rights, in each case the factors must be evaluated to see what adjustment should be made or whether the guidelines are safe to use at all.[83]

5 *Future loss*

Where no further employment has been secured, tribunals will have to speculate how long the employee will remain unemployed. Here the tribunal must utilise its knowledge of local market conditions as well as considering personal circumstances. According to the EAT, employees who have become unfit for work wholly or partly as a result of unfair dismissal are entitled to compensation for loss of earnings, at least for a reasonable period following the dismissal, until they might reasonably have been expected to find other employment.[84] If another job has been obtained, tribunals must compare the employee's salary prospects for the future in each job and see as best they can how long it will take the employee to reach in the new job the salary equivalent to that which would have been attained had he or she remained with the original employer.[85] Where the employee is earning a higher rate of pay at the time compensation is being assessed, the tribunal should decide whether the new employment is permanent, and if so, should calculate the loss as between the date of dismissal and the date the new job was secured.[86]

Awards and the Jobseeker's Allowance

Finally, mention must be made of Employment Protection (Recoupment of Jobseeker's Allowance and Income Support) Regulations 1996,[87] which were designed to remove the state subsidy to employers who dismiss unfairly. Such benefits had the effect of reducing the losses suffered by dismissed persons. These regulations provide that a tribunal must not deduct from the compensation awarded any sum which represents jobseeker's allowance received, and the employer is instructed not to pay immediately the amount of compensation which represents loss of income up to the hearing (known as the 'prescribed element'). The National Insurance Fund can then serve the employer with a recoupment notice which will require him or her to pay the Fund from the prescribed element the amount which represents the jobseeker's allowance paid to the employee prior to the hearing.[88] When the amount has been refunded by the employer, the remainder of the prescribed element becomes the employee's property. It is important to note that private settlements do not fall within the scope of these Regulations.

CALCULATING A REDUNDANCY PAYMENT

The size of a redundancy payment depends on the employee's length of continuous service, his or her age and the amount of a week's pay. A week's pay is calculated in accordance with sections 220–9 ERA 1996 (see Chapter 16) and in this context means gross pay.[89] However, it does not take into account increased wage rates agreed subsequently to the employee's dismissal but backdated to a date prior to the dismissal.[90] Unless the contrary is shown, employment is presumed to have been continuous (see Chapter 16), but this only applies in relation to the dismissing employer (except when a business or undertaking has been transferred[91] or an employee has been taken into employment by an associated employer). If continuity is not preserved on a transfer, an assurance given by one employer that the obligations of another will be met will not confer jurisdiction on a tribunal to award a payment based on overall service. However, an employee may be able to show that there was a contract to the effect that he or she would retain the benefit of previous employment.[92]

Redundancy payments are calculated according to the following formula, with a maximum of 20 years' service being taken into account. Starting at the end of the employee's period of service and calculating backwards:

■ one and a half weeks' pay is allowed for each year of employment in which the individual was between the ages of 41 and 64.[93] Those who are aged 64 have their entitlement reduced by one-twelfth in respect of each month they remain in employment

■ a week's pay for each year of employment in which the individual was between the ages of 22 and 40

■ half a week's pay for each year of employment between the ages of 18 and 21.[94]

On making a redundancy payment the employer must give the employee a written statement indicating how the amount has been calculated. An employer who, without reasonable excuse, fails to do so can receive a fine not exceeding level 3 on the standard scale.[95]

EMPLOYEE RIGHTS ON INSOLVENCY

If an employer becomes insolvent or bankrupt, an employee's wages in respect of the four months beforehand, up to a maximum of £800, become a preferential debt.[96] In addition, Schedule 6 of the Insolvency Act 1986 provides that the following shall be treated as wages for these purposes: a guarantee payment; remuneration payable under suspension on medical or maternity grounds; remuneration payable during a protective award; and a payment for time off for union duties, antenatal care, or to look for work or make arrangements for training in a redundancy situation.

Section 182 ERA 1996 gives employees the right to make a written request to the Secretary of State for a payment out of the National Insurance Fund to meet certain other debts which arise out of the employer's insolvency.[97] These debts are:

■ arrears of pay up to a maximum of eight weeks; this includes any of the matters treated as wages for the purposes of the Insolvency Act 1986

■ wages payable during the statutory notice period. It should be noted that employees are still required to mitigate their loss

■ holiday pay up to a maximum of six weeks, provided the entitlement accrued during the preceding 12 months

■ a basic award of compensation for unfair dismissal

■ any reasonable sum by way of reimbursement of the whole or part of any fee or premium paid by an apprentice or articled clerk.

A financial limit is imposed on the amount that can be recovered in respect of any one week[98] (£270 per week in 2004).

Before reimbursing the employee the Secretary of State must be satisfied both that the employer has become insolvent[99] and that the employee is entitled to be paid the whole or part of the debt claimed.[100] The Secretary of State is liable only to the extent to which the employee is legally entitled to make a claim against the employer.[101] Also, a payment cannot be made unless a 'relevant officer' appointed in connection with the insolvency – eg a liquidator, receiver or trustee in bankruptcy – has supplied a statement of the amount owed to the employee. However, this requirement may be waived if the Secretary of State is satisfied that the statement is not necessary to determine the amount owing.[102] If the Secretary of State fails to make a payment or if it is less than the amount which the employee thinks should have been made,[103] a complaint may be presented to an employment tribunal within three months of the Secretary of State's decision being communicated.[104] Where a tribunal finds that a payment ought to have been made under section 182 ERA 1996, it must make a declaration to that effect and state the amount that ought to be paid. Finally, it should be noted that when the Secretary of State makes a payment to the employee, the rights and remedies of the latter in relation to the employer's insolvency are transferred to the Secretary of State.[105]

KEY POINTS

- Complaints of unfair dismissal must normally arrive at an employment tribunal within three months of the effective date of termination.
- Employees who have not received a redundancy payment will normally be entitled to make a claim within six months of the relevant date.
- ACAS will assist the employee and the employer by conciliating to try to reach an agreement to settle the complaint.
- Remedies for unfair dismissal include reinstatement, re-engagement or compensation.
- Compensation for unfair dismissal will consist of a basic award and a compensatory award.
- The maximum compensatory award is £53,500 in 2003 and is linked to the retail price index.
- The size of a redundancy payment depends upon the employee's age, length of service and the amount of a week's pay.
- If an employer becomes insolvent, some liabilities will pass to the Secretary of State for payment out of the National Insurance Fund.

NOTES

1 See paragraphs 6 and 9 Schedule 2 EA 2002
2 Section 111(2) ERA 1996
3 Section 239(2) TULRCA 1992
4 See *Swainston* v *Hetton Victory Club* (1983) IRLR 164
5 Section 111(4) ERA 1996; see *Patel* v *Nagesan* (1995) IRLR 370
6 See *Palmer* v *Southend BC* (1984) IRLR 119
7 See *Schultz* v *Esso Petroleum Co Ltd* (1999) IRLR 488
8 See *London Underground* v *Noel* (1999) IRLR 621
9 See *Marley Ltd* v *Anderson* (1996) IRLR 163
10 See *Palmer* v *Southend BC* (note 5)
11 (1978) IRLR 499
12 (1983) IRLR 187; see also *Post Office* v *Sanhotra* (2000) IRLR 866
13 See *London International College* v *Sen* (1993) IRLR 333
14 See *Pruden* v *Cunard Ltd* (1993) IRLR 317
15 See *Consignia plc* v *Sealy* (2002) IRLR 624 where detailed guidance is provided
16 See *Camden and Islington NHS Trust* v *Kennedy* (1996) IRLR 381
17 Section 164(1) ERA 1996; see *Duffin* v *Secretary of State* (1983) ICR 766
18 See *Price* v *Smithfield Group Ltd* (1978) IRLR 80
19 See *Secretary of State* v *Banks* (1983) ICR 48 and *Swainston* v *Hetton Victory Club* (note 3)
20 Section 164(2) ERA 1996
21 (1982) IRLR 31
22 Section 18(4) ETA 1996
23 See *Slack* v *Greenham* (1983) IRLR 271
24 Section 18(6) and (7) ETA 1996

25 See *Hennessy* v *Craigmyle Ltd* (1985) IRLR 446

26 See *Freeman* v *Sovereign Chicken Ltd* (1991) IRLR 408

27 See *Gilbert* v *Kembridge Fibres Ltd* (1984) IRLR 52

28 Section 203(2)(e) ERA 1996

29 Section 203(3A) ERA 1996 defines 'relevant independent adviser' as a qualified lawyer; an officer, official, member or employee of a trade union who has been certified to give advice by the union; an authorised advice centre worker; or others specified by the Secretary of State

30 Section 203(2)(f) and 203(3) ERA 1996

31 See *Rock-It Cargo Ltd* v *Green* (1997) IRLR 582. See *Sutherland* v *Network Appliance* (2001) IRLR 12

32 See ACAS Arbitration Scheme (England and Wales) Order 2001 SI No.1185

33 See *Constantine* v *Cory Ltd* (2000) IRLR 939

34 Section 112 ERA 1996

35 Section 116(1) ERA 1996

36 Section 116(4) ERA 1996

37 See *Rank Xerox* v *Stryczek* (1995) IRLR 568

38 See *Port of London Authority* v *Payne* (1994) IRLR 9

39 Section 13(2) ETA 1996

40 (1986) IRLR 485

41 (1998) IRLR 680

42 See *Enessy Co* v *Minoprio* (1978) IRLR 489

43 Section 114(2) ERA 1996

44 Section 114(3) ERA 1996

45 Section 115(2) ERA 1996

46 See *Artisan Press* v *Strawley* (1986) IRLR 126 on the difference between not re-employing and not fully complying with an order

47 Section 117(2) ERA 1996

48 See section 124(4) ERA 1996

49 Section 117(3) and (4) ERA 1996

50 See *Port of London Authority* v *Payne* (note 37)

51 Section 117(3)(b) ERA 1996

52 See *Motherwell Railway Club* v *McQueen* (1989) ICR 419

53 Section 122(4) ERA 1996; see *Boorman* v *Allmakes Ltd* (1995) IRLR 553

54 Section 120 ERA 1996

55 Section 122(1) and (2) ERA 1996

56 See *RSPCA* v *Cruden* (1986) IRLR 83

57 Section 121 ERA 1996

58 Section 123 ERA 1996

59 (1998) IRLR 653

60 See *Devonshire* v *Trico-Folberth* (1989) IRLR 397

61 See *Nelson* v *BBC (No.2)* (1979) IRLR 304; *Morrison* v *ATGWU* (1989) IRLR 361

62 See *Polentarutti* v *Autokraft Ltd* (1991) IRLR 457

63 See *Crosville Ltd* v *Tracey & anor (No.2)* (1996) IRLR 916

64 See *Parker Foundry Ltd* v *Slack* (1992) IRLR 11

65 See *Slaughter* v *Brewer Ltd* (1990) IRLR 426

66 See *Warrilow* v *Walker Ltd* (1984) IRLR 304

67 See *Rao* v *Civil Aviation Authority* (1994) IRLR 240

68 See *Heggie* v *Uniroyal Englebert Tyres Ltd* (1998) IRLR 425

69 See *Savage* v *Saxena* (1998) IRLR 182

70 See *Fyfe* v *Scientific Furnishings Ltd* (1989) IRLR 331 An unreasonable refusal of an offer of re-employment and the failure to mitigate loss see: *Wilding* v *BT plc* (2002) IRLR 524

71 Section 124A ERA 1996

72 Section 123(5) ERA 1996

73 See *TGWU* v *Howard* (1992) IRLR 170

74 Section 124(5) ERA 1996; see *Braund Ltd* v *Murray* (1991) IRLR 100

75 See *Digital Equipment Co Ltd* v *Clements (No.2)* (1998) ICR 258

76 See *Cox* v *London Borough of Camden* (1996) IRLR 389

77 See *Britool Ltd* v *Roberts* (1993) IRLR 481

78 See *Tele-trading Ltd* v *Jenkins* (1990) IRLR 430

79 See *Puglia* v *James & Sons* (1996) IRLR 70 and *Rubenstein* v *McGloughlin* (1996) IRLR 557

80 See *Pagetti* v *Cobb* (2002) IRLR 861

81 *Dunnachie* v *Hull City Council* (2003) IRLR 384

82 See *Guinness Ltd* v *Green* (1989) IRLR 289 and *Puglia* v *James & Sons* (note 77)

83 See *Clancy* v *Cannock College* (2001) IRLR 331

84 On compensating for career-long loss see *Kingston upon Hull City Council v Dunnachie (No.3)(2003) IRLR 843*

85 See *Devine* v *Designer Flowers Ltd* (1993) IRLR 517

86 See *Tradewind Airways Ltd* v *Fletcher* (1981) IRLR 272

87 See *Fentiman* v *Fluid Engineering Ltd* (1991) IRLR 150

88 SI 1996/2439; see also sections 16 and 17 ETA 1996

89 See *Homan* v *A1 Bacon Ltd* (1996) ICR 846

90 See *Secretary of State* v *Woodrow* (1983) IRLR 11; the maximum amount of a week's pay is £270 in 2004

91 See *Leyland Vehicles Ltd* v *Reston* (1981) IRLR 19

92 See *Lassman* v *Secretary of State* (1999) ICR 416 where continuity was preserved by the Transfer Regulations 1981, even though, at the time of the transfer, the employees received statutory redundancy payments

93 See *Secretary of State* v *Globe Elastic Ltd* (1979) IRLR 327

94 Section 162(1) and (2) ERA 1996. On age discrimination see Chapter 7

95 Section 165 ERA 1996; see *Barnsley MBC* v *Prest* (1996) ICR 85

96 Section 386 Insolvency Act 1986

97 Insolvency is defined in section 183 ERA 1996; see *Secretary of State* v *Stone* (1994) ICR 761

98 See *Benson v Secretary of State (2003) IRLR 748*

99 See *Morris* v *Secretary of State* (1985) IRLR 297

100 See *Secretary of State* v *Walden* (2001) IRLR 168

101 See Section 182 ERA 1996

102 See *Mann* v *Secretary of State* (1999) IRLR 566

103 Section 187(2) ERA 1996; the 'time-limit escape clause' applies here

104 See *Potter* v *Secretary of State for Employment* (1997) IRLR 21 on the ability of the Secretary of State to set off protective awards against the claims of the employees

105 Section 189 ERA 1996

106 Section 189 ERA 1996

Continuity of Employment, Normal Working Hours and a Week's Pay

OVERVIEW

In this chapter we are concerned with the concepts of continuity of service, including the effect of the TUPE Regulations, normal working hours and a week's pay. They are important because many statutory rights are dependent upon minimum length of service, and payments are related to statutory concepts of normal working hours and a week's pay. We begin by looking at continuity of employment and what impact different types of gaps in service have on these statutory rights. We then look briefly at normal working hours. (Aspects of the regulation of working time are dealt with in Chapter 10.) Lastly we examine the concept of a week's pay which is used for computing many payments under ERA 1996, such as redundancy payments and compensation for unfair dismissal.

CONTINUITY OF EMPLOYMENT

Continuous employment is an important concept because many statutory rights are dependent on a minimum service qualification, and certain benefits – for example redundancy payments and basic awards – are calculated by reference to length of service. For the purposes of ERA 1996 an individual's period of employment is to be computed in accordance with sections 210–219. Continuity of employment is a statutory concept[1] and the courts will look to see whether there has been a break in service. In *Morris* v *Walsh Western UK Ltd*[2] the employer agreed to ignore a month's break in employment and treat the employee as having been continuously employed. Despite this, the EAT held that the month's gap had constituted a break in service.

Section 210(5) ERA 1996 states that employment is presumed to have been continuous unless the contrary is shown, although this is not so where there is a succession of employers.[3] Apart from redundancy payment purposes, these provisions also apply to periods of employment wholly or mainly outside Great Britain.[4] Continuity is normally assessed in relation to the particular contract on which a claim is based. However, it may be possible for an employer to deliberately subject employees to a combination of separate contracts which amount to a series of fixed-term contracts with a break in between.[5] The EAT concluded that any anomalies or avoidance of the legislation is a matter for Parliament rather than the Courts. For the effect of the Fixed-term Employees/Prevention of less Favourable Treatment/Regulations 2002 on continuity of employment see Chapter 4.

A period of continuous employment, which begins with the day on which the employee 'starts work',[6] is to be computed in months, and except in so far as is otherwise provided, a week which does not count breaks the period of continuous employment.[7] A person accrues a period of continuous service only if he or she is employed under a legal contract of employment. Thus, if for a period of time the contract is illegal, then for that period the contract cannot be relied on.[8] Where there is a dispute over continuity, employees have to establish that there was a week which counted, but in respect of subsequent weeks they can rely on the presumption contained in section 210(5) ERA 1996 that employment is continuous (unless there is evidence to the contrary).[9]

Weeks that count

According to section 212(1) ERA 1996, any week[10] during the whole or part of which a person has a contract of employment will count. In *Sweeney* v *J & S Henderson Ltd*[11] an employee resigned on a Saturday and was re-engaged on the following Friday. Despite the fact that the employee had left voluntarily, continuity was preserved for the purposes of a subsequent unfair dismissal claim. A week counts if one of the following applies for the whole or part of that week:

■ The employee is incapable of work as a consequence of sickness or injury.[12] Not more than 26 consecutive weeks can be counted under this head.[13] In this context the expression 'incapable of work' does not mean incapable of work generally, nor does it refer to the particular work provided for in the contract which has ended. According to the Court of Appeal, where the work on offer by the employer differs from that for which the employee was previously employed, the tribunal must consider whether the work offered was of a kind which the employee was willing to accept or, even if the employee was unwilling, was suited to his or her particular circumstances.[14]

■ The employee is absent from work on account of a temporary cessation of work.[15] In this context the phrase 'absent from work' does not necessarily mean physical absence but means not performing in substance the contract that previously existed between the parties.[16] The words 'on account of' refer to the reason when the employer dismissed, and the fact that the unavailability of work was foreseen and the employee took another job will not prevent a tribunal holding that this provision applies. 'Cessation of work' denotes that a quantity of work has for the time being ceased to exist and was therefore no longer available to be given to the employee. Thus, when a member of a pool of casual cleaners was not allocated work under a pool arrangement, that absence was not on account of a temporary cessation of work.[17]

According to the House of Lords, 'temporary' means lasting a relatively short time and whether an interval can be so characterised is a question of fact for the employment tribunal. Where there is a succession of fixed-term contracts with intervals between them, continuity is not broken unless 'looking backwards from the date of expiry of the fixed-term contract on which the claim is based, there is to be found between one fixed-term contract and its immediate predecessor an interval that cannot be characterised as short relative to the combined duration of the two fixed-term contracts'.[18] In *Flack* v *Kodak Ltd*[19] the EAT held that where an employee has worked intermittently over a period of years in an irregular pattern, tribunals ought to have regard to all the circumstances and should not confine themselves to the mathematical approach of looking at each gap and immediately adjoining periods of employment. The fact that cessation is not permanent does not mean that it must be temporary for these purposes.[20]

■ The employee is absent from work in circumstances such that by arrangement or custom he or she is regarded as continuing in the employment of the employer for all or any purposes.[21] Although an arrangement must normally exist at the time the absence began, the EAT has held that the period between dismissal and voluntary reinstatement may be covered by this provision.[22] For section 212(3)(c) ERA to preserve continuity of employment by arrangement or custom there needs to be a mutual recognition, by the employer and the employee, that, although the employee is absent from work, he or she continues to be employed by the employer. A recognition that there is some other kind of continuing relationship is not enough. Thus a child break scheme which guaranteed the employee a post similar to that which she had previously held and which had arrangements for keeping the parties in contact during the absence was held not to be an arrangement preserving continuity because the employee was required to resign her employment at the beginning of the scheme.[23]

It would appear that the cause of the absence is immaterial. Thus employees who have been loaned to a third party may be protected as well as those given leave of absence for personal reasons. In *Colley* v *Corkindale*[24] the EAT held that employees who worked alternate weeks were to be regarded as being absent by arrangement on their weeks off.

It should be noted that continuity of employment where employees are absent from work for family reasons is now dealt with under the Maternity and Parental Leave Regulations 1999 and the Paternity and Adoptions Leave Regulations 2002 (see Chapter 8).

Strikes and lock-outs

Days on which an employee is on strike neither count nor break the employee's period of continuous service.[25] By virtue of section 235(5) ERA 1996 for this purpose 'strike' means:

(a) the cessation of work by a body of persons employed acting in combination, or

(b) a concerted refusal or a refusal under a common understanding of any number of persons employed to continue to work for an employer in consequence of a dispute, done as a means of compelling their employer or any person or body of persons employed, or to aid other employees in compelling their employer or any person or body of persons employed, to accept or not to accept terms and conditions of or affecting employment.

Where an employee is absent from work because of a lock-out, again continuity is not broken and if the contract of employment subsists, the period of absence could be counted under section 212(1) ERA 1996.[26] 'Lock-out' means:[27]

(a) the closing of a place of employment

(b) the suspension of work

(c) the refusal by an employer to continue to employ any number of persons employed by him in consequence of a dispute, done with a view to compelling those persons, or to aid another employer in compelling persons employed by him, to accept terms or conditions of or affecting employment.

It makes no difference that employees were dismissed during a strike or lock-out; as long as they were subsequently re-engaged, their period of continuous employment will be preserved. Any attempt to provide otherwise – for example, by introducing a specific term relating to previous employment – will be construed as an attempt to exclude or limit the operation of this paragraph and will be ineffective as a result of section 203 ERA 1996.[28]

Change of employer

Usually when an employee leaves one employer and starts working for another, his or her period of continuous service will be broken. However, in certain circumstances a person will be regarded as having been employed by the new employer as from the date his or her previous employment commenced. Apart from the situation where an employer voluntarily agrees to give credit for service with a previous employer (which does not bind the Secretary of State),[29] there are six main types of case in which employment is deemed to be continuous despite a change of employer:

■ if there is a transfer of a trade, undertaking, business or part of a business.[30] The words 'trade' and 'undertaking' are not defined in ERA 1996, but 'business' includes a trade or profession and any activity carried on by a body of persons, whether corporate or unincorporated.[31] In relation to business transfers the critical question is whether there has been the transfer of a 'going concern' which could be carried on without interruption or merely the disposal of assets. If the latter, continuity of employment is not maintained. A transfer is not an event that necessarily happens all at once. A trade or business has different elements such as goodwill, property and stock in trade, as well as the employees. The transfer, for continuity purposes, does not therefore take place at a precise moment in time.[32]

If the transfer is a relevant transfer for the purposes of the Transfer Regulations 1981 (see below), the fact that the employees were dismissed and given redundancy payments at the time of the transfer will not necessarily affect continuity of employment.[33]

- if an Act of Parliament results in one corporate body replacing another as employer[34]

- if the employer dies and the employee is then re-employed by the personal representatives or trustees of the deceased[35]

- if there is a change in the partners, personal representatives or trustees who employ the individual[36]

- if the individual is taken into the employment of an associated employer.[37] 'Associated employer' is defined in section 231 ERA 1996 as follows: 'Any two employers are to be treated as associated if (a) one is a company of which the other (directly or indirectly) has control; or (b) both are companies of which a third person (directly or indirectly) has control.' The expression 'has control' is used in the company-law sense of controlling 51 per cent or more of the shares. However, the register of shares does not conclusively establish the identity of the possessor of control because the person registered as owner might be a nominee.[38] According to the EAT, tribunals should look at the way in which control had in fact been exercised.[39] While there must not be a gap between the employments (unless it is covered by the statute), it is not necessary that the move to an associated employer be made with the acquiescence of either employer.

- if the employee is employed by the governors of a school maintained by a local education authority or by the authority itself and he or she is transferred to another school or local education authority.[40]

TRANSFERS OF UNDERTAKINGS

The Transfers of Undertakings (Protection of Employment) Regulations 1981[41] (the Transfer Regulations 1981) were introduced as a result of the Acquired Rights Directive.[42] The Directive was amended in 1998 and these amendments will result in changes to the Transfer Regulations. The intention of the Directive and the Transfer Regulations 1981 was to protect the contract of employment and the employment relationship of employees who were transferred from one employer to another. When a transfer takes place, it is as if the employee's contract of employment was initially agreed with the transferee employer. All rights contained in the contract of employment, except pension benefits,[43] are transferred, as are all outstanding claims and liabilities of the employer to the employees.[44] This may include non-contractual obligations such as in *DJM International Ltd* v *Nicholas*.[45] In this case the EAT held that liability for an alleged act of sex discrimination transferred from the transferor company to the transferee employer.

When does a relevant transfer of an undertaking take place?

There is no satisfactory definition in the Directive or the Transfer Regulations of what a transfer actually consists of, although the government's proposed changes should make this much clearer. The European Court of Justice supplied a definition in *Berg and Busschers* v *Besselsen*[46] in which it stated that a transfer happened as soon as a change occurs of the natural or legal person operating the undertaking and that a change of ownership is not needed. Thus a change in the natural or legal person running a business, or part of it, will constitute a transfer of an undertaking. This can even apply to two separate businesses which are subsidiaries of the same holding company. Provided that each has its own legal identity it is possible that the Transfer Regulations will apply to transfers between them.[47] Transfers have been held to take place in a wide variety of such situations as:

- the sale of an abattoir by an insolvent company to another, even though the abattoir was closed for a period during the sale[48]

- the outsourcing to a contractor of the internal catering operations of a company[49]

- the transfer of the work of caring for drug-dependent immigrants after the local authority switched its funding from one charity to another[50]
- the contracting out of a local authority refuse collection and street cleaning service.[51]

Actual ownership is not, therefore, important. A relevant transfer does not take place if there has merely been a change in the shareholders. This was shown in *Brookes* v *Borough Care Services Ltd and CLS Care Services Ltd.*[52] In this case there were 335 employees of Borough Care Services Ltd, a company set up by Wigan Council to manage care homes for the elderly. The Borough wanted to transfer the operation to the voluntary sector and CLS Ltd. The transfer was effected by the CLS directors' becoming directors of BCS and the shares being transferred. The EAT held that there had not been a relevant transfer because there had been no change in the natural or legal person who was the employer.[53]

Because of the lack of a definition, the ECJ has developed the meaning of a transfer. In *Spijkers*[54] the ECJ stated that it was necessary to take all the factual circumstances of the transaction into account, including:

- the type of undertaking or business in question
- the transfer or otherwise of tangible assets such as buildings or stocks
- the value of intangible assets at the date of transfer
- whether the majority of staff are taken over by the new employer
- the transfer or otherwise of customers
- the degree of similarity between activities before and after the transfer, and
- the duration of any interruption in those activities.

The Court of Justice held that one had to consider these factors and look at the entity before and after the transfer to see whether the operation continued. Since this case there have been a number of further cases at the ECJ that have developed this definition. In *Schmidt* v *Spar und Leihkasse*[55] this process led to the ECJ concluding that the transfer of a contract using one part-time cleaner in a bank branch office constituted a transfer of an undertaking for the purposes of the Directive.

This has been qualified by the case of *Süzen*[56] which concerned the competitive tender for a school cleaning contract. The Court of Justice considered whether the taking over of a school cleaning contract could be a relevant transfer and concluded that one had to distinguish between the transfer of an entity (as in *Spijkers* above) and an activity only. If there is no transfer of tangible or intangible assets or the taking over by the new employer of a major part of the workforce, in terms of their numbers and skills, then there has not been a transfer of an entity, only the transfer of an activity (in this case the cleaning of a school). As a result of this judgment there was continuing uncertainty as to whether the Directive, and hence the Transfer Regulations, applied when one contractor took over a labour-intensive contract from another contractor. If there was no transfer of equipment or other assets and no transfer of the employees or their skills, then there appeared to be no protection offered to the affected employees.

This has led to apparently contradictory judgments in the English courts. In *Betts* v *Brintel Helicopters*[57] the question was whether the transfer of a helicopter contract ferrying supplies to North Sea oil rigs was a relevant transfer or not. The Court of Appeal decided that because no employees were transferred, nor any tangible assets, then according to the *Süzen* judgment there was no relevant transfer. Thus the employees working for the contractor who lost the contract received no protection from the Transfer Regulations. In *ECM Ltd* v *Cox*[58] there was a change of contractor running a car-delivery contract. Like *Betts* there was no transfer of employees or of tangible or intangible assets. In this case, however, the Court of Appeal concluded that there was a relevant transfer and concluded that employers could not escape the effects of the

Transfer Regulations by failing to take on the previous contractor's employees.[59] This latter view has had some support from the ECJ, which looked at the transfer of a number of contracts that were labour only so that there could be no transfer of assets.[60] The ECJ concluded that there could be a transfer in circumstances where there were few assets to transfer, only employees who had been dedicated to a particular contract.

Who is protected by the Transfer Regulations?

Regulation 2 of the Transfer Regulations defines an employee as 'anyone who works for another person whether under a contract of service or otherwise, but [it] does not include anyone who provides services under a contract for services'. Thus the Regulations apply only to employees. Indeed, the ECJ has held that the Directive extends extra protection only to those who already receive protection under national law as employees.[61] There are a number of qualifications to be considered:

- Regulation 5(3) states that it is only employees who are employed immediately before the transfer who are protected. This has been interpreted broadly by the House of Lords. In *Litster* v *Forth Dry Dock Engineering*[62] an employer dismissed the workforce one hour before the transfer took place and claimed that there were no employees at the time of the transfer. The House of Lords took a purposive approach and held that being employed immediately before the transfer also included those who would have been so employed if they had not been unfairly dismissed before the transfer for a reason connected to the transfer.

- There is no obligation upon employees to transfer. Although employees employed immediately before the transfer are protected, those employees may choose not to move to the new employer.[63] Regulation 5(4B) of the Transfer Regulations states that 'Where an employee so objects, the transfer of the undertaking or part in which he is employed shall operate so as to terminate his contract of employment with the transferor but he shall not be treated, for any purpose, as having been dismissed by the transferor.'

  The result is draconian, for the transferor no longer employs the worker concerned, who is now unemployed because his contract of employment has not transferred. There is no right of redress against the transferor because there has been no dismissal.[64]

- Regulation 8(1) of the Transfer Regulations states that if a person is dismissed for a reason connected to the transfer, he or she has a claim for unfair dismissal as in Part X of the ERA 1996.

- If a change to an employee's contract is for an economic, technical or organisational reason[65] (ETO reasons), then a change may be protected by the Transfer Regulations. In *Wilson* v *St Helens Borough Council*[66] a community home was being transferred from one local authority to another. At the same time there was a reorganisation of staff and a number were made redundant while others suffered pay cuts. The claim that the employees were protected was not upheld by the House of Lords because the changes, which were aimed at making the homes economically viable, were held to be for economic, technical or organisational reasons even though they happened at the same time as the transfer. It is not always easy to distinguish between a change that results from the transfer and one that results from ETO reasons.

Proposed changes to the Transfer Regulations

The government has proposed the following amendments to the Transfer Regulations:

- In outsourcing situations there will be a relevant transfer if there is a change in service provision. A service provision is where a party enters into an arrangement to contract out to another organisation the ongoing provision of a service or services. This can include the initial contracting out of the service or a change of contractors who provide it. The key issue is whether there are employees assigned to an organised group providing the service. If the answer is yes, then they will transfer with the service.

■ There is to be widespread application of the Transfer Regulations to all potential transfers in the public sector.

■ There will be an obligation placed upon the transferor employer to notify the new employer of all outstanding liabilities that are to transfer.

■ Many transfers take place because businesses become insolvent and need to be rescued. Sometimes the need to transfer all the employees on their current terms and conditions inhibits the rescue. The proposals will allow employers and employee representatives to negotiate changes to terms and conditions in order to help any rescue.

■ Pensions have always been excluded from the scope of the Directive and the Transfer Regulations. The government proposes that an entitlement to pension provision should transfer.

■ Only minor changes to the information and consultation requirements.

NORMAL WORKING HOURS[67]

For all statutory purposes normal working hours and a week's pay are to be ascertained by reference to section 234 and sections 220–229 ERA 1996. Normal working hours are the number of hours employees are required to work by their contracts, and where they are expressly stated, this will usually be conclusive even if longer hours are actually worked.[68] Where the contractual terms have not been expressed by the parties, to determine the number of hours the contract normally involves it is necessary to look at the way the parties have acted. If it was a term that employees should work the hours they were asked to, then one looks at the hours actually worked.[69] Normal working hours will not include overtime unless that overtime is included in the minimum number of hours of employment.[70] In *London Borough of Newham v Skingle*[71] a retired school caretaker claimed that his final earnings, from which his pension was calculated, should include the overtime that he had worked. His contract of employment had contained his normal working hours and the rate that would be paid for working overtime. The provision of information about what rate of pay would be paid for overtime did not make that overtime contractual. The school caretaker was not under a contractual obligation to work overtime and, therefore, the pay did could not be counted for pension purposes.

A WEEK'S PAY

This concept is used for computing many payments under ERA 1996 – for example, redundancy payments and the basic award of compensation for unfair dismissal. Where there are normal working hours:

■ if remuneration does not vary with the amount of work done, a week's pay is the gross amount payable for a week's work under the contract of employment in force on the calculation date.[72] Calculation dates are laid down in section 225 ERA 1996 and vary according to the particular statutory rights being enforced.

■ if the remuneration varies with the amount of work done, a week's pay is the remuneration for the number of normal working hours payable at the average hourly rate.[73] The average hourly rate is ascertained by calculating the total number of hours actually worked in the 12 calendar weeks preceding the calculation date, the total amount of remuneration paid for these hours, and then deducing the average hourly payment. The 12 calendar weeks preceding the calculation date consist of weeks during which the employee actually worked even though for some of this time he or she might have earned less than usual. However, a week in which no remuneration was required to be paid must be disregarded.[74] In *British Coal* v *Cheesebrough*[75] the average hourly rate was calculated by taking into account all remuneration paid in respect of all hours worked, including overtime, except that the premium element in respect of overtime was disregarded.

■ and they are worked at varying times and in varying amounts in different weeks – for example, in the case of shift-workers – both the average rate of remuneration and the number of hours worked in a week will have to be computed in the 12 calendar weeks preceding the calculation date. In these circumstances, a week's pay is the average weekly number of normal working hours payable at the average hourly rate of remuneration.[76]

Where there are no normal working hours, a week's pay is the average weekly remuneration received over the period of 12 calendar weeks preceding the calculation date.[77]

If an employee has not been employed for a sufficient period to enable a calculation to be made under any of the above provisions, a tribunal must decide what amount 'fairly represents a week's pay'. Section 228(2)–(3) ERA 1996 sets out some matters for consideration in this respect. Where an individual's actual rate of pay is less than the national minimum wage (see Chapter 5) then the tribunal will use the higher figure when computing basic and compensatory awards for unfair dismissal.[78]

Annualised hours contracts can present a problem here. In *Ali v Christian Salvesen Food Services Ltd*[79] the employees agreed a total number of hours per annum as part of a collective agreement. The arrangement, however, did not deal with the situation where employees left during the year, after they had worked in excess of the notional weekly hours on which their standard rate of pay was based. The Court of Appeal refused to fill the gap in the agreement so that the employees could claim for the hours actually worked.

Finally, the word 'remuneration' has not been statutorily defined for these purposes but it has been held to include any payments made on a regular basis – eg commission, bonuses and attendance allowances. The payment of commission does not, however, override the need for the amount of work done in normal working hours to vary in order for it to be taken into account. Thus, if commission is earned as a result of successful sales during normal working hours, it may not necessarily be taken into account when working out the average hourly rate. The Court of Appeal held, in *Evans v Malley Organisation Ltd*[80], that time spent attempting unsuccessfully to sell to a client was as much work as that spent successfully selling. Remuneration did not, therefore, vary with the amount of work done, so just the basic pay was to be used in the calculation (in this case holiday entitlement under the Working Time Regulations 1998 – see Chapter 10). Payments in kind are excluded – eg free accommodation – as are payments received from a third party, such as tips. However, gratuities added to cheques and credit card vouchers are paid to the employer and may be treated as remuneration for these purposes.[81]

KEY POINTS

■ Continuity of employment is a statutory concept and the courts look to see whether there has been a break in service.

■ A person accrues a period of continuous service only if he or she is employed under a legal contract of employment.

■ Any week during the whole or part of which a person has a contract of employment will count. One day's employment in a week is sufficient to preserve continuity.

■ Days on which an employee is on strike neither count nor break the employee's period of continuous service.

■ There are circumstances in which an employee leaves one employer and starts working for another where continuity is preserved – for example, where the Transfer Regulations 1981 apply.

■ Normal working hours are the number of hours employees are required to work by their contracts of employment and exclude non-contractual overtime.

■ A week's pay is normally the gross amount payable for a week's work under the contract of employment. Where there is a variation in the amount paid for work, the average hourly rate will apply.

NOTES

1　See *Collison* v *BBC* (1998) IRLR 239
2　(1997) IRLR 562
3　See *Secretary of State* v *Cohen* (1987) IRLR 169
4　See section 215 ERA 1996 and *Weston* v *Vega Space Ltd* (1989) IRLR 509
5　See *Booth* v *United States of America* (1999) IRLR 16; on fixed-term contracts see Chapter 5
6　See *General of the Salvation Army* v *Dewsbury* (1984) IRLR 222
7　Section 210(4) ERA 1996
8　See *Hyland* v *J. Barker Ltd* (1985) IRLR 403
9　See *Nicoll* v *Nocorrode Ltd* (1981) IRLR 163
10　'Week' means a week ending with Saturday; see section 235(1) ERA 1996
11　(1999) IRLR 306
12　Section 212(3)(a) ERA 1996
13　Section 212(4) ERA 1996
14　See *Pearson* v *Kent County Council* (1993) IRLR 165
15　Section 212(3)(b) ERA 1996
16　See *Stephens & Son* v *Fish* (1989) ICR 324
17　*Byrne* v *City of Birmingham DC* (1987) IRLR 191
18　*Ford* v *Warwickshire County Council* (1983) IRLR 126
19　(1986) IRLR 255
20　See *Sillars* v *Charrington Ltd* (1989) IRLR 152 on seasonal work
21　Section 212(3)(c) ERA 1996
22　*Ingram* v *Foxon* (1985) IRLR 5
23　*Curr* v *Marks and Spencer plc* (2003) IRLR 75
24　(1995) ICR 965
25　Section 216(1) and (2) ERA 1996
26　Section 216(3) ERA 1996
27　Section 235(4) ERA 1996
28　See *Hanson* v *Fashion Industries* (1980) IRLR 393
29　See *Secretary of State* v *Globe Elastic Thread Co. Ltd* (1979) IRLR 327
30　Section 218(2) ERA 1996; for a generous interpretation of this provision see *Tuck Ltd* v *Bartlett* (1994) IRLR 162 and *Justfern Ltd* v *D'Ingerthorpe* (1994) IRLR 164
31　Section 235(1) ERA 1996
32　See *Astley* v *Celtec Ltd* (2002) IRLR 621
33　See *Secretary of State* v *Lassman* (2000) IRLR 411
34　Section 218(3) ERA 1996
35　Section 218(4) ERA 1996
36　Section 218(5) ERA 1996; see *Jeetle* v *Elster* (1985) IRLR 227
37　Section 218(6) ERA 1996
38　See *Payne* v *Secretary of State* (1989) IRLR 352 and *Strudwick* v *JBL* (1988) IRLR 457
39　*Tice* v *Cartwright* (1999) ICR 769
40　Section 218(7) ERA 1996; see also section 218(8)–(10) on certain types of employment in the health service
41　SI 1981/1794
42　Directive 77/187/EEC, now consolidated into Directive 2001/23/EC
43　See *Adams* v *Lancashire County Council* (1996) IRLR 154
44　Regulation 5(1) Transfer Regulations 1981
45　(1996) IRLR 76
46　(1988) ECR 2559
47　See Case 234/98 *Allen* v *Amalgamated Construction Ltd* (2000) IRLR 119

48   *Spijkers* v *Gebroeders Benedik Abattoir* (1986) ECR 1119
49   *Rask* v *ISS Kantineservice* (1993) IRLR 133
50   *Sophie Redmond Stichting* v *Bartol* (1992) IRLR 366
51   *Wren* v *Eastbourne Borough Council* (1993) IRLR 425
52   (1998) IRLR 636
53   See Case C-171/94 *Merckx* v *Ford Motor Co Belgium SA* (1996) IRLR 467
54   See note 105
55   (1994) IRLR 302
56   *Süzen* v *Zehnacker Gebäudereinigung* (1997) IRLR 255
57   (1997) IRLR 361
58   (1999) IRLR 559
59   See also *Adi (UK) Ltd* v *Willer* (2001) IRLR542
60   See *Francisco Hernandez Vidal* v *Gomez Perez* (1999) IRLR 132
61   See *Mikkelson* (1985) ECR 2639
62   (1989) IRLR 161
63   See *Katsikas* v *Konstantidis* (1992) ECR 6577
64   See *Hay* v *George Hanson Ltd* (1996) IRLR 427
65   Regulation 8(2) Transfer Regulations 1981
66   (1998) ICR 387
67   See also Chapter 11 on the regulation of working time
68   See *Gascol Conversions* v *Mercer* (1974) IRLR 155
69   See *Dean* v *Eastbourne Fishermen's Club Ltd* (1977) IRLR 143
70   Section 234(3) ERA 1996; see *Lotus Cars Ltd* v *Sutcliffe and Stratton* (1982) IRLR 381
71   (2003) IRLR 72
72   Section 221(2) ERA 1996; see *Keywest Club* v *Choudhury* (1988) IRLR 51
73   Section 221(3) ERA 1996
74   Section 225 ERA 1996; see *Secretary of State* v *Crane* (1988) IRLR 238
75   (1990) IRLR 148
76   Section 221 ERA 1996
77   Section 224 ERA 1996
78   *Paggetti* v *Cobb* (2002) IRLR 861
79   (1997) IRLR 17
80   (2003) IRLR 156
81   See *Nerva* v *UK* (2002) IRLR 815

Human Rights and Data Protection

OVERVIEW

Article 8(1) of the European Convention on Human Rights, incorporated into UK law by the Human Rights Act 1998, states that 'Everyone has the right to respect for his private and family life, his home and his correspondence.' We examine here the provisions of the Human Rights Act 1998, the Data Protection Act 1998 and the Access to Medical Records Act 1988, and consider their effect upon employment law and practice. In particular, we examine the Data Protection Principles, which provide a framework for regulating the activities of those who control and process personal data, and the rights of employers to monitor and record the communication of employees.

THE HUMAN RIGHTS ACT 1998

The Human Rights Act 1998 (HRA 1998) incorporates a substantial part of the European Convention for the Protection of Human Rights and Fundamental Freedoms, which was originally agreed in Rome in 1950. It is unlawful for public authorities, which include courts and tribunals, to act in a way that is incompatible with a Convention right.[1] From October 2000 courts and tribunals in the United Kingdom have been required to take into account any 'judgment, decision, declaration or advisory opinion' of the European Court of Human Rights[2] (ECHR) or the European Commission of Human Rights. In addition, all primary and subordinate legislation must be read and interpreted in a way that is compatible with Convention rights.[3] If a court is satisfied that a piece of legislation is incompatible with a Convention right, it may make a declaration of incompatibility,[4] after which the government may amend the legislation concerned to bring it into line.[5]

The Articles of the Convention that might have an effect on employment law in the United Kingdom are listed below, with some illustrations of what impact they may, or may not, have.

Article 8: The right to respect for private and family life

This Article has two parts. The first, quoted in the introductory paragraph to this chapter, states the right to privacy. Article 8(2) forbids the interference by any public authority with the exercise of this right, except for:

- the interests of national security
- public safety or the economic well-being of the country
- the prevention of disorder or crime
- the protection of health and morals
- the protection of the rights and freedoms of others.

The application of Article 8

These are important exceptions. In *Halford* v *United Kingdom*[6] the Assistant Chief Constable of Merseyside Police brought a claim that she had been discriminated against on the grounds of her sex when on a number of occasions she unsuccessfully applied for promotion. During the proceedings, Ms Halford complained to the ECHR that the interception of telephone calls from her office and home breached her rights to privacy and freedom of expression.[7] The UK Government argued that interception of office telephone calls fell outside the protection of Article 8 because there could not be a reasonable expectation of privacy in relation to them. They argued that in principle employers should be able to monitor phone calls without the employees' knowledge on equipment provided by them. The court refused to accept this argument and awarded her compensation. Because she had received no warning, Article 8 applied to protect her privacy. Thus the entitlement to privacy extends to calls made from the office as well as home, unless there has been prior warning that such calls are liable to be monitored.

Article 8 has also been effectively used to re-enforce the rights of transsexuals. In *Goodwin v United Kingdom*[8] a male to female transsexual complained about her legal status in the United Kingdom. Under UK law, transsexuals were treated for social security and employment purposes as the same gender as that which they were born with. She was often required to produce evidence of her birth sex, e.g. when applying for life assurance or employment. This, she claimed, had caused her to suffer discrimination and humiliation. The European Court of Human Rights decided that this was an unsatisfactory situation and that her rights under Article 8 and Article 12 (the right to marry) had been breached. This decision was applied in another case[9] which concerned a male to female transsexual who applied to join the West Yorkshire Police Force. She was turned down particularly because of concerns about the need sometimes to carry out intimate body searches and that this needed to be done by someone of the same sex as the person being searched. The Court of Appeal stated that after the *Goodwin* decision a post-operative male to female transsexual was to be treated as female for the purposes of employment law. The Police Force were required to treat her as a female applicant. This, however, does not apply to pre-operative transsexuals.[10]

The right to privacy is closely connected with the protection given to employees by the Data Protection Act 1998. This right to privacy is not unlimited and employers are given some rights to monitor employees' activities, particularly by the Regulation of Investigatory Powers Act 2000 (see below).

Article 9: Freedom of thought, conscience and religion

Article 9(1) establishes the right of a person to 'freedom to change his religion or belief, and freedom, either alone or in community with others and in public or private, to manifest his religion or belief, in worship, teaching, practice and observance'. The limitations to this right are those:

- in the interests of public safety
- for the protection of public order, health or morals
- for the protection of the rights and freedoms of others.

One issue is when the practice of religion or religious beliefs clashes with the requirements of a contract of employment. It is not clear whether Article 9 will be helpful in this respect.

In *Ahmad v Inner London Education Authority*[11] a school teacher who was a devout Muslim worked under a contract of employment which required his full-time service. The contract incorporated a staff code which allowed for time off with pay on special days in which a religion held that no work should be done. The employers would not allow him a 45-minute period of absence each Friday for him to be able to attend at a mosque. The claim for unfair dismissal was lost in the Court of Appeal, which held that the dismissal was fair because the employee's absence occurred during working hours and was not for reasons of religious belief. Lord Denning considered the issue with regard to Article 9 and concluded that 'It is drawn in such vague terms that it can be used for all sorts of unreasonable claims and provoke all sorts of litigation.' He then stated that he could see nothing in the Convention that would give an employee the right to participate in religious activity on Friday afternoons in derogation of a contract of employment. Lord Scarman dissented from the majority view and decided that the Convention required a broad view to be taken, and that Article 9 would help people exercise their religious beliefs during working hours without losing pay.

In *Stedman* v *United Kingdom*[12] an employee lost a claim for breach of Article 9 as a result of her dismissal for refusing to work on a Sunday, which was against her religious beliefs. A similar case was cited of an employee of Finnish State Railways who had lost a job because a requirement to work after sunset on a Friday clashed with the employee's beliefs as a member of the Seventh-Day Adventist Church. The court had held that this was for economic reasons and had nothing to do with the person's religious beliefs. Ms Stedman lost for similar reasons.[13]

After the adoption of the Employment Equality (Religion or Belief) Regulations 2003 (see Chapter 7), employees are also able to rely upon these Regulations as well as the European Convention.

Article 10: Freedom of expression

According to Article 10(1), the right to freedom of expression shall include the right to hold opinions and receive and impart information and ideas without interference from public authorities and regardless of frontiers. Again there is an important list of limitations to this right. They are restrictions in the interests of:

- national security
- territorial integrity or public safety
- the prevention of disorder or crime
- the protection of health or morals
- the protection of the reputation or the rights of others
- the prevention of disclosure of information received in confidence
- maintaining the authority and impartiality of the judiciary.

Camelot v *Centaur Communications*[14] concerned a leak of information about Camelot, who ran the national lottery, to the press. The information was a draft set of accounts which contained potentially embarrassing information. Among other matters, Camelot sought the return of the documents partly to help them identify the source of the leak, which they believed to be an employee. The Court of Appeal stated that weight had to be given to the Convention and decisions of the ECHR. The Contempt of Court Act of 1981 restricted the court's right to compel disclosure unless it was in the interests of, among other factors, justice or national security.[15] The Court decided that the public interest in enabling the employer to discover the identity of the person who had made the leak outweighed the public interest in 'enabling the person to escape detection'. A slightly broader approach was evident in a case which concerned employees distributing leaflets outside a supermarket to urge the public not to buy their employer's goods.[16] Lord Justice Neill stated that the court should bear in mind the Convention whenever it is asked to exercise its discretion in a way which restricts freedom of expression.

In *Ahmed* v *United Kingdom*[17] there was a challenge by local government officers against regulations which restricted the right of senior local government employees to participate in political activities. They claimed that the regulations were in breach of Article 10 of the Convention. The ECHR held that such restrictions were not in breach because they were prescribed by law for a legitimate aim – namely, to protect the rights of others, such as local councillors and the electorate, to effective political democracy at the local level. The ECHR accepted that for a restriction of Article 10 there had to be a pressing need and that Member States had a certain 'margin of appreciation'. This restriction was a valid response to a social need within the UK's margin of appreciation.

Article 11: Freedom of assembly and association

Article 11(1) states that everyone has the 'right to freedom of peaceful assembly and to freedom of associ-ation with others, including the right to form and to join trade unions for the protection of his interests'. There is an exception allowed for the armed forces, the police and 'the administration of the state'.[18] Other restric-tions are:

- for the interests of national security or public safety
- for the prevention of disorder or crime
- for the protection of health or morals
- for the protection of the rights and freedom of others.

The attitude of the United Kingdom towards this Article was tested in the decision, in 1984, to forbid employees at the Government Communications Headquarters (GCHQ) to be members of a trade union. The UK government argued that there was a national security justification for this action.[19] The matter was subsequently considered by the European Commission of Human Rights.[20] The trade unions argued that the exceptions should be strictly interpreted and that assertions of national security did not create a 'blan-ket exception to the Convention guarantees'. The Commission accepted that the staff serving at GCHQ could be considered members of the administration of the state and that 'they were concerned with vital functions of national security'. As a result the measures were held to come within the exceptions in Article 11(2).

In *Wilson v United Kingdom*[21] the European Court of Justice reviewed UK laws which did not prohibit employers from offering financial inducements to employees who give up their right to collective represen-tation, even if the purpose of such inducements was end collective bargaining and weaken the trade unions in an establishment. The Court held that this amounted to a violation of Article 11 of the Convention and that the United Kingdom had failed in its positive obligation to ensure that individuals should be able to enjoy their rights under Article 11.

Article 14: Non-discrimination

Article 14 states that 'the enjoyment of the rights and freedoms set forth in this Convention shall be secured without discrimination on any grounds such as sex, race, colour, language, religion, political or other opin-ion, national or social origin, association with a national minority, property, birth or other status'.

This right to non-discrimination reinforces the other rights in the Convention. It can only be relied upon inso-far as it relates to the rights set out elsewhere in the Convention. The Article is potentially wide in its effect. It mentions specifically a number of grounds upon which discrimination is not permitted, but uses the phrase 'on any grounds such as . . .', which suggests that its effect could be much broader. Thus the appli-cant needs to show preferential treatment for other persons in a comparable position and that there is no objective justification for the difference.

Although this right depends upon alleged infringement of other rights, it does not depend upon the suc-cessful prosecution of those other rights. In *Inze v Austria,*[22] for example, the allegation that Article 1 of the first protocol was infringed failed, but a breach of Article 14 was still held to have taken place.

DATA PROTECTION

The collection and holding of information on workers is an important role of management. The potential for misuse of this information is evident. Employers will hold much personal and other information which, if used for the wrong purposes, may have a detrimental effect upon employees' working and personal lives.

In the United Kingdom the Data Protection Act 1984 provided some protection by giving rights to individuals about whom information is recorded on computers. The Directive on the Protection of Personal Data[23] 1995 (PPD Directive) led to the passing of the Data Protection Act 1998, which replaced the 1984 Act.

The Directive on personal data protection

The PPD Directive is aimed at seeking a high level of protection in the European Community and is partly justified by Article 8 of the European Convention on Human Rights, which is concerned with the right to privacy.[24] Article 1(1) of the Directive states that:

> **Member States shall protect the fundamental rights and freedoms of natural persons, and in particular their right to privacy with respect to the processing of personal data.**

It applies not only to the processing of personal data wholly or partly by automatic means, but also to data that is part of a non-automated filing system.[25] Obligations are imposed upon the data controller, ie the natural or legal person or body 'which determines the purposes and the means of the processing'.[26] Data controllers are required to observe a number of principles. These are that data should be processed fairly and lawfully; it should be collected for specified purposes and used accordingly; it should be adequate, relevant and not excessive for the purpose proposed; it should be accurate and up to date; and individuals should not be identifiable from the data longer than is necessary.[27]

The Directive also sets out the criteria which makes the processing of data legitimate.[28] These are that:

- the data subject has unambiguously given his or her consent
- data processing is necessary for the performance of a contract or in order to enter into a contract requested by the data subject
- processing is required by law
- processing is necessary to protect a vital interest of the data subject
- processing is necessary in the performance of tasks carried out in the public interest or by official authorities where necessary
- data can be processed where the data controller has a legitimate interest to do so and this interest is not overridden by the interest of protecting the fundamental rights, including that of privacy, of data subjects.

More stringent rules apply to the processing of sensitive data relating to racial or ethnic origin, political opinions, religious or philosophical beliefs, and trade union membership, and the processing of data concerning personal health or sex life.[29]

The Data Protection Act 1998

The use, or misuse, to which information held by employers can be put was illustrated by *Dalgleish* v *Lothian and Borders Police Board*.[30] In this case an employer was asked by the local authority to provide details of employee names and addresses in order to help the local authority in identifying those who were in arrears with their community charge.[31] The employees succeeded in obtaining an interim interdict (injunction) stopping the employer revealing this information. The Court of Session held that the names and addresses of employees were confidential and therefore protected against disclosure. The information was held by the employer for the purpose of the employment relationship. That an individual residing at a particular address was an employee of the employer was information that was generally not available to the public.

'Data' in the Data Protection Act 1998 (DPA 1998) means information which:

- is processed by equipment operating automatically in response to instructions given for that purpose
- is recorded with the intention that it should be processed by means of such equipment
- is recorded as part of a relevant filing system or with the intention that it should be part of that system[32]
- is not one of the above, but is an accessible record such as a health, educational or other accessible public record.[33]

It is important to note that the Act applies to data that is kept in a manual filing system which is structured 'either by reference to individuals or by reference to criteria relating to individuals, in such a way that specific information relating to a particular individual is readily accessible'.[34]

The data protection principles

The DPA 1998[35] lists a number of data protection principles. Every data controller has an obligation to comply with these principles in relation to all personal data that he or she controls and/or processes.[36] The principles are:

Principle 1 – Personal data is to be processed fairly and lawfully
In order for personal data to be processed fairly and lawfully, either the data subject[37] must give consent to the processing or the processing must be held to be necessary for a variety of other reasons, such as protecting the vital interests of the data subject or performing a contract to which the data subject is a party.

There are rules in relation to the processing of 'sensitive personal data'. This is data relating to the racial or ethnic origin of the data subject; the subject's political opinions; the subject's religious or similar beliefs; whether the subject is a member of a trade union; the subject's physical or mental health or condition;[38] the subject's sexual life; the subject's commission, or alleged commission, of any offence; any proceedings against the subject for committing, or allegedly committing, an offence, and the outcome of those proceedings.[39] The processing of this sensitive personal data can take place only if the data subject has given consent or there is a necessity as defined in schedule 3 DPA 1998. This includes any processing necessary to protect the vital interests of the data subject or any processing that consists of racial or ethnic monitoring for the purposes of an equal opportunities policy.[40]

It is necessary to provide data subjects with information about the purpose for which data is being processed. Without this the processing is not likely to be 'fair'.[41]

Principle 2 – Personal data is to be obtained only for specified and lawful purposes
It must not be further processed in any manner incompatible with those purposes. The purpose or purposes for which data is obtained may be specified in a notice given by the data controller to the data subject.

Principle 3 – Personal data is to be adequate, relevant and not excessive in relation to the purpose for which it is processed
In employer/employee terms this may mean that the employer should take care only to collect information that is relevant to the employment relationship.

Principle 4 – Personal data should be accurate and, where necessary, kept up to date
This is not to say that the data controller is necessarily at fault if the data is inaccurate, as long as it is an

accurate record of the data provided by the data subject or a third party. There is a need for the data controller to take all reasonable steps to ensure the accuracy of the data and to record any views of the data subject about the inaccuracy of the data.[42]

Principle 5 – Personal data processed for any purposes is not to be kept longer than is necessary for those purposes
This may be a difficult issue with regard to ex-employees. It may be necessary to keep information in order to be able to provide references to future employers and for other purposes with regard to an employee. The difficult questions centre on how long this information should be kept and how much information really has to be kept (perhaps not as much as for a current employee).

Principle 6 – Personal data is to be processed in accordance with the rights of the data subject under this Act

Principle 7 – Appropriate technical and organisational measures must be taken against unauthorised or unlawful processing of personal data and of accidental loss, destruction or damage to this data
This is about the security of the data. Data controllers must ensure a level of security appropriate to the harm that might be caused from unlawful or unauthorised processing or loss or damage. The cost of implementing any measures and the nature of the data to be protected are also relevant.[43] Measures are likely to include controls on access to records by restricting the information to those who need to know it – for example, by the controlled use of passwords. There is an obligation upon the data controller to take reasonable steps to ensure the reliability of any employees who have access to the data.[44]

Principle 8 – Personal data is not to be transferred outside the European Economic Area (EEA) unless that country ensures adequate levels of protection for the rights and freedoms of data subjects

Data subjects have certain rights:[45]

- to be informed by the data controller whether personal data about the subject is being processed, and if so, the content of that data. Some personal data is exempt if it consists of, for example, a reference to be given in confidence by the data controller for the purposes of education, training or employment, or prospective education, training or employment, of the data subject; or the appointment, or prospective appointment, of the data subject to any office.
  Thus references provided to prospective employers, given in confidence, are exempt and the employee may not apply to examine them under the provisions of the DPA 1998. This exemption does not apply to other parties, and so does not apply to references given by a former employer.
- to request in writing that a data controller should cease or not begin processing data which may cause substantial damage or substantial distress to the data subject when such damage or distress is unwarranted
- to request that the data controller cease processing personal data for the purposes of direct marketing
- by a written notice, to require the data controller to ensure that no decision which significantly affects the data subject should be based upon the processing by automatic means of personal data. Such decisions may relate to performance at work, creditworthiness, reliability or conduct.

The DPA re-established the post of Data Protection Commissioner, first established by the Data Protection Act 1984.[46] The office was subsequently re-designated as the Information Commissioner. The Commissioner has a variety of duties, including the promotion of good information-handling and the encouragement of codes of practice, such as that on the 'Use of personal data in employer/employee relationships'. This Code has four parts being developed. These are

- recruitment and selection; employment protection
- records of management
- monitoring at work
- medical informtion

There is a requirement for data controllers to register with the Commissioner, although there is an exemption for certain human-resource-related processing, such as appointments or removals, pay, discipline, superannuation, work management or other personnel matters of the staff of the data controller.[47] This exception relates only to past, present or prospective members of staff of the data controller.

REGULATION OF INVESTIGATORY POWERS ACT 2000 (RIP 2000)

It is unlawful[48] for a person, without lawful authority, to intentionally intercept a communication in the course of its transmission by way of a public or private telecommunications system, although such an interception will not be unlawful if the interceptor believes that both parties had agreed to the interception.[49]

Section 4(2) RIP 2000 provided for the introduction of The Telecommunications (Lawful Business Practice) (Interception of Communications) Regulations 2000 (the LBPIC Regulations).[50] These Regulations authorise conduct which involves the monitoring or recording of communications, on the employer's telecommunications systems, without consent, for the purposes of:[51]

- establishing facts; this may involve the recording of messages and telephone conversations in order to establish the facts of an event
- ascertaining compliance with regulatory or self-regulatory practices or procedures; this might include monitoring to ensure that the employer's business is complying with any established rules or guidelines, whether such guidelines are external or internal
- ascertaining or demonstrating the standards that are to be achieved, or ought to be achieved, by the persons using the system; this could mean for the purposes of quality control and employee training[52]
- maintaining national security
- preventing or detecting crime
- investigating or detecting the unauthorised use of the telecommunications system
- securing the effective operation of the system; this may include detection for the purposes of checking bugs or any other threat to the system.

Systems controllers are also authorised to monitor:[53]

- communications for the purpose of determining whether they are communications relevant to the system controller's business;[54] this will clearly permit employers to examine individual employee's e-mail accounts
- communications made to confidential telephone counselling or support services or helplines. This may be done to support counselling staff, but the potential implications in interfering with confidential calls is significant.

The apparent contradiction between these rules and the right to privacy contained in the HRA 1998 would suggest that the powers of employers to monitor and record will have to be treated with caution. The LBPIC Regulations 1998 provide some limitations. The ability to monitor or record communications can be authorised only if:

- the interception is solely for the purpose of monitoring and recording communications relevant to the business; it is difficult to see, however, how an employer could distinguish between e-mails relevant to the business and those not relevant without examining them all
- the telecommunications system in question is provided for use wholly or partly in connection with the business
- the systems controller has made all reasonable efforts to inform every person using the system that communications may be intercepted; it should be noted that there is no requirement for the user's consent to the interception, only that every effort has been made to inform him or her of the fact.

There is also a potential conflict with the requirements of the Data Protection Act 1998, which imposes important restrictions on the processing of such data once it has been recorded. The Information Commissioner's guidance is that such monitoring should take place only after it has been established that there is a problem which needs examining and that the methods used should not be too intrusive into an individual's privacy.

The real difficulty for employers lies in monitoring and then processing any data collected with regard to infringing the right to privacy of individuals. One solution is, of course, to make explicit reference to the subject in the contract of employment or as part of any disciplinary procedure and rules. The lack of any explicit description of an employer's IT policy may contribute to making a dismissal unfair.

THE ACCESS TO MEDICAL REPORTS ACT 1988

This Act provides a right of access to any medical report relating to an individual which is to be, or has been, supplied by a medical practitioner for employment or insurance purposes. The AMRA 1988 applies to 'medical reports' which are commissioned both before employment commences and during employment from 'a medical practitioner who is or has been responsible for the clinical care of the individual'.[55]

An employer who wishes to apply for a medical report covered by this legislation is required to notify the individual that he or she proposes to make an application, and must obtain that person's consent.[56] In addition, the employer must inform the individual in writing of the following rights created by the Act:

- the right to withhold consent to such an application[57]
- if the individual does consent, the right to state that he or she wants access to the report. Where the individual so states, the employer must notify the medical practitioner of this fact at the time the report is sought[58]
- the right of access is to the report before it is supplied to the employer[59] and to any medical report relating to him or her that the practitioner has supplied during the previous six months.[60] A person who wants access to the report before it is supplied to the employer has 21 days to contact the medical practitioner about arrangements for access. For these purposes, giving access to a report means supplying the individual with a copy of it or making the report (or a copy) available for inspection. A reasonable fee may be charged for the cost of supplying a report
- the right to request the amendment of, or record a difference of opinion over, any details contained in the report which the individual regards as misleading or incorrect. If the individual requests in writing that the medical practitioner should attach to the report a statement of that individual's views about any part of the report which the doctor refuses to amend, the doctor is obliged to do so[61]

- the right to refuse consent to the disclosure of the report to the employer.[62]

Doctors' duty of care is to the person for whom a report is made – not to the applicant

An employer who applies for a medical report from a doctor must also inform that doctor of certain matters.[63] However, there is nothing to prevent employers from using standard forms for notifying either employees or doctors. The courts have held that medical practitioners who carry out pre-employment medical assessments and examinations do not owe a duty of care to the potential employee. The duty of care is owed to the person for whom the report is made and who is relying on it. The case of *Kapfunde* v *Abbey National plc*[64] concerned a part-time employee who applied for a full-time position with the same employer. She was asked to complete a medical questionnaire and disclosed that she suffered from sickle-cell anaemia. The questionnaire was referred to a general practitioner to whom the employer paid an annual retainer. The GP stated that the medical evidence showed a likelihood of higher-than-average levels of absenteeism and the employer declined to give the employee a full-time post. The court held that the GP was under a contract of service with the employer when assessing medical questionnaires and that there was no special relationship from which a duty of care to the applicant could be shown. This approach was also followed in *London Borough of Hammersmith & Fulham* v *Farnsworth*,[65] where an occupational health physician was held to be an agent of the employer when preparing a report on a potential employee.

An individual can be denied access to the whole or part of a report if the medical practitioner thinks that its disclosure would be likely:

- to cause serious physical or mental harm to the individual involved, or
- to reveal information about another individual, or
- to reveal the intentions of the practitioner in relation to the individual, or
- to reveal the identity of another non-medical person who has supplied information to the medical practitioner.[66]

Where the medical practitioner decides that access to the report should be withheld (wholly or in part) because of one or more of the statutory exemptions, he or she must notify the individual of that fact. If a person is unhappy about the disclosure of information in these circumstances, he or she may choose to refuse consent to the report being supplied to the employer. Obviously, both job-seekers and job-holders will think hard about the conclusions that employers might draw from the withholding of consent to a medical report.

People who feel that their rights under this Act have been infringed can complain to the County Court.[67] If the court is satisfied that a person has failed (or is likely to fail) to comply with a requirement relating to the complainant, it may order compliance. Thus if a medical report has already been supplied without the individual's consent or access to it has been denied, all that can be enforced is the right of access to the report and to have a statement of views attached to it.

KEY POINTS

- The Human Rights Act 1998 incorporates a substantial part of the European Convention for the Protection of Human Rights and Fundamental Freedoms into UK law.
- The Articles that may have particular effect upon employment law are Article 8 on respect for private and family life, Article 9 on freedom of thought, conscience and religion, Article 10 on freedom of expression, and Article 11 on freedom of assembly and association.
- Employment tribunals and courts must interpret legislation in a way that is compatible with Convention rights.
- The Directive on the Protection of Personal Data 1995 aims to achieve a high level of protection of the 'fundamental rights and freedoms of natural persons, and in particular their right to privacy with respect to the processing of personal data'.
- The Data Protection Act 1998 regulates the processing of data whether done automatically or through a manual filing system.
- The Access to Medical Records Act 1988 provides some rules for employers and medical practitioners seeking a pre-employment medical assessment or examination.
- Medical practitioners who carry out such assessments owe a duty of care not to the employee but to the employer who is relying on the report.

NOTES

1 Section 6 HRA 1998
2 Section 2(1)(a) HRA 1998
3 Section 3(1) HRA 1998
4 Section 4 HRA 1998; the courts referred to include the House of Lords, the Court of Appeal, the High Court and the Court of Session
5 Section 10 HRA 1998
6 (1997) IRLR 471
7 Articles 8 and 10 of the Convention, respectively
8 (2002) IRLR 664
9 *A v Chief Constable of West Yorkshire* (2003) IRLR 32
10 See *Croft v Consignia plc* (2003) IRLR 592
11 (1977) ICR 490
12 (1997) 23 EHRR CD 168
13 Sections 45 and 101 ERA 1996 protect shop workers and betting workers who refuse to work on a Sunday from suffering detriment or dismissal because of this refusal
14 (1998) IRLR 81
15 Section 10 Contempt of Court Act 1981
16 *Middlebrook Mushrooms Ltd v TGWU* (1993) IRLR 232
17 (1999) IRLR 188
18 Article 11(2) HRA 1996
19 See *CCSU v Minister for the Civil Service* (1985) ICR 374
20 See *CCSU v United Kingdom* (1987) EHRR 269
21 (2002) IRLR 568
22 (1987) 10 EHRR 394
23 Directive 95/46/EC
24 Preamble, paragraph (10) DPP Directive 1995
25 Article 3 DPP Directive 1995
26 See Article 2(d) DPP Directive 1995

27   Article 4 DPP Directive 1995
28   See Article 7 DPP Directive 1995
29   Article 8 DPP Directive 1995
30   (1991) IRLR 422
31   Community charge was the method of collecting local taxes at the time. It was levied on the individ-
     ual, rather than the household
32   Section 1(1) DPA 1998
33   See section 68 DPA 1995
34   Section 1(1) DPA 1998
35   Part 1 Schedule 1
36   Section 4(4) DPA 1998
37   An individual who is the subject of the personal data; section 1(1) DPA 1998
38   It is permissible to process sensitive data concerning the holding of different beliefs and different states
     of physical or mental health, or physical and mental conditions, for the purpose of keeping or review-
     ing equality of opportunity or treatment between persons; see The Data Protection (Processing of
     Sensitive Personal Data) Order 2000 SI 2000/417
39   This list is contained in section 2 DPA 1998
40   Provided that it is carried out with 'appropriate safeguards for the rights and freedoms of data sub-
     jects'; schedule 3 para 9(1)(c) DPA 1998
41   Schedule 1 Part II para 2 DPA 1998; this notification may not be necessary if the provision of the infor-
     mation would involve a disproportionate effort; schedule 1 Part II para 3(1). However, this option is
     limited by The Data Protection (Conditions under Paragraph 3 of Part II of Schedule 1) Order 2000 SI
     2000/185
42   Schedule 1 Part II para 7 DPA 1998
43   Schedule I Part II para 9 DPA 1998
44   Schedule I Part II para 10 DPA 1998
45   These rights are listed in schedule 1 Part II para 8 of the DPA 1998
46   Section 6 DPA 1998
47   See The Data Protection (Notification and Notification Fees) Regulations 2000 SI 2000/188 schedule
     I para 2
48   Section 1 RIP 2000
49   Section 3 RIP 2000
50   SI 2000/2699
51   Regulation 3(1)(a) LBPIC Regulations 2000
52   The first three purposes are only permitted insofar as they are authorised by Article 5 of Directive
     97/66/EC concerning the processing of personal data and the protection of privacy in the telecommu-
     nications sector; Regulation 3(3) LBPIC Regulations 2000
53   Regulations 3(1)(b)–(c) LBPIC Regulations 2000
54   Communications that are entered into in the course of business or otherwise relate to that business;
     see Regulation 2(b)(i) LBPIC Regulations 2000
55   Section 2(1) AMRA 1988
56   Section 3(1) AMRA 1988
57   Section 3(2) AMRA 1988
58   Section 4(1) AMRA 1988
59   Section 4(2) AMRA 1988
60   Section 6(2) AMRA 1988
61   Section 5(2) AMRA 1988
62   Section 5(1) AMRA 1988
63   Section 4(1) and (2) AMRA 1988
64   (1999) ICR 1 CA

65   (2000) IRLR 691 CA
66   Section 7 AMRA 1988
67   Section 8 AMRA 1988

Information and consultation

CHAPTER 18

OVERVIEW

Some of the current mandatory requirements for employers to consult their employees in the United Kingdom are as a result of European Union measures. The European Union has had a policy of trying to introduce a comprehensive and harmonised approach to consultation for a number of years and there are a number of levels at which this policy works. These are the at the EU level itself, at a transnational level amongst employers who operate at this level, and at the national level within Member States of the Community. This has resulted in a number of measures which have required, and will require, employers, who may not previously have had one, to set up a formal information and consultation process with their employees. This includes European Works Councils at transnational level and the Information and Consultation Directive at the national level.

TRANSNATIONAL INFORMATION AND CONSULTATION

The measures considered here are those concerned with the establishment of European Works Councils and those dealing with the information and consultation requirements in a European Company (SE).

The European Works Council Directive

The European Works Council Directive (EWC Directive) was finally adopted after some 14 years of debate. It was originally adopted under the Agreement on Social Policy 1992 and so did not bind the United Kingdom. After the 1997 general election, and a willingness of the United Kingdom to accept the Social Policy Agreement, the Council adopted an extension Directive with a requirement for it to be transposed into UK national law by December 15 1999.[1] The purpose of the Directive was to improve the right to information and to consultation of employees in Community-scale undertakings and Community-scale groups of undertakings.[2]

A Community-scale undertaking is one that has at least 1000 employees within the Member States and at least 150 employees in each of at least two Member States. A Community-scale group of undertakings is one where a group of undertakings has at least 1000 employees within the Member States with at least two group undertakings in different Member States employing at least 150 employees.[3] The EWC Directive was transposed into national law by The Transnational Information and Consultation of Employees Regulations 1999 (TICE Regulations), which came into effect on January 15 2000.[4]

Consultation is defined in the TICE Regulations as meaning the exchange of views and the establishment of a dialogue in the context of an EWC or in the context of an information and consultation procedure.[5] The central management of an undertaking is responsible for creating the conditions and the means necessary for setting up an EWC, where the central management is situated in the United Kingdom; where it is situated outside the country, but has its representative agent based in the United Kingdom; or, if neither of these, has its biggest group of employees in the United Kingdom.

The number of UK employees is to be calculated by taking an average over a two year period, with provision for counting some part-timers as a half number. The number of employees in undertakings in other Member States is to be calculated in accordance with whatever formula that State has adopted in its law implementing the EWC Directive. Employee representatives are entitled to information on these calculations so that they can decide whether the employer qualifies. If the information given to them is incomplete or inadequate, they may present a complaint to the Central Arbitration Committee (CAC).

If central management does not act on its own initiative, the whole process of establishing an EWC can be started with a request from 100 employees, or their representatives, in two undertakings in two Member States. If there is a dispute as to whether a valid request has been made, this can be referred to the CAC for a decision.

The first stage is the establishment of a special negotiating body (SNB), whose task is to negotiate, with central management, a written agreement covering 'the scope, composition, functions and terms of office' of an EWC or the arrangements for implementing an information and consultation procedure. The SNB must consist of at least one representative from each Member State and there is a weighting formula to increase representation from bigger units in different States. The UK representatives are to be elected by a ballot of UK employees and any complaints about the ballot are to be made to the CAC. Where there is already an elected body in existence with whom consultation takes place, then that body can nominate from its membership the representatives.

The two parties are to negotiate in 'a spirit of co-operation with a view to reaching an agreement'. They may negotiate an agreement to set up an EWC or to establish an information and consultation procedure. The EWC agreement must include agreement on

1　the undertakings which are covered by the agreement
2　the composition of the EWC
3　the functions and procedures for information and consultation
4　the venue, frequency and duration of meetings
5　the financial and material resources to be allocated to the EWC
6　the duration of the agreement and the procedure for re-negotiation.

If the parties decide to establish an information and consultation procedure instead of an EWC, then this agreement must specify a method by which the information and consultation representatives[6] 'are to enjoy the right to meet and discuss the information conveyed to them'.

The information conveyed to the representatives must relate in particular to 'transnational questions which significantly affect the interests of employees'. If negotiations do not start within 6 months of a valid request by employees or fail to finish within three years from the date of that request, the Regulations provide for a default agreement, which is contained in the Schedule. These provide for an EWC of between 3 and 30 members, with at least one member from each Member State where there are undertakings. This representation is weighted according to the relative size of the undertakings in different States. The rules cover the election or appointment of UK delegates and provide that the EWC should meet at least once per annum.

Complaints about the failure of the negotiating process, either because of lack of agreement or a failure to start the process, or because of a failure to keep to the agreement, are to be referred directly to the EAT. The EAT may order the defaulter to remedy the failure and impose a fine of up to £75.000. Central management will have a defence if they are able to show that the failure resulted 'from a reason beyond the central management's control or that it has some other reasonable excuse for its failure'.

One concern related to statutory rights to information is the revealing by management of 'confidential' information. Regulation 24 TICE Regulations provides that central management is not required to disclose any information or document which, 'according to objective criteria', would seriously prejudice or harm the functioning of the undertaking concerned. It is interesting to speculate as to what this actually means. Would the sale of a subsidiary undertaking in one Member State be such information,

if it would prejudice the price received, even though it might have important effects for employees? There is an obligation for a representative, or an adviser to a representative, not to disclose confidential information unless it is a protected disclosure under section 43A ERA 1996 (whistleblowing). The Central Arbitration Committee has the responsibility of settling disputes about confidentiality and can order information to be disclosed by management or order a representative not to disclose information.

Information and consultation representatives, members of EWCs, SNBs and candidates for relevant elections have certain rights. These are:

- the right to reasonable time off with pay during working hours;
- protection against unfair dismissal; dismissal as a result of performing any of the functions or duties related to any of these bodies will make the dismissal automatically unfair.
- the right not to be subject to detriment as a result of performing any of the duties or functions related to the bodies

Complaints about any infringement of these rights are to be made to an employment tribunal.

The Company Statute

On December 20 2000 the Council of Ministers reached agreement on a proposed Regulation establishing a European Company Statute. The European Parliament agreed its support for the proposal at its meeting on September 4 2001. This gives companies operating in more than one Member State the option of establishing themselves as 'European companies' (Societas Europea or SE) operating under EU rules rather than a variety of national rules as at present. An SE can be established by the merger or formation of companies with a presence in at least two different Member States.

One concern in establishing this procedure was that companies previously based in countries with strong requirements for information and consultation might be able to avoid these requirements by establishing themselves as an SE, especially if they were merging with companies from countries with weak consultation requirements. As part of this agreement, therefore, there is a directive[7] establishing rules for information, consultation and, possibly, participation of workers employed by the SE.

Information is defined as informing the representatives of the employees
in a manner and with a content which allows the employees' representatives to undertake an in-depth assessment of the possible impact and, where appropriate, prepare consultations with the competent organ of the SE.[8]

Consultation is defined as
The establishment of dialogue and exchange of views between the body representative of the employees . . . .and the competent organ of the SE, at a time, in a manner and with a content which allows the employees' representatives, on the basis of information provided, to express an opinion on measures envisaged by the competent organ which may be taken into account in the decision-making process within the SE.[9]

When the SE is created there will need to be a special negotiating body to discuss the arrangements for employee involvement. In the absence of any agreement there will be standard rules established by the directive which will need to be followed. These require information and consultation on matters such as

- the structure, economic and financial situation
- the probable development of the business and of production and sales
- the situation and probable trend of employment and investment
- substantial changes concerning organisation, introduction of new working methods or production processes
- transfers of production, mergers, cut-backs or closures of undertakings, establishments or important parts thereof
- collective redundancies

There are also provisions for employee participation for those SE's which include companies from countries where there are such rules. Participation can include the right to elect or appoint, or oppose the election or appointment, of members of the supervisory or administrative board.

It remains to be seen how many such organisations will be established.

INFORMATION AND CONSULTATION REQUIREMENTS IN THE UNITED KINGDOM

Apart from the consultation requirements related to European Works Councils and the European Company there are a number of other areas where there already exists mandatory rules on consultation with employees. Those considered here relate to collective redundancies, transfers of undertakings and health and safety.

COLLECTIVE REDUNDANCIES

Employers proposing to dismiss as redundant 20 or more employees at one establishment within a period of 90 days or less must consult appropriate representatives of employees affected by the proposed dismissals or who may be affected by measures taken in connection with those dismissals.[10] The consultation must begin 'in good time' and in any event:

- where the employer is proposing to dismiss 100 or more employees, at least 90 days, and
- otherwise, at least 30 days before the first of the dismissals takes effect.[11]

Appropriate representatives are representatives of trade unions recognised for the purposes of collective bargaining. If there are no such representatives, the employer may choose to consult either employee representatives who have been elected or appointed by the affected employees for the purpose of this consultation or existing employee representatives who may have been elected or appointed by the employees for another purpose.[12] Employers have a responsibility for ensuring that elections for employee representatives are fair and may determine the number of representatives to be elected.[13] If the affected employees fail to elect or appoint representatives, employers may fulfil their obligations by giving them the appropriate information.[14] Conversely, if there is a complaint that an employer has failed in its duty with regard to the election of employee representatives, it is for that employer to show that it has satisfied the requirements in section 188 TULRCA 1992.[15] According to section 188(5A) TULRCA 1992, employers must allow appropriate representatives access to the employees whom it is proposed to dismiss and must provide the representatives with appropriate accommodation and facilities.[16]

Redundancy where no jobs are actually lost

In this context, redundancy is defined as 'dismissal for a reason not related to the individual concerned or for a number of reasons all of which are not so related'. This might include, for example, dismissals resulting from a refusal to accept a change in terms and conditions of employment. It will also be presumed that a dismissal is by reason of redundancy unless the contrary is proved.[17] In *GMB* v *Man Truck & Bus UK Ltd*[18] a new company was formed by the merger of two independent businesses. In order to harmonise the terms and conditions of the employees of the two businesses, the company wrote to all the employees terminating their contracts of employment on a particular day. They also wrote to all the employees offering to re-employ them from the same day, but on the new harmonised terms and conditions. The EAT held that these were not 'technical' dismissals but genuine dismissals for reasons of redundancy, as defined in section 195 TULRCA 1992 (see Chapters 13 and 14).

It is important to note that the employees covered need not be employed for any minimum number of hours per week. However, those who work under a contract for a fixed term of three months or less will be excluded unless the employment lasted for more than three months.[19]

Defining 'establishment'

'Establishment' is not defined by the statute and the EAT has ruled that this is a question for the tribunal acting as an industrial jury using its common sense on the particular facts of the case. In *Bakers' Union* v *Clark's of Hove Ltd*[20] it was accepted that separate premises could be regarded as one establishment if there was common management and accounting. The ECJ has indicated that the word 'establishment' must be understood as designating the unit to which the workers made redundant are assigned to carry out their duties. It is not essential for that unit to be endowed with a management that can independently effect collective dismissals.[21]

The consultation procedure

The consultation required must include consultation about ways of:

- avoiding the dismissals,
- reducing the numbers to be dismissed, and
- mitigating the consequences of the dismissals,

and must be undertaken 'with a view to reaching agreement with the appropriate representatives'.
An employer is required to consult on each of the three aspects individually. It is not enough just to consult on ways of reducing the numbers of employees to be dismissed and mitigating the consequences of dismissals, without consulting on ways of avoiding the dismissals. In such a case the employer would not have met the statutory requirements.[22] The employer is not required, however, to consult on the economic background for the proposed redundancies.[22A]

According to the EAT, employers are required to begin consultation before they give notice of dismissal,[23] but notices can be issued during the consultation period so long as the dismissals do not take effect until after the period has elapsed. Of course, if an employer gives notice of dismissal immediately after consultation has begun, it could be argued that no meaningful consultation took place.[24] A fundamental question in relation to these provisions is: how concrete does the intention to make employees redundant have to be before the duty applies? In *Hough* v *Leyland DAF*[25] the EAT suggested that the duty to consult arose when matters had reached a stage where a specific proposal had been formulated. This is a later stage than the diagnosis of a problem and the appreciation that one answer would be redundancies. Hence an employer must have formed some view as to how many employees are to be dismissed, when this is to take place, and how it is to be arranged.

It is important to note that Article 2 of the Collective Redundancies Directive[26] requires consultation where an employer is 'contemplating' collective redundancies. According to the EAT, the word 'contemplating' is far wider than the word 'proposing'. It suggests that a number of options are being considered, including redundancies. In *Scotch Premier Meat Ltd* v *Burns*[27] an employer decided on two options, which were either the sale of the business as a going concern or its closure and sale as a development site. The latter option would have led to all the employees' being dismissed as redundant. The meeting at which these options were decided upon was the occasion when the employer was contemplating (and proposing) redundancies. In *MSF v Refuge Assurance plc*[28] the court held that it was not possible to construe the word 'proposing' as same as the word 'contemplating'. The word 'proposing 'relates to a state of mind which is much more certain and further along the decision making process than contemplates'.

What employers must disclose in writing

The employer must disclose in writing the following matters at the beginning of the consultation period, although a lack of information should not be allowed to delay the start of consultation.[29]

(a) the reason for the proposals

(b) the number and description of employees whom it is proposed to dismiss

(c) the total number of employees of any such description employed by the employer at that establishment

(d) the proposed method of selecting the employees who may be dismissed

(e) the proposed method of carrying out the dismissals, with due regard to any agreed procedure, including the period over which the dismissals are to take effect

(f) the proposed method of calculating the redundancy payment if this differs from the statutory sum.

This information must be delivered to each of the appropriate representatives, or sent by post to an address notified by them or, in the case of union representatives, to the union head office. In *E. Green Ltd* v *ASTMS and AUEW*[30] it was held that items (d) and (e) had not been complied with when the method of selecting employees who might be dismissed was given as 'to be in consultation with union representatives'.

'Special circumstances' permitting employers to depart from consultation requirements

If there are 'special circumstances' which render it not reasonably practicable for the employer to comply with the above-mentioned provisions, an employer must take 'all such steps towards compliance' as are reasonably practicable in the circumstances. 'Special circumstances' mean circumstances which are uncommon or out of the ordinary, so insolvency by itself will not provide an excuse, as it may well be foreseeable.[31] However, that the employer has continued trading in the face of adverse economic pointers in the genuine and reasonable expectation that redundancies would be avoided can justify non-compliance.[32] Additionally, a pending application for government financial aid, the withdrawal of a prospective purchaser from negotiations combined with a bank's immediate appointment of a receiver, and the need for confidentiality in negotiating a sale, have all constituted 'special circumstances'. By way of contrast, the following have not been accepted as being 'special':

- the alarm and chaos caused by the disclosure of information about the proposed redundancies

- a genuine belief that the union had not been recognised: in *Wilson & Bros Ltd* v *USDAW*[33] it was held that such a belief must be reasonable

■ the fact that the employer had been informed by the relevant government department that there was no duty to consult in the particular case.[34]

Section 188(7) TULRCA 1992 also states that where the decision leading to the proposed dismissals is that of a person controlling the employer, a failure on the part of that person to provide information to the employer will not constitute 'special circumstances'. In addition, if the employer has invited any of the employees who may be dismissed to elect employee representatives, and this invitation was issued long enough before the time when consultation must begin to allow them to elect representatives by that time, the employer is not in breach of the statute if he or she complies with the consultation requirements as soon as reasonably practicable after the election of the representatives.[35]

Protective awards

Where the employer has failed to comply with any of the requirements of section 188 TULRCA 1992, employee representatives can complain of any failure relating to them and the union can complain where there is a failure relating to its representatives. In any other case, employees who have been or may be dismissed as redundant can complain. Claims can be made to an employment tribunal before the proposed dismissal takes effect or within three months of its doing so unless the 'time-limit escape clause' applies (see Chapter 14).[36] Employers wishing to argue that there were 'special circumstances' justifying non-compliance must prove that these circumstances existed and that they took all such steps towards compliance as were reasonably practicable. If a complaint is well-founded, the tribunal must make a declaration to that effect and may also make a protective award. A protective award refers to the wages payable for a protected period to employees who have been dismissed or whom it is proposed to dismiss. The protected period begins with the date on which the first of the dismissals to which the complaint relates takes effect (ie the proposed date of dismissal)[37] or the date of the award (whichever is the earlier) and will be of such length as the tribunal determines 'to be just and equitable in all the circumstances having regard to the seriousness of the employer's default'. The protected period is a maximum of 90 days.[38]

One object of an award is to compensate employees for their employer's failure to consult with the union even where compliance with the statute would have made no difference.[39] A consequence of focusing on the loss of days of consultation rather than the loss or potential loss of remuneration during the relevant period is that it becomes possible to make a protective award in favour of employees who have suffered no pecuniary damage – for example, where alternative employment was immediately secured.[40] The rate of remuneration payable under a protective award is a week's pay for each week of the protected period, with proportionate reductions being made in respect of periods less than a week.[41]

Where protected awards will not apply

If during the protected period employees are fairly dismissed for a reason other than redundancy, or if they unreasonably resign, then their entitlement to remuneration under the protective award ceases on the day the contract is terminated. Similarly, employees who unreasonably refuse an offer of employment on the previous terms and conditions or an offer of suitable alternative employment will not be entitled to any remuneration under a protective award in respect of any period during which, but for that refusal, they would have been employed.[42] Employees who are of a description to which a protective award relates may complain to a tribunal, within three months unless the 'time-limit escape clause' applies, that their employer has failed, wholly or in part, to pay the remuneration under that award. If the complaint is well-founded, the employer will be ordered to pay the amount due to the complainant.[43] The three-month period runs from the last day of the protected period to which the award relates. This is a problem for many applicants because the order for the award will often not be obtained until some considerable time has passed. In such cases the tribunal is likely to accept that it was 'not reasonably practicable' to present the complaint in time.[44]

Finally, it may be of interest to note that section 198 TULRCA 1992 enables the parties to a collective agreement to apply to the Secretary of State for an exemption order in respect of the consultation provisions.

Notification

An employer proposing to dismiss as redundant 100 or more employees at one establishment within a period of 90 days, or more than 20 employees within 30 days, must notify the Secretary of State in writing of the proposal within 90 or 30 days respectively.[45] There is thus no obligation to notify if fewer than 20 employees are to be dismissed. In addition, the employer must give a copy of the notice to appropriate representatives. The written notice must be in such form and contain such particulars as the Secretary of State may direct, but it is expressly provided that where there are representatives to be consulted under section 188 TULRCA 1992 the employer must identify them and state when consultation began.[46] At any time after receiving a notice under this section the Secretary of State may require the employer to give further information.[47]

If there are special circumstances rendering it not reasonably practicable for an employer to comply with the requirements of section 193 TULRCA 1992, the employer must take all such steps as are reasonably practicable in the circumstances. Again, where the decision leading to the proposed dismissals is that of a person controlling the employer, a failure on the part of that person to provide information to the employer will not constitute 'special circumstances'.[48] Employers who fail to give notice in accordance with this section may be prosecuted and suffer a fine not exceeding level 5 on the standard scale.[49]

TRANSFERS OF UNDERTAKINGS

The purpose of the Acquired Rights Directive[50] and the Transfer Regulations[51] is contained in Article 3(1) of the amended Directive. Article 3(1) states that the transferor's rights and obligations arising from a contract of employment or from an employment relationship existing on the date of the transfer shall be transferred to the transferee employer. It is as if the contract of employment was originally made between the transferee and the employee (see Chapter 16).

Regulation 10 of the Transfer Regulations is concerned with the duty to inform and consult employee representatives and regulation 11 with the consequences of failing to do so. Information should be provided 'long enough before a relevant transfer to enable the employer of any affected employees to consult all the persons who are appropriate representatives of any of those affected employees'. The High Court, in *Institution of Professional and Civil Servants v Secretary of State for Defence*[52] decided that the words 'long enough before' a transfer to enable consultation to take place meant as soon as measures are envisaged and if possible long enough before the transfer. The court held that the words did not mean as soon as measures are envisaged and in any event long enough before the transfer. This case concerned the introduction of private management into the Royal dockyards at Rosyth and Devonport. A measure which was opposed by the trade unions. Before consultation could take place there needed to be some definite plans or proposals by the employer around which consultation could take place.

The information to be provided should consist of:

- the fact that a relevant transfer is to take place,
- approximately when it is to take place
- the reasons for it
- the legal, economic and social implications for the affected employees

- the measures which are envisaged to take place in connection with the transfer, in relation to the affected employees or the fact that there are no such measures envisaged.

The rules on who are appropriate representatives and the requirements concerning their election are contained in regulations 10(2A) and 10A Transfer Regulations. These are identical to those rules concerning the appointment of appropriate representatives for the purposes of consultation in collective redundancies (see above). The representatives are the independent trade union which is recognised by the employer. If there is no such trade union, then there are employee representatives to be elected or appointed by the affected employees, whether for the purpose of these consultations or for some other purpose.

It is, of course, both the transferor and the transferee that need to consult and there is an obligation upon the transferee to provide the transferor with information about their plans, so that the transferor can carry out their duty to consult. Where the employer actually envisages taking measures in relation to any of the affected employees, then the employer must consult the appropriate representatives 'with a view to seeking their agreement to the measures to be taken'. In the course of these consultations the employer will consider the representations made by the appropriate representatives and, if any of those representations are rejected, the employer must state the reasons for so doing.

There is a special circumstances defence for the employer if it renders it not reasonably practicable to perform the duty to consult and inform. In such a case the employer must take all such steps as are reasonable in the circumstances. There is also a defence for the employer if the employees fail to elect representatives. In such a case the duty to consult is fulfilled if the employer gives each employee the necessary information.

Complaints to an employment tribunal may be made for a breach of the rules concerning consultation. If the complaint is well-founded the employment tribunal may make an award of up to a maximum of 13 weeks pay to each affected employee.

The European Council Directive on the introduction of measures to encourage improvements in the safety and health of workers[53] has specific requirements both for the provision of information to workers and for consultation and participation of workers. Article 10 ensures that workers receive information from the employer about the safety and health risks of their jobs, or their workplaces, as well as information about what protective and preventive measures are to be taken. Article 11 of the Directive provides that employers shall consult workers and /or their representatives 'and allow them to take part in discussions' on all questions relating to safety and health at work. Protection is also offered to the workers or workers' representatives who take part in this process, including the right to time off work with pay for the purpose of carrying out their duties.

HEALTH AND SAFETY

The Health and Safety (Consultation with Employees) Regulations 1996 (HSCE Regulations) were introduced to ensure that the information and consultation requirements of the SRSC Regulations were extended to those workplaces where there was no trade union recognised for collective bargaining purposes.

Regulation 5 requires employers to make available to those employees or representatives such information as is necessary to enable them to participate fully and effectively in the consultation. Representatives of employee safety must also be given information to enable them to carry out their functions.[54] In addition, inspectors are obliged, in circumstances in which it is necessary to do so for the purpose of assisting in keeping employees adequately informed about health, safety and welfare matters, to give employees or their representatives factual information relating to an employer's premises, as well as information with respect to any action which they have taken or propose to take in connection with those premises. Such information must be conveyed to the employer, and inspectors can also give a written statement of their observations to anyone likely to be a party to any civil proceedings arising out of any accident, etc.[55]

The words 'instruction' and 'training' suggest that employees should be taught to understand the duties imposed by legislation. Indeed, Regulation 13 of the MHSW Regulations stipulates that in entrusting tasks to their employees, employers must take into account their capabilities in relation to health and safety. In particular, employers have a duty to ensure that their employees are provided with adequate health and safety training when recruited or if they are exposed to new or increased risks. As regards supervision, it would seem to follow that if the employer's efforts do not persuade an employee to adopt safe working practices, disciplinary or other action may have to be taken.

Safety representatives

Section 2(4) HASAWA 1974 provides for the appointment by recognised trade unions of safety representatives from among the employees.[56] Where such representatives are appointed, employers have a duty to consult them with a view to the making and maintenance of arrangements that will enable the employer and employees to co-operate effectively in promoting and developing measures to ensure the health and safety at work of the employees, and in checking the effectiveness of such measures.[57] In particular, employers must consult union safety representatives in good time with regard to:

- the introduction of any measure which may substantially affect the health and safety of the employees represented
- the arrangements for appointing or nominating competent persons in accordance with Regulations 7(1) and 8(1)b of MHSW 1999
- any health and safety information that the employer must provide to the employees represented
- the planning and organisation of any health and safety training the employer is required to provide for the employees represented
- the health and safety consequences for the employees represented of the planning and introduction of new technologies.[58]

Employers' duty to consult

Union safety representatives may be elected or appointed. If there are employees who are not covered by union safety representatives under the SRSC Regulations, the employers must consult the employees directly or 'representatives of employee safety', who have been elected by employees, about the matters listed above. In either case employers must make available such information within their knowledge as is necessary to enable full and effective participation in the consultation.[59] Where employers consult representatives of employee safety, they must inform the employees represented of the names of the representatives and the groups they represent.[60] Similarly, if employers discontinue consultation with a representative of employee safety, they must inform the employees in the group concerned of that fact.[61]

Trade union safety representatives

The SRSC Regulations stipulate that if an employer has received written notification from a recognised independent trade union of the names of the people appointed as union safety representatives, such persons have the functions set out in Regulation 4 of the SRSC Regulations (below). So far as is reasonably practicable, union safety representatives will either have been employed by their employer throughout the preceding two years or have had at least two years' experience in similar employment.[62] Employees cease to be union safety representatives for the purpose of these regulations when:

- the trade union which appointed them notifies the employer in writing that their appointment has been terminated
- they cease to be employed at the workplace[63]
- they resign.

Functions of union safety representatives

Apart from representing all employees (not only trade union members) in consultation with the employer under section 2(6) HASAWA 1974, union safety representatives are given the following functions by Regulation 4(1) SRSC Regulations:

- to investigate potential hazards and dangerous occurrences at the workplace (whether or not they are drawn to their attention by the employees they represent) and to examine the causes of accidents at the workplace
- to investigate complaints by any employee they represent relating to that employee's health, safety or welfare at work
- to make representations to the employer on general matters affecting the health, safety or welfare at work of the employees at the workplace
- to carry out inspections in accordance with Regulations 5, 6 and 7 SRSC Regulations
- to represent the employees they are appointed to represent in consultation at the workplace with inspectors from the enforcing authorities
- to receive information from inspectors in accordance with section 28(8) of HASAWA 1974
- to attend meetings of safety committees where they attend in their capacity as safety representatives in connection with any of the above functions.

Functions of representatives of employee safety

By way of contrast, representatives of employee safety have only the following functions:[64]

- to make representations to the employer on potential hazards and dangerous occurrences at the workplace which affect, or could affect, the group of employees represented
- to make representations to the employer on general matters affecting the health and safety at work of the group represented and, in particular, on such matters as he or she is consulted about by the employer under Regulation 3 of the HSCE Regulations 1996, and
- to represent the group of employees in consultations at the workplace with inspectors appointed under section 19 HASAWA 1974.

Further points to note are:

- None of these functions imposes a duty on safety representatives, although they will be liable for the actions they take as ordinary employees.
- Employers who consult representatives of employee safety have a duty to ensure that those representatives are provided with such training in respect of their functions as is reasonable in all the circumstances. The employer must also meet any reasonable costs associated with such training, including travel and subsistence costs.[65]

Regulation 5 SRSC Regulations entitles safety representatives to inspect the workplace at least every three months, but they must give reasonable notice in writing of their intention to do so. Of course, inspections may take place more frequently if the employer agrees. Additional inspections may be made if there has been a substantial change in the conditions of work or new information has been published by the HSC or

HSE relevant to the hazards of the workplace. Inspections may also be conducted where there has been a notifiable accident or dangerous occurrence or a notifiable disease[66] contracted, for the purpose of determining the cause. The employer must provide reasonable facilities and assistance for the purpose of carrying out an inspection, including facilities for independent investigation by the union representatives and private discussion with the employees. However, there is nothing to prevent the employers or their representatives from being present during an inspection.

Time off for safety representatives

According to Regulation 4(2) of the Safety Representatives and Safety Committee Regulations 1977[67] (SRSC Regulations) and Regulation 7(1)(b) of the Health and Safety (Consultation with Employees) Regulations 1996 (HSCE Regulations) a trade union safety representative or a representative of employee safety[68] is entitled to time off, with normal or average pay,[69] during working hours to perform his or her functions and to undergo such training as may be reasonable in the circumstances. In relation to trade union safety representatives elected or appointed under the SSRC Regulations, regard has to be had for the provisions of an approved code of practice. In *White* v *Pressed Steel Fisher*[70] the EAT held that if employers provide an adequate in-house course it is not necessarily reasonable for them to be required to grant paid time off for safety representatives to attend a union course. The Code recommends that as soon as possible after their appointment union safety representatives should be permitted time off with pay for basic training approved by the TUC or the independent union which appointed the representatives. Further training, similarly approved, should be undertaken where the safety representative has special responsibilities or where such training is necessary to meet changes in circumstances or relevant legislation. Aggrieved safety representatives or representatives of employee safety can complain to an employment tribunal that their employer has failed to permit them to take time off or that they have not been paid in accordance with the Regulations. If the complaint is well-founded, the tribunal must make a declaration and may make an award of compensation.[71]

Safety committees

Where at least two union safety representatives submit a written request, employers must establish a safety committee, but before doing so they must consult the union safety representatives who made the request and the representatives of recognised trade unions. Such a committee must be formed within three months of the request being made, and a notice must be posted stating the composition of the committee and the workplaces covered.[72] Under section 2(7) HASAWA 1974 the function of safety committees is to keep under review the measures taken to ensure the health and safety at work of employees.

It should be noted that the Code of Practice advises employers, recognised unions and union safety representatives to make full and proper use of existing industrial relations machinery to reach the degree of agreement necessary to achieve the purpose of the SRSC Regulations and to resolve any differences. However, where an employee suffers a detriment as a result of health and safety activities, a complaint may be brought under section 100 ERA 1996 (if the individual was dismissed) or section 44 ERA 1996. The remedies available for infringement of section 44 mirror those available for detriment on trade union grounds (see Chapter 20). In *Shillito* v *Van Leer*,[73] for example, an employee who was a safety representative for one production line became involved, in a belligerent way, in safety issues affecting another production line, for which the employee was not a representative. The employee was disciplined and given a formal warning. A complaint to the tribunal about suffering a detriment failed because the person involved was not a safety representative in the area concerned. In *Goodwin* v *Cabletel*[74] a construction manager who had responsibility for health and safety matters on site was unhappy with one subcontractor and took an aggressive approach. The manager's employer, however, wished to be more conciliatory. The construction manager was demoted and claimed constructive dismissal. The EAT subsequently confirmed that protection extended to the way duties were carried out.

THE INFORMATION AND CONSULTATION DIRECTIVE

Directive 2002/14/EC of the European parliament and of the Council establishing a general framework for informing and consulting employees in the European Community[75] was finally unanimously adopted by the Council of Ministers in December 2001 after some years of debate. It is the first EU Directive to introduce a generalised requirement to provide information and to consult with employees or their representatives. All other information and consultation measures have been concerned with specific situations, such as collective redundancies, transfers of undertakings or in situations where companies have a European Works Council.

The Directive will eventually apply to all undertakings with 50 or more employees. This represents less than 3% of all EU companies, but about 50% of all employees.

In the preamble to the Directive the European Commission provides the justification for the measure. Some of the reasons given are that

- the existence of current legal frameworks at national and Community level concerning the involvement of employees have not always prevented serious decisions, that affect employees, from being taken and made public without adequate consultation;[76]
- there is a need to strengthen dialogue in order to promote trust within undertakings. The result of this will be an improvement in risk anticipation, making work organisation more flexible and facilitate employee access to training within the undertaking. It will also make employees more flexible in their approach and involve them in the operation and future of the undertaking as well as increasing its competitiveness;[77]
- timely information and consultation is a pre-requisite for successful restructuring and adaptation of undertakings to the needs of the global economy, especially through the new forms of organisation at work;[78]
- the existing legal frameworks for employee information and consultation are inadequate, because they 'adopt an excessively a posteriori approach to the process of change, neglect the economic aspects of decisions taken and do not contribute either to genuine anticipation of employment developments within the undertaking or to risk prevention'.[79]

It is likely that HRM practitioners will play a central role in introducing and administering the new information and consultation procedures. The CIPD itself supported the principle of legislation on the subject, but called for the regulations to be as flexible as possible so that organisations may develop arrangements that are best suited to their circumstances.[80] The Directive's provisions are, however, quite specific:

Article 1 Object and principles
The purpose is set out as being to establish a general framework for the right to
information and consultation of employees in undertakings or establishments within the European Community.

The practical arrangements for defining and implementing this are to be left to the Member States, who must carry out their obligations in such a way as to ensure their effectiveness. In doing this the employer and the employees' representatives must work 'in a spirit of co-operation'.

Article 2 Definitions
There are some interesting definitions, particularly with regard to the distinction between undertakings and establishments.

Information means transmission by the employer to the employees' representatives of data to help them acquaint themselves with the subject matter and to examine it.

Consultation means the exchange of views and establishment of dialogue between the employer and the employees' representatives.

Article 3 Scope
The Directive will apply either to undertakings employing at least 50 employees in any one Member State or to establishments employing at least 20 employees in any Member State. The method for calculating the thresholds of employees is left to the Member State.

Article 4 Practical arrangements for information and consultation
As mentioned above the practical arrangements are to be left to the individual Member State. There are, however, rules concerning what information and consultation will cover, when it is to take place and what its objectives are. The subject matter is to be

(i)   information on the recent and probable development of the undertaking's or establishment's activities and economic situation

(ii) information and consultation on the situation, structure and probable development of employment and on any anticipatory measures envisaged, especially those that threaten employment

(iii) information and consultation on decisions likely to lead to substantial changes in work organisation or in contractual relations (including those covered in Article 9 below).

Information shall be given at such time, and in such fashion, as to enable employee representatives to conduct an adequate study and, where necessary, prepare for consultation.

Consultation shall take place

- while ensuring that timing, method and content are appropriate;
- at the relevant level of management, depending upon the subject under discussion;
- on the basis of information provided by employer and of the opinion of employee representatives;
- in such a way as to enable employee representatives to meet the employer and obtain a response, the reasons for that response, to the employee representative's opinion
- with a view to reaching agreement on decisions within the scope of the employers' powers.

Article 5 Information and consultation deriving from an agreement
As with the European Works Council Directive, there is the opportunity for management and labour to negotiate their own information and consultation arrangements, providing that they meet the requirements of the Directive and national legislation. Thus any agreements existing at the transposition date of March 23 2005 will be able to continue as will any other agreements subsequently negotiated.

Article 6 Confidential information
This has always been an important concern of employers and the question of what is confidential and what is not will be part of the interest in watching this Directive put into practice. There are two aspects to confidentiality. One is imposing an obligation upon the parties to maintain a confidence. The second is the decision as to what material is so confidential that it cannot be revealed at all.

In dealing with the first of these, Member States may provide that employee representatives, and any experts who assist them, may not reveal information to employees or third parties if provided in confidence 'in the legitimate interest of the undertaking or establishment', unless that other party is bound by a duty of confidentiality. This obligation may continue after the expiry of a term of office.

Member States may also provide that the employer need not provide information or consult when the nature of the information or consultation is such that, 'according to objective criteria', it would seriously harm the functioning of the undertaking or establishment or would be prejudicial to it.

Member States shall provide for judicial review of situations where employer requires confidentiality or does not provide information or consult in accordance with above. This is the case with the TICE Regulations implementing the European Works Council Directive. The independent body is the Central Arbitration Committee.

Article 7 Protection of employees' representatives
Member States must protection for employee representatives and guarantees to enable them to perform the duties which have been assigned to them.

Article 8 Protection of rights
This Article obliges Member States to have suitable judicial processes in place to enable the obligations of employers and employees to be enforced. It also requires adequate sanctions to be available for infringement of the Directive. These sanctions must be 'effective, proportionate and dissuasive'. This is going to be an interesting provision of any UK regulations. There are potentially large sums of money which may be involved in, for example, a merger or an acquisition. If an employer decided that it wished not to consult the employees is a fine of the sort contained in the TICE Regulations going to be a sufficient deterrent. If it is not, then the might be an issue related to a bigger fine as to whether it would be proportionate.

Article 9 Link with other provisions
The Directive must not lessen existing protection (not an issue in the United Kingdom) and must be without prejudice to other Directives with requirements to consult, namely the Collective Redundancies Directive, The Acquired Rights Directive and the European Works Councils Directive.

Article 10 Transitional provisions
Although Article 11 stipulates March 23 2005 as the deadline for transposition, there
is an extension for Member States who do not have a general, permanent and statutory system of information and consultation (such as the United Kingdom). In such a case the Directive will only apply to undertakings employing at least 150 people or establishments employing 100 people until March 23 2007 (a two year extension). Thereafter, for one year, it may apply to undertakings employing 100 people or establishments with 50 employees. The full application of the Directive, to undertakings with 50 or more employees and establishments with 20 or more employees, will not therefore take effect until March 23 2008.

After this date industrial relations practices in the United Kingdom will look very different to those in existence today. They will look far more like those that exist in other Member States of the European Union.

KEY POINTS

- Community-scale undertakings with at least 1000 employees within the EU and at least 150 employees in two Member States must establish a European Works Council
- A company that establishes itself as a 'Societas Europa', is required to negotiate an information and consultation procedure with representatives of employees
- Mandatory requirements to consult, in the United Kingdom, include matters in relation to health and safety, transfers of undertakings and collective redundancies
- The Information and Consultation Directive will require the establishment of information and consultation procedures in all Uk organisations employing 50 or more people

NOTES

1   Council Directive 97/74/EC OJ L 010/22
2   Article 1(1) EWC Directive
3   Article 2(a) and (c) EWC Directive
4   SI 1999/3323; the Regulations are some 57 pages long, so what follows can only be regarded as a summary of the main points
5   Regulation 2 TICE Regulations 1999
6   Defined in Regulation 2 TICE Regulations as a person who represents employees in the context of an information and consultation procedure
7   Directive 2001/86/EC
8   Article 2(i)
9   Article 2(j)
10 Section 188(1) TULRCA 1992 as amended by the Collective Redundancies and Transfers of Undertakings (Protection of Employment) (Amendment) Regulations 1999 SI 1999/1925
11 Section 188(1A) TULRCA 1992
12 Section 188(1B) TULRCA 1992
13 Section 188A TULRCA 1992
14 Section 188(7B) TULRCA 1992
15 Section 189(1B) TULRCA 1992
16 On time off for employee representatives see Chapter 11
17 Section 195 TULRCA 1992
18 (2000) IRLR 636
19 Section 282(1) TULRCA 1992
20 (1978) IRLR 366
21 *Rockfon* (1996) IRLR 168
22 See *Middlesborough Borough Council* v *TGWU* (2002) IRLR 332
22A *Securicor Omega Express Ltd* v *GMB* (2004) IRLR 9
23 See *NUT* v *Avon County Council* (1978) IRLR 55
24 See *TGWU* v *Ledbury Preserves* (1985) IRLR 412 and *Sovereign Distribution* v *TGWU* (1989) IRLR 334
25 (1991) IRLR 194
26 Directive 98/59
27 (2000) IRLR 639
28 (2002) IRLR 324
29 Section 188(4) TULRCA 1992 and *GMB and AMICUS* v *Beloit Walmosley Ltd* (2004) IRLR 18
30 (1984) IRLR 135
31 See *GMB* v *Rankin* (1992) IRLR 514
32 See *APAC* v *Kirwin* (1978) IRLR 318
33 (1978) IRLR 20

34   See *UCATT* v *Rooke & Son Ltd* (1978) IRLR 204
35   Section 188(7A) TULRCA 1992
36   Section 189(1) and (5) TULRCA 1992
37   See *E. Green Ltd* v *ASTMS and AUEW* (1984) IRLR 435
38   Section 189(4) TULRCA 1992 as amended by the CRTUPEA Regulations 1999
39   See *Sovereign Distribution* v *TGWU* (1989) IRLR 334
40   See *Spillers-French Ltd* v *USDAW* (1979) IRLR 339
41   Section 190(2) TULRCA 1992
42   Section 191(1–3) TULRCA 1992
43   Section 192 TULRCA 1992
44   See *Howlett Marine Services Ltd* v *Bowlam* (2001) IRLR 201
45   Section 193 TULRCA 1992
46   Section 193(4) and (6) TULRCA 1992
47   Section 193(5) TULRCA 1992
48   See section 193(7) TULRCA 1992
49   Section 194 TULRCA 1992
50   Now Directive 2001/23/EC
51   Transfer of Undertakings (Protection of Employment) Regulations 1981
52   (1987) IRLR 373
53   Directive 89/391/EC
54   For exceptions see Regulation 5(3) HSCE Regulations 1996
55   Section 28(8)(b) HASAWA 1974
56   In this context 'recognition' means recognition for the purposes of collective bargaining. See Regulation 2 SRSC Regulations and *Cleveland County Council* v *Springett* (1985) IRLR 131
57   Section 2(6) HASAWA 1974
58   Regulation 4A SRSC Regulations
59   Regulation 5(2) of HSCE 1996. 'Representatives of employee safety' are defined in Regulation 4(1)(b) HSCE Regulations 1996
60   Regulation 4(2) HSCE Regulations 1996
61   Regulation 4(3) HSCE Regulations 1996
62   Regulation 3(4) HSCE Regulations 1996
63   Defined by Regulation 2(1) SRSC Regulations
64   Regulation 6 HSCE Regulations 1996
65   See Regulation 7(1)(a) HSCE Regulations 1996
66   For definitions see Regulations 6(3) SRSC Regulations
67   SI 1977/500
68   See Chapter 11
69   See the Schedule to the SRSC Regulations 1977 and the HSCE Regulations 1996
70   (1980) IRLR 176
71   Regulation 11 SRSC Regulations and Schedule 2 HSCE Regulations 1996
72   Regulation 9 SRSC Regulations. See also the Guidance notes on safety committees
73   (1997) IRLR 495
74   (1997) IRLR 665
75   OJ L80/29 23.3.02
76   Preamble para (6)
77   Preamble para (7)
78   Preamble para (9)
79   Preamble para (13)
80   CIPD (2001) *Response of the CIPD to the Government's consultation on implementation of the EU directive on information and consultation*

The Legal Framework of Collective Bargaining

CHAPTER 19

OVERVIEW

The general and specific duties of ACAS, the functions of the Central Arbitration Committee (CAC) and the role of the Certification Officer were all outlined in Chapter 1. In this chapter we examine the legal definition of an employers' association and a trade union, and describe the mechanism by which a union can obtain a certificate of independence. We also consider the question of recognition, including the statutory right to recognition of trade unions, and the duty placed upon employers to disclose information for the purpose of collective bargaining. Finally, the legal enforceability of collective agreements is discussed.

EMPLOYERS' ASSOCIATIONS

According to section 122 TULRCA 1992 an employers' association is an organisation that consists either:

■ wholly or mainly of employers or individual proprietors whose principal purposes include the regulation of relations between employers and workers (or trade unions), or

■ wholly or mainly of constituent or affiliated organisations with these purposes or representatives of such organisations

and in either case is an organisation whose principal purposes include the regulation of relations between employers and workers (or trade unions) or between constituent and affiliated organisations.[1]

Thus whether a trade association is or is not to be legally regarded as an employers' association will depend on its particular objectives. The Certification Officer is responsible for maintaining a list of employers' associations containing the names of those organisations that are entitled to have their names entered on it.[2] Whether listed or not, employers' associations are granted immunity in respect of the doctrine of restraint of trade, although the immunity of incorporated associations is only in connection with the regulation of relations between employers (or employers' associations) and workers (or trade unions).[3] Like trade unions, employers' associations are required to keep accounting records, to make annual returns and to have their accounts audited.[4] Part 1 Chapter 3 of TULRCA 1992 deals with the administrative provisions relating to employers' associations and trade unions.

TRADE UNIONS AND CERTIFICATES OF INDEPENDENCE

A trade union is an organisation, whether permanent or temporary, which consists either:

■ wholly or mainly of workers whose principal purposes include the regulation of relations between workers and employers (or employers' associations), or

■ wholly or mainly of constituent or affiliated organisations with those purposes, or representatives of such organisations

and in either case is an organisation whose principal purposes include the regulation of relations between workers and employers (or employers' associations) or include the regulation of relations between its constituent or affiliated organisations.[5]

This definition covers not only individual and confederated unions and the TUC, but also the union side of a joint negotiating committee. Section 10 TULRCA 1992 states that a trade union 'shall not be, or be treated as if it were, a body corporate', yet it is capable of making contracts, suing and being sued in its own name, and being prosecuted. However, in *EETPU* v *Times Newspapers*[6] it was held that the union could not sue for libel because it did not have the necessary legal personality to be protected by an action for defamation. All property belonging to a trade union must be vested in trustees, and any judgment, order or award is enforceable against the property held in trust.[7] Trade unions are protected against the doctrine of restraint of trade, in respect of both their purposes and their rules[8] (on immunity from certain actions in tort see Chapter 21).

'Listed' trade unions

The Certification Officer maintains a list of trade unions, and a trade union which submits the appropriate fee, a copy of its rules, a list of officers, the address of its head office and the name under which it is known may apply for inclusion on this list.[9] A listed union is entitled to a certificate stating that its name is included on the list and such listing is a prerequisite for obtaining a certificate of independence. The Certification Officer makes copies of the lists of trade unions and employers' associations available for public inspection and must remove the name of an organisation if requested to do so by that organisation or if he or she is satisfied that the organisation has ceased to exist.[10] Any organisation that is aggrieved by the refusal of the Certification Officer to enter its name on the relevant list, or by a decision to remove its name, may appeal to the EAT on a question of fact or law.[11]

Certification of independence for unions

A trade union whose name is on the relevant list can apply to the Certification Officer for a certificate that it is independent. The Certification Officer is responsible for keeping a record of all applications and must decide whether the applicant union is independent or not.[12] Section 5 TULRCA 1992 deems a trade union to be independent if:

- it is not under the domination or control of an employer or a group of employers or of one or more employers' associations, and
- it is not liable to interference by an employer or any such group or association, arising out of the provision of financial or material support or by any other means whatsoever, tending towards such control.

A certificate constitutes conclusive evidence for all purposes that the union is independent. If a question arises in any proceedings as to whether a trade union is independent and there is no certificate in force and no refusal, withdrawal or cancellation of a certificate recorded, the body before whom the issue arose cannot decide the matter but may refer it to the Certification Officer.[13]

Employer control of or domination over a union

Over the years, certain criteria have evolved for assessing whether a union is under the domination or control of an employer. In *A. Monk Staff Association* v *Certification Officer and ASTMS*[14] the EAT confirmed that the following matters should be considered:

- the union's history (was it originally the employer's creation?)
- its organisation and structure (is it likely to be controlled by senior members of management?)
- its finances (to what extent is it subsidised by the employer?)

- the extent of employer-provided facilities (are there free premises, etc?)
- its collective bargaining record.

Here there had been significant changes since the Certification Officer investigated the matter, including the appointment of an independent consultant/negotiator. In this case it was also held, on appeal against the Certification Officer's decision, that the question of independence should be decided on all the evidence available and not confined to the material that was before the Certification Officer.

As regards 'liable to interference', the Court of Appeal has ruled that the Certification Officer is not required to assess the likelihood of interference by the employer. The Certification Officer's interpretation of the words as meaning 'vulnerable to interference' was the correct one – ie the degree of risk is irrelevant so long as it is recognisable and not insignificant. Thus in *GCSF v Certification Officer*[15] the staff federation was denied a certificate because its continued existence depended on the approval of the GCHQ director.

Finally, it is worth documenting the major advantages that accrue to independent trade unions:

- If recognised, they have the right to appoint safety representatives (see Chapter 18).
- If recognised, their representatives are entitled to receive information for collective bargaining purposes (see below).
- If recognised, their representatives may be consulted in respect of redundancies and transfers of undertakings (see Chapter 18).
- If recognised, their officials can take time off for union activities (see Chapter 10).
- They can make and apply for exemption for a 'dismissal procedures agreement' (see Chapter 13).
- Employees cannot have action taken against them because they seek to join, have joined, or have taken part in the activities of such a union. Interim relief is available to members who have been dismissed.

RECOGNITION

An independent trade union must be recognised by the employer in order to enjoy a number of statutory rights. The same definition applies in respect of each of these rights, namely, 'Recognition in relation to a trade union means the recognition of the union by an employer, or two or more associated employers, to any extent for the purpose of collective bargaining.'[16]

Collective bargaining means negotiations relating to or connected with one or more of the matters specified in section 178(2) TULRCA 1992.[17] Although the question of recognition is one of fact for a court or employment tribunal to decide, it would appear that there must be an express or implied agreement between the union and the employer (but see statutory rights to recognition below) to negotiate on one or more of the matters listed in section 178(2) TULRCA 1992. For agreement to be implied there must be clear and unequivocal conduct over a period of time.[18] Thus although recognition has been inferred from consultations on discipline and facilities for union representatives despite the absence of formal agreement,[19] a discussion on wages which took place on a particular occasion was held to be insufficient to establish recognition, particularly when the employer's attitude was one of refusing to bargain.[20] Neither the fact that the union has a right of representation on a national body responsible for negotiating pay[21] nor the fact that the employers' association to which the employer belongs recognises the union will, by itself, constitute recognition by the employer.[22]

STATUTORY RECOGNITION PROCEDURES

The rules regarding the statutory right of trade unions[23] to recognition for collective bargaining purposes were introduced by the ERel Act 1999 and are now contained in Schedule A1 of TULRCA 1992. In this the meaning given to collective bargaining by section 178(1) TULRCA 1992 (see above) does not apply. Unless otherwise agreed by the parties, collective bargaining that is the result of the statutory recognition procedure relates to negotiations on pay, hours and holidays only.[24]

Request for recognition

A union seeking recognition must make a request for recognition to the employer. The request must be in writing, identify the union and the bargaining unit and state that it is made under this Schedule.[25] The basic rules concerning the parties are:

- The union must have a certificate of independence (see section 6 TULRCA 1992).[26]
- The employer, including associated employers, must employ at least 21 workers on the day of the request, or have employed an average of 21 workers in the 13 weeks ending on the day of the request.[27]

The parties agree[28]

If, before the end of a 10-day period, starting on the day the employer received the request, the parties agree on a bargaining unit and that the union is to be recognised for collective bargaining purposes on behalf of that unit, then the matter is complete.

If, before the end of the first period of 10 working days the employers inform the union that they do not accept the request but are willing to negotiate, then negotiations may continue into a second period. This second period lasts for 20 working days, starting on the day after the first period ends, or longer if both parties agree.

Negotiations fail[29]

If, before the end of the first period of 10 days the employers fail to respond or inform the union that they do not accept the request (and show no willingness to negotiate), then the union may apply to the Central Arbitration Committee (CAC) to decide two important issues. These are:

- whether the proposed bargaining unit is appropriate or some other bargaining unit is appropriate
- whether the union has the support of a majority of the workers constituting the bargaining unit.

If the employers refuse the request for recognition or no agreement is reached by the end of the second period of 20 working days, then the union may apply to the CAC to decide the two issues described above.

If the employers inform the union that they intend to request ACAS to assist in the negotiations and this proposal is rejected by the union or the union fails to respond, the application to the CAC must be delayed.

Appropriate bargaining unit[30]

If the CAC accepts an application from a trade union, it is obliged to help the parties reach an agreement, within the appropriate period, on what the appropriate bargaining unit is. In deciding whether a bargaining unit is appropriate the CAC must consider the trade union's proposal first. If it thinks that the proposed unit is appropriate, then that will be enough. Employers' proposals can be considered but only in respect of whether the trade union's proposal is appropriate or not. They need only be considered further if the trade union proposal is not considered appropriate.[31]

The appropriate period is 20 working days, beginning with the day after that on which the CAC accepts the application, or a longer period, if the CAC specifies, with reasons. If there is no agreement within the appropriate period, then the CAC has 10 working days, or a longer period, if the CAC specifies, beginning with the day after the end of the appropriate period, to make a decision.

In making the decision the CAC must take into consideration the need for the bargaining unit to be compatible with effective management and, provided they do not conflict with this consideration, with:

- the views of the employer and the union
- existing national and local bargaining units
- the desirability of avoiding small, fragmented bargaining units within an undertaking
- the characteristics of workers falling within the proposed bargaining unit and of any other employees the CAC considers relevant
- the location of the workers.

It is possible for a bargaining unit to consist of more than one employer. If the reality is that technically separate employers were really one and the same employer, then it might be possible to join them into one bargaining unit. Indications of this might be standard contracts of employment, interchangeability of employees and a unitary management in parts of the two organisations.[32]

Ballots for union recognition[33]

Once the appropriate bargaining unit has been decided upon by agreement between the parties or by CAC decision, the CAC must decide whether the union is likely to have the support of a majority of the workers in the unit. The CAC can only proceed if it is satisfied that the union is likely to have support.

If the union shows that a majority of the workers in the unit are members of the union, then the CAC must issue a declaration that the union is recognised for collective bargaining purposes. In *Fullarton Computer Industries Ltd* v *CAC*[34], for example, a slender majority of 51.3% of employees being trade union members was sufficient for there not to be a ballot called.

If one of three qualifying conditions is fulfilled, the CAC will hold a ballot rather than make a declaration. The three qualifying conditions are:

- the CAC is satisfied that a ballot is in the interests of good industrial relations
- a significant number of union members within the bargaining unit inform the CAC that they do not want the union to conduct collective bargaining on their behalf
- membership evidence is produced which leads the CAC to doubt whether a significant number of union members want the union to represent them. This evidence is about the circumstances in which employees became members and evidence about the length of time for which union members have belonged.

The CAC will appoint a qualified independent person to conduct the ballot within a period of 20 working days, starting the day after the appointment.[35] If it gives reasons, the CAC may specify a longer period. The ballot can be conducted at a workplace, or workplaces, or by post. In deciding which method to select, the CAC must take into account:

- the likelihood of unfairness or malpractice if the ballot is conducted at a workplace

- costs and practicality
- any other matters it thinks appropriate.

As soon as practicable the CAC must inform the parties of its decisions. Once the employers are informed, they must comply with three duties:

- to co-operate with the union and the independent person in connection with the ballot
- to give the union access to the workers so that they can inform them of the ballot and seek support. The Code of Practice on Access to Workers during Recognition and Derecognition Ballots[36] recommends that consideration should be given to establishing an agreement, preferably in writing, on access arrangements. Such an agreement should include the union's programme for where, when and how it will access workers, together with a mechanism for resolving any disputes that might arise
- to provide the CAC, within 10 working days, with the names and home addresses of the workers concerned, together with the names and addresses of any workers who join or leave after this.

The CAC will pass this information to the independent person who is conducting the ballot. This person will send out material provided by the union to the workers concerned, at the union's expense. If the CAC is satisfied that the employer has failed to comply with any of the three duties, it may order the employer to take steps to do so, or it may declare that the union is recognised for collective bargaining purposes. The costs incurred in the ballot will be shared equally between the employer and the union.

As soon as practicable the CAC will inform the parties of the result of the ballot. It will issue a declaration that the union is recognised if:

- a majority of those voting support recognition, and
- at least 40 per cent of the workers constituting the bargaining unit supported recognition.

The consequences of recognition[37]

Following the declaration from the CAC the parties may negotiate, within a certain period, about the way in which they will conduct collective bargaining. The negotiating period is 30 working days from when the parties were notified of the declaration. The parties may agree to a longer period.

If no agreement is reached, the employer or the union may ask the CAC for assistance. There is then an agreement period of 20 working days, or longer if the CAC decides (with the agreement of the parties), in which the CAC will try to help the parties reach an agreement. If no agreement is reached, the CAC may specify the method by which they are to conduct collective bargaining. The CAC is obliged to take into account the method specified in The Trade Union Recognition (Method of Collective Bargaining) Order 2000.[38] This method recommends that the employer and the union establish a joint negotiating body to discuss and negotiate pay, hours and holidays of the workers in the bargaining unit. There should be at least three employer and three union representatives on this body and each side will take turns in chairing the body for 12 months at a time.

This agreement will be a legally enforceable contract between the parties. It may be varied by the parties agreeing, but it will remain a legally enforceable agreement. The only remedy available for breach of this agreement will be that of specific performance, by which the court will order an employer to carry out the terms of the agreement. The CAC may stop the whole process prior to issuing its ruling at the joint request of the parties.

General provisions

The CAC will not accept an application:

- if it is satisfied that there is already a union recognised on behalf of any of the workers in the bargaining unit
- if it decides that members of the union constitute at least 10 per cent of the workers and there is *prima facie* evidence that a majority of the workers are likely to favour recognition; the CAC will decide whether this is so within 10 working days of receiving the application
- if the employer alleges that they are below the 21-employee threshold (see above); in this case they may have up to 10 working days in which to produce the evidence; the CAC will consider the views of the union before making a decision
- where there is more than one union involved, if the CAC is not yet satisfied that the unions 'will co-operate with each other in a manner likely to secure stable and effective bargaining' or will make, if the employer so wishes, joint negotiating arrangements
- where there is another application within a period of three years for substantially the same bargaining unit by the same union.

Voluntary recognition

If the parties reach a voluntary agreement on recognition, they may still apply to the CAC to specify the method by which collective bargaining is to be carried out.[39] The CAC will accept the application, provided the employee threshold has been met (see above) and it is clear that the parties have either not agreed a method or have failed to implement a method to which they have agreed. There is an agreement period of 20 working days, or longer if both the parties agree, in which the CAC will help them to reach an agreement. If no agreement is reached, the CAC may specify the method to be used. The same rules about legally enforceable contracts and the remedy of specific performance apply (see above).

Changes affecting the bargaining unit[40]

There will be situations where the original bargaining unit becomes inappropriate. If either the employer or the trade union believes that this has happened, they may apply to the CAC to make a decision as to what the appropriate bargaining unit should be. For such an application to be admissible, the reason must be that there has been:

- a change in the organisation or structure of the business carried on by the employer
- a change in the activities pursued by the employer in the course of the employer's business
- a substantial change in the number of workers employed in the original unit.

If the parties cannot agree on new arrangements, then the CAC is empowered to issue a declaration on the changes to be made.

Employers may also give notice to the union, with a copy to the CAC, that they believe that the original bargaining unit has ceased to exist. If the CAC accepts this, it may make a declaration ending the bargaining arrangements or may make a decision on a more appropriate bargaining unit.

De-recognition[41]

This applies where the CAC has issued declarations on recognition and/or the method to be used for collective bargaining purposes. The process is the reverse of that for recognition, albeit with different initiators and a different question in the application to the CAC. The relevant date is the expiry of a three-year period after the date of the CAC's declaration or the parties' agreement.

Protection against detriment and dismissal[42]

Detriment
A worker has the right not to be subject to any detriment by any act, or any deliberate failure to act, by the employer if the act or failure takes place on any of the following grounds:

- the worker acted with a view to obtaining or preventing recognition of a union
- the worker indicated that he or she supported or did not support recognition of a union
- the worker acted with a view to securing or preventing the ending of bargaining arrangements
- the worker indicated that he or she supported or did not support the ending of bargaining arrangements
- the worker influenced or sought to influence the way in which votes were to be cast by other workers in a ballot
- the worker influenced or sought to influence other workers to vote or abstain in the ballot
- the worker voted in such a ballot
- the worker proposed to do, failed to do, or proposed to decline to do, any of the above.

The worker is not protected, however, if the ground is an unreasonable act or omission by the worker.

The only remedy available to a worker is complaint to an employment tribunal, normally within three months of the act, or failure to act, which constitutes the detriment. The tribunal may issue a declaration and award compensation 'such as the tribunal considers just and equitable in all the circumstances having regard to the infringement complained of and to any loss sustained by the complainant which is attributable to the act or failure'.

Workers have a duty to mitigate their loss, and there will be a reduction in compensation if the worker contributed to the act or failure. Compensation for ending a contract is subject to the limits on compensation for unfair dismissal specified in the ERA 1996.

Dismissal
For the purposes of Part X of the ERA 1996, which is concerned with the right not to be unfairly dismissed (see Chapter 12), the dismissal of an employee shall be regarded as unfair if it takes place for any of the reasons listed above (under Detriment). This applies only to employees rather than those covered by the wider definition of worker, as in Section 296(1) TULRCA 1992, but includes those on fixed-term contracts.

The dismissal of an employee for redundancy shall also be unfair if it is shown to be for one of the reasons listed above or if it is shown that there are others in a similar position and the same circumstances who were not dismissed for reasons of redundancy.

DISCLOSURE OF INFORMATION FOR COLLECTIVE BARGAINING

For the purposes of all the stages of collective bargaining between employers and representatives of recognised independent trade unions, employers have a duty to disclose to those representatives, on request, all such information relating to their undertakings as is in their possession or that of any associated employer which is both:[43]

- information without which the union representatives would be to a material extent impeded in carrying on such collective bargaining, and

- information which it would be in accordance with good industrial relations practice that they should disclose.

An employer can insist that a request for information must be made in writing, and likewise the information itself must be in written form, if that is the wish of the union representatives.[44] According to section 181(1) TULRCA 1992, a 'representative' is an 'official or other person authorised by the trade union to carry on such collective bargaining'. However, an 'undertaking' is not defined for these purposes.

Unions' right to information on matters not connected with collective bargaining

The phrase 'of all the stages' means that information can be sought in order to prepare a claim, although it must relate to matters in respect of which the union is recognised. In *R v CAC ex parte BTP Tioxide*[45] the High Court held that the CAC had misdirected itself in concluding that the union was entitled to information relating to a job evaluation scheme In respect of which it had no bargaining rights but only the right to represent its members in re-evaluation appeals:

In essence, for information to be disclosed under these provisions it must be both relevant and important.

> There is no obstacle under the Act to an agreement which recognises the union's right to collective bargaining, that is negotiating, in respect of one aspect of terms and conditions of employment and also recognises a right to some form of dealings with employers which does not answer to the description of collective bargaining, about another aspect.

Although each case must be judged on its merits, unions may be entitled to information about groups not covered for collective bargaining purposes. Thus in Award 80/40 the CAC held that information about a productivity scheme for management not covered by the union was relevant and important to negotiations over a scheme for technical staff because of the similarity of the work of some employees within both groups.

'Good practice' and the ACAS Code

In determining what constitutes 'good industrial relations practice' attention must be paid to the ACAS Code of Practice,[46] although other evidence is not to be excluded.[47] Thus unions may seek to demonstrate good practice by referring to the approaches taken by comparable employers. To decide what information is relevant, negotiators are advised to take account of the subject matter of the negotiations and the issues raised during them, the level at which negotiations take place, the size of the company, and its type of business.[48] There is no list of items that should be disclosed in all circumstances, but the following examples of information which could be relevant in certain situations are given as a guide:[49]

- pay and benefits
- conditions of service
- manpower
- performance
- finance.

This is not an exhaustive list and other items may be relevant in particular negotiations. The underlying philosophy of the code is that employers and unions should endeavour to reach a joint understanding on how the disclosure provisions can be implemented most effectively: 'In particular, the parties should endeavour to reach an understanding on what information could most appropriately be provided on a regular basis.'[50]

The duty to disclose is subject to the exceptions detailed in section 182 TULRCA 1992. Employers are not required to disclose:

(a) any information the disclosure of which would be against the interests of national security

(b) any information which could not be disclosed without contravening other legislation

(c) any information which has been communicated to the employer in confidence

(d) any information relating specifically to an individual unless he or she has consented to its disclosure

(e) any information the disclosure of which would cause substantial injury to the employer's undertaking for reasons other than its effect on collective bargaining

(f) information obtained by the employer for the purpose of bringing or defending any legal proceedings.

Where disclosure may lead to 'substantial injury'

Although (c) applies to standard form tenders headed 'In confidence',[51] it should be noted that it does not protect an employer who discloses information in confidence to lay union representatives and restricts them from communicating it to union members and full-time officials. Where a union seeks disclosure about individual salaries without the consent of the individuals concerned, in order to avoid the impact of (d) it must be clear that the information relates to the posts involved and not to the individuals who fill them. As regards (e), paragraph 14 of the Code offers some examples of information which, if disclosed in particular circumstances, might cause substantial injury. This would cover such matters as cost information on individual products, detailed analysis of proposed investment, marketing or pricing policies, price quotas, and the make-up of tender prices. Further guidance is offered in paragraph 15:

> ... substantial injury may occur if, for example, certain customers would be lost to competitors, or suppliers would refuse to supply necessary materials, or the ability to raise funds to finance the company would be seriously impaired as a result of disclosing certain information. The burden of establishing a claim that disclosure of certain information would cause substantial injury lies with the employer.

By virtue of section 182(2) TULRCA employers are not obliged to produce, allow inspection of, or copy, any document other than a document conveying or confirming the information disclosed, and are not required to compile any information where to do so would involve an amount of work or expenditure out of reasonable proportion to the value of the information in the conduct of collective bargaining.

Redress to unions for failure to disclose

A union which feels that its representatives have not received the information to which they are entitled can complain in writing to the CAC, and if the CAC is of the opinion that the complaint is 'reasonably likely to be settled by conciliation' it must refer it to ACAS. Where no reference to ACAS is made or no settlement or withdrawal is achieved, the CAC must hear the complaint, make a declaration stating whether it is well-founded, wholly or in part, and give reasons for its finding. If the complaint is upheld, the declaration will specify the information in respect of which the CAC believed the complaint to be well-founded, the date on which the employer refused or failed to disclose information, and the period within which the employer ought to disclose the information specified.[52]

At any time after the expiry of this period the union may present a 'further complaint' that the employer has failed to disclose the required information. Again, the CAC must hear and determine the complaint and declare whether it holds it to be well-founded.[53] On or after presenting the further complaint the union may submit a claim that the employees' contracts should be amended to include the terms and conditions detailed in the claim – eg for more pay. However, no such claim can be lodged, or if presented it will be treated as withdrawn, if the relevant information is disclosed at any time before the CAC has adjudicated on the further complaint. If the further complaint is well-founded, the CAC may, after hearing the parties, award the terms and conditions detailed in the claim or others which it considers appropriate. Such an award will relate only to matters in respect of which the trade union is recognised. The terms and conditions awarded take effect as part of the contracts of employment of the employees covered, except in so far as they are superseded or varied by:

- a subsequent award under these provisions
- a collective agreement between the employer and the union
- an individual agreement, express or implied, effecting an improvement in the terms and conditions laid down in the award.[54]

It should be observed that these statutory provisions do not enable a union to force the disclosure of information.

THE LEGAL ENFORCEABILITY OF COLLECTIVE AGREEMENTS

In this section we are concerned with the legal enforceability of collective agreements between employers and trade unions and not the effect of such agreements on individual contracts of employment. It is important to remember that the legal status of the arrangements made between the employer and the union has no bearing on the relationship between the employer and his or her workers. The mechanisms by which the terms of a collective agreement may be enforced between the parties to a contract of employment have been described in Chapter 2.

A collective agreement is statutorily defined as any agreement or arrangement made by or on behalf of one or more trade unions[55] and one or more employers, or employers' associations, which relates to one or more of the matters mentioned in section 178(2) TULRCA 1992.[56] A collective agreement is conclusively presumed not to have been intended by the parties to be a legally enforceable contract unless the agreement is in writing and contains a provision which states that the parties intend the agreement to be a legally enforceable contract,[57] or the agreement has been specified by the CAC as a result of the statutory recognition procedures. Equally, the parties may declare that one or more parts only of an agreement are intended to be legally enforceable.[58] Nevertheless, it should not be assumed that a collective agreement which declares the parties' intention to create legal relations is necessarily legally binding, because agreements exist which are too vague or uncertain to be enforced as contracts.

KEY POINTS

- The Certification Officer maintains a list of employers' associations and of trade unions and makes them available for public inspection.
- The Certification Officer decides if a trade union is entitled to a certificate of independence.
- An independent trade union must be recognised by an employer in order to enjoy a number of statutory rights, such as the right to the disclosure of information for collective bargaining purposes.
- The statutory recognition procedures apply to firms with 21 or more employees on the day an independent trade union requests recognition.
- Establishing the bargaining unit is a necessary prerequisite for the recognition procedure. The CAC will assist and take into account, amongst other factors, the need for bargaining units to be compatible with effective management and the desirability of avoiding small fragmented units within an undertaking.
- Employers have a duty to disclose to trade unions recognised for collective bargaining purposes such information without which the union representatives would be to a material extent impeded in carrying on collective bargaining with them.
- A collective agreement is conclusively presumed not to be a legally enforceable contract unless it is in writing and contains a provision that the parties intend it to be a legally enforceable contract.

NOTES

1　The words 'employee', 'employer' and 'worker' are defined in sections 295–6 TULRCA 1992; the expression 'associated employer' is defined in section 297 TULRCA 1992
2　Section 123 TULRCA 1992
3　Section 128 TULRCA 1992
4　Section 131 TULRCA 1992
5　Section 1 TULRCA 1992
6　(1980) 1 All ER 1097
7　Sections 12 and 13 TULRCA 1992
8　Section 11 TULRCA 1992
9　Section 3 TULRCA 1992
10　Section 4 TULRCA 1992
11　Section 9(1) TULRCA 1992
12　Section 6(2) and (5) TULRCA 1992
13　Section 8 TULRCA 1992
14　(1980) IRLR 431
15　(1993) IRLR 260
16　Section 178(3) TULRCA 1992
17　Section 178(1) TULRCA 1992
18　See *NUGSAT* v *Albury Bros* (1978) IRLR 504
19　See *J. Wilson & Albury Bros* v *USDAW* (1978) IRLR 20
20　See *NUGSAT* v *Albury Bros* (note 18)
21　See *Cleveland County Council* v *Springett* (1985) IRLR 131
22　See *NUGSAT* v *Albury Bros* (note 18)
23　All references in this section to a trade union should also be taken as references to more than one union if there is more than one union involved in the application for recognition
24　Schedule A1 para 3(3) TULRCA 1992; see also *UNIFI* v *Union Bank of Nigeria* (2001) IRLR 712 which held that pay includes matters related to the group pension scheme

25 Schedule A1 para 8 TULRCA 1992
26 Schedule A1 para 6 TULRCA 1992
27 Schedule A1 para 7 TULRCA 1992 The meaning of worker is defined in section 296(1)(b) TULRCA 1992; see *R* v *CAC* (2003) IRLR 460
28 Schedule A1 para 10 TULRCA 1992
29 Schedule A1 para 12 TULRCA 1992
30 Schedule A1 para 18 TULRCA 1992
31 (2001) IRLR 752
32 See *Graphical, Paper and Media Union* v *Derry Print Ltd* (2002) IRLR 380
33 Schedule A1 paras 20–29 TULRCA 1992
34 (2001) IRLR 752
35 See the Recognition and Derecognition Ballots (Qualified Persons Order) 2000 SI 2000/1306, which describes those who are qualified persons
36 Introduced by SI 2000/1443
37 Schedule A1 paras 30–31 TULRCA 1992
38 SI 2000/1300
39 Schedule A1 paras 58–63 TULRCA 1992
40 Schedule A1 Part III TULRCA 1992
41 Schedule A1 Part IV TULRCA 1992
32 Schedule A1 Part VIII TULRCA 1992
43 Section 181(1) and (2) TULRCA 1992
44 Section 181(3) and (5) TULRCA 1992
45 (1982) IRLR 61
46 Disclosure of Information to Trade Unions for Collective Bargaining Purposes, HMSO, 1997
47 Section 181(4) TULRCA 1992
48 Code of Practice paragraph 10
49 Code of Practice paragraph 11
50 Code of Practice paragraph 22
51 See *CSU* v *CAC* (1980) IRLR 274
52 Section 183 TULRCA 1992
53 Section 184 TULRCA 1992
54 Section 185(5) TULRCA 1992
55 See *Edinburgh Council* v *Brown* (1999) IRLR 208, where an agreement between the employer and the joint consultative committee constituted a collective agreement
56 Section 178(1) TULRCA 1992
57 Section 179(1) TULRCA 1992
58 Section 179(3) TULRCA 199

Trade Unions and Their Members

OVERVIEW

In this chapter we look at discrimination against employees or prospective employees on grounds of trade union membership or non-membership and consider the issues of unlawful refusal of employment, the right not to suffer a detriment and dismissal. We also examine the way in which the relationship between trade unions and their members is regulated. This includes controls over what discretion trade unions have to admit, discipline and expel members. We look at the detailed statutory rules that regulate union elections. Finally, we describe the important role played by the Certification Officer in settling disputes.

TRADE UNION MEMBERSHIP OR NON-MEMBERSHIP

Unlawful refusal of employment

Section 137(1) of TULRCA 1992 makes it unlawful to refuse employment to people because:

- they are or are not members of a trade union
- they refuse to accept a requirement that they become a member or cease to be a member, or a requirement that they suffer deductions if they fail to join.[1]

People are deemed to have been refused employment with an employer if that employer:

- refuses or deliberately omits to entertain the application or enquiry
- causes the applicant to withdraw or cease to pursue the application or enquiry
- refuses or deliberately omits to offer employment
- makes an offer of employment the terms of which are such as no reasonable employer who wished to fill the post would offer, and which is not accepted
- makes an offer of employment but withdraws it or causes the applicant not to accept it
- offers employment on terms which include a requirement within section 137(1), and the applicant declines the offer because of this requirement.

As regards job advertisements,[2] if an advertisement indicates, or might reasonably be understood as indicating, that employment is open only to people who are or are not union members, or that there is a requirement applying to the post of the sort mentioned in section 137(1)(b), then if people who do not meet the relevant condition are refused employment, it will be conclusively presumed that this was because they failed to satisfy the condition. Where it is the practice for trade unions to supply job applicants, non-members who are refused employment are deemed to have been so refused on account of their non-membership.

Section 138 makes it unlawful for an agency which finds employment for workers, or supplies employers with workers, to refuse its services to people because they are or are not union members or are unwilling to accept a condition or requirement of the type mentioned in section 137(1)(b). The provisions relating to advertisements also apply to such agencies.

Compilation of lists of trade union members

Section 3 of the ERel Act 1999 allows the Secretary of State to make regulations prohibiting the compilation of lists which:

- contain details of members of trade unions or persons that have taken part in the activities of trade unions
- are compiled with a view to being used by employers or employment agencies for the purposes of discrimination in relation to the recruitment or treatment of such workers.

This measure seeks to end the practice by some employers and employers' associations of maintaining lists of trade union members and activists who are seen as potential troublemakers and who are therefore turned down for any positions applied for with the employer or employers holding the list. In February 2003, the Government published a consultation document on draft Regulations. However, it was made clear that regulations will not be put before Parliament for approval until there is evidence that individuals or organisations are planning to draw up such lists or if there is any evidence that there is a demand from employers for them. It remains to be seen how effective such a measure can be against the informal exchange of information between employers, as against the keeping of formal lists.

Complaints about unlawful refusal of employment

A complaint about the infringement of these provisions must normally be presented to an employment tribunal within three months of the date of the conduct complained about. Under section 139 TULRCA 1992, the date of the conduct complained of will be:

- in the case of an actual refusal, the date of the refusal
- where there was a deliberate omission to offer employment or deal with an application or enquiry, the end of the period within which it was reasonable to expect the employer to act
- in the case of conduct that causes the applicant to withdraw or cease to pursue an application, the date of that conduct
- in a case where an offer was made but withdrawn, the date when it was withdrawn
- in a case where an offer was made but not accepted, the date the offer was made.

Provision is made for conciliation, but if a complaint is upheld, the tribunal must make a declaration to that effect and may make such of the following remedies as it considers just and equitable.[3]

- an order obliging the respondent to pay compensation, which is to be assessed on the same basis as damages for breach of statutory duty and may include damages for injury to feelings
- a recommendation that the respondent takes such action as the tribunal thinks practicable to obviate or reduce the effect on the complainant of the conduct to which the claim relates. If such a recommendation is not complied with, any award of compensation can be increased, although the total award cannot exceed the amount stipulated in section 124 ERA 1996 (£55,000 in 2004).

Finally, it should be noted that a trade union may be joined as a defendant in tribunal proceedings where an employer or agency maintains that it was induced to act in the manner complained of by union pressure.[4] If compensation is awarded, the union may be ordered to pay all or part of it.

Subject to detriment short of dismissal

Section 146 TULRCA 1992 gives employees the right not to be subjected to any detriment as an individual by any act, or any deliberate failure to act, by an employer if the act or failure takes place for the purpose of:

- preventing or deterring them from being or seeking to become members of an independent trade union or penalising them for doing so

- preventing or deterring them from taking part in the activities of an independent trade union at any appropriate time, or penalising them for doing so

- compelling them to become members of any trade union or of a particular trade union or of one of a number of particular trade unions

- enforcing a requirement that in the event of their failure to become, or their ceasing to remain, members of any trade union or a particular trade union or one of a number of particular trade unions, they must make one or more payments. For this purpose, any deduction from remuneration which is attributable to the employee's failure to become, or his or her ceasing to be, a trade union member will be treated as a detriment.

As regards the requirement that the action must be taken against an employee as an individual, the Court of Appeal has offered the following guidance: 'If an employee is selected for discrimination because of some characteristic which he shares with others, such as membership of a particular trade union, then the action is ... taken against him as an individual.'[5] Thus de-recognition of an individual shop steward by an employer can be action taken against the shop steward as an individual, rather than action taken against the trade union.[6]

The words 'for the purpose of'[6A] connote an object that the employer seeks to achieve, and the purpose of an action must not be confused with its effect. Thus when a full-time union official was turned down for promotion, the Court of Appeal accepted that section 146 had not been infringed because the employer's purpose had been to ensure that only those with sufficient managerial experience were promoted.[7] By way of contrast, when a full-time branch secretary was offered promotion without the usual salary increase, it was held that the employer's purpose was to deter the individual from engaging in union activities.[8] It is clear that employees have the right to join any independent trade union of their choice.[9] Thus in *Carlson*'s case[10] the EAT decided that the denial of a car-park permit to a member of a non-recognised independent trade union constituted a form of penalisation outlawed by the section. In this context 'penalising' was held to mean 'subjecting to a disadvantage'.

Tribunal definitions of the activities of an independent trade union

Because there is no statutory definition, tribunals have the task of determining what the 'activities of an independent trade union' are. The following have been accepted as such: attempting to recruit new members or form a workplace union branch, taking part in union meetings, and consulting a union official. Thus those claiming that they have suffered because of their activities do not have to show that they were authorised union representatives, although individual complaints or group meetings which have no union connection will not be protected. It is not conclusive that workers did not get together at a committee or formal branch meeting; it would appear sufficient that union members have discussed matters with which an independent trade union is concerned.[11] However, in *Therm-a-Stor* v *Atkins*[12] the Court of Appeal drew a distinction between the employer's reaction to a trade union's activities and reaction to an individual employee's activities in a trade union context. Where a union district secretary's letter asking for recognition led to dismissal it was therefore held that the reason for dismissal had nothing to do with anything the employee concerned had personally done or proposed to do. As a result, the employment tribunal had no jurisdiction to hear Mr Atkins's complaint. The expression 'activities of an independent trade union' refers to the activities of a specific trade union rather than the activities of unions generally.

According to the EAT, an employment tribunal must establish:

- the belief held by the employer upon which the decision was taken
- that such a belief was genuinely held
- whether the facts upon which the belief was based, judged objectively, fell within the 'activities of an independent trade union'.[13]

In the light of the European Court of Human Rights' decision in *Wilson* v *UK*,[14] a more generous approach to what constitutes "trade union activities" will have to be adopted. In this case it was held that, by permitting employers to use financial incentives to induce employees to surrender their right to representation, the UK had violated Article 11 of the European Convention on Human Rights (or freedom of association) in relation to both the applicants and their unions. According to the court, in order to protect their interests, individual members have the right to have their union represent them in attempts to regulate their relations with their employers.

Industrial action as an activity

Can industrial action be regarded as an activity? In *Rasool's* case[15] the EAT was prepared to accept that attendance at an unauthorised meeting for the purpose of considering the views of employees in relation to impending wage negotiations was such an activity. Nevertheless, such activity is not normally taken at an 'appropriate time' since this is defined as being outside working hours or within working hours in accordance with arrangements agreed with, or consent given by, the employer. Such consent may be express – for example, in a collective agreement – or may be implied from the conduct of the parties. Unless there is an arrangement that covers the situation, however, it would seem that a shop steward who is unaccredited by management at the relevant time cannot be taken to have implied permission to call a meeting during working hours.[16] Activities carried out at an 'appropriate time' means activities occurring during the period of employment and excludes activities during a prior period. Nevertheless, the statute is infringed if the employee suffers detriment short of dismissal on the basis of previous trade union activities when the only rational basis for his so suffering is a subsequent employer's fear that those activities will be repeated in the present employment.[17] The phrase 'working hours' is defined as meaning any time when an employee is required to be at work, but in order to protect union activities carried out during paid tea breaks it has been construed as meaning the time when work is actually performed.[18]

A claim that there has been detriment short of dismissal must normally be presented within three months of the date on which the act complained of occurred, or if the act complained of is spread over a period, then the last day of that period.[19] When section 32 EA 2002 comes into force, an employee wishing to complain under this legislation must first submit a statement of grievance to their employer.[20] A failure to act shall be treated as occurring on the date when it was decided upon. If there is an absence of evidence to the contrary, employers shall be deemed to have failed to act:

- when they do something distinctly different from what they should have done (ie an act inconsistent with doing the failed act); or
- if there has been no inconsistent act, when the period expires within which the employer might have been expected to do the failed act.[21]

The burden is on employers to show the purpose for which they acted or failed to act. In deciding on this purpose, the tribunal must not take into account any pressure exerted on the employer by the threat or organisation of industrial action.[22] Where an employment tribunal finds an employee's complaint to be well-founded, it must make a declaration to that effect and may make an award of compensation. The amount awarded must be such as the tribunal considers 'just and equitable in all the circumstances having regard to the infringement of the complainant's right' and 'to any loss sustained by the complainant which is attributable to that action.[23] In this context 'loss' is taken to include any expenses reasonably incurred and any benefit which the applicant might have received but for the unlawful action. Compensation can be reduced if employees fail to mitigate their loss, or cause or contribute to the action taken against them. In *Brassington's* case[24] the EAT ruled that the statute did not impose a quasi-fine, so that compensation could be awarded only if the employee could show that an injury resulted. Yet this injury is not restricted to pecuniary loss. The stress engendered by the situation may have caused injury to the employee's health, or a sincere desire to join a union – with all the benefits of help and advice which that might entail – could have been frustrated. It might also include a sum for injury to feelings, as in *Cleveland Ambulance NHS Trust* v *Blane*[25] where a trade union activist was not short-listed for promotion because of trade union activities.

Dismissals relating to trade union membership

According to section 152(1) TULRCA 1992 a dismissal is unfair if the reason for it (or if more than one, the principal reason) was that the employee:

- was or proposed to become a member of an independent trade union
- had taken, or proposed to take, part in the activities of an independent trade union at an appropriate time
- was not a member of any trade union or of a particular trade union, or had refused or proposed to refuse to become or to remain a member.

Section 152(3) TULRCA 1992 states that dismissals are to be treated as falling within the last point above if one of the reasons for them was that employees:

- refused (or proposed to refuse) to comply with a requirement that in the event of their failure to become, or their ceasing to remain, a trade union member they must make some kind of payment
- objected, or proposed to object, to the operation of a provision under which their employer was entitled to deduct sums from their remuneration if they failed to become or remain a trade union member.

It would seem that if an employee is dismissed because of her or his proposal to leave an independent trade union, that will be unfair, even though the proposal is conditional on something occurring or not occurring.[26]

The usual qualifying period and upper age-limit for claiming unfair dismissal do not apply if the reason, or principal reason, for dismissal was one of those specified in section 152 TULRCA 1992.[27] This being so, the burden is on employees to prove that their dismissal related to trade union membership. However, where the question of jurisdiction does not arise, the only burden on the employee is to produce some evidence that casts doubt upon the employer's reason.[28]

Where employees allege that their dismissals were unfair by virtue of section 152 TULRCA 1992, they can seek 'interim relief'.[29] This is available where employees present their claims within seven days of the effective date of termination and, where sections 152(1)(a) or (b) TULRCA 1992 are relied on, they submit written certificates signed by an authorised union official which state that there appears to be reasonable grounds for supposing that the reason for dismissal was the one alleged in the complaints. The tribunal must hear such an application as soon as practicable,[30] and, if it thinks it 'likely' (ie there is a pretty good chance) that the complainant will be found to have been unfairly dismissed by virtue of Section 152 TULRCA 1992, it must ask whether the employer is willing to reinstate or (if not) to re-engage the employee pending the determination of the complaint. If the employer is willing to reinstate or the employee is willing to accept re-engagement, the tribunal should make an order to that effect. Where the employer fails to attend the hearing or is unwilling to re-employ, the tribunal must make an order for the continuation of the employee's contract of employment. In essence, such an order amounts to suspension on full pay.[31]

Where there has been pressure to dismiss on the grounds of non-membership of a trade union, section 160 TULRCA 1992 enables the person who applied the pressure to be joined (by either the employer or the employee), ie be brought in as a party to the unfair dismissal proceedings. A request that a person be joined must be acceded to if it is made before the hearing but can be refused if it is made after that time. No such request can be entertained after a remedy has been awarded, and the tribunal is empowered to apportion compensation in a 'just and equitable' manner.

Refusal to opt out of a collective agreement

The ERel Act 1999 permits the Secretary of State to make regulations about cases where a worker is subject to detriment or dismissal on the grounds that the worker refuses to enter into a contract which includes terms which differ from an applicable collective agreement.[32] If an employer wishes to persuade employees to agree to an individual contract of employment which excludes or changes the terms of a relevant collective agreement, the employer may try to do so as long as those that refuse to sign such contracts are not subjected to detriment or dismissal. Specifically excluded as a detriment, however, is the payment of higher wages or bonuses to those employees who sign, so long as they are not prevented, as a result, from being members of any trade union.[33]

ADMISSION

A union is entitled to stipulate the descriptions of persons who are eligible for membership, but provided it observes its own rules no union can be ordered by a court to admit a particular applicant. However, the anti-discrimination legislation makes it unlawful for an organisation of workers to discriminate in the terms on which it is prepared to admit into membership, or on which it refuses or deliberately omits to accept an application for membership. Equally, it is unlawful for an organisation of workers to discriminate on the prohibited grounds against a member in the way it affords access to any benefits, facilities or services, or subjects him or her to any detriment, including deprivation of membership.[34]

Section 174 TULRCA 1992 gives employees the right to join the union of their choice. It states that an individual may not be excluded from a union unless the reason is one of the following:

- The individual fails to satisfy an enforceable membership requirement in the union's rules. A requirement is 'enforceable' if it restricts membership solely by reference to one or more of the following criteria:
- employment in a specified trade, industry or profession
- occupational description (including grade, level or category)
- possession of specified qualifications or work experience.[35]
- The individual does not qualify for membership by reason of the union operating only in particular parts of Great Britain.
- The union operates only in relation to one employer or a number of associated employers, and the individual is not employed by that employer or one of those employers.
- The exclusion is entirely attributable to the individual's conduct. For these purposes conduct does not include being or ceasing to be:
- a member of another trade union
- employed by a particular employer or at a particular place

- a member of a political party.
- Nor does it include any conduct for which an individual may not be disciplined by a trade union (see below).[36]

In this context 'exclusion' refers to a refusal to admit into membership, not to suspension of the privileges of membership.[37]

Redress for non-admission

A person excluded in contravention of these provisions can complain to an employment tribunal. This must normally be done within six months of the date of exclusion. However, where a tribunal finds that it was not reasonably practicable to comply with this time-limit, the period may be extended by such amount as is considered reasonable.[38] If the claim is upheld, the tribunal will make a declaration to that effect. Complainants who are admitted or re-admitted to the union can apply to the tribunal for compensation after a four-week period and must do so before six months have elapsed from the date of the declaration. If there is no admission or re-admission, applications for compensation must be made to the EAT. The employment tribunal and EAT will award such compensation as is considered 'just and equitable in all the circumstances' subject to a maximum as set out in section 176(6) TULRCA 1992. Currently, however, compensation fixed by the EAT must be at least £5,500.[39]

DISCIPLINE, EXPULSION AND RESIGNATION

The rules of a trade union constitute a contract between the union and its members and must be strictly adhered to. A trade union wishing to take disciplinary action must therefore ensure that its rule-book contains the necessary powers.[40] Although a court can infer a power to discipline a member, it will do so only where there are compelling circumstances to justify it.[41]

Section 64 TULRCA 1992 gives members the right not to be unjustifiably disciplined by the union, and section 65 deems disciplinary action by a union to be unjustifiable for the following types of conduct:

- failing to participate in industrial action or criticising such action; what 'industrial action' is for these purposes is a mixed question of fact and law; it is necessary to look at all the circumstances, including the contracts of the employees concerned and whether any breaches of the terms are involved, the effect on the employer of what is done or omitted, and the object that the union or employees seek to achieve[42]
- alleging that the union or an official is acting unlawfully; this protects members who bring legal proceedings against the union
- encouraging or assisting others to perform their contracts of employment (for example, during industrial action) or encouraging others to make an allegation of the type mentioned in the previous point
- asking the Certification Officer for advice or assistance on any matter, or consulting another person about an allegation against the union or its officers
- refusing to comply with a requirement imposed by a union (for example, during disciplinary proceedings) which amounts to an infringement of the above rights
- proposing or preparing to engage in any conduct mentioned above
- resigning or proposing to resign from the union or another union, joining or proposing to join another union, refusing to join another union, or being a member of another union
- working with, or proposing to work with, individuals who are not members of the union or who are not members of another union

- working for, or proposing to work for, an employer who employs or has employed individuals who are not members of the union, or who are not members of another union

- requiring the union to do an act which it is required to do under TULRCA 1992 when requested to do so by a member.

In this context disciplinary action covers virtually all forms of detrimental treatment.[43] Thus in *NALGO* v *Killorn*[44] a member was subjected to a detriment when suspension deprived her of the benefits of membership and she was named as a strike-breaker in a branch circular with the intention of causing her embarrassment.

Compensation for unjustifiable discipline

Those wishing to complain about unjustifiable discipline may choose between making a complaint to an employment tribunal or the Certification Officer (see below). The complainant must normally apply to an employment tribunal within three months of the relevant union decision.[45] Not surprisingly, individuals cannot be prevented from complaining by their union rule-book and any settlement will be binding only if ACAS has been involved or the conditions regulating compromise agreements are satisfied.[46] If a tribunal upholds a complaint, it will make a declaration to that effect. Compensation is available if a separate application is lodged not earlier than four weeks and not later than six months from the date of the tribunal's declaration.[47] If the union has revoked its disciplinary action, compensation will be assessed by an employment tribunal; otherwise, applications must go to the EAT.[48] Both tribunals are empowered to award such compensation as is just and equitable in the circumstances. As with unfair dismissal, compensation can be reduced on the grounds of contributory fault or a failure to mitigate loss.[49] The remedies for unjustifiable discipline are not available where the complainant could bring an action under section 174 TULRCA 1992 (see below). However, if the exclusion or expulsion is for any of the reasons listed above, it is not to be attributed to the conduct of the individual.[50]

If the rules specify the grounds on which disciplinary action may be taken, it will be unlawful for the union to rely on any other grounds, and where the rules provide for a procedure to be adopted, that procedure must be rigidly followed. Ultimately, a court's interpretation of the rules will take precedence over that of the union, although occasionally the judges have acknowledged that union rules should not be construed literally but should be given a reasonable interpretation which accords with their intended meaning.[51]

The supremacy of the courts over union rules

The court's jurisdiction as final arbiters on questions of law cannot be ousted. Thus a rule which purports to make a decision of a union appeal body 'final and binding' will be of no effect if challenged.[52] Even where there is an express provision that internal remedies must be exhausted before a member goes to law, a court will not be bound by such a requirement. Indeed, section 63 TULRCA 1992 gives union members a right to start legal proceedings in connection with any matter which can be dealt with under the rule-book so long as a valid application to resolve the matter within the union's rules has previously been made. However, the court proceedings cannot be commenced within six months of the date of the application to the union, and this period can be extended if a court is satisfied that any delay in operating the internal procedure resulted from the applicant's unreasonable conduct. If these conditions are met, the court is bound to deal with the matter, but if they are not, the burden will be on complainants to show why they should not first exhaust the internal procedures.[53]

At one time, judges were of the opinion that the essential fairness or otherwise of union rules was not for them to decide, although a different view is that if such rules are contrary to natural justice they should be declared invalid. In this context natural justice requires that a member should be given notice of the charge and a reasonable opportunity of meeting it. Yet there is no legal obligation on a union to give notice of a decision to terminate membership or to grant an opportunity of being heard if there is nothing the member could say that would affect the outcome.[54] Where hearings are granted they must be fairly conducted and *bona fide* decisions reached on their merits – in other words, without the slightest appearance of bias.[55] However, unless contained in the rule-book, there would appear to be no right to legal representation. As regards appeals, the courts have decided that because they do not constitute a rehearing, appeals cannot correct defects at the initial hearing.

The right not to be expelled

Under common law, a person who is wrongfully expelled may seek a declaration that he or she is still a union member, an injunction to prevent the expulsion from being put into effect, and damages for breach of contract. In addition, section 174 TULRCA 1992 establishes a right not to be expelled from a trade union unless there is a statutory permitted reason for expulsion.[56] This precisely parallels the right not to be excluded, and the method of enforcement is as described in relation to a refusal to admit (see above). It should be noted that although the employment tribunal procedure will be cheaper, the common law remedies may prove more attractive. There are three main reasons for this: first, an injunction may be obtained to compel the union to treat the plaintiff as still being a member; second, damages cannot be reduced on the grounds of contributory fault; third, a court is unlikely to condone breaches of the union's rules and procedures.

As regards resignation, section 69 TULRCA 1992 implies into every contract of membership of a trade union a term conferring a right on the member, on giving reasonable notice and complying with reasonable conditions, to terminate his or her membership of the union.

ELECTIONS

Section 46 TULRCA 1992 stipulates that irrespective of its rule-book, every trade union must elect its president, general secretary and members of its executive by ballot at least once every five years.[57] The election results must be given effect within a reasonable period (not exceeding six months), although the actions of the principal executive committee remain valid even if that body is not elected in accordance with the statute.[58] In conducting such elections unions must satisfy the following conditions:

(a) members must be given equal entitlement to vote unless they belong to a specified class which is excluded by the union rules from voting

(b) members who are entitled to vote must be allowed to do so in secret by marking a voting paper without interference from the union (or any of its members, officials or employees), and so far as is reasonably practicable they should do so without incurring any direct cost to themselves[59]

(c) ballot papers and a list of candidates must be sent by post to a member's address and each member must be given an opportunity to vote by post

(d) votes must be fairly and accurately counted, although any inaccuracy can be disregarded if it is 'accidental and on a scale which could not affect the result of the election', and the result of the election must be determined solely by counting the number of votes cast directly for each candidate[60]

(e) no member must be unreasonably excluded from standing as a candidate, unless she or he belongs to a class which has been excluded by the union rules, and no candidate can be required to be a member of a political party.[61] In *Ecclestone* v *National Union of Journalists*[62] the claimant was held to have been unreasonably excluded from a short-list for election to the post of deputy general secretary. The national executive committee of the union had imposed a qualification which amounted to having the confidence of that committee. The High Court held that this created a class of excluded persons which was created purely by reference to whom the executive committee decided to exclude. This was deemed to be arbitrary and not in accordance with good employment practice.

Election addresses by candidates

Section 48 TULRCA 1992 gives candidates in union elections the right to prepare an election address and to have it distributed with the ballot papers. Unions cannot impose a word-limit of fewer than 100 words, and the address can be edited only with the permission of the candidate. There is also a duty to ensure, so far as is practicable, that the same facilities apply equally to all candidates. Section 24 TULRCA obliges trade unions to compile and maintain a register of the names and addresses of their members and to ensure, so far as is reasonably practicable, that entries in the register are accurate and kept up to date.

The role of the scrutineer

Prior to an election, a trade union must appoint a qualified independent person (a 'scrutineer').[63] Before the scrutineer begins performing his or her functions, a trade union must either personally inform all its members, so far as is reasonably practicable, of the scrutineer's name or notify the members of the name in such other way as is in keeping with the union's practice. A trade union must supply the scrutineer with a copy of the register of members' names and addresses as it applies to the particular election. The scrutineer must inspect the register (see above) whenever it appears appropriate to do so and, in particular, if requested to do so by a member who suspects that the register is not accurate or up to date. The latter requirement does not apply where the scrutineer considers that the suspicion is ill-founded.[64]

The scrutineer must supervise the production and distribution of voting papers; make a detailed report on the conduct of an election, indicating any matters about which he or she is dissatisfied; and retain custody of the returned voting papers for at least a year after the ballot result has been announced. Once the candidate with the largest number of votes has been declared elected, following a favourable report by the scrutineer, a trade union cannot cancel the election unless there is express power under the union rules to do so or it can be shown that the whole election process was a nullity.[65]

The handling of voting papers

The storage and distribution of the voting papers and the counting of votes must be undertaken by 'independent persons' appointed by the union. Such a person may be the scrutineer or a person whom the union believes will carry out his or her functions competently, and whose independence cannot reasonably be called into question.[66] Finally, in addition to the detailed statutory provisions, the Secretary of State is empowered to issue codes of practice on union elections.[67]

If a trade union fails to comply with any of the above provisions, within a year from the date the election result was announced a member may apply to the Certification Officer or the High Court for a declaration. The High Court can also make an enforcement order requiring the union to take remedial action. The period for ensuring compliance with an enforcement order will be specified by the court, and any person who was a member when the order was made is entitled to enforce obedience to it.[68]

THE ROLE OF THE CERTIFICATION OFFICER (CO)

The ERel Act 1999 added a new Chapter VIIA to Part I TULRCA 1992. The effect was to establish an alternative to the courts for trade union members to seek remedies in relation to certain alleged breaches of union rules. Chapter VIIA consists of three sections: 108A, 108B and 108C.

Section 108A specifies the circumstances under which a complaint can be made to the CO and gives the CO the authority to make declarations dealing with the complaint. The alleged breach or intended breach of union rules must relate to:

- the appointment or election of a person to any office in the union
- the removal of a person from an office of the union

Essentials of Employment Law

- disciplinary proceedings by the union (including expulsion)
- the balloting of union members other than in respect of industrial action
- the constitution or proceedings of union executive committees and other decision-making meetings
- any other matter which the Secretary of State may specify from time to time.

Complaints to the CO on these matters can be made only by members of the union or individuals who were members of the union at the time of the alleged or threatened breach.[69] Complaints about a breach of the rules concerning dismissal or disciplining employees of the union, however, are excluded from the CO's jurisdiction.[70] Sections 108A(6) and (7) TULRCA 1992 set out the timetable for complaints to the CO. In cases where the internal disputes procedure of the union was not used, complaints must be made within six months of the alleged breach or intended breach. Where the internal complaints procedure of the union was used within six months of the alleged or intended breach, the complaint to the CO must be made within six months of the ending of that internal procedure, or 12 months after the procedure was commenced, whichever is the sooner. It is not possible to complain to the court and the CO. A complainant will need to choose, and having made that choice will not be able to take parallel action with either the court or the CO.

According to section 108B the CO may refuse to accept applications unless the applicant satisfies the CO that all reasonable steps have been taken to use the union's internal complaints procedure.[71] The CO also has the power to make declarations.[72] Sections 108B(3) and (4) give the CO the power to make enforcement orders imposing requirements on the union to remedy the breach or withdraw the threat of a breach within a specified time period. Any declarations of the CO are to be relied upon as if they were a declaration of the court and can be enforced as if they were court orders.[73]

Section 108C allows for appeals against the CO's decisions to be made to the EAT. These appeals can be made only on questions of law.

POLITICAL FUNDS

Contribution to a union's political fund cannot be made a condition of admission to a union, and members who wish to contract out of a political levy must be free to do so. Similarly, the contracted-out members cannot be excluded from any benefit or disqualified from holding any office, except for a position connected with the management of a political fund.[74] According to sections 73–8 TULRCA 1992, unions wishing to maintain political funds must ballot their members at least once every 10 years and observe the same conditions as apply to elections (see above). Where a political fund resolution has ceased to have effect, members who were exempt from the obligation to contribute must not be excluded from any benefits or placed in any respect, either directly or indirectly, under any disadvantage compared with other union members by reason of being so exempt.[75] Similarly, where a resolution has lapsed but the union has continued to collect contributions, it must pay a refund of any contribution made after the date of cessation to any member who applies for one.[76]

Unions must first seek the approval of the CO for the rules under which they propose to conduct the ballot. The CO will give an opportunity for both the complainant and the union to be heard and take into account decisions on similar issues that have previously been made by the courts. The CO has the power to make an enforcement order on the union to remedy a failure to comply with the law on political fund ballots and/or to abstain from repeating the failure in the future. The CO's order can be enforced in the same way as an order from the court.

Section 86 TULRCA 1992 imposes a duty on employers not to deduct contributions to a political fund from the emoluments payable to a member who has either informed the employer in writing that he or she is exempt from paying the political levy or has given written notification to the union of his or her objection to paying it. Employers must comply as soon as is reasonably practicable and will be in breach of the Act if they deduct any union dues from the pay of the person who submitted a certificate under this section. Aggrieved employees may apply to the county court for a declaration that the employer has failed to comply, and the court can make an order requiring the employer to take remedial action within a specified period.[77]

INTER-UNION DISPUTES

There is no legal machinery for handling inter-union disputes, and relations between TUC-affiliated unions are regulated by the Bridlington Principles.[78] According to Principle 2, TUC affiliates 'accept as a binding commitment ... that they will not knowingly and actively seek to take into membership the present or 'recent' members of another union by making recruitment approaches, either directly or indirectly, without the agreement of that organisation'. Where there is dispute over recruitment, 'The effort at resolution will include a moral obligation on the part of the respondent union to offer compensation to the complainant union for any loss of income that it has suffered as a consequence of any knowingly and active recruitment of its members.' Principle 3 provides that 'No union shall commence organising activities at any establishment or undertaking in respect of any grade or grades of workers in which another union has the majority of workers employed and negotiates terms and conditions, unless by arrangement with that union.'[79] Principle 4 obliges unions to involve the TUC before industrial action occurs over an inter-union dispute and, where necessary, to take steps to secure a return to normal working. Where unions are unable to resolve a dispute and it is referred to the TUC, the General Secretary may refer it to a Disputes Committee which is empowered to make an award. Finally, it should be noted that an employer who is affected by an inter-union problem may seek assistance from ACAS.

KEY POINTS

- Employees have the right to join the union of their choice and cannot be excluded unless they fail to meet an enforceable membership requirement, the union operates only in another part of Great Britain, the union deals with only one employer, or the exclusion is attributable to the individual's conduct.
- The rules of a trade union constitute a contract between the union and its members and must be strictly adhered to. A trade union wishing to discipline a member must have the power to do so in its rule-book.
- If the union rules specify the grounds on which disciplinary action may be taken, and the procedures to be taken, it will be unlawful for the union to rely on other grounds, or not rigidly follow its own procedures.
- Irrespective of its rule-book, every trade union must elect its president, general secretary and members of its executive by ballot at least once every five years.
- There are detailed rules governing union elections, including candidates having the right to prepare election addresses and have them distributed with the ballot papers, plus the need to appoint independent persons to distribute and store ballot papers, and the need for an independent scrutineer.
- The Certification Officer can be used as an alternative to the courts for union members who wish to make complaints about disciplinary action by their union. The Certification Officer has the power to make enquiries, hear the parties and issue declarations which can be enforced in the same way as court orders.
- It is unlawful to refuse employment to a person because they are or are not members of a trade union.
- Employees have the right not to be dismissed or subjected to a detriment for the purposes of preventing them from becoming a member or taking part in the activities of a trade union or, conversely, for not wanting to be a member or take part in union activities.

NOTES

1 These provisions do not apply if the employee ordinarily works outside Great Britain
2 Defined by Section 143 TULRCA 1992
3 Section 140 TULRCA 1992
4 Section 142 TULRCA 1992
5 *Ridgway* v *NCB* (1987) IRLR 80
6 See *Farnsworth* v *McCoid* (1998) IRLR 362
6A The Employment Relations Bill 2003 proposes to replace the word 'purpose' by 'sole or main purpose'
7 *Gallagher* v *Department of Transport* (1994) IRLR 231
8 See *Southwark London Borough Council* v *Whillier* (2001) ICR 142
9 See *Ridgway* v *NCB* (note 5)
10 *Carlson* v *Post Office* (1981) IRLR 158
11 See *British Airways* v *Francis* (1981) IRLR 9
12 (1983) IRLR 78
13 See *Port of London Authority* v *Payne* (1992) IRLR 447
14 (2002) IRLR 568
15 *Rasool* v *Hepworth Pipe Ltd (No.2)* (1980) IRLR 135
16 See *Marley Tile* v *Shaw* (1980) IRLR 25
17 See *Fitzpatrick* v *British Rail* (1991) IRLR 376
18 See *Zucker* v *Astrid Jewels* (1978) IRLR 385
19 Section 147(2) TULRCA 1992
20 See paragraphs 6 & 9 Schedule 2 EA 2002
21 Section 147(3) TULRCA 1992
22 Section 148(2) TULRCA 1992
23 Section 149 TULRCA 1992
24 See *Brassington* v *Cauldon Wholesale Ltd* (1977) IRLR 479
25 (1997) IRLA 332
26 See *Crosville Motor Ltd* v *Ashville* (1986) IRLR 475
27 Section 154(1) TULRCA 1992. See p247 for the requirement to submit a statement of grievance when Section 32 EA 2002 comes into force
28 See *Maund* v *Penwith District Council* (1984) IRLR 24
29 Section 161 TULRCA 1992
30 Section 162 TULRCA 1992
31 See section 164 TULRCA 1992
32 Section 17 ERel Act 1999
33 Section 17(4) ERel Act 1999
34 See for sample, Section 12 SDA 1975, section 11 RRA 1976 and section 13 DDA 1995; see also EOC Code of Practice, paragraphs 6–8, CRE Code of Practice, part 3, and Code of Practice on the Duties of Trade Organisations to Their Disabled Members and Applicants
35 Section 174(3) TULRCA 1992
36 Section 174(4) TULRCA 1992
37 See *NACODS* v *Gluchowski* (1996) IRLR 252
38 Section 175 TULRCA 1992
39 Section 176 TULRCA 1992
40 See *Clarke* v *Chadburn* (1984) IRLR 350
41 *McVitae* v *Unison* (1996) IRLR 33
42 See *Knowles* v *Fire Brigades Union* (1996) IRLR 617
43 Section 64(2) TULRCA 1992
44 (1990) IRLR 464
45 Section 66(2) TULRCA 1992

46 Section 288 TULRCA 1992

47 Section 67(3) TULRCA 1992

48 On the requirement to take all necessary steps to secure the reversal of an expulsion, see *NALGO* v *Courteney-Dunn* (1992) IRLR 114

49 Section 67(6) and (7) TULRCA 1992

50 Section 174(4) TULRCA 1992

51 See *Jacques* v *AUEW* (1986) ICR 683

52 See *Leigh* v *NUR* (1970) IRLR 60

53 See *Longley* v *NUJ* (1987) IRLR 109

54 *Cheall* v *APEX* (1983) IRKLR 215

55 See *Roebuck* v *NUM* (1976) ICR 573 and *Hamlet* v *GMBATU* (1986) IRLR 293

56 See *McGhee* v *TGWU* (1985) IRLR 199 on the meaning of expulsion

57 Section 46(3) TULRCA 1992 defines a 'member of the executive'. On exemptions for certain presidents and general secretaries, see section 46(4) TULRCA 1992

58 Sections 59 and 60 TULRCA 1992

59 See *Paul* v *NALGO* (1987) IRLR 43

60 See *R* v *Certification Officer ex parte EPEA* (1990) IRLR 98

61 Section 47 TULRCA 1992

62 (1999) IRLR 166

63 Defined by section 49(2) TULRCA 1992

64 See sections 49 and 52 TULRCA 1992. On the confidentiality of the register, see section 24A TULRCA 1992

65 See *Douglas* v *GPMU* (1995) IRLR 426

66 Section 51A TULCRA 1992

67 Section 203 TULRCA 1992

68 Section 54 TULRCA 1992. On the contractual right of a member to complain of a breach of the rules, see *Wise* v *USDAW* (1996) IRLR 609

69 Section 108A(3) TULRCA 1992

70 Section 108A(5) TULRCA 1992

71 Section 108B(1) TULRCA 1992

72 Section 108B(2) TULRCA 1992

73 Sections 108B(6) and (8) TULRCA 1992

74 Section 82 TULRCA 1992

75 Section 91(4) TULRCA 1992

76 Section 90 TULRCA 1992

77 Section 87 TULRCA 1992

78 See TUC booklet *TUC Disputes, Principles and Procedures*, 1993

79 The process of statutory recognition of trade unions is stopped if there is an unsettled dispute between unions over representation (see Chapter 19)

Liability for Industrial Action

OVERVIEW

It has already been explained that all forms of industrial action are likely to constitute a breach of an individual's contract of employment. In this chapter we shall be concentrating more on the liability of those who organise industrial action than those who participate in it. In this respect we shall be examining the nature of the common-law liabilities and the extent to which statutory provisions can be used to negate their effect. We begin with an examination of the economic torts and then consider the protection offered by statute for action that takes place in contemplation or furtherance of a trade dispute. This is followed by a consideration of the statutory hurdles that have to be overcome before lawful action can take place. We shall be focusing mainly on the civil law, but it will also be necessary to deal with the possibility of criminal prosecutions.

THE 'ECONOMIC' TORTS

Inducing a breach of contract

There are two forms of inducement: direct and indirect.

Direct inducement may occur when a union official puts direct pressure on an employer to breach a commercial contract. Thus if A induces B to break the contract of supply with C and C suffers loss as a result, C could sue B for breaking the contract (but is unlikely to in the circumstances), or could sue A if the following matters are shown:

- that A knew of the contract which would be broken or was 'recklessly indifferent' as to its existence
- that A's conduct was intentional; here, once sufficient knowledge has been established, the intention to produce a breach will be presumed
- that there was clear evidence of inducement; in this context inducement means pressure, persuasion or procuration and must be distinguished from the giving of advice, information or a warning.[1]

Indirect inducement is when A induces union members to break their contracts of employment so that B is forced to break the contract with C. C can sue A if the requirements of knowledge, intention and inducement are met and the use of unlawful means is proved. It makes no difference that A believed that the functions performed by the members were voluntary rather than contractual.[2] For the purposes of all the economic torts, unlawful means may be either tortious, eg breaking a contract or inducing a breach of statutory duty, or criminal acts, eg the use of violence.

Thus the essential difference between direct and indirect inducement is one of causation. Where the person immediately responsible for bringing the pressure to bear was the defendant or someone for whose acts he or she was legally responsible, the inducement is direct. If it was a third party responding to the defendant's inducement or persuasion but exercising his or her choice (and not being a person for whom the defendant was legally responsible), the inducement is indirect.[3]

Section 219(1)(a) TULRCA 1992 provides that an act done in contemplation or furtherance of a trade dispute – the so-called 'golden formula' (see below) – will not be actionable in tort on the ground only that it induces another to break a contract. In *Norbrook Ltd* v *King*[4] it was pointed out that the effect of the phrase 'on the ground only' is that the use of unlawful means to induce a breach of contract deprives the user of statutory protection. However, it is clear that section 219 does not provide immunity against prosecution in respect of acts which are in themselves criminal.[5]

Contracts of supply

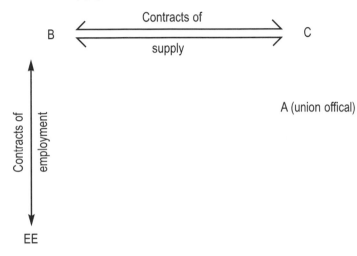

Intimidation

This tort is committed where C suffers as a result of action taken by B in response to an unlawful threat made to B by A. In this situation C or B can sue A at common law, whether the threat is of tortious or criminal conduct.[6] However, section 219(1)(b) TULRCA 1992 states that an act done in contemplation or furtherance of a trade dispute shall not be actionable in tort on the ground only that it consists of a person 'threatening that a contract (whether one to which he is a party or not) will be broken or its performance interfered with, or that he will induce another person to break a contract or interfere with its performance'.

Conspiracy

Again, this tort could take one of two forms:

- a combination to injure with illegitimate objectives. This is where two or more persons combine in order to harm the plaintiff by use of means which are lawful in themselves but with a predominant purpose other than that of advancing their own legitimate interests. Thus if those combining can show a genuine trade union reason behind their action (for example, protecting jobs), the conspiracy will not be actionable despite any loss caused to an employer.[7]

- a situation in which people combine in order to harm the plaintiff by using unlawful means. In this way a tort is committed irrespective of the purpose of the combination. The use of unlawful means eliminates the justification of self-interest.

Because almost all strikes involve combinations of workers inflicting loss on employers, section 219(2) TULRCA 1992 provides that a combination to do any act in contemplation or furtherance of a trade dispute is not actionable in tort if the act is one which, if done by one person alone, would not be actionable.

Interference with business by unlawful means

This tort was developed to take account of the practice of inserting *force majeure* clauses into commercial contracts. The effect of such a clause is to exempt a party from liability where a breach of contract would otherwise have arisen as a result of industrial action. The Court of Appeal has stated that to succeed in establishing the tort of wrongful interference with contractual rights, five conditions must be fulfilled. These are:

- It must be shown that the defendant persuaded or procured or induced a third party to break its contract with the plaintiff.
- It must be shown that the defendant when so acting had knowledge of that contract.
- The defendant must be shown to have had the intent to persuade or induce a breach of that contract.
- The plaintiff must show that it suffered more than nominal damage.
- If justification is put forward as a defence, the plaintiff must be able to rebut this.[8]

Statutory immunity is provided by section 219(1)(a) TULRCA 1992, which states that so long as the 'golden formula' applies, an act is not to be actionable in tort on the ground only that it 'interferes or induces any other person to interfere' with the performance of a contract. In *Hadmor Productions* v *Hamilton*[9] the House of Lords held that inducing, or threatening to induce, a breach of contract could not be regarded as unlawful means for the purpose of establishing liability for interference with the business of a third person.

Inducing a breach of statutory duty

In *Meade* v *Haringey LBC*[10] two Court of Appeal judges expressed the opinion that persons inducing a public body to act in breach of its statutory duty would be committing a tort for which there would be no statutory immunity. If this view were adopted, it would be relatively easy to restrain action taken by workers in the public sector.

ECONOMIC DURESS

If the financial consequences to an employer of not acceding to the request of a trade union or another person are catastrophic, it could be argued that there was such coercion of the employer's will as to vitiate consent to any agreements made with, or payments made to, the union (or person) applying the pressure. Contracts made in these circumstances will be voidable and it will be possible to claim restitution of money paid under them. The rationale is that the employer's apparent consent was induced by pressure exercised by that other party which the law does not regard as legitimate. In *Universe Tankships Inc of Monrovia* v *ITWF*[11] the House of Lords accepted that sections 219 and 244 TULRCA 1992 afforded an indication of where public policy requires the line to be drawn between the kind of commercial pressure by a trade union which ought to be treated as legitimised and the kind that amounts to economic duress. The events which gave rise to this case occurred in 1978 and it is safe to say that subsequent legislation will have encouraged the judiciary to take a narrower view of what is regarded as legitimate pressure.

THE 'GOLDEN FORMULA'

We have observed that statutory immunity in tort for various types of industrial action depends on that action taking place in contemplation or furtherance of a trade dispute. Although we shall be outlining later the requirement to conduct a ballot before industrial action (see below), it should be noted that so long as the action taken is in contemplation or furtherance of a trade dispute the TULRCA 1992 immunities apply irrespective of whether or not the action is in breach of a disputes procedure. However, if the 'golden formula' does not apply, it will be relatively easy for an employer to show that one of the economic torts is being committed, and to obtain an interim injunction on that basis.

The meaning of 'trade dispute'

Section 244 TULRCA 1992 defines a trade dispute as a dispute between workers and their employer which relates wholly or mainly to one or more of the following:

- terms and conditions of employment, or the physical conditions in which any workers are required to work[11A]. These are not confined to contractual terms and conditions, and the House of Lords has held that a dispute about the reasonableness of an employer's instruction may be covered[12]

- engagement or non-engagement, or termination or suspension of employment, or the duties of employment of one or more workers. This might include a dispute about a proposal to transfer an undertaking and its employees.[13] However, if the reason or one of the reasons for calling industrial action is 'the fact or belief that the employer has dismissed one or more employees in circumstances such that by virtue of section 237 TULRCA 1992 (dismissal in connection with unofficial industrial action) they have no right to complain of unfair dismissal', the immunity provided by section 219 TULRCA 1992 is lost[14]

- allocation of work or the duties of employment as between workers or groups of workers

- matters of discipline

- the membership or non-membership of a trade union on the part of a worker. Nevertheless, there will be no immunity from liability in tort where the purpose of the industrial action is to enforce union membership or persuade employers to insert recognition or consultation requirements in contracts for the supply of goods or services[15]

- facilities for officials of trade unions

- the machinery for negotiation or consultation and other procedures relating to any of the foregoing matters, including the recognition by employers or employers' associations of the right of a trade union to represent workers in any such negotiation, or consultation, or in the carrying out of such procedures.

In *University College London Hospital NHS Trust* v *Unison*[16] the union gained an overwhelming majority in favour of strike action in support of a demand for employment guarantees associated with the building of a new hospital under the Private Finance Initiative. This would have involved the transfer of some workers to a new employer. The Court of Appeal held that the dispute was about terms and conditions which would apply to workers not currently employed by the NHS Trust and that such a dispute about future employment with a new employer was outside the provisions of section 244. Subsequently the European Court of Human Rights has ruled that in these circumstances the UK did not exceed the margin of appreciation accorded to it in regulating trade union action.[17]

Clearly, where there is a dispute between a union and an employer there is a dispute between those workers on whose behalf the union was acting and that employer.[18] In addition, section 244(2) TULRCA 1992 provides that in certain circumstances a dispute between a Minister of the Crown and any workers is to be treated as a dispute between those workers and their employers.[19]

A 'worker' is defined to cover only those employed by the employer in dispute.[20] However, the 'golden formula' will not apply if the dispute concerns a former employee unless either the employment was terminated in connection with the dispute or the termination was one of the circumstances giving rise to the dispute. A realistic view of who is an employer was taken in *Examite Ltd* v *Whittaker*[21] where it was stated that 'the Act applies to employers whatever particular hat these particular employers may wear from time to time.'

A trade dispute can exist even though it relates to matters occurring outside the UK:

> so long as the person or persons whose actions in the UK are said to be in contemplation or furtherance of a trade dispute relating to matters occurring outside the UK are likely to be affected in respect of one or more of the matters specified in section 244(1) TULRCA by the outcome of that dispute.[22]

It is also stated that an act, threat or demand done or made by a person or organisation against another which, if resisted, would have led to a trade dispute with that other, 'shall, notwithstanding that because that other submits to the act or threat or accedes to the demand no dispute arises, be treated as being done or made in contemplation or furtherance of a trade dispute'.[23]

Contemplation or furtherance

The word 'contemplation' refers to something imminent or likely to occur, so the 'golden formula' cannot be invoked if the action was taken too far in advance of any dispute. 'Furtherance' assumes the existence of a dispute and an act will not be protected if it is not for the purpose of promoting the interests of a party to the dispute (for example, if it is in pursuit of a personal vendetta) or occurs after its conclusion.[24] In *MacShane and Ashton* v *Express Newspapers*[25] the House of Lords held that while the existence of a trade dispute had to be determined objectively, the test for deciding whether an act is in furtherance of such a dispute is a subjective one: 'If the person doing the act honestly thinks at the time he does it that it may help one of the parties to the dispute to achieve their objective and does it for that reason, he is protected.' Apparently there is no requirement that a union should act exclusively in furtherance of a trade dispute; it is sufficient if the furtherance of a trade dispute is one of its purposes. Indeed, the presence of an improper motive is relevant only where it is so overriding that it negates any genuine intention to advance the trade dispute.[26]

SECONDARY ACTION

In this book 'primary action' refers to action taken directly against the employer in dispute and 'secondary action' is that taken against the employer's suppliers and customers. Section 244 defines secondary action as being an inducement to break or interfere with a contract of employment or a contract for personal services, or a threat to do so, where the employer under that contract is not party to the dispute. For these purposes an employer is not to be regarded as a party to a dispute between another employer and its workers. Similarly, where more than one employer is in dispute, the dispute between each employer and its workers is to be treated as a separate dispute.[27]

The protection afforded against certain tort liabilities by section 219 TULRCA 1992 will not be available unless the secondary action satisfies the requirements of section 224. These can be met only if the secondary action is taken in the course of such attendance as is declared lawful by section 220 TULRCA 1992:

- by a worker employed (or last employed) by the employer who is party to the dispute, or
- by a union official whose attendance is lawful by virtue of section 220(1)(6) TULRCA 1992 (on peaceful picketing and section 220 TULRCA 1992, see below).

UNION RESPONSIBILITY FOR THE ACTS OF THEIR MEMBERS AND OFFICIALS

Trade unions are to be treated in law as ordinary persons. This means that they get the benefit of the immunities conferred by section 219 TULRCA 1992 but can be sued if they are responsible for unlawful industrial action. However, a union will be held liable for the torts mentioned in section 20(1) TULRCA 1992 only if the acts in question were authorised or endorsed by the union. Where other torts are committed, the ordinary principles of vicarious liability apply.[28] Irrespective of union rules, acts are to be regarded as authorised or endorsed if there was authorisation or endorsement by:[29]

- any person empowered by the rules to do, authorise or endorse acts of the kind in question
- the principal executive committee or the president or general secretary, or
- any other committee of the union or any other official of the union (whether employed by it or not).

In this context 'rules' means the 'written rules of the union and any other written provisions forming part of the contract between a member and other members'. 'President' and 'general secretary' are defined to include, where there is no such office in the union, the person who holds the 'nearest equivalent' office.[30] For these purposes any group of persons constituted in accordance with the rules of the union is a committee of the union and 'an act shall be taken to have been done, authorised or endorsed by an official if it was done, etc' by any member of a group whose purposes include organising or co-ordinating industrial action.[31] These provisions apply irrespective of anything in the union rules that prevents particular officials or committees from calling industrial action.

How unions may repudiate members' and officials' acts

A union can avoid liability for the actions of union committees and officials if those actions are repudiated by the principal executive committee or the president or general secretary 'as soon as reasonably practicable after coming to the knowledge of any of them'. However, a repudiation will be effective only if:

- written notice of the repudiation is given to the official or committee in question without delay, and
- the union has done its best to give individual written notice of the fact and date of repudiation without delay to every member who the union has reason to believe is taking part, or might otherwise take part, in the industrial action. The notice to members must contain the following statement: 'Your union has repudiated any call for industrial action to which this notice relates and will give no support to such action. If you are dismissed while taking unofficial industrial action, you will have no right to complain of unfair dismissal.' This notice must also be given to the employer of every such member.[32]

An act shall not be treated as repudiated if the union's principal executive committee, president or general secretary subsequently behaves in a manner inconsistent with that repudiation. Additionally, if a request is made to any of these bodies within three months by a person who is party to a commercial contract that has been, or may be, interfered with and who has not been given notice of the repudiation, that body must immediately confirm the repudiation in writing.[33] Finally, in any injunction proceedings arising out of this section, the courts are empowered to require unions to take such steps as are considered appropriate for ensuring that:

- there is no inducement of persons to take part in industrial action, and
- no person engages in any conduct after the grant of the injunction by virtue of having been induced before it was granted to take part in industrial action.[34]

BALLOTS AND NOTICE OF INDUSTRIAL ACTION

Trade unions and their officials can benefit from immunity provided by section 219 TULRCA 1992 only if the union has authorised or endorsed the industrial action, having gained majority support in a ballot of the members concerned not more than four weeks before the start of the action.[35] It is the Court of Appeal's view that once industrial action has begun it should continue 'without substantial interruption' if reliance is to be placed on the result of the original ballot. Whether the original action has come to an end is a matter of fact and degree.[36]

For section 219 TULRCA 1992 immunity to be available, the following requirements must be met:

- Trade unions must take such steps as are reasonably necessary to ensure that at least seven days before the start of the ballot a written notice is received by 'every person who it is reasonable for the union to believe . . . will be the employer of persons who will be entitled to vote in the ballot'. This notice must

    - state that the union intends to hold a ballot

    - specify the date which the union reasonably believes will be the opening day of the ballot

    - provide the employer with such information in the union's possession which 'would help the employer to make plans and bring information to the attention of those of his employees who it is reasonable for the union to believe will be entitled to vote in the ballot'.[37] If the union possesses information as to the number, category or workplace of the employees concerned, then this information should be included in the notice.[38] Thus in *RMT v London Underground*[39] the Court of Appeal held that a notice relating to proposed strike action by 'all members of the union employed in all categories at all workplaces' did not comply with the statutory requirements. Additionally, at least three days before the opening of the ballot, the union must take such steps as are reasonably necessary to ensure that the same employer receives a sample voting paper.[40]

- Conditions (b) and (d) on union elections must be satisfied (see Chapter 20).

- Entitlement to vote must be given equally to those, and only those, who the union reasonably believes will be called upon to take strike or other industrial action.[41] In *London Underground v RMT*[42] the Court of Appeal accepted that a union could call for newly recruited members to take part in industrial action even though they had not been balloted.

- There must be a separate ballot at each workplace unless the ballot is limited to all the members of a union who

    - according to the union's reasonable belief have an occupation of a particular kind or have any of a number of particular kinds of occupation, and

    - are employed by a particular employer, or by any number of particular employers, with whom the union is in dispute.[43]

- So far as is reasonably practicable, all members entitled to vote must be sent a voting paper at his or her registered address, and be given a convenient opportunity to vote by post.[44]

- The voting paper must

    - state the name of the independent scrutineer appointed to carry out the functions described above[45]

    - specify the address to which, and the date by which, it is to be returned

    - be marked with a number which is one of a series of consecutive whole numbers

    - contain the following statement:

> If you take part in a strike or other industrial action you may be in breach of your contract of employment. However, if you are dismissed for taking part in a strike or other industrial action which is called officially and is otherwise lawful, the dismissal will be unfair if it takes place fewer than eight weeks after you started taking part in the action, and depending on the circumstances may be unfair if it takes place later.

- invite a 'yes' or 'no' answer to the question whether members are prepared to participate in a strike or other industrial action. According to the Court of Appeal, the questions on the ballot paper must be framed so that members can draw a distinction between their willingness to take strike action and their willingness to take action short of a strike.[46] In *Connex South Eastern Ltd v NURMTW*[47] employees voted for strike action and the employer was notified by the union that they proposed to start a ban on overtime and rest-day working. The employer claimed that this discontinuous action was not strike action and was therefore unlawful. The Court of Appeal held that the action was lawful because strike action was not restricted to stoppages of all work, but could include stoppages on particular days and at particular hours. The position has been modified by the ERel Act 1999 which states that overtime bans and call-out bans are forms of industrial action short of a strike.[48] Each question has to be voted on individually and the majority in respect of each question considered separately[49]

- identify the person(s) authorised to call industrial action and that person must be one of those specified in section 20(2) TULRCA (see above).

- Industrial action will not be regarded as having the support of a ballot if a member who was likely to be induced into taking part in the action was not accorded the right to vote.[50]

- As soon as is reasonably practicable after the ballot, the union must take such steps as are reasonably necessary to ensure that all those entitled to vote and every relevant employer are informed of the number of votes cast, the numbers voting 'yes' and those voting 'no', and the number of spoiled ballot papers.[51] If there is a failure to inform one or more relevant employers, the ballot and subsequent action will still be valid in relation to the other employers who were informed correctly.[52]

- Trade unions must take all reasonably necessary steps to ensure that the employer of those to be called upon to take industrial action receives written notice of the action. This notice must be received after the employer has been informed of the ballot result and at least seven days prior to the date on which the action is to commence. The notice must contain

  - such information 'as would help the employer to make plans and bring information to the attention of those of his employees whom the union intends to induce or has induced to take part, or continue to take part, in the industrial action'[53]

  - a statement of whether the industrial action is intended to be continuous or discontinuous[54]

  - where there is continuous action, the date on which it is intended to start; where the action is discontinuous, the dates on which it is intended to take place. The ballot will cease to be effective after a period of four weeks, or up to eight weeks if the union and the employer agree[55]

  - a statement that the notice is given for the purposes of section 234A TULRCA 1992.

If there are accidental and minor failures to comply with all the balloting requirements, these may be ignored as long as they are unlikely to affect the ballot outcome.[56]

Where industrial action ceases to be authorised or endorsed (other than in compliance with a court order or undertaking), and is subsequently re-authorised or re-endorsed, the union must give another notice to the employer before the industrial action is resumed.

Finally, where a member has been (or is likely to be) induced by the union to take part in any industrial action which does not satisfy the ballot requirements of Part V TULRCA 1992, he or she can apply to the High Court for an order requiring the union to stop authorising or endorsing the industrial action without the support of a valid ballot.[57] It should be noted that although a court can order the union to ensure that there is no further inducement, it has no power to compel the union to conduct a valid ballot.

REMEDIES

Damages

Section 22(2) TULRCA 1992 limits the amount of damages that can be awarded 'in any proceedings in tort' against a trade union which is deemed liable for industrial action.[58] The words 'in any proceedings' are crucial, since separate proceedings may be brought by all those who have suffered from the industrial action. The limits set are:

- £10,000, if the union has fewer than 5,000 members
- £50,000, if the union has 5,000 or more members but fewer than 25,000
- £125,000 if the union has 25,000 or more members but fewer than 100,000
- £250,000 if the union has 100,000 or more members.

It should be noted that interest on such damages may be available.[59] Finally, it should be noted that damages, costs or expenses cannot be recovered from certain 'protected property'. This includes union provident funds and political funds, which cannot be used for financing industrial action.[60]

INJUNCTIONS

If an employer is suffering economic harm as a result of unlawful industrial action, the logical remedy is to seek an injunction so as to prevent further loss being incurred. An injunction may be sought against a trade union or some other person, although section 236 TULRCA 1992 prevents a court from compelling an employee to do any work. The general principle that if damages would provide an adequate remedy an injunction must be refused will not apply in this context: 'Where it is clear that the defendants were acting unlawfully, it would require wholly exceptional circumstances to be a proper exercise of discretion to allow such conduct to continue.'[61]

There are two basic types of injunction that should be mentioned:

- In situations of extreme urgency an *interim* injunction can be sought. This is a temporary measure which endures until a named day and can be obtained on the basis of sworn statements submitted by the applicant alone. If the respondent is absent, this is known as an *ex parte* (one-sided) injunction.
  According to section 221 TULRCA 1992, a court shall not grant an application if the party against whom the injunction is sought claims (or in the court's opinion might claim) that the act was done in contemplation or furtherance of a trade dispute unless all reasonable steps have been taken to give that party notice of the application and an opportunity of being heard.
- A *permanent* injunction is one which is granted at the end of the trial.

Before granting an interim injunction, a judge will have to consider the following questions:

- Is there a serious question to be tried?
- Does the balance of convenience lie with the plaintiff? In *NWL* v *Nelson*[62] Lord Diplock argued that

judges should not blind themselves to the practical realities by pretending that an injunction merely preserves the *status quo* until the trial is heard: 'It is the nature of industrial action that it can be promoted effectively only so long as it is possible to strike while the iron is hot; once postponed, it is unlikely that it can be revived ... The grant or refusal of an interim injunction generally disposes finally of the action.' In such a case the court has to balance the risk of doing an injustice to either party and evaluate the public interest.[63]

■ Where the party against whom the injunction is sought claims that the action was in contemplation of furtherance of a trade dispute, is there a likelihood of the defendant establishing a defence to the action under section 219 or 220 TULRCA 1992?[64] It has been held by the House of Lords that the effect of section 221(2) TULRCA 1992 is that in exercising its discretion a court should put into the balance of convenience the degree of likelihood of the defendant's succeeding in establishing a trade dispute defence.[65] Thus in *Health Computing* v *Meek*[66] no injunction was granted because there was a 'substantial probability' that the defendants would establish that they were acting in contemplation or furtherance of a trade dispute. By way of contrast, in *RJB Mining* v *NUM*[67] an interim injunction was granted because it was at least arguable that the union was in breach of section 227 TULRCA 1992 by omitting to ballot all of its members who might be involved in the industrial action. However, that it is likely that a trade dispute defence would be established should not be regarded as an overriding or paramount factor precluding the granting of an injunction. There may be cases where the consequences to the plaintiff or to others may be so serious that the court feels it necessary to grant this form of remedy. In the *Duport Steels* case[68] the Law Lords confirmed that there is a residual discretion to grant an injunction notwithstanding the likelihood of a trade dispute defence succeeding at trial. Nevertheless, the opinion was expressed that it required an exceptional case in which the consequences of the threatened act might be disastrous.

■ What good will be done to the plaintiff by the grant of the injunction sought? In *Hadmor Productions* v *Hamilton*[69] the House of Lords held that the High Court judge had been entitled to attach great weight to the view that an injunction would not have been of practical use to the plaintiff. It is not sufficient ground for granting an injunction to argue that if the defendants had no intention of engaging in unlawful conduct the injunction would do them no harm![70]

Failure by union officials to comply with an injunction may amount to contempt of court, for which the union is vicariously liable. Indeed, it would appear that a delay in complying with a court order cannot be justified by reference to the union's internal constitution.[71] Where there is deliberate defiance of a court order, a substantial fine may be imposed.[72] In this context it should be observed that section 15 TULRCA 1992 makes it unlawful for a union to use its property to indemnify an individual on whom a penalty has been imposed for contempt or a criminal offence. Additionally, where it is alleged that a union's trustees have unlawfully applied union property or complied with an unlawful direction given under the union rules, a member can seek a High Court order to remove the trustees, recover the property or appoint a receiver.[73]

INDUSTRIAL ACTION THAT AFFECTS THE SUPPLY OF GOODS OR SERVICES TO AN INDIVIDUAL

Section 235A TULRCA 1992 gives an individual the right to apply to the High Court for an order if:

■ a trade union or other person has done, or is likely to do, an unlawful act to induce a person to take part in or continue with industrial action, and

■ an effect, or likely effect, of the industrial action is, or will be, to prevent or delay the supply of goods or services, or to reduce the quality of goods or services supplied to the claimant.

For these purposes an act is unlawful if it is actionable in tort by anyone, or if it could form the basis of an application by a union member under section 62 TULRCA 1992 (see above). It is immaterial whether or not the individual concerned is entitled to be supplied with the goods or services in question.

PICKETING

Civil law aspects

According to section 220 TULRCA 1992, it shall be lawful for a person in contemplation or furtherance of a trade dispute to attend:

- at or near their own place of work, or
- if they are an official of a trade union, at or near the place of work of a member of that union whom they are accompanying and whom they represent

for the purpose only of peacefully obtaining or communicating information, or peacefully persuading any person to work or abstain from working.

'Place of work' is not statutorily defined but it would seem to refer to a person's principal place of work or base.[74] As regards the words 'at or near', the Court of Appeal has confirmed that a geographical approach should be taken and that the matter will be one of fact and degree in each case.[75] If people normally work at more than one place or at a place where it is impracticable to picket, their place of work is any of their employer's premises from which they work or from which their work is administered.[76] Unemployed workers whose last employment was terminated in connection with a trade dispute, or whose dismissal was one of the circumstances giving rise to a trade dispute, are entitled to picket at their former place of work. It should be observed that section 220 TULRCA 1992 does not necessarily provide employees with a place that they can effectively picket – for example, if their place of work is closed down. A trade union official who has been elected or appointed to represent some of the members is to be regarded for the purposes of picketing as representing only those members; otherwise, a union official is regarded as representing all the union's members.[77]

Section 220 TULRCA 1992 protects mere attendance only for one of the designated purposes. If an act is done in the course of picketing which is not lawful by virtue of section 220, then section 219 TULRCA 1992 will not prevent an action in tort from being brought. Thus pickets acting within the scope of section 220 TULRCA 1992 may be liable for conspiracy to use unlawful means if they are accompanied by pickets who are not so acting. Equally, a person who is not picketing at a permitted place may be sued for trespass to the highway as well as all the economic torts. This is so even if the employer at the premises picketed has accepted the work of the primary employer in dispute. Peaceful picketing at one's own place of work may also result in civil liability – for example, if it is in support of workers in dispute with another employer.

Mass picketing and intimidation

In *Thomas v NUM (South Wales)*[78] Mr Justice Scott refused to distinguish between 'so-called pickets who are stationed close to the gates of the colliery and the rest, so-called demonstrators, who stand near by'. The judge held that whether the presence or conduct of pickets represents a tortious interference with the right of those who wish to go to work depends on the particular circumstances of the case. In his view, where feelings run high, substantial numbers of pickets are almost bound to have an intimidatory effect on those going to work. Thus while picketing *per se* is not a common-law nuisance, mass picketing is – ie picketing so as by sheer weight of numbers to block the entrance to premises or prevent the entry of vehicles or people.[79]

Injunctions to stop unlawful picketing

An employer whose contracts are interfered with by picketing which falls outside section 220 TULRCA 1992 may bring an action for damages against those responsible and ask a court to make an order stopping the unlawful picketing. An injunction will normally be sought against the person or union on whose instructions or advice the picketing is taking place, but it will also restrict the activities of any others who act on behalf of that person or union (see above on a union's responsibility for the acts of its officials). While the police are not obliged to help an employer identify pickets, a court can ask the police to assist its officers in enforcing injunctions.

The impact of the criminal law

The immunity provided by the civil law cannot protect a picket who commits a criminal offence, and even peaceful picketing can lead to criminal proceedings if it is not lawful by virtue of section 220 TULRCA 1992:

> The criminal law protects the right of every person to go about his lawful daily business free from interference by others. No one is under any obligation to stop when a picket asks him to do so, or if he does stop, to comply with the picket's request, for example, not to go into work. Everyone has the right, if he wants to do so, to cross a picket line to go into his place of work or to deliver or collect goods. A picket may exercise peaceful persuasion, but if he goes beyond that and tries by means other than peaceful persuasion to deter another person from exercising those rights, he may commit a criminal offence.[80]

Paragraph 43 of the Department of Employment Code of Practice on Picketing lists a range of criminal offences that may be committed by pickets:

(a) using threatening, abusive or insulting words or behaviour, or disorderly behaviour within the sight or hearing of any person ... likely to be caused harassment, alarm or distress by such conduct

(b) using threatening, abusive or insulting words or behaviour towards any person with intent to cause fear of violence or to provoke violence

(c) using or threatening unlawful violence

(d) obstructing the highway or the entrance to premises or to seek physically to bar the passage of vehicles or persons, etc

(e) being in possession of an offensive weapon

(f) intentionally or recklessly damaging property

(g) engaging in violent, disorderly or unruly behaviour or taking any action which is likely to lead to a breach of the peace

(h) obstructing a police officer in the execution of his duty.[81]

The police may limit picket numbers

Although it is not the function of the police to take a view of the merits of a particular trade dispute, the law gives them the discretion to take whatever measures may reasonably be considered necessary to ensure that picketing remains peaceful and orderly. Hence the police are entitled to limit the number of pickets at any one place where they have reasonable cause to fear disorder.[82] Having identified the main causes of violence and disorder on the picket line as excessive numbers, the Code of Practice exhorts pickets and their organisers to ensure that 'in general the number of pickets does not exceed six at any entrance to, or exit from a workplace; frequently a smaller number will be appropriate'.[83] The code also has paragraphs dealing with the functions of a picket organiser and the safeguarding of essential supplies and services.[84]

Trespass: liability under civil and criminal law

Apart from the law relating to picketing, the criminal law does not generally play an important role in regulating industrial conflict. However, if employees occupy their employer's premises they become trespassers under the civil law and the employer may invoke a specified procedure to regain possession. In addition, persons occupying a workplace may be charged under the Criminal Law Act 1977 with using violence to secure entry and trespassing with a weapon of offence – eg ordinary working tools if they are intended to be used offensively.[85] Of the remaining statutory provisions which could give rise to criminal liability, the most important today are probably sections 240–41 TULRCA 1992. According to section 240:

> A person commits an offence who wilfully and maliciously breaks a contract of service or hiring, knowing or having reasonable cause to believe that the probable consequence of his so doing, either alone or in combination with others, will be (a) to endanger human life, or cause serious bodily injury, or (b) to expose valuable property whether real or personal to destruction or serious injury.

Establishing guilt

Anyone found guilty of such an offence is liable to pay a fine not exceeding level 2 on the standard scale or to be imprisoned for up to three months, or both. This provision is less likely to form the basis of a prosecution than an action for an injunction to prevent a breach of it by someone who expects that serious injury will result from industrial action.

Section 241 TULRCA 1992 states that:

> A person commits an offence who, with a view to compelling another person to abstain from doing or to do any act which that person has a legal right to do or abstain from doing, wrongfully and without legal authority:
>
> (a) uses violence to or intimidates such other person or his wife or children, or injures his property, or
>
> (b) persistently follows such other person about from place to place, or
>
> (c) hides any tools, clothes or property owned or used by such other person, or deprives him of or hinders him in the use thereof, or
>
> (d) watches or besets the house or other place where such other person resides, or works, or carries on business, or happens to be, or the approach to such house or place, or
>
> (e) follows such other person with two or more other persons in a disorderly manner in or through any street or road.

A person found guilty of this offence is liable to imprisonment for a term not exceeding six months or a fine not exceeding level 5 on the standard scale, or both.

To establish guilt under this section it must be proved that the conduct relied on was wrongful and that the intention with which it was done was, at least in part, to compel others from doing specified acts which they had a legal right to do.[86] In *Galt v Philp*[87] it was held that employees who locked and barricaded the entrance to the premises where they were employed so as to prevent others from working were guilty of 'besetting' within (d) above.

KEY POINTS

- The economic torts considered here are inducing a breach of contract, intimidation, conspiracy, interference with business by unlawful means and inducing a breach of statutory duty.
- Statutory immunity from these torts depends on the action's taking place in contemplation or furtherance of a trade dispute. This is known as the 'golden formula'.
- A union will be held liable for the actions of its committees and officials unless those actions are repudiated by the principal executive committee, the president or the general secretary, and the union has done its best to inform the officials, and those taking part in the industrial action, of its repudiation.
- Trade unions and officials can claim immunity only if the union has authorised and endorsed the industrial action after a ballot of members has shown a majority in support of that action.
- Trade unions must take all reasonably necessary steps to ensure that the employer of those to be called upon to take part in industrial action receives written notice of both a ballot and any proposed action. The union must also provide information which would help the employer to make plans and bring information to the attention of those employees that the union believes will be entitled to vote in the ballot and take part in industrial action.
- Remedies available for unlawful action are damages, and interim and permanent injunctions.
- Picketing is lawful in contemplation or furtherance of a trade dispute if it takes place near the employee's own place of work, or if the picket is an official of the union accompanying a member, with the intention of peacefully persuading someone to work or abstain from working.

NOTES

1 See *Camellia Tanker Ltd v ITWF* (1976) IRLR 183
2 See *Metropolitan Borough of Solihull v NUT* (1985) IRLR 211
3 See *Middlebrook Mushrooms v TGWU* (1993) IRLR 232
4 (1984) IRLR 200
5 See *Galt v Philp* (1984) IRLR 156
6 See *Messenger News Group v NGA* (1984) IRLR 397
7 See *Crofter Harris Tweed Co v Veitch* (1942) AC 435
8 See *Timeplan Education Group Ltd v NUT* (1997) IRLR 457
9 (1982) IRLR 103
10 (1979) ICR 494; see also *Barretts & Baird Ltd v IPCS* (1987) IRLR 3
11 (1982) IRLR 200; see also *Dimskal Shipping v ITWF* (1992) IRLR 78
11A See *British Telecommunications v CWU* (2004) IRLR 58
12 See *P v NAS-UWT* (2003) IRLR 307
13 See *Westminster City Council v Unison* (2001) IRLR 524
14 Section 223 TULRCA 1992; see Chapter 13 on dismissal during industrial action
15 Sections 222 and 225 respectively TULRCA 1992
16 (1999) IRLR 31
17 See *Unison v UK* (2002) IRLR 497
18 *ABP v TGWU* (1989) IRLR 291
19 See *London Borough of Wandsworth v NAS-UWT* (1993) IRLR 344

20 Section 244(5) TULRCA 1992
21 (1977) IRLR 312; compare *Dimbleby & Sons* v *NUJ* (1984) IRLR 161
22 Section 244(3) TULRCA 1992
23 Section 244(4) TULRCA 1992
24 See *Huntley* v *Thornton* (1957) 1 WLR 321; also *Stratford* v *Lindley* (1965) AC 307
25 (1980) IRLR 35
26 See *ABP* v *TGWU* (1989) IRLR 305
27 Section 224(4) TULRCA 1992
28 See *News Group* v *SOGAT* (1986) IRLR 227
29 Section 20(2) TULRCA 1992
30 Section 119 TULRCA 1992
31 Section 20(3)(b) TULRCA 1992
32 Sections 21(1)–(3) TULRCA 1992. See *Balfour Kilpatrick* v *Acheson* (2003) IRLR 683
33 Section 21(5) and (6) TULRCA 1992
34 Section 20(6) TULRCA 1992
35 This can be extended to eight weeks with agreement by the employer; section 234 TULRCA 1992; see also *RJB Mining* v *NUM* (1997) IRLR 621
36 *Post Office* v *UCW* (1990) IRLR 143
37 See section 226A(2)(c) TULRCA 1992
38 Section 226A(3A) TULRCA 1992. See *British Telecom* v *CWU* (2004) IRLK 58
39 (2001) IRLR 228; see also *Westminster City Council* v *Unison* (2001) IRLR 524
40 Section 226A TULRCA 1992
41 Section 227 TULRCA 1992; see *RMT* v *Midland Mainline Ltd* (2001) IRLR 813
42 (1995) IRLR 636
43 Section 228A TULRCA 1992
44 Section 230(2) TULRCA 1992. See *P* v *NAS-UWT* (2003) IRLR 307
45 See sections 226B and 131B TULRCA 1992
46 *Post Office* v *UCW* (note 35)
47 (1999) IRLR 249
48 See section 229(2A) TULRCA 1992
49 See *West Midlands Travel* v *TGWU* (1994) IRLR 578
50 Section 232A TULRCA 1992; see *P* v *NAS-UWT* (2003) IRLR 307
51 See sections 231 and 231A TULRCA 1992
52 Section 226(3A)
53 Section 234A TULRCA 1992
54 See *Connex South Eastern Ltd* v *NURMTW* (1999) IRLR 249 (note 46)
55 See section 234(1) TULRCA 1992
56 Section 232B TULRCA 1992. See *P* v *NAS-UWT* (2003) IRLR 307
57 Section 62 TULRCA 1992
58 For exceptions see section 22(1) TULRCA 1992
59 See *Boxfoldia Ltd* v *NGA* (1988) IRLR 383; on aggravated and exemplary damages, see *Messenger News Group* v *NGA* (note 6)
60 Section 23 TULRCA 1992
61 *Express Newspapers* v *Keys* (1980) IRLR 247 per Griffiths J
62 (1979) IRLR 478
63 *ABP* v *TGWU* (note 25)
64 See section 221(2) TULRCA 1992
65 See *NWL* v *Nelson* (1979) IRLR 478
66 (1980) IRLR 437
67 See note 34

68 *Duport Steels* v *Sirs* (1980) IRLR 112
69 See note 9
70 See *Shipping Company Uniform Inc* v *ITWF* (1985) IRLR 71
71 See *Kent Free Press* v *NGA* (1987) IRLR 267
72 See *Read Transport* v *NUM (South Wales)* (1985) IRLR 67
73 Section 16 TULRCA 1992
74 See *Union Traffic* v *TGWU* (1989) IRLR 127
75 See *Rayware Ltd* v *TGWU* (1989) IRLR 134
76 See section 220(2) TULRCA 1992
77 See section 220(4) TULRCA 1992
78 (1985) IRLR 136
79 See also *News Group* v *SOGAT* (note 27) where the torts of nuisance and intimidation were committed
80 Department of Employment Code of Practice on Picketing paragraph 42
81 See also the Public Order Act 1986 for the offences of disorderly conduct, riot, violent disorder, affray and threatening behaviour
82 See *Moss* v *McLaughlan* (1985) IRLR 76
83 Department of Employment Code paragraph 51; see *Thomas* v *NUM (South Wales)* (1985) IRLR 136
84 Department of Employment Code paragraphs 54–57 and 62–64
85 See sections 6 and 8 Criminal Law Act 1977
86 See *Elsey* v *Smith* (1983) IRLR 293
87 See note 6

Index